READER'S DIGEST

Condensed

BOOKS

READER'S DIGEST

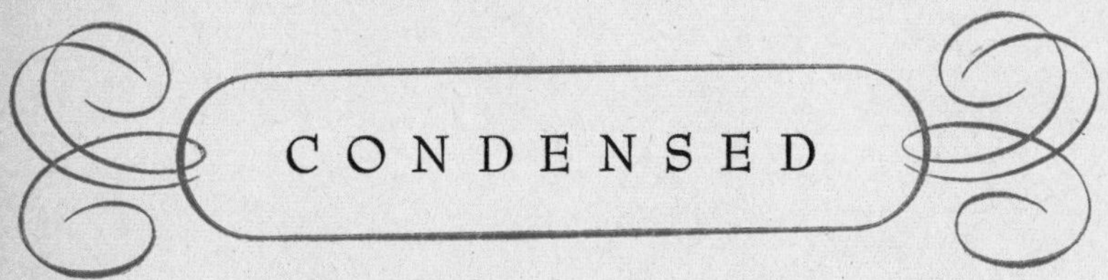

BOOKS

Summer 1954 Selections

Volume Eighteen

THE READER'S DIGEST ASSOCIATION

Pleasantville, N.Y.

The condensations reprinted in this book
are used by permission of and special arrangement with
the publishers holding the respective copyrights

FIRST EDITION

PRINTED IN THE UNITED STATES OF AMERICA

Contents

THE DESPERATE HOURS . . . Page 7

By Joseph Hayes

PUBLISHED BY RANDOM HOUSE, INC.

GENERAL DEAN'S STORY . . . . Page 111

By William F. Dean, as told to William L. Worden

PUBLISHED BY THE VIKING PRESS

MR. HOBBS' VACATION . . . . Page 199

By Edward Streeter

PUBLISHED BY HARPER & BROTHERS

THE POWER AND THE PRIZE . . Page 231

By Howard Swiggett

PUBLISHED BY BALLANTINE BOOKS, INC.

THE DUCHESS AND THE SMUGS . Page 381

Condensed from A WREATH FOR THE ENEMY

By Pamela Frankau

PUBLISHED BY HARPER & BROTHERS

TOMORROW! . . . . Page 427

By Philip Wylie

PUBLISHED BY RINEHART & CO., INC.

Illustrations by GUSTAVSON

The DESPERATE HOURS

A condensation of the book by

JOSEPH HAYES

"The Desperate Hours," copyright 1954 by Marrijane and Joseph Hayes, is published at $3.50 by Random House, Inc., 457 Madison Ave., New York 22, N. Y.

When Eleanor Hilliard answered the doorbell on that quiet fall afternoon, she never suspected who the shy young man on the porch could be. She never guessed that the next three days would be filled with terror and uncertainty for herself, for Dan, her husband, and for Cindy and Ralphie, their two children.

Deputy Sheriff Jesse Webb knew from experience what that ringing doorbell could mean. He wanted to help, to end the Hilliards' nightmare, but he had no way of knowing that their house had been chosen.

The Desperate Hours is a novel of extraordinary suspense. What happened to the Hilliards could happen to any of us. *What would you have done in their place?*

"Convincing and spellbinding . . ."
—Lewis Gannett in the
New York *Herald Tribune*

"Don't begin it after midnight unless you have company."
—C. V. Terry in the New York *Times*

BE ON LOOKOUT FOR GLENN GRIFFIN, HANK GRIFFIN
AND S. ROBISH---ESCAPED FROM FEDERAL PRISON
TERRE HAÛTE AN HOUR AGO---
BELIEVED HEADED NORTHEAST---USE CAUTION
THESE MEN MAY BE ARMED---

CHAPTER 1

THEY emerged from the woods a few minutes after dawn, a cold, moist dawn with a mist billowing up from the fields. There were three of them, their uniforms blending with the yellowing autumn green. They paused only briefly, scanning the deserted highway that lay flat across the flat Midwestern country. At a signal from one—the tall, lean, young-looking man who walked slightly ahead of the other two, with his head tilted and his shoulders lifted at a defiant and slightly triumphant angle—they proceeded swiftly, but not running, behind a screen of trees and underbrush, in a line parallel to the highway. In a very short time, and before anyone else appeared on the road, they reached a farm. In the barn lot, one detached himself from the others, moving quickly, a small young man, even younger than the tall one but without the other's jaunty manner, and began to work on the wires under the hood of the late-model, gray-colored sedan parked there. The other two moved swiftly but with stealth toward the barn. Inside, they came upon a middle-aged farmer, wearing blue overalls, shifting with pail and stool from one cow to another. The shorter of the two men — who was middle-aged and slower, but powerful-looking, with the ponderous, forward-leaning gait of a bear — picked up an axe handle and stepped across the straw-littered, concrete floor. Before the startled farmer could utter a cry, the tremendous arms went up once, there was an ugly sound and the farmer sprawled. The heavy man lifted the handle again, but the other stopped him with a short, commanding gesture similar to the one he had used on the highway. He knelt down by the unconscious but still breathing farmer and stripped him of his overalls.

They then went out of the barn, rejoined the boy who was now seated behind the wheel of the car with the motor purring. With no eyes upon it, the sedan slipped out of the barn lot, turned south and became lost in the thinning mist.

All this had been accomplished with a minimum of effort, no waste motion and in the most precise and machinelike manner imaginable.

Word of this incident, and all that had preceded it, reached Indianapolis, 72 miles to the east, less than half an hour later. Almost immediately then a telephone rang in a small, neat cottage in one of the suburbs northwest of the city.

A rangy young man rolled over in bed, yawning, reached across his unawakened wife and picked up the telephone. He spoke into it curtly, then listened briefly. "I'll be down," he said quietly. Wide-awake now, he replaced the telephone in its cradle and turned to the woman in the bed.

Her eyes were open now, and she crinkled her nose at him to cover up the sharp cut of apprehension that such phone calls always caused in her. She sat up, watching her husband climb into his dark suit. He was an extremely tall man, in his early 30's, with thin arms and legs that in no way betrayed the wire-like twist of muscles that lay below the surface. He was talking as he dressed, and he spoke in a laconic sort of drawl.

"Glenn Griffin, his kid brother and another con, a lifer named Robish," Jesse Webb was saying. "Not more than an hour ago.

From the federal prison in Terre Haute." He strapped on his gun, then pulled on his suit jacket, flipping it back once with an automatic gesture so that the deputy sheriff's badge showed briefly. "I'll catch a shave downtown, Kathie."

"You'll eat, too," she reminded him, and he turned to the bed, grinning slowly, his face suddenly very young.

"I'll eat, Kathleen Webb," he drawled, "if you say so."

He bent quickly, kissed her and turned.

Her voice caught him. "Is Glenn Griffin the one you — " She broke off when he paused in the bedroom doorway.

"He's the one," he said. "He had twelve years to go. I hope he heads straight for his old home town." Kathleen rose from the bed and walked with him to the front door. "But isn't this the last place he *would* come?" she asked reasonably.

Jesse Webb, of the Marion County Sheriff's office, in charge this week because his superior, Sheriff Masters, was away, turned to his wife and explained why he thought that Glenn Griffin would come to Indianapolis. In the first place, he said, you had to bank on the homing-pigeon instinct in the criminal mind; a familiar town gives criminals an illusion of security. Then, too, there was the woman, name of Helen Lamar; Jesse had a hunch she had the money.

"If she's still in Indianapolis, I'll lay two to one she's the beacon will lead us straight to those three," Jesse said. Again he kissed Kathleen's lips, still warm with sleep, then strode toward the car, waiting for the inevitable words from the door.

They came, floating in the sharp air: "Good luck, darling."

He waved and backed the Sheriff's car into the street.

AT THAT moment the gray sedan was cruising along in farm country with Glenn Griffin, wearing the faded blue overalls, at the wheel. The middle-aged man sat beside him, his enormous hulk of head sunk between two permanently upthrust shoulders. The boy, Glenn's younger brother, lay stretched out on the back seat, his eyes closed.

But Hank Griffin was not sleeping. He was remembering the slow, flat crawl in darkness over the hundred yards of bare ground with the walls and gun towers behind them; he was remembering the crash of the three bodies through the dark woods. There was a gash across his forehead and it had begun to throb. But worst of all, he was shuddering. They were beyond earshot of the bloodcurdling, shrieking sirens but he could imagine the sound. His body had begun to shake with crawling vibrations, and there was nothing he could do to stop it as he lay there listening to Glenn and Robish.

"You're going south," Robish was complaining. "Indianapolis is northeast."

"I'm going southeast now," Glenn Griffin said easily.

"Didn't you say Lamar was in Indianapolis? With the dough?"

"She moved last week to Pittsburgh. If they can't locate her in Indianapolis, it'll take the heat off."

"Where the hell we heading then?"

"Indianapolis," Glenn said quietly. "I got some business there, remember? But we're not walking into a roadblock from the west, pal. We'll circle all the way around and come in from the northeast."

"Then what?"

"Then we'll find us a cozy spot. And I'll contact Helen."

"A cozy spot — like where?"

"You name it, Robish. Only no hangouts. They'll be watching all of them. Pick a nice quiet house on a nice quiet street on the edge of town with no other houses close by. Make it a big place with soft furniture. Comfortable, scared people. Some place to take the stir-taste out of our mouths."

"Then what?"

"We wait till Helen gets there from Pittsburgh. Now shut up, Robish; let a guy enjoy his freedom."

In the back seat Hank heard Robish swear under his breath. Hank had to hand it to Glenn: he could certainly handle Robish. Robish had complained about not carrying a gun: it made him feel helpless. Glenn had said they couldn't afford to pull a job and tip off their whereabouts; besides, Glenn had one, didn't he? A .38 revolver, taken from a guard now in the prison infirmary with a bump on his head. Relax, Robish, and enjoy yourself.

Hank was picturing a house such as Glenn had described. After the clank of lock, the concrete floors and metal bunks, he was imagining himself sinking down again into a soft chair, his feet planted on deep-tufted carpet, the warm and intimate reality of ordinary walls with framed pictures on them.

THE Hilliards' house on Kessler Boulevard, while fairly convenient to shopping centers and bus lines, was remote enough from other homes to give the family a sense of privacy. In the eight years that they had occupied the house, they had come, without any of them ever being quite aware of it, to love every corner, stairstep and shingle. True, the furniture showed some evidence of wear and tear by two growing youngsters. Cindy, who was now 19, thought they should replace the living-room suite as soon as possible, but her mother, Eleanor, wasn't just sure. Even though they could get a discount because Dan was now personnel manager of the largest department store in town, Eleanor argued that these were inflationary times and the furniture *was* comfortable. Besides, as she pointed out to Dan, Cindy might be getting married soon.

As Dan came down the stairs at 7:40 on this particular Wednesday morning, he was trying to look ahead to the office rather than give in to the nagging uncertainty he had begun to feel about his daughter. Not that he had anything against Charles Wright. Perhaps, he chided himself, only a banked-down sort of envy. Dan had had to work for everything, every cent. Without an education past the second year in high school, he had come to this. And he was proud. On the other hand, Charles Wright, or Chuck — as Cindy had come to call him after going to work as secretary in the law office where young Wright was already a junior partner — had had it all handed to him, everything easy. He was lucky. But he was also, Dan knew from hearsay, an irresponsible young man, more interested in fast sports cars, beautiful girls and wine-drenched parties than in finding a solid place for himself in the community. Very well then, Dan was acting like a typical father or, as Cindy had chided, "a conservative old fogy."

In the kitchen Ralphie, who dawdled over breakfast as though it were some sort of punishment for past crimes, was glaring at a half-full glass of milk. He looked up when Dan came in. Eleanor, small, blonde and still slender, smiled and placed Dan's steaming ham and eggs at his place, then sat down across from him.

"Lucille is sick," she announced, explaining the absence of the maid who usually came on Wednesdays and Saturdays.

"Again?" Dan said. "Any gin missing?"

Ralphie lifted his eyes from the milk and grinned. "She's probably blotto," he said sagely.

"Where does he learn his language?" Dan inquired.

"Comic books," Eleanor said, buttering toast. "Television. Do you know what blotto means, Ralphie?"

"My name," Ralphie announced, "is Ralph. R-a-l-p-h. There's no 'y' on the end of it. And blotto means tight. Tight means drunk. Have I drunk enough milk?"

Eleanor was laughing and nodding. Ralphie was up, kissing his mother's hair swiftly; then he turned grave eyes on Dan, gave him a swift salute and turned on his heel.

"I'll ride my bike. I've got a whole half hour, almost." He disappeared onto the rear porch, and was gone. Dan heard the garage door sliding up.

Eleanor said, "Our son Ralph, spelled R-a-l-p-h, is too old to kiss a man — that's you — good-bye or good night."

"Well," Dan said wryly, but feeling a pinch somewhere inside, "that seems to be that."

Eleanor's eyes were on Dan steadily now, studying him. What she saw was a man of average height with heavy shoulders; she looked into the familiar deep-blue eyes and was conscious of the mahogany-red hair above and the freckles climbing over and across the rather broad nose and the deep fine lines that added so much character to a very appealing face.

Reading his mind, she said, "Cindy'd like to ask him for Thanksgiving dinner, Dan. Should she?"

Dan stood up and shrugged. "Ellie, I don't want to start opposing this thing and get Cindy's back up. But — well, Thanksgiving's a sort of family day."

Eleanor lifted her face for his kiss, then Dan went out the rear door.

As she set a fresh place for Cindy, Eleanor decided against mentioning Chuck Wright this morning, especially in view of Dan's unspoken rejection of the Thanksgiving-dinner idea. Then she flipped on the radio for a news report.

After listening for perhaps five minutes — her attention not caught by the report of the three escaped convicts or by the warning that these men were armed and dangerous — she heard Cindy descending the back stairs. Eleanor turned off the radio. As soon as Cindy was out of the house, Eleanor's own day would really begin.

In the office of the Sheriff, in downtown Indianapolis, the day had started long before. Through the morning Jesse Webb had kept in close contact with the state police, the city police, the teletypes, the news reports and the local office of the FBI. They had now an accurate description of the gray sedan, its license number and the approximate time of its theft from a farm south of Terre Haute.

Jesse hated waiting. There was a helplessness about it that worked like sandpaper on his nerves. The roadblocks had been set up on all the main highways; everything that could be done was being done. But Jesse was not satisfied.

His uncle, Frank Pritchard, telephoned him after the ten-o'clock radio news. Jesse listened to the tired voice, nodding his lean head occasionally. Then he said, "I haven't forgotten a thing, Uncle Frank. Go to sleep."

"Was that Frank P?" Tom Winston, the deputy who shared the small office, had heard the conversation. "Bet he'd like to be back in the business today."

"Yeah," Jesse said slowly, "with two good hands and his gun."

"Why'd you tell him to go to sleep?"

Jesse Webb turned on him, biting off the words. "I told him to go back to sleep because he's got a job he has to keep. A night-watchman job at the meat-packing plant. I don't want him to lose *that* one because of Glenn Griffin."

Winston picked up a sheaf of papers and retreated. "I didn't know what had become of old Frank P," he said apologetically.

Jesse stared after his friend as Winston slouched down the corridor. Don't blame Winston, Jesse reminded himself; blame the guy who did it. He could see it happening again.

Uncle Frank had been behind the parked car when Glenn Griffin came out of the little apartment hotel. Even in his blue uniform, Uncle Frank had looked too old and wispy for the .38 he held in his hand. Then he shouted. Glenn Griffin had whirled, firing, and two bullets had ripped into Uncle Frank's right arm, permanently injuring a nerve. Now the arm was a hanging, limp, useless thing.

Jesse had blamed himself for not letting go then, blasting; but he had been temporarily stunned and surprised to hear Uncle Frank scream like a child, a terrible shriek that still haunted Jesse. Glenn Griffin had leaped back inside the doorway, graceful as a dancer, despite the roar and whine of the other guns. Then Glenn Griffin, while Uncle Frank lay writhing on the ground, had shouted for a chance to surrender, throwing his gun into the street.

Jesse recalled the blank wall of unreason that had come down on him as he stepped over the gun on the pavement and approached the unarmed young hoodlum; he had been helpless despite the shouts of his lieutenant, ordering him to stop. It was not until he had yanked the cowering Glenn Griffin to his toes with one hand and brought his other full into the prisoner's handsome but distorted face that Jesse Webb had felt a momentary relief from the grip of rage.

Thinking about it now, more than two years later, left him pale and shaken. He remembered the way Uncle Frank had been eased off the city force because of his withered arm. He recalled, too, the trial of Glenn Griffin, with the boy smiling blandly through the bandages that held his broken jaw in place while his attorney pointed dramatically to this "indisputable evidence of police brutality." Even after the jury had brought in the guilty verdict — it was Griffin's third major conviction — the young man had kept up his front. At the sentencing, his kid brother, captured with him that same night, had begun to tremble. But not Glenn.

The only time Glenn Griffin had shown any emotion was that day when the Federal Marshal was taking him away. Jesse had made a point of being present. The boy spoke carefully, stiffly.

"You got yours coming, copper," he said — not spitting out the words, nothing dramatic or violent about it.

Jesse Webb stood up now from his desk. He rubbed the back of his neck with the palm of his hand; it came away wet. Then he left the office and the building and walked toward the State House.

Lt. Van Dorn of the State Police grinned at Jesse's scowl from behind the counter. "The city can't pick up any trace of this Helen Lamar, Jess. They've ripped whole buildings apart. We can't get anything from the roads except the usual — the car's been spotted thirty-two times since seven o'clock. But not officially. My guess is the woman's out West somewhere and they're on their way to her, probably all the way across Illinois by now."

Then he turned his head and peered at Jesse from the corner of his eyes. "You look awful. Bad night?"

"No," Jesse answered slowly, thinking of Kathleen.

Then something struck him between the eyes. It was only a possibility, and a very slight one at that, but he was taking no chances. He picked up the telephone and dialed his office.

"Tom," he said when Winston answered, "send a car out to bring my wife to the office. Tell her I just want to see her. Don't scare the girl, hear?"

Anything was possible. You could never tell when it came to a mind like Griffin's.

Eleanor Hilliard was about to go up the front stairs to change into her gardening clothes when she heard the step on the porch. The front doorbell rang. She sighed. It was that blissful moment after lunch when Ralphie had returned to school and she felt a certain treasured sense of freedom until 3:30. It annoyed her that anyone had come to the front door. The family and tradesmen normally used the side entrance.

The man who faced her on the porch, a very young man with short-cropped, glistening black hair, wore faded blue farmer's overalls and he was smiling almost apologetically. He looked boyish, and so miserable about his errand that Eleanor smiled, too.

"Sorry to bother you, ma'am," he said in a voice that was almost a whisper, "but I guess I've lost my way. I'm trying to get to the Bulliard Dairy. I know it's in the neighborhood, but — "

Then he stopped, and now he was looking over her shoulder into the hall, a subtle alteration taking place around the edges of his mouth. Involuntarily, she turned.

After that, everything happened so fast and with such precision that she was paralyzed, mind and body.

She heard the door behind her open, felt the knob hard against her ribs, then heard it close. The older man, who must have entered through the back door, turned from her and stomped up the stairs. A third man, much younger, who wore the same strange gray-green garb as the big fellow, appeared in the dining-room door, then walked swiftly through the downstairs section of the house, opening doors, closing them. Eleanor saw, without really comprehending, the black gun in the hand of the young man in overalls who remained with her in the hall. She thought of the small automatic upstairs, concealed in the spring under Dan's bed. She felt then a scream accumulating, powerful and uncontrollable, in her throat.

"Take it easy, lady," the young man advised. "You open your mouth, your kid'll come home from school and find your body."

She lifted her hand to her mouth and bit down hard on the back of it, choking off the scream in the back of her aching throat.

The youngest man returned, not looking at her, and said, "All clear down here, Glenn." Without another word, he turned and went through the dining room toward the kitchen.

Eleanor heard the back door open and close and then a motor grind over in the driveway. Then she heard a familiar sound: the garage door descending on the metal runners.

In the silence that followed, the middle-aged man came down the stairs; he carried one of Dan's suits over one arm. His animal-like face wore an expression that might have denoted pleasure, but his yellowish-green eyes, lost between the slits in the bulbous pouches, seemed as opaque as marbles.

"Nobody home but the missus," the man reported.

Staring at Dan's tweed suit, Eleanor thought of her husband, big, calm, reserved, never roused to anger. Even in the swift flood of panic and disgust—as she saw the older man's eyes crawl hungrily over her—the thought of Dan calmed her.

"Get in there, Robish," Glenn Griffin said, "and keep an eye open out front."

Robish, pulling his eyes from her, went into the living room. The back door opened and closed again. All three of them were in the house, the car concealed in the Hilliard garage.

"Now," said the one named Glenn. "Now, lady. We got a phone call to make, you and me. I guess you know what'll happen, you let go with anything fishy while you're talking. Case not, though, listen. We don't want to hurt nobody, specially kids. But when the little guy who owns that bike out there gets home..."

"What do you want me to do?" Eleanor asked.

Glenn Griffin grinned again. "Smart little lady. Hope the whole family's smart as you. Now."

Leaning against the telephone table, Eleanor listened to the directions, then picked up the phone and dialed Long Distance. She gave the operator a number that she knew she should remember but could not. A number in Pittsburgh, Pennsylvania...

"PITTSBURGH!" Jesse Webb uttered an oath and stood up from his desk after talking to Carson, the studious-looking young FBI man assigned to the case. "They've located Helen Lamar."

Tom Winston didn't turn from his desk. "They got her?"

"She checked out over an hour ago. They're still questioning the hotel people but, as far as they can dope it, she didn't receive a phone call, at least not at the hotel. She'd be too smart for that, figuring we might be watching." He was striding up and down. "But maybe he didn't have to call. They could have it all timed. You know where that leaves us, Tom? Nowhere. That leaves us with a license number and the description of a car. A car they'll ditch soon enough, but they're taking their time on that, too. No trail. They can't melt into the ground!" He sat down abruptly and cracked the top of the desk with his fist. "Where is that car?"

Ralphie arrived home at 3:30. Eleanor detained him in the living room, speaking swiftly. She had a terrible headache, she said; she had to have absolute quiet all afternoon; he would have to go out and play until suppertime and he was not to come back until then. But Ralphie was hungry—as usual. Then he was to go to the drugstore, get a sandwich; she gave him the money. Pleased at the chance to buy a drugstore sandwich on his own, Ralphie went off on his bicycle.

"Nice work, lady," Glenn said, pocketing his gun.

She looked at him without expression, feeling nothing now but the hard stone in the pit of her stomach.

"I got a few more questions now, Mrs. Hilliard."

Then the process started all over again. The questions . . . This daughter, what time did she get home? Did she drive her own car? Was she ever late? Okay, just let her walk in.

"You won't have to do a thing but keep quiet, see."

At 5:18 Cindy came into the living room through the sun porch. Eleanor was sitting stiff and still on the sofa. Glenn was standing by the television set; the gun was in his hand. Robish was in the small den in the rear of the house, watching the driveway through the side windows. Eleanor knew that the young one, named Hank, was still in the kitchen, his eye on the back yard, listening to news on the radio.

Cindy burst in, her checked coat flying, her hair flowing behind her. When she caught sight of her mother, she stopped, her hazel-flecked, blue eyes snapping around the room, remaining a split second on Glenn Griffin.

Glenn grinned. "Come right in, redhead."

Cindy whirled and started to run.

"Okay," Glenn Griffin said, "we still got your old lady."

Robish burst in from the den as Cindy's step faltered at the sun-porch door. She turned slowly, catching sight of Robish. Dismissing him instinctively, she faced Glenn Griffin.

"That's better, redhead," he said, grinning. As his eyes flicked over her, the grin faded.

Cindy did not in any way indicate that she was terrified. She glared. "What do you want?"

Without taking his gaze from the girl, Glenn said, "Robish, get back to the window. The old guy's due any minute."

"I need a gun," Robish said.

"Get back there," Griffin told him, not glancing at him.

"You think you can — "

"Now."

Robish turned and disappeared into the den.

"Sit down, redhead," Glenn said. "Sit down and let me explain the facts of life. With that hair, you might feel like getting real brave. You might even get away with it. But that's not saying what'll happen to the old lady . . . or the kid brother . . . or the father. We're waiting for him now, see, so take off your coat and sit down."

Without removing her coat as commanded but glancing at Eleanor with a hint of a reassuring smile that failed to come off, Cindy sat down. She even lighted a cigarette, steadily.

"How long have these animals been here, Mother?" she asked.

Glenn laughed, a short, explosive snort of sound.

"I've lost track of time," Eleanor said. "Some time after noon. There's another one in the kitchen."

"In other words," said Cindy, blowing smoke, "the house is crawling with them."

Eleanor was watching Glenn Griffin's face at that moment, and she felt a tightening of her own terror. The young man's face went icy-white, colorless, and the flesh around his even white teeth drew back into a stiff grin. He stood there perhaps half a minute; then he turned and, in that graceful feline glide of his, walked toward the muffled chatter of the radio in the kitchen.

There he remained until the sound for which Eleanor's nerves had been tensed reached her.

"Griffin!" Robish barked from the den.

Glenn Griffin materialized again. "No lights now, not a word out of either of you. Got that?"

Eleanor nodded dumbly.

"Got that, redhead?"

Cindy seemed to look through Glenn Griffin as though he were simply not present. Eleanor longed to put out a hand. This was no time for Cindy's stubborn temper.

"He's trying to open the garage," Robish said. "You want me to grab him now?"

"Not with all those cars going by," Glenn said. "He'll come in." He lifted his voice. "You watching, Hank?"

"He's not coming in this way," the other's voice called from the kitchen.

Again Eleanor felt a scream gathering in her chest. She listened to the familiar footsteps: up the two steps, across the tiled sun porch. Glenn pointed the gun directly at the door.

First, Dan saw his wife, pale and haggard. He stopped short.

The room was filled with the fading twilight. Then he saw Cindy, sitting straight, her face angry and defiant. Only then, because there was the faintest sort of shadow movement from the direction of the hall, did Dan see Glenn Griffin. And the pointed gun.

He felt his breath hold and, before anyone could move or speak, although he felt Eleanor straining half out of her chair, he had the whole picture clear. He recalled the news reports on the car radio; he realized he had been a fool for not comprehending as soon as he saw the gray sedan through the windows of the garage. But such a farfetched thought would not have occurred to him.

Eleanor saw the unnatural redness mounting in her husband's craggy face. Dan's mind, she knew, moved straight ahead, but with caution, into whatever faced him.

"I suggest you put the gun away, Griffin," Dan said. "If you fire it, you'll have the whole neighborhood down on you in less than three minutes."

Dan felt a movement from the direction of the den, but he did not shift his eyes from Glenn Griffin's.

"What do you want?" he demanded.

"I don't want anybody to get hurt," Glenn Griffin said. "What do *you* want, Pop?"

Dan crossed then, despite the gun, toward his wife. He placed a hand on her shoulder. "That's what I want, too."

Glenn let go with a laugh at that; he dropped the arm holding the gun. "Now you talk sense. So I'm going to talk sense, too."

The room was deep in shadow now, and Dan listened in silence. Glenn, striding in that slender catlike manner of his up and down the room, spoke in the manner of one who has known for months exactly what he wants to say. Dan listened while the helplessness of his position seeped into him like some benumbing drug.

All they wanted was a safe place to stay till about midnight; at the latest, two or three in the morning. They had some money coming, and when it arrived they would go. It was as simple as that. In the meantime, life in the Hilliard house was to go on normally.

"Just like normal, see? You got it straight, folks?"

He spoke like an actor. He moved around the room and his brows lifted and his face worked as though some invisible camera were on him, as though he were trying to live up to some picture of himself that he carried in his mind. Dan recorded all this in his own mind and reached one stone-hard conclusion: these were not idle threats. This boy would kill one or all of them if anything went wrong. Dan could feel his body frozen and numb with helplessness.

"We'll do what you say, Griffin," Dan said. "Only — "

"Yeah?"

"Griffin, what if I could get you the money you want right away? *Before* midnight? Would you leave then?"

"You couldn't do it, Pop. I had a look at your bankbooks. You just don't have it."

"That sounds like a deal to me," Robish said from the den. "We could get the hell out of here."

Dan noted the urgency behind the invisible man's tone. "Maybe I could raise it. Somehow. What then, Griffin?"

"We're sticking," Glenn said.

"Yeah," Robish muttered sourly. "You'd risk our necks just to see that dame again."

Having unexpectedly created the breach, Dan stepped into it. "If this woman knows where to come, how do you know the police won't be following her?"

"What about that?" This time Robish emerged, planting himself at the far end of the room in threatened mutiny. "The guy talks sense, Griffin. Hell, you can pick up a woman anywheres."

A flicker of bewilderment passed over Glenn Griffin's face. He glanced from Dan to Robish. Then he whirled to Robish, the movement a dancer-shadow in the room. "I'm running the show, Robish. I thought we had that straight. We're staying, see, till Helen gets here. She's too smart to let the cops get on her tail. And I got to have the dough here, see. Right in this town."

"You got no right to take these chances just so you can get a copper knocked off. What do I care somebody broke your jaw? That was a long time ago, anyway, and — "

"No!" The word crackled. "You heard me, both of you."

Slowly Glenn stepped toward Dan. "You, Hilliard, you lay off. I don't need no ideas from you. I got my own all worked out fine."

"Ain't worth it," Robish snorted.

"I say it is, Robish. Where'd you be if it wasn't for me?" He spoke with his back to Robish, his eyes on Dan. "You'd be sitting down to that stew again with a guard breathing down your neck." He was rubbing his cheek, feeling the hard ridge of tissue that now protected the mended bone. "And you, Hilliard, you're going to keep your trap closed. You're going to play ball. Any cops show up in front of this joint, it's not going to be pretty."

Mrs. Kathleen Webb was smiling at her husband across what was left of a very thick steak. He was talking excitedly as he ate, and the ripple of excitement reached across the restaurant table.

"She left Pittsburgh at approximately four o'clock this afternoon. That much is for certain. Driving south on U. S. 19. Less than an hour later, she was spotted on U. S. 40, heading west. West — that's here. I told you they were homing pigeons. She's sailing along now in her nice maroon two-door job, and they're holed up somewhere here thinking how smart they were to get her out of town so she could backtrack to them without being watched. Not so smart." He shoved the platter back. "Every town she goes through, there's going to be a pair of eyes on her. But nobody's going to bother her. Oh no. Along about Greenfield, they'll put a real tag on her and she'll breeze in here tonight and lead us right to the hole. Just like that."

"Jess," his wife said gently, with a faint wonder in her face, "you want to kill that man, don't you?"

Jesse knew the truth, the blank fact: yes. But suddenly it seemed important to explain and justify this feeling. "Look, all I know is that as long's a guy like Glenn Griffin is running around free and with a gun in his hand — well, it's not safe for the rest of us, any of us. It's like that, hear?" He leaned across the table. "That's why you're going to sleep in my office tonight. Or at a hotel. Which do you prefer?"

"I'll take the jail. I'd like to be near you."

Jesse smiled, taking her hand on the table. She cast an embarrassed glance around the restaurant, then turned to see a scowl replace the smile on her husband's narrow face. By an accidental association of images and fears, Jesse's mind had pounced upon a picture that was true in its general outline if not in detail. He was imagining Glenn Griffin with that gun pointed at frightened and innocent people. But where? If he only knew where . . .

As Dan Hilliard stared at the gun held so casually in the hand of the young man, he was caught in a sickening helplessness. If the police came, it would be tragic; if they did not come, it might be worse.

"The kid's coming up on his bike," Robish reported.

Dan could hear the sound of a tire skidding on the gravel of the driveway. "With the lights off like this, the boy will be scared to death. You can't . . ."

Glenn Griffin took two swift, silent strides and jabbed the gun point with bruising force into Dan's ribs. Dan gasped for breath.

He heard quite distinctly the few short carefree steps on the back porch, the back door opening, the small cry of astonishment and sudden fear. He stiffened. As though his own insane and suicidal impulse had communicated itself through the gun against him, that point once again rammed itself with force into his ribs.

There was a brief and one-sided scuffle and then Ralphie was standing in the hall, held in the grip of a young man whom Dan had not seen before but whom he recognized as Glenn Griffin's brother.

"Let *go!*" Ralphie said, twisting out of the man's grasp.

"Hank." Glenn switched the gun idly so that it was directed at the hall. "Turn on the hall light, pull the blinds in the dining room and get back to the kitchen." As he spoke he stepped into the hall, out of view of the front windows.

Anyone on the street outside could see the Hilliards in their living room. They could not see the small straight figure of the boy in the hall, outrage written on his play-streaked face. Nor could they see Glenn Griffin beside the boy.

"What's that guy doing in our kitchen?" Ralphie demanded.

"It's all right, Ralphie," Dan said quickly. He then saw terror leap to the boy's face as the eyes fell on the gun in Glenn's hand. "I'll explain it to you, Ralphie."

With startling suddenness, the boy whirled, leaped to the front door, turned the knob and tugged.

"Take it easy now, kid," Glenn said in a single breath.

Still tugging, Ralphie began to cry. Then he gave up on the locked door. It appeared that he was going to turn to face them, but what he did was so abrupt and ridiculous that even Griffin seemed startled into inaction. Ralphie darted into the living room, passed Dan and reached the unlocked sun-porch door.

"Ralphie!" Eleanor screamed in terror.

Dan was after the boy but, before he could reach him, Robish, cursing, grabbed Ralphie. Glenn flipped off the lights almost as soon as Robish appeared in the living room. In semidarkness, the big man twisted Ralphie about, the enormous hands spinning him, then slipping down to his shoulders and shaking the small body. Dan heard Glenn draw the front-window curtains. All he saw was his son's head snapping up and down against his chest and the heavy shoulders of the man half-turned away from him.

It was enough. Dan forgot the gun and Glenn Griffin completely. In that blank moment of wildness he took two more steps, felt the lights come up in the room, saw Ralphie's tear-filled, incredulous eyes and the hate-twisted face of the man looming over him. Dan whirled Robish's hulking body about as though it were a toy one third its size. The eyes in the bulbous pouches glittered with surprise. Then they closed completely as Dan's fist exploded in the square face.

Before, all had been silence; now the bone-against-bone sound of that single blow filled the whole house. The body straightened slightly, then collapsed into a soft heap.

What broke the silence again was Eleanor's cry as she saw Glenn Griffin move in behind Dan, lift the gun and bring it down full force against the top of his shoulder.

The whole right side of Dan's body went numb and cold, and he felt himself staggering sidewise. He felt, too, a rough hand shoving him backward into the enveloping softness of the sofa. The blackness closed in.

When he could see again, and hear, he saw Glenn Griffin facing the man Robish, the gun directed at Robish's stomach.

"... not going to be like this, see!" Griffin was almost shouting.

Robish was muttering incomprehensible words and his greenish-yellow eyes were fixed on Dan.

"Get to the kitchen, Robish, fast!"

"You think I'm gonna let him get away with that?"

"Nothing's going to foul this up!" Glenn cried. "Got that, Robish? *Nothing."*

After that, the blackness threatened to return. Dan's next impression was of Glenn Griffin reaching into his pocket and drawing out something small which Dan could not see. The young man crossed to Eleanor and Dan felt himself stiffen. In that instant he knew that under similar circumstances he would be unable to do anything but what he had just done when Robish grabbed Ralphie. That or worse.

"Read it," Glenn said. "Loud enough so he can hear it."

Dan heard his wife's tight voice begin to read the yellow newspaper clipping, and he had to concentrate to catch the words.

What she read was a dispassionate news-service story of an occurrence in New York state. A convict, attempting to escape from a house in which he was hiding, had climbed into a pickup truck, holding a small girl in front of him. Even though wounded himself by police fire, he had shot the child through the stomach and she had died.

When Eleanor had finished reading, there was silence. Eleanor held Ralphie's hand. Cindy's face was ashen. Dan could picture Glenn Griffin carefully clipping this from a newspaper months ago — looking ahead to just this moment of his life.

Dan realized now that he was consumed by hatred of this young criminal who stood carelessly, letting the significance of that newspaper account sink in. A sharp warning twisted in Dan: he must not let himself become the victim of his emotions again.

"Now, Hilliard," Glenn said, "you got a gun in the house?"

Without hesitation, Dan nodded. He had no choice. He couldn't afford to fight; too much was at stake. "Upstairs. In the coils of bedspring. My bed."

Glenn shouted for Hank, who came into the room at once; Glenn spoke quietly to his brother and Hank disappeared up the stairs.

When he returned, Glenn said in a whisper, "Put it in your pocket, Hank. Don't tell Robish." He turned to Dan. "You agree with that, Hilliard?"

Dan nodded. He had reached the conclusion that, in addition to playing *their* game, he must also concentrate on Glenn: he was the leader, the one to watch and to fear and to depend on.

"One thing, Griffin," Dan said when Hank had gone again. "I'll handle my family. We'll all do anything you say. Anything within reason. But if one of you touches one of us again — "

"I don't go for threats, Pop."

"Griffin," Dan said, his breath paining him, "this is no threat. I'm stating facts. If one of you touches one of us again, you're done for. So are we, but that's just the way it'll have to be. I'm not just talking tough. I'm saying we'll help you if you can control your men."

This was the sort of challenge which Glenn Griffin was capable of comprehending.

"I handled Robish, didn't I?"

"And very well," Dan said. "I think we understand each other, Griffin." He glanced at Eleanor. "I think we all know what we have to do, don't you, Eleanor?"

Eleanor could only nod her head.

CHAPTER 2

THE curtains had been drawn open, but the headlights passing on the boulevard seemed unreal. Dan Hilliard, by lifting his eyes from the photographs on the front page of the evening paper, could look across the hall into the dining room and see two of the faces reproduced there: the Griffin brothers bent over road maps at the table. Although he was not able to see it, the third face was in the den beyond the open door at the end of the living room.

Cindy, on the sofa with Ralphie, who pretended to be reading a book, turned her back purposefully and contemptuously on that door. Eleanor was seated in her usual chair so, if any casual passer-by should glance in, he would see a perfectly normal family group.

It was all very carefully arranged. From the front windows in the dining room, Glenn commanded a view of the street and the lawn. From the den, Robish could keep watch on the back yard, the garage and the driveway along the side of the house.

Dan was stiff; his rib was bruised and aching, and with each breath there was a stab of pain in his lungs. The two and a half hours that had passed had filled him with a slow, banked-down fury. It was directed not only at the three men themselves but at something larger and less tangible: an incredible accident that had caused these men to choose *his* house. Because they had seen Ralphie's bicycle in the driveway? Because the closest neighbors were two city lots away? Yes, but why *this* house? There must be others as ideally situated for their purposes.

Dan glanced at his watch. 8:34. Three hours and twenty-six minutes until midnight. He had made it so far; he would get through the rest.

The evening had been more or less without incident. It had been shortly after dinner that Robish had demanded to know where Dan kept the liquor. There was none in the house. Robish had muttered that Dan was lying; he had crashed about in a fruitless search, snarling threats of what would happen if he found any. Robish was emotional, twisted, ugly and unpredictable. Dealing with him was like trying to talk to an animal.

The telephone shrilled. In the shock of silence that followed, the house came alive. Dan rose. Glenn Griffin came into the hall, gun in hand, and Hank went up the stairs to listen on the bedroom phone.

"Okay, redhead, answer it, and be careful. If someone asks for a Mr. James, that's me. If it's for anyone in the family, let 'em talk. Quick now."

Cindy picked up the phone.

"Hello . . . oh . . . yes, Chuck. I'm . . . well, I'm not feeling very well . . . Oh, a cold, I guess. You know. No, I can't." She listened a long moment. "No, Chuck, but please understand. You do, don't you? . . . Tomorrow, then. G'night." She replaced the telephone and then faced Glenn Griffin. "Do I pass, teacher?" she inquired, her tone acid and scornful.

Glenn looked up the stairs as Hank descended, nodding.

"You pass, sis," Glenn said. "Maybe you got more sense than I figured. Who was that, the boy friend?"

"It was Anthony Eden," Cindy said and returned to the sofa.

Dan said, "Ralphie. Bedtime, pal."

Without protest, Ralphie said good night and went into the hall to mount the stairs. Dan followed, according to ritual. Glenn didn't object, watched them both unsmiling. Dan happened to glance at Hank Griffin then, caught a strange expression lurking in those dark eyes. The expression, as Dan saw it, was one of longing, or envy, or both.

In the bedroom, with the model airplanes dangling from the ceiling, Ralphie undressed, donned his pajamas, went into the bathroom, brushed his teeth quickly – while Dan sat on the side of the bed, in silence. How could a man explain a thing like this to a ten-year-old boy?

In bed, Ralphie spoke. "They don't look so tough."

"They're . . . tough, Ralphie. Don't you fool yourself."

"You're scared." It was not a question but an accusation.

"Yes, son," Dan said softly, "I'm scared. You should be, too."

"Mother's scared, too. But Cindy isn't. And I'm not."

There was nothing else to do then but to speak the truth, fully. So Dan leaned forward on the bed and whispered steadily and firmly for a few moments. When he finished, he met disillusion.

"I could sneak down the back stairs," Ralphie said. "That guy Robish is in the den, but he wouldn't even hear me open the back door. Nobody's in the kitchen now."

"Now listen, Ralph," Dan growled. "You want to be considered a grown boy in this house, don't you? Then you've got to act like one and *think* like one. If you went running out of here and got the police, do you know what would happen? They'd shoot your mother and your sister."

The boy's face clouded; suddenly there were tears in his eyes. "I don't want them to take me along," he blurted.

"Take you . . ?"

"You heard what Mother read. That newspaper thing about the little girl. What's going to happen when they go, Dad?"

"They're not going to take you," Dan said slowly. The fear in his son's eyes lashed knifelike at his rational control. Perhaps he had known all along and had been afraid to face it. Well, he was facing it now. "They're not taking you, or anyone, Ralphie. I'll see to that."

"But — what can you do? Now you don't even have a gun?"

"You heard me!" Dan reached for control of his voice. "I said not to worry. Go to sleep. You ought to know I wouldn't let them take you along, Ralphie."

Dan reached out and took hold of Ralphie's shoulder and held it a brief moment; then he went into the hall, turning off the light, closing the door.

Dan descended the front stairs slowly, the fierce new hatred choking him. In the living room again, he looked at Eleanor, sitting quiet, her face wan. He saw Cindy whose head was resting on her arm along the back of the sofa.

You can't let rage force you into action, he warned himself.

He sat down again. Three minutes to nine. He stared incredulously at his watch, then lifted it to his ear. It was still running.

In the Sheriff's office, Jesse Webb had been waiting for the telephone to ring. Even so, the sound echoing in the night stillness startled him. He spoke his name into the phone, listened. In less than one minute, he said, "Check" and replaced the phone.

From now on, even waiting was a waste of time. Helen Lamar had disappeared. Jesse Webb smashed his right fist into his left palm.

Driving the maroon two-door sedan, she had been sighted east of Columbus, Ohio, approaching the city. It was quite a proposition to follow her progress through a large city but, as it turned out, all the precautions had been unnecessary and useless.

Helen Lamar had made one simple mistake. She had exceeded the speed limit and a traffic-patrol car had attempted to stop her. She must have grown panicky then and stepped on the gas. The patrol car gave chase.

And yet, Jesse thought angrily, they had their instructions, all of them: DO NOT ARREST REPEAT DO NOT ARREST. The order was on every teletype between Pittsburgh and Indianapolis.

"Speeding, for heaven's sake!" Jesse said bitterly.

She gave the pursuit car the slip. She was taking no chances because she was hauling money, and she couldn't let herself be stopped. How could she know that the fools only wanted to give her a traffic-violation ticket?

The police had found the car, but not soon enough. Helen Lamar was gone. There you have it, Jess. She's gone. She had slipped somehow, in the snakelike way of the criminal, down a hole, into hiding, protected somewhere by others of her kind. Right now she was probably trying to think of a safe way to contact Griffin.

What would Griffin do then? No money now, no means of escape in the clever manner he'd planned, all his neatly laid calculations gone haywire—what would he do?

GLENN GRIFFIN remained in the Hilliard house, but Dan was now out of it. It was 9:15.

He sat in the family car while a service-station attendant filled the gas tank and checked the oil and water. He was following orders now. The car was needed for a getaway. Robish had called Glenn a fool for letting Dan leave the house, but Glenn was confident that Dan would do what he had to do, simply because his wife, his daughter and his son remained in the house.

Glenn was right, as usual. Dan was staring at a telephone inside the service station. He could speak to the police now in less than 30 seconds. Would they realize that it would be irresponsible murder of innocent people for them to attempt to move in at once? Could he make them understand this fact?

Perhaps. But, even if they did, what precautions would they take? They would have to set up roadblocks in the neighborhood in the hope of stopping Griffin. Their job was to capture the two Griffin boys and Robish. His was to protect his family. And certainly Glenn Griffin had not overlooked any danger inherent in letting Dan leave the house. He had certainly looked ahead.

He knew that he needed the Hilliard car. But Glenn must have realized that, as soon as he had gone, leaving the Hilliards behind, that blue car would become as well known as the gray one — once Dan had notified the police. How did Griffin hope to prevent this?

Dan tore his gaze from the telephone. Glenn hoped to prevent it in the same way that he was now making sure that Dan did not telephone the police: by keeping one of the family in the escape car. *I don't want them to take me along,* Ralphie had said.

If Dan brought the police into it, he was running a risk; if he did not, he was no better off and perhaps even more at the mercy of Glenn Griffin's design. Now, instead of looking forward to the time when the money and the woman would arrive, he dreaded it. Less than three hours. Perhaps, in the interim . . .

Perhaps what?

In the interim, he told himself grimly, you will do as you have been told and you will hope that, by the time the moment of departure arrives, you will have thought of some threat to hang over Glenn Griffin's head that will make him change his plans.

Dan paid the attendant. The car purred easily. A fine car, efficient, fast. Dan had to concentrate very hard in order to avoid imagining the holes that bullets would make in the rear window and the stain that blood would leave on the upholstery. If only it was the blood of the three men.

Dan brought the car to a halt near a liquor store. He bought a fifth of bourbon. Then he was in the car again and turning it in the direction of his house. Soon he caught sight of the yellow flare from the front windows. He parked the car as he had been instructed to park it: nose pointed toward the boulevard. He climbed out, feeling eyes upon him, crawling over him like insects. He went into the house through the side door, crossed the sun porch and then the living room toward Glenn Griffin waiting in the hall, out of sight of the front windows. Robish clumped in from the dining room and snatched the bottle.

"Didn't get any ideas, did you, Pop?" Glenn proceeded to search Dan.

Dan's eyes returned to the living room. At once a question surged up, hot and choking: "Where's Cindy?"

"She's out with Charles Wright," Eleanor said. "He came anyway. Cindy went out before he could get inside."

"I talked to her, Hilliard," Glenn Griffin explained easily. "She won't make any mistakes. I told her what would happen if she did. Robish, now, he thinks I'm a fool. What about you, Hilliard? You don't think I'm a fool, do you?"

"Not a fool," Dan said slowly. "No."

Glenn laughed. "Pop, you're all right. You're a real funny guy. Now you sit down while I have a little drink with Robish."

Dan felt himself moving into the living room.

"Cindy won't take any chances, Dan," Eleanor said, trying to smile. "You're not worried about that, are you?"

"Of course not," Dan lied, recalling the defiant contempt in his daughter's eyes. "Cindy's too smart."

"Dan..." Eleanor whispered. "Dan, you didn't..?"

Dan shook his head.

Eleanor relaxed slightly. "Because it's such a short time now, dear, till they go."

Dan stared at her. What if Cindy made some foolish attempt to get help? Certainly she would go over all the possibilities with which he had struggled. But what would Cindy conclude? You could never be sure that someone else might not examine the same set of facts and arrive at the opposite conclusions.

THERE was a cold glint in Cindy's eyes—very puzzling to Charles Wright. Sitting beside her in his sports car in a drive-in restaurant—where he had brought her finally, after suggesting almost every place else in the city—Chuck sipped his coffee and let the evening's silence gather around again.

Over and over she had assured him, finally with some impatience, that it was just this cold nagging her. But Chuck had never seen her behave like this before. Even at the office she managed a secret smile occasionally. And tonight, her eyes were clear, with no evidence of a cold in them.

Cynthia wasn't the sort of girl Chuck normally chose for a playmate. Since coming home from the Marines, he had steered clear of the ones who might want to turn a nice thing into a permanent,

and therefore, in his book, a not-so-nice thing. Chuck had worked out for himself a very neat little philosophy: life is short, marriage is long, and love is something no one can depend on, ever. If this was the cynicism of youth, so be it. He was stuck with it.

But with Cindy, things had been different from the beginning. This fact bewildered him and continued to fill him with an odd high-running excitement, whether he was with her or not. What did it mean? And why was he sticking around to find out, since he already suspected that she could not fit into his pattern?

Tonight now, she had lied to him on the telephone and she had been lying ever since she had leaped out the door of her house before he could so much as touch the doorbell. Now she had fallen into a silence that shut him out completely.

"Look, I don't mind being ignored," he said, twisting around in the small seat, "but you might give me a hint."

"I'm sorry, Chuck." Just that.

Chuck shrugged.

Slowly — very slowly then — Cindy turned to him. The small face trembled, fell apart, going all wrong. She was lowering her head, her lip shaking, and, before he could speak, she was against him, full against his chest.

His heart tightening, Chuck held her. He could feel her shuddering. Though the questions surged in him, he said nothing. When she didn't speak or cry, the suspicions of the last few weeks hardened into words: "Your people don't think I'm worth much, do they?"

Cindy, her mind battering like a trapped wild bird against her stiff helplessness, decided that she had to tell him. Chuck would know what to do. "Chuck, I have to tell you. Chuck — "

But then, with the words already forming in her throat, she remembered Glenn Griffin whispering hastily into her ear as he half shoved her toward the door an hour ago: "You tell anyone, we'll take your mother along on our little ride after a while, red-head. Maybe the kid, too, in case the cops get wise to when we're blowing out of here tonight. Any shooting, you folks get it first, see."

"Yes, Cindy?" Chuck prompted.

"Take me home."

"What?"

"Please, Chuck, no more questions. Take me home."

"Not now. What were you going to say?"

"Please, please, please."

She was sitting up straight again, in her own corner.

He took her home. What the devil, he was thinking, with the irritation erupting through him. Mr. Hilliard looked upon him as reckless, irresponsible. Probably Papa Hilliard had had his say: Chuck Wright isn't going to marry you, Cindy, you or any one else. And she had believed him. This was the brush-off.

Mr. Hilliard was right, wasn't he? You don't intend to marry her, do you? That much was for sure. Then why the resentment?

He turned into the Hilliard driveway, and noted a small but, to him, interesting fact: Mr. Hilliard had failed, for the first time within Chuck's memory, to put his car in the garage for the night. Tsk-tsk, he thought satirically, what will happen to our world if we start breaking with our little ironclad habits?

Chuck jumped out, came around to open Cindy's door. She looked unable or unwilling to move. He felt a strange melting sensation in the pit of his stomach. His youthful anger gone, he touched her arm. For a split second he was sure that she was going to crumple against him again.

"Chuck," she whispered suddenly, "do you have a gun?"

He couldn't speak. The question seemed to come from nowhere, staggering him, taking his breath.

"Cindy, what do you mean? *Cindy!"*

But she was already running toward the house. He followed her to the rear door, the one she always used at night. She turned there, while her hand fumbled at the lock. "Forget it, Chuck. Can you forget everything?"

"No," he said and took the key from her trembling hand and unlocked the door. "Cindy, you can't go in now, like this. Let me come in with you. We've got to — "

"No!" The whisper threatened to grow loud. "Just stay away and leave me alone, that's all!"

She slipped into the house, closed the door. Chuck strode to the car. He discovered that he still held the key to the back door of the Hilliard house in his palm. He shoved it into his pocket, stepped into the car, maneuvered it onto the boulevard. What would a girl like Cindy Hilliard want with a gun? He'd get the answer to that one tomorrow morning, first thing.

DAN heard the back door open and close. He had come up to bed at 11, following orders. Since then, he had lain there with his hand stretched between the twin beds, holding Eleanor's.

There was a low, indistinct rush of voices in the kitchen. Dan got up and went into the upstairs hall. "Cindy?" he called.

Behind him Eleanor inquired with taut concern, "Dan?"

"Stay in there, dear," Dan warned her, then called again: "Cindy?"

The dining-room light clicked on and a flow of light reached the downstairs hall. Dan was going down the stairs when he heard Robish's voice, blurred with whisky: "What's it to you, Hank?"

Dan paused in the front hall and looked into the dining room. He heard Glenn Griffin approach from behind him, and he knew the gun was on him. But what he saw before him made him forget that. Cindy was backed against the buffet. Robish was in front of her, his head twisted, his small eyes on Hank Griffin, who sat at the table. The room reeked with whisky. Dan took in everything in a sickening and terrifying flash.

"What's the matter?" Robish demanded again of Hank. "Got to search her, don't I? Searched the old man, didn't we?"

Dan could see Hank's profile as the boy stood up at the table; his dark eyes were sharp. "Get upstairs to bed, miss," Hank Griffin said, each word clipped off and distinct.

"Oh no, oh no," Robish said hazily, "gonna search her, might have a gun, got to search the pretty little redhead."

Hank's words were still soft: "Let her by, Robish."

Robish turned fully. "You giving orders, too, Hank?"

"This time."

Ignoring Hank, Robish turned again to Cindy. But Hank reached him in two steps, whirled him about, and then Dan saw Robish's head snap back; he saw the sudden blood.

Hank stepped away then. "You going up to bed now, miss?"

Cindy joined Dan in the hall as Robish shook his head.

Then there was a low roar from that broad, working throat. One arm went out to Hank, but Hank stepped easily aside.

Out of nowhere the automatic appeared in Hank's hand.

"Hank, you damn fool," Glenn Griffin breathed harshly.

Robish was blinking at the gun in Hank's hand, Dan's automatic, the one Robish didn't know existed. He didn't move. He stared owlishly at the two brothers.

"Turning on *me,* huh," Robish muttered at last. "Turning on your old pal." The words seeped from between thick, moist lips. He was staring at Hank. "You better stay away from me."

Still muttering, he disappeared into the living room. Glenn glared at his brother.

"Get to bed," he said, his tone hard and resentful.

"Thank you, Mr. Griffin," Cindy said then, her eyes on Hank.

She held Dan's arm. They turned to the stairs. Eleanor was halfway down.

It was at that moment that they heard a door closing. It took several seconds for the significance of that sound to reach them.

Glenn understood first. "Stay down here," he barked to Dan. Then to Hank: "Cover 'em."

Glenn ran across the dark living room, through the sun porch, cursing as his leg struck furniture twice, delaying him.

Robish was outside. Glenn was outside. Dan, frowning, realized that for the first time he was in the house and two of them were not. The pressure of her hand on his arm told him that the same thought had taken hold of Cindy. He could depend on Cindy's acting fast now; he could depend on Eleanor's getting upstairs to the telephone. In the dark, and inside, he had as good a chance as Glenn who was outside and unprotected.

His first and immediate problem was to get hold of Hank's gun. In less than half a minute, he made the decision. In the house, all doors locked and the family safely huddled upstairs in one room out of range of Glenn's gun, Dan had a chance to hold off Glenn and Robish, perhaps to force them to get in the car and leave. A slight chance, perhaps, but he had no other.

It came to him then how he would get hold of Hank's gun.

"Faint," he whispered to Cindy.

Cindy, not waiting even a second, collapsed on the floor.

CHAPTER 3

DAN HILLIARD uttered a small breath of surprise as Cindy fell and, stooping over her, he watched Hank Griffin out of the corner of his eye. The boy looked bewildered, uncertain.

"Give me a hand, Griffin," Dan said, attempting to lift his daughter.

The boy hesitated, straining to hear whatever sounds Glenn and Robish might be making outside the house.

"Come on," Dan said. "Can't you see this child is sick?"

Hank made up his mind then. With the gun in one hand, he came forward, placed his other arm under Cindy's shoulders.

The gun was directed toward the front door. It was the second Dan had anticipated. He struck out, fast and smoothly. The automatic clattered to the floor. Dan made a dive for it.

The metal felt moist and warm in his hand. Behind him he heard a small cry of astonishment and pain and turned to see Cindy sitting up now, her mouth clamped over the boy's wrist, biting hard. Hank's face writhed in pain.

"Get out," Dan said curtly. "Cindy, lock the other doors and get upstairs. Ellie! Ellie, get on the phone up there, fast, and keep Ralphie with you, away from the windows."

Cindy was already up, flipping off the dining-room light. Dan heard the click of the side-door lock and watched Hank stepping toward the front door.

"Hurry it up," Dan said to young Griffin.

Hank opened the front door. Dan shoved him out and locked the front door. He was turning toward the stairs when he heard, from above, Eleanor's scream. He bounded up the stairs as Eleanor appeared from Ralphie's room.

"Ralphie . . . Dan . . . Ralphie's gone!"

Cindy came up the stairs behind him, flipped off the hall light, plunging them into total darkness. They seemed frozen there then, the three of them – mute figures, caught, trapped.

"Maybe he got away," Cindy said at last. "Maybe he – "

But Glenn's voice reached them then from outside. "We ain't going, Hilliard. Open up the back door and throw that gun out." Dan automatically dropped down. Cindy crouched low.

"Hilliard," Glenn cried outside, and there was a note of cruel desperation behind the call. "Hilliard, listen!"

At first, Dan couldn't believe the voice that reached him. But Eleanor recognized it and uttered a faint cry of defeat.

"Dad?" The one word came from outside. There was no childish valor in it; the word was high with terror. "Dad."

"If we go, Hilliard," Glenn Griffin's voice said, "we're taking the kid. Open up and we'll forget the whole business."

Dan flicked the safety latch on the gun and stood up. "I'm coming down to the back door," he called to Glenn Griffin.

It was not a shout that reached him then from the darkness, but a laugh, a thin and arrogant gust of triumph.

"Lock the bedroom door, Cindy. If you hear a shot downstairs, make the call anyway. If you don't, keep Eleanor up here. No matter what else you hear, don't call."

Dan descended the uncarpeted back stairs and walked through the tiny pantry; then he threw open the door.

"Toss the gun first, Hilliard," Glenn Griffin advised.

Dan tossed the gun. Again he had no choice.

Glenn appeared first out of the darkness. Then Ralphie. Dan heard the stifled sob as the boy leaned against him.

"Go upstairs, son," Dan said.

The boy obeyed, running on bare feet up the stairs. A door opened and Dan heard Ralphie taken in with the others.

Now Glenn was standing before him, tall and angular. Behind Glenn, Hank Griffin appeared from the darkness.

"We got Robish, too," Glenn Griffin said, pushing Dan backward into the pantry. "I had to put him on ice for a while so he'd learn who was boss around here." The young man spoke coolly.

Then the blow struck. It was a vicious swipe, the barrel of the revolver catching him on the forehead. Dan went down.

He had no idea how much later it was that he awakened in his own bedroom in the darkness. He stirred with a groan. Then he felt Eleanor's hand on his face, over his mouth, gentle and cool.

"Dan," she whispered, "Dan, don't talk, don't move, darling. Dan, you hear me?" His head nodded under her hand. "Dan, I gave you some pills to make you sleep. It's almost morning. If you can hear me, listen to me."

"Ralphie?"

"He's all right, Dan. Sleeping."

"And . . . *them?*"

"They're still here. Cindy's with Ralphie and one of them's in her bedroom up here. The other two are downstairs. Dan, you did a foolish and terrible and wonderful thing, and I love you. Can you hear me, darling? You must never do anything like that again. You might have been killed. Dan, I'm pleading with you. Promise me, darling. Never again."

"I promise," he whispered, dully.

"We don't want you to be brave, darling," his wife said. "We want you well and alive with us."

There were things that Dan knew vaguely at this moment, but he couldn't arrange them in his mind and he couldn't explain them. "Didn't the woman come?"

"Telephoned," Eleanor said softly. "After midnight. She's not coming, Dan. I don't know what it means, but they're staying. Now try to sleep again, dear."

He felt then her lips closing over his, soft and full, and he felt his love for her stirring deeply, more deeply perhaps than ever before. He slept.

NEXT MORNING Glenn Griffin sat at the head of the table, one of Dan's hats pushed back from his face. A cigarette dangled between his lips. Dan studied his own large freckled hands. Beside him, Eleanor pressed her leg against his. Cindy was across from Dan, her eyes black and determined. Beside her, Ralphie was alert, his gaze soft and bewildered as he stared at the gash on his father's forehead.

"Things've changed, folks," Glenn was saying. "My friend who was coming can't make it. Some coppers tried to pick her off." Outside, the rain gurgled in the drains. "Now I got things to do before I can go. We're going to stick a little longer."

"How much longer?" Dan asked.

"Until I get a certain envelope in the mail, Hilliard; that's how much longer."

"When will that be?"

"It might get here today. Meanwhile, everything goes on around here just like normal. You and the redhead go to work, just like usual. Only Junior here's too smart a boy. He stays home. He's sick today."

"I'm sorry, Griffin," Dan said then, slowly. "I'm not going to work today. I'm sick, too."

Glenn's laugh died. "You could be a lot sicker, Hilliard."

"I can call my office. No one will think anything of it."

"Then how'm I going to get the envelope, Pop? With the dough in it." He was grinning faintly. "That envelope's addressed to you at your office, see."

Dan considered this, feeling the pressure increase along Eleanor's leg. Then he shook his head. "I can't leave my wife in the house with that drunken friend of yours, Griffin. Not after what happened last night."

A poisonous silence hung over the room.

Then Glenn said, "Mrs. Hilliard can stay upstairs all day. I'll keep Robish down here."

"I can't take that chance. After last night."

"Dammit, Hilliard, I said I'm making a promise! Don't push, Hilliard. Don't push too far!" Glenn's chest was heaving. "I took orders all my life from smart-eyed characters like you. Now. You're going to that office of yours, Hilliard, and, as soon as that dough comes, you take it to your bank and get it changed into small bills, nothing over twenty, and then you call me and tell me you're on your way home. Just that, Hilliard. Only listen: I been in touch with a pal of mine, see. And this guy's going to do a little job for me. Before you come home, I'll think of some way for you to pay him off for me. You think you want to try something different, the kid and the wife'll be here." He stopped and began to grin. "Pop, you're a tough guy, but you be careful, see."

Eleanor reached for Dan's hand. She said quietly, "Dan, if one of them starts up the stairs all day, I'll scream so loud they'll have to use their guns, and that'll be the end of it. Do you understand me, dear? It's only a little time now." She stood up. "I'll get your raincoat. Isn't it an awful day?"

Dan happened to be watching Hank Griffin's face when Eleanor went into the hall: the boy stared after her with a strange expression of admiration.

In the hall, Dan climbed into the coat she held, then turned around and took his wife into his arms. He drew her to him and kissed her, unmindful of the eyes. Glenn's mocking laugh reached from the dining room, raucous and coarse. It was then that Hank Griffin spoke. "What's so funny?" the boy demanded of his brother.

The laughter broke off jaggedly.

"I don't see anything so funny you should break your neck laughing, that's all," Hank said, but his voice was shaky now.

"I laugh when I feel like it, Hank," Glenn said evenly. "You got nothing to say about it. Now go wake up Robish. I need some shut-eye. And you, Hilliard — what are you waiting for? Wouldn't want to be late and get docked at that store, would you?"

Dan was looking past Glenn; then he took a step toward his son. "Ralphie, you heard what Mr. Griffin said. You stay with your mother upstairs and out of trouble." Ralphie nodded.

Abruptly, Dan raised a hand in brief salute and went out into the bone-chilling rain toward Cindy's car. Cindy joined him at once, sliding under the wheel, shooting the coupé down the driveway. Dan didn't look back.

Robish would wake up now, drunk, groggy. Would he turn on Glenn? Could Glenn handle him?

THE MAIL arrived in three large canvas bags at 9:31. The mail clerks worked fast, because Mr. Hilliard was standing in the mail room. He remained there until all of the mail had been sorted. The senior mail clerk handed Dan all the envelopes addressed to Personnel Department or to Mr. Daniel Hilliard. The recognition of the return addresses on every envelope caused Dan to turn away abruptly, his whole body packed solid with defeat.

The next mail was five hours away, and no power on earth could hurry it. He went into his office, sat down behind the familiar desk and, working on some impulse that he dared not question, he reached for a blank piece of paper and his pen.

> *To Whom It May Concern,* he wrote. *Innocent people will be in the automobile with the three escaped convicts you want. If you shoot, you will be responsible for taking the lives of people who have done no harm. To attempt to trace this letter will endanger these same people.*

He studied what he had written. Then he folded the paper, drew a plain envelope from his desk, sealed it over the note and addressed it: *Police Headquarters, South Alabama St., City.*

He picked up the phone and dialed his home number.

"Ellie? Where are they?"

"Downstairs. I'm with Ralphie. Are you all right, dear?"

"Anything happen? Anything at all?"

"No. Only Mr. Patterson, the trash collector, came to the back door. He wanted to get in the garage, but I told him we'd lost the key and not to bother. He seemed awfully disappointed in a funny way, but that's all."

"He didn't notice anything odd?"

"No, I'm sure not. But Mr. R. thought he did. I was worried for a few minutes. That's all, Dan."

Dan heard a familiar, taunting laugh: Glenn Griffin, listening on the downstairs phone.

"Nothing in the morning mail," Dan said. "Perhaps this afternoon. Two-forty-five. Good-bye, dear."

Dan replaced the instrument on his desk. He sat bent forward, every nerve crying out for him to go home, to murder those men, to get it over with. But all he could do was sit, trying to devise a way to have that anonymous note delivered to the police without answering any questions about it.

"I SAW him snooping around those damn windows," Robish said. "We got to grab him, Griffin. Listen! He was up on his toes, looking in the garage."

"Mr. Patterson?" Eleanor said. "He just came to collect. He picks up the trash every Thursday morning and then he comes back after lunch for his check."

"I know what I seen," Robish said, his voice murky. "He saw the car. I'm going to get him. Let me have your gun."

"Hank," Glenn shouted, "where'd the old guy go?"

"House next door. I can see the back end of the truck."

"Then maybe I can catch him, Glenn," growled Robish.

"Glenn," Hank called, "why take chances? Let's just blow."

Eleanor's eyes were fixed on Glenn. "Mr. Patterson wouldn't be suspicious. He . . . you saw him . . . a man like that . . ."

"Shut up," Glenn Griffin said and extended his gun toward Robish. "Mrs. Hilliard, you want the old guy to bring the cops up on your lawn? Use your head."

Robish shoved the gun into the side of Dan's gray jacket. He took a step toward the back door. Glenn's voice halted him.

"If you get into trouble, don't come back here, Robish."

"Me? I don't know what trouble is."

Just before she collapsed over the table, Eleanor thought that she had never heard Robish's voice so lighthearted, so excited.

AT approximately this time Dan Hilliard stepped into a hotel where he was not likely to be known, asked for a messenger, then spoke to him quickly. The man nodded, showing no surprise as he accepted from Dan a white envelope and a five-dollar bill. In less than a minute the messenger was walking toward the offices of the city police department, directly across the street from the offices of the Sheriff.

The Wallings were not at home. Mr. Patterson returned to his truck and started to climb in, a little stiffly because of his arthritis; then he saw the man sitting in the cab of his truck.

"Just get in, Jack," the man said.

Mr. Patterson saw the revolver as he lifted himself up.

"Drive, Jack, and no hurry. Drive out east."

Mr. Patterson started the motor and glanced sideways at the huge man in the seat beside him. Mr. Patterson recognized the face, after perhaps ten seconds, and then he remembered the car parked in the Hilliard garage and the radio reports.

"Good Lord," he said aloud, "those poor people."

The man seemed pleased at this; he chuckled heavily.

Mr. Patterson had forgotten everything but Mrs. Hilliard's face as she wrote out his check a few minutes ago. The gun must have been pointed at her then, from the next room. Why hadn't he guessed that?

If he'd gone straight to a drugstore and called Jesse Webb, he might have helped them. Mr. Patterson had even jotted down the license number on a scrap of paper that was now in his pocket; he meant to ask Jesse Webb — Jesse would remember him because many was the night he'd played pinochle with young Jesse's father — whether the license was the one Mr. Patterson suspected it might be. Jesse'd have that sort of information.

But he had done nothing. If anything happened to those people, he'd never forgive himself. It was then that he realized that what was going to happen now was to happen to him. His breathing became irregular, and the arthritis pain clenched in his right knee. But he didn't grow panicky. He made a silent plan.

They were east of the city now, on a country road. With his left elbow, very quietly, he pressed down on the door handle. Timing the click, he spoke simultaneously with it and in a loud tone: "Mister, I swear I'm not going to say a word to anybody!"

The man beside him laughed then. "Why don't you get down on your knees and pray, Jack?"

The door was open now. Ahead, Mr. Patterson saw two blue gasoline pumps set alongside the road, fairly close to the edge. There was a deserted and boarded-up service-station building, too.

Mr. Patterson waited till he was almost abreast of the pumps, then in one movement he whipped the wheel to the right, tramped hard on the accelerator and fell from the truck just as its nose struck the first pump. He hit the gravel and rolled, the stiffness of his leg forgotten, hearing the metallic crash above and behind him. He kept his body crouched low and ran toward the building.

He was within two yards of the weathered building when the first bullet reached him; then he heard the cracking, ear-bursting sound. He knew he had been hit; but what surprised Mr. Patterson, in the only moment he had left for surprise or any other emotion, was that the bullet did not burn or sear or scorch. It was more like a paralyzing but painless blow against his back. He didn't feel the second bullet at all. Nor the third.

In his office, Dan Hilliard received a phone call from home. He listened, frowning. Then he said, "How can I do that, Ellie? The money should be here in less than an hour now. It's almost two o'clock."

He listened again. He couldn't believe what his wife told him; the incredibility of what she said smashed into the tension of his mind that had been straining toward 2:45 for hours now.

When he replaced the instrument and stood up, Dan Hilliard did not know why he was being instructed by Glenn Griffin, through Eleanor, to do what he was now going to do. He felt a sour rage rise in him. He had been tricked. The money had not been mailed until after Griffin had talked to that woman on the phone last night. It could not be delivered until tomorrow. Griffin had known all along. He had lied in order to get him out of the house today, in order to make it appear a normal day, without incident.

Now, however, there was an incident of some sort. In half an hour he and Cindy were to be parked in an area in front of a shopping center on the far east of the city. Why they were to be there, what would happen—Glenn Griffin had not told him.

The panting was over now, the wild, animal terror was behind Robish. Back there a bit, crashing through the woods after he realized the truck wouldn't start, he had been scared. And sore. Mostly sore at that old guy, thinking he could pull a fast one. Remembering the old guy sent a warm, pleasant flush down Robish's massive body: the way the old guy'd tried to run, stiff-like, and then the way he stopped, kicking up the gravel with one foot, those skinny little arms going up, and then the way he sprawled. That memory had caused Robish to grin.

Glenn thought he was dumb. But was he? Hadn't he come out of the edge of the woods, picked the shopping center, found the telephone in the service station, made his call? Wasn't he waiting here now, cozy and tight in the men's room, until the little redhead's car came for him? Robish was feeling great.

Glenn had said a half hour. Robish had no way to estimate time, but he figured maybe ten minutes had passed since he talked to Griffin, maybe twenty.

Then he heard, very faintly, the wail of a siren. It made him grin. But the grin twisted and left his face sagging. A lot could happen in half an hour. Maybe those cops'd work their way through the woods out onto the street.

Where was that redhead!

"Cindy'll be back in a minute, Mr. Hilliard," Chuck Wright said. "She's taking dictation from Mr. Hepburn right now."

Chuck hadn't missed the sleepwalking aspects of Dan Hilliard's appearance and manner.

"How much longer?"

Chuck felt a twitch of annoyance at the man. "I couldn't say," he said, the irritation roughing his words. But he felt it ebb. "Won't you sit down, sir?" he said.

"Could you interrupt her?" Dan asked. "It's—important."

"Mr. Hilliard," Chuck said, "is something wrong? I mean — with Cindy? Or you? Someone?" Chuck shook his head in a bewildered way. "I don't mean to pry. At first I thought maybe Cindy was just giving me the brush. Now — "

"Now what?"

"I'm damned if I know."

And there it rested. It stayed there because all Dan Hilliard would say was what Cindy had said earlier in the afternoon: "You're imagining things, Chuck." Her father used the same words now.

"It started last night," Chuck said stubbornly. He went over it all for Dan — the way she'd leaped out at him from the house, the way she'd insisted on being taken home after sitting in silence all evening, the abrupt tears in the car and the question about a gun.

"It doesn't figure, sir. That's all."

"It's not your business, Chuck."

"Maybe not, but — "

"No *maybes*. This is not your affair. Stay out of it."

"It's my business if it concerns Cindy, Mr. Hilliard."

The blue eyes snapped to attention. "So it's like that, is it?"

"It's like that," Chuck said, "whether you like it or not."

"I've no time to talk about it now. Or to think about it." The earlier urgency returned to the man. "Where's Hepburn's office?"

"I'll get her," Chuck said. He tapped on Mr. Hepburn's door. Whatever this thing was, it was bigger than any feeling Mr. Hilliard might bear toward him. It was beyond that, more desperate. He spoke a few brief words, saw Cindy rise without so much as turning to Mr. Hepburn, and run out the door. He followed. He saw Cindy join her father; there were a few muttered words between them. Cindy reached for her coat. Dan Hilliard was moving toward the corridor and Cindy followed.

Chuck stood staring at the closed door. All right. Now he'd have to find out on his own. *"It's my business if it concerns Cindy,"* his own words echoed back at him. That's the way it came to him. He loved Cynthia Hilliard.

He grabbed his own raincoat and strode from the office.

CHAPTER 4

After he had seen Dan Hilliard and Cindy turn into the parking lot where Cindy kept her car, Chuck Wright had a quick moment of panic. Would he lose them before he could get his car onto the street behind them? Cindy, he saw, did the driving and she was not wasting time; she swung north, and shot out of sight before Chuck could ease his low-slung sports job out of the parking lot.

In the midtown area no turns were permitted between noon and six, and it was this accident of timing that allowed him to narrow the distance until he saw the black coupé turn east. He followed. It was not difficult to keep Cindy's car in view, but he was careful to stay out of line of her rear-vision mirror.

A siren was such an ordinary and expected sound on a city thoroughfare that Chuck felt no surprise when the Sheriff's car whizzed past. But when an ambulance followed he began to think of an accident east of the city. Were the Hilliards now on their way to the scene? But, of course, that didn't explain last night, Cindy's startling tears and the question about the gun.

When, not 20 minutes later, Cindy's black coupé edged itself into a parking space before a new shopping center on the edge of the city, the siren wails were distant, well beyond the woods to the northeast. Chuck drew to a halt behind the service station on the corner; he waved the attendant away and worked with the air hose at his rear wheels while he watched.

Almost at once, a man emerged from the service station—a ponderous bulk of man in a rain-soaked gray suit. The man approached Cindy's car, waited while Mr. Hilliard climbed out of the car, then slid his great body into the seat beside Cindy. Mr. Hilliard, with not so much as a nod of recognition, stepped back in and closed the door. The car shot forward.

Chuck didn't wait. He was well behind, but with the coupé in clear vision. The square mass of the strange man's head was between the other two. Who was he? What could a man like that have to do with the Hilliards? The black-sheep uncle? The family drunkard? He'd probably find the explanation that simple in the end.

Then what about the gun?

Chuck trailed the coupé all the way north, aware that it was the least populated way to Kessler Boulevard. He remained far behind, knowing that Cindy could recognize his car at once.

In the end, Chuck had no answer; the coupé pulled into the Hilliard driveway as he knew it would. Where does this leave you? he asked himself. Dead end.

"Where does it leave us, Jess?" Tom Winston asked, moving away from the frail outstretched body of the dead man.

Jesse Webb stepped to the two uprooted blue gasoline pumps and half leaned against the red truck. He spread out on the flat top of the fender the few pitiful belongings he had taken from Mr. Patterson's pockets: a dog-eared wallet, four single dollar bills in another pocket, a chewed-at stub of pencil, odd scraps of paper, and nine checks, each made out for $2 payable to Floyd Patterson.

Jesse unfolded the scraps of paper, flattening them out: a grocery list, a garage repair bill marked paid, and one other.

"Shot in the back. Three times. Why, Jess?" asked Tom Winston.

Jesse rubbed the back of his neck. "It's a good question, Tom. Why'd he try to smash into those pumps? Or was that an accident? You tell me, Tom."

"The truck won't go, so I figure the killer had to take off on foot. They've got ten men in those woods and more coming. My hunch is — "

"Hold it," Jesse Webb said, and then, very quietly, "Lord." He was holding between his long fingers the last small scrap of soiled paper from Mr. Patterson's pocket. "Lord, Tom."

Winston bent over, studied the figures printed in pencil on the paper, then looked up into the thin face of Jesse Webb.

Far off a siren wailed. The sound cut through Jesse.

"He might've got just a quick glance," Winston said, beginning to breathe a little tightly himself. "He might've been in a hurry, y'know. That'd explain the 3."

"Maybe he heard it on the radio," Jesse drawled. "Maybe he jotted it down from the radio, just in case."

"People do that," Winston conceded. "But if you change the 3 to an 8, you got it. I reckon he was in a hurry, y'know, and his eyes not what they once was."

"Just for a while," said Jesse Webb slowly, "we're going to change that 3 to an 8. We'll just kind of pretend Mr. Patterson doesn't have a radio. We're going to pretend he saw that license, and then we're going to locate that car. I'm going to find out where he's been today, Tom, and you're going to start working backward on those checks—and all the rest of Mr. Patterson's customers. The works. That might include a hundred, two hundred people. This might be it." He was moving toward the Sheriff's car, in long swift strides. "We got the license. Now we're going to get that car. If they pick up anybody in the woods, give it to me fast. Tell 'em who we're looking for now."

"Now. What are we going to do about that farmer's car out there in the garage? The car's hot now, Pop. Not like it was before, see. Our pal Robish here, he got jumpy and he didn't go through the old guy's pockets way he should."

"If you think I'm going to do any more of your dirty work for you, you're wrong." Hilliard's voice was level and empty and dry.

Glenn thought this was funny; he laughed; he even threw an arm over Hilliard's wide, thick shoulders. "Pop, you're smart and you got guts. But you got to be reasonable. Look at my position. The kid's been yammering at me all day to go. I can't go, I tell him. That dough'd come to your office tomorrow morning and I'd be miles away, and no chance to get my little job here in town taken care of. I worked for that money, Pop. Me and Hank. We can't throw any of it away."

The money wasn't worth it, thought Hank Griffin. He was leaning against the paneled wall of the den, listening to them in the living room. Paying off Jesse Webb wasn't worth it. Nothing was worth sticking here now with a man dead and the cops liable to close in any minute! Another part of Hank's mind also cried, *"These people have had enough!"* His muscles throbbed with the certainty that they should go, move, get out. But Glenn always made the decisions. And he was usually right.

Dan Hilliard was shaking his head. "I don't know what to tell you. The car's safe enough in the garage. No one else is likely to come and if you try to take it out — "

"I'm not going to take it out, Hilliard. *You* are." The words silenced the room. "Soon as it gets good and dark out, you're going out there to the garage and you're going to take the license plates off and put on the ones from the redhead's coupé. You're too wise to start talking even if you get caught. Me, I trust you — because I got you where the hair's short. You listening, Hank? That's the only time you ever take a chance trusting anybody."

Lesson noted, Hank thought bitterly. He had to admit the truth of it, too. Glenn was reminding him that the last time he'd pleaded with his brother to go, Glenn had warned him that Hilliard couldn't be trusted once they didn't have one of the family right alongside. This was why Glenn planned to take the wife and the girl along when they did leave. Hank had balked; not the girl. But Glenn's smile had withered his rebellion, even as Glenn had agreed with a shrug: *We'll take the kid then, it make you feel any better, Hank. Only don't go soft on me, see.*

Hank's eyes drifted again to the girl. She was watching her father. Hank remembered the way, last night, she'd said, *Thank you, Mr. Griffin.* That memory and the expression of pity on her beautiful face now caught Hank like a double blow to the stomach.

As Dan Hilliard said, "I'll dump the car in the river for you, Griffin; I know just the place," Hank couldn't take his eyes from the girl's lovely face, even though that was the source of his pain. It was almost, he realized, as if he wanted to suffer; he had never before had a chance to suffer about a girl, and he needed it. That need was part of his hunger.

"You play square with me, Pop," Glenn was saying, "and I'll play square with you, see."

Square? *Square!* When you plan to use his child as a shield! Not for the first time, but for the first time in this cold and single-minded way, Hank hated his brother. Glenn was the only person who had ever shown him any real kindness. Glenn had protected him from his father's brutal violence, from his mother's disdain. Yet under all the twisted trust and love, Hank hated him now. Facing that fact made Hank Griffin forget everything else, even the eternal prodding fear that perhaps the police were moving closer even now. . . .

WORKING with the city directory Jesse had, by five o'clock, located the exact sites of the homes of those people who had written checks to Mr. Patterson in payment for trash removal. It was safe to assume that those who paid by cash were nearby. He had drawn a red-ink marking around the neighborhood, consisting of approximately ten square city blocks – perhaps two hundred homes, three stores, several vacant lots.

He shifted the map about on his desk. "I don't say they're in there, Tom. If they knocked off Mr. Patterson, they'd be damn fools to stay. But three human beings can't disappear into thin air. We got four cars up there, right? Tell 'em to park. Put one here, another here, and here and here. That covers the main roads out. My hunch is they won't go through the city to get away." He straightened and took a breath.

"Sorry to intrude, gentlemen," a voice said from the doorway. Carson, the FBI man, entered. "The city police, for some reason that I don't get, have been sitting on this since noon." He handed Jesse a sheet of white paper with a few words written on it in ink. "It came in at the station some time during the noon hour. A bellhop from one of the hotels brought it, and he gave four different descriptions of the man who paid him to deliver it."

Jesse read it, then passed it over to Tom Winston. Reading, Winston whistled softly. "Now we know," he said, at last.

"The idiot," Jesse Webb muttered.

"The man's on a spot, friends," Carson said.

"But he ought to know!" Jesse said. "He can't play ball with savages like that!"

"Easy now," Tom Winston said.

"But think of that poor guy, trapped in his own house – "

"What's this?" young Carson put in. He picked up the map.

"That's guesswork," Jesse Webb said, slumping into his chair.

"Plain and not-so-fancy guesswork by Deputy Sheriff Webb. Look, Carson, isn't there some way to get word to that guy, whoever he is, that he can't play their game with them? They'll tear him to ribbons before they're done."

Carson lit a cigarette. "What would you do, Webb? Put yourself in his place. I think he was smart to write this thing. It might keep some itchy-fingered young cop from shooting a woman or a child. What would you do under the circumstances?"

"He'd play ball," Tom Winston told Carson, touching Jesse's shoulder with his fist.

"Yeah," said Jesse slowly. "I'd do just that, Tom."

DAN HILLIARD was aware that he drove a car that was wanted by the police; but the license plates from Cindy's coupé might throw off a questioning policeman, if, by some evil chance, a patrol car should notice him. He had tossed the old plates into a thicket along the side of a small street on which there were no houses and felt reasonably sure that he had not been seen.

Dan was within three blocks of the river bridge when he realized that a pair of headlights had been following him. He made a sharp left turn down a shabby street, then a right. He slowed then, carefully.

The twin lights swung into view in the mirror.

Dan felt no panic; he had passed beyond all that now. He took the next right, and chose a driveway that ran close alongside a dark house. Before his pursuer turned the corner, he flipped off his headlights, whipped the gray sedan into the driveway, and let it glide to a stop under the deeper shadow of a small frame garage. He waited, trying to hold his breath, looking out the rear window.

Light flooded the street as the car that had been following picked up speed; the motor roar reverberated through the neighborhood. After the car had passed, Dan could hear the motor slowing, hesitating. In the moment that it passed, he could see nothing but its shape: it was a huge convertible.

Without stopping now to puzzle this out, he felt only a sharp relief that it was not a police car. When the convertible made a turn, Dan backed into the narrow street and nosed away, in the direction from which he had come.

Only when he was crossing the river bridge, did Dan begin to wonder again about the identity of the convertible and its driver. Here was a whole new element, and his mind could not quite bring it fully into the picture. Who could it be?

He dismissed the conjecture as he approached the place that he had in mind — a high cliff perhaps a hundred yards beyond the smooth wide pavement. He was searching for a place where he would turn off the road but he had only the vaguest impression of the area. Slowly he followed car ruts into a clump of trees and underbrush; to his relief, they led to the edge of the bluff.

He set the brake and clambered out, stood listening in the silence, with the headlight beams stabbing the darkness over the water. Down below, the river was almost soundless. He studied the grassy and bush-tangled shelf; there were no obstacles. The crash would be loud and there was the chance that it would attract attention. But Dan, at this point, had grown accustomed to calculating risks.

Sliding into the seat, his shoes clogged with mud, Dan backed so that he was far enough away from the edge of the cliff to gain the necessary momentum. Then he threw the car into forward gear, felt with his left elbow to make sure the door was open, bore down on the gas, released the clutch, held the wheel steady, saw the black void rushing toward him. His ears filled with the crackling of tree limbs and roar of motor and the angry grind of tires in soggy earth.

He plunged sideways, feeling the jolt of hard earth under his body. Then the whole world filled to bursting with the thundering descent of the car. The sound echoed and reverberated, gnashing, crushing and ugly. The splash was abrupt; then came a series of gurgles and gasps, as though some living monster were battling for life below the edge of the bluff. Finally, the bubbling slackened into utter stillness.

Dan crawled to the precipice. Below, there was nothing. He stood up unsteadily, shaking. He was faced now with the hours-long walk back to the house.

DAN WAS crossing the river bridge, returning on foot by the same route he had traveled an hour ago in the gray sedan. Griffin, grinning, had been cruelly specific: "No cabs, Pop. Walk it. Do you good." Each step drove shocks of pain up his legs. He sagged against the stone buttress of the bridge, under a garish street lamp that cast his shadow before him. He caught a glimpse of the slump-shouldered figure of himself, outlined darkly on the wet pavement, small-looking and shriveled. He straightened, and plunged forward again. He found that, if he swung his legs forward, attaining a certain balance, he didn't drive the shafts of burning pain so high up into his body.

Without warning, then — he didn't even see the flash of headlights — a car screamed to a stop across the gleam of dark pavement. It looked familiar in a misty sort of way, as Dan stared at it. The police? A giddiness rose in him. When the door opened and a man stepped out and strode across toward him, he knew that he should turn and run. But he couldn't move.

"Mr. Hilliard. Let me take you home." Dan recognized Chuck Wright. "Come on, sir, I'll give you a lift."

Dan didn't reply. The impossibility of the encounter still held him and he was without will as he crossed the damp pavement, opened the door of the car and slid into the seat. The seat was soft, incredibly soft and giving, and he lowered his body into it with gratitude. He closed his eyes then and gave himself over to the luxury of softness and the close warmth of the car.

The young man's voice lifted him from it. "I'll have to know now, you see," Chuck Wright was saying.

Dan opened his eyes reluctantly. Chuck Wright drove a miniature sports car of foreign design. This was a larger car. "Is this your car?" Dan said.

"My father's. I borrowed it."

"Why?"

Chuck shrugged. "Carburetor on mine's acting up."

A lie, Dan Hilliard's mind cried, with renewed alertness. He had it now. This large car, a convertible, was the one he'd eluded back there before he crossed the river in the gray sedan. Chuck Wright had been following him then. Why?

"If you don't want to talk, sir, it can wait till we get to your house."

The significance of the young man's intention struck Dan for the first time then. How much had he guessed? Of one thing Dan was certain: Chuck Wright must be prevented from taking him all the way home. The boy wanted an explanation. He was stubborn and he would go into the house and demand to know what this was all about. Well then, Dan would give him an explanation.

The idea came to him from nowhere. "You haven't got a little drink on you, have you?" Dan asked.

He heard the abrupt catch of breath. "Not a drop," Chuck Wright said quietly.

"Damnation," Dan said. "Thought you were the drinking type, Chuck. You never know, do you?"

"No, you don't," Chuck agreed thinly.

"Shows to go you," Dan said. "Tell you what, Chuck, old fellow – now that you're into my little family secret, y'see, you can skip taking me home. Just drop me off at the liquor store nearest the house and I'll walk the rest of the way."

"Anything you say, Mr. Hilliard."

"Not shocked, are you, Chuck? You won't hold it against Cindy, will you? I'm always discreet about it. Notice the neighborhood I was in tonight? Nobody knows me there." He halted himself, for fear of going too far. He had made his point; the effect was in young Wright's set face. But what had he forgotten?

Then it came to him, in the long silence, and he spoke again: "Lost my car tonight. Gray car." He lowered his voice: "Own private car, for own private pleasures."

After that, more silence as the miles rolled by. Had he covered everything now? Did Chuck believe him?

The stiff silence held until Chuck stopped in front of the lighted store in which, only last night, Dan had bought the whisky for Robish.

"It's a long walk from here to your house," Chuck said.

"Wouldn't want to embarrass Cindy, would we, Chuck?" he said in conspiratorial tones. "Cindy already embarrassed enough about her father. Worried sick. Poor Cindy."

Standing unsteadily but not drunkenly on the sidewalk, Dan heard Chuck Wright's "good night," clipped and short – no "sir" now. When the red taillights had blurred in the distance, he stepped from the curb, crossed the still-damp street.

A cloud of astonishment filled his brain: where had the cunning come from? How had he thought to make up that story? And, more important, had he been believed?

Even though he stayed on a dim and untraveled street, walking east, he saw a police car halfway down the second block. But the possible meaning of what he saw didn't strike him fully until, three blocks later, he saw another. A wide white stripe ran down the side of the car, and he made out the words "State Police." This time he almost broke into a run.

An awesome urgency drove him forward. A few minutes later,

he was turning into his own driveway. Nothing moved, inside the house or out. The profound quiet sent him charging the last few yards to the side door. The living room was deserted. What did it mean? He rattled the door handle, calling in a whisper. Cindy appeared then, coming across the living room swiftly. When she faced him, he knew that it had not been his approach that had caused the terrible silence.

Cindy was white. Not pale. White. "It's Ralphie," she said, her voice quivering.

CHAPTER 5

For possibly five seconds Dan Hilliard stood motionless in the hall, held rigid in the shock of stark terror over the nightmare scene before him.

He saw Eleanor on the lower steps, her eyes unrecognizable with fright. He heard Cindy pause behind him on the edge of the living room. Glenn Griffin lounged in the dining-room doorway across the hall. Dan saw Robish then, his face a blackish red now. The big man turned the revolver on Dan.

"Where's Ralphie?" Dan asked.

"Upstairs," Eleanor said quickly. "Sleeping."

Glenn Griffin's dark eyes glinted. "This time I ought to let Robish handle him. That kid's going to foul up everything."

"Put that gun away," Dan said in a dry whisper.

It might have been the whispered tone, or it might have been the squared hulk of Dan's body; whatever caused it, Glenn took a step toward Robish.

"Forget it, Robish," Griffin advised. "The old lady covered it on the phone. That teacher don't suspect a thing."

It occurred to Dan to ask what all this meant, but everything was happening too fast. He saw Robish lower the gun then, almost automatically; but the downward arc broke. Something came over the brute face; there was a hardening of his jaw muscles. "You don't give the orders any more," the heavy voice said. "I got this now." Not so slowly then, he brought the gun up again, and this time it was directed at Glenn Griffin's belt.

Robish had forgotten Ralphie now — and whatever Ralphie had done to rouse that murderous instinct — and Dan could see the slow grinding of that dull and unpredictable mind behind the massive forehead. Glenn Griffin saw it, too.

With the gun inching toward his stomach, clutched in the dark hairy hand of the big man, he began to laugh. At first it was a defiant crackle of sound, but staring at the intensity on Robish's face, he seemed abruptly to lose control and the laugh died in a series of odd gurgles. His hands came up to his face, fluttered there, and then his jaw was working without sound.

Glenn Griffin uttered a long but broken breath that sounded like, "Come on, now, Robish — "

At this Robish bellowed — a wild, animal cry, vast and awesome and hollow, the cave of mouth open.

Glenn Griffin's terror-stricken words caught and reflected Dan's immediate thought: "You're nuts, Robish." But as he heard the words, Dan knew at once that Griffin could not have said anything more dangerous. Robish brought the point of the revolver against the young man's stomach in a vicious jab that doubled Griffin over with a cry of pain. Then he began to slither toward the floor, his hands still fluttering in that odd terrified way at his chin.

"Yeh, I'm nuts, Griffin!" Robish bawled. "Doing your dirty work. You, you're the general, ain't you? I konk the guard, I plug the old guy, I — "

Then, from above, from the darkness of the upper hall, another voice cut across Robish's low snarl: "Throw it on the floor, Robish."

Robish turned his head, peered unseeing into those shadows. Hank Griffin, still invisible above, spoke again.

"Throw it on the floor, Robish. Now."

Dan was watching Robish, wondering. He saw the temptation to whirl firing; he saw that slow, prison-broken mind tearing its attention from Glenn Griffin who half lay against the doorframe. Then he saw Robish toss the gun to the rug.

At the head of the stairs there was no movement. The whole house seemed locked in unnatural stillness. Finally, Glenn reached out and picked up the revolver. He stood up, very slowly, reached for his swagger, lifted his shoulders. Then his eyes met Dan's.

With a start Dan caught the furious glare of shame: the memory of those few moments of clawing terror and the knowledge that Dan and the others had stood witness to the cowardice. What would this mean? In what direction would it push Griffin?

Behind him, Dan heard his daughter take a deep draught of breath. Then, breaking the silence, Hank Griffin came down the stairs, stepping quickly. He paused on the bottom step, glanced at Robish who stood bearlike and still now, his arms dangling; then at his brother. What Dan heard then was not so much the content of the younger Griffin boy's words as the flattened note of finality in his tone: "Let's go, Glenn."

Glenn Griffin frowned, said nothing.

"This is our chance, Glenn," Hank said. "We can't hold them and Robish, too. This is going on too long. The cops are bound to get here sooner or later. They're not dumb. And that teacher. The one the kid slipped the note to. How do you know there wasn't some smart cop right at her elbow?"

"Don't get jumpy, kid."

"I'm not jumpy!" Hank Griffin cried suddenly, and Dan saw his mouth trembling oddly. "But I'm not going to the chair just 'cause Robish got trigger-happy and you let him. You think the cops ain't working on that right now?"

"Shut up," Glenn Griffin said softly.

Hank shook his head deliberately. "Come with me, Glenn."

Glenn lifted his shoulders. "After we get the dough."

"What good's the dough gonna do you in the death house?" Hank was shouting then, his mouth twisting and out of control.

Robish watched this with no expression.

"You heard me," Glenn Griffin said then. "We're gonna stay, see. I'm going to pay off Webb. I got to have that dough for Flick so he'll take care of Webb."

"Then I'm going, Glenn. By myself."

After that, the silence came back, intensified.

Finally Glenn Griffin grinned. "Go ahead, kid. On your own they'll have you back in stir in less'n an hour."

Hank Griffin moved into the lighted living room.

"Damn it!" Glenn Griffin yelled. "You'll do what I say, you

little jerk! I got you this far, both you dumb cons, and I'll get you the rest of the way!"

Hank did not pause until he reached the door of the sunroom; then he turned. "Yeh," he said bitterly, low, "you got me this far. And where is that, I'm asking you. We're all headed for the chair, that's where. Only count me out." Then his voice dropped even lower: "Come along, Glenn."

"I oughta — " Both guns came up at the same instant. Hank Griffin was shaking his head.

"It'd break my heart, Glenn, but I'd do it. So long, Glenn."

Hank Griffin backed through the sunroom door, turned and ran, his steps sharp on the tiled porch.

"He's gonna take the car," Robish said.

Glenn Griffin touched the light switch, plunged them all into darkness; Dan felt him brush past, heard the window overlooking the driveway grind open. "Stay away from that car, you dumb punk!"

Outside, a door on Cindy's coupé slammed. The motor turned over, caught, purred.

Above this sound Dan heard another. It was Glenn Griffin shouting wildly, a long series of blasphemy and lewdness erupting from the frustration in him.

HANK traveled west four full blocks before he saw the first patrol car. He made a sharp right turn, so that he wouldn't have to pass it. A half block farther on he saw another. This time there was no way for him to avoid passing it.

He touched the automatic in his pocket. He'd use it if he had to. His palms were cold and moist.

As he drove directly in front of the nose of the patrol car which was at right angles to the street, he knew that he was forgetting something about Cindy's coupé, something important that made it dangerous. He should have taken the blue sedan. But why? Whatever it was about this car, though, the coppers didn't notice. He watched his rear-view mirror. They didn't follow.

He turned west again, at the first street he saw, and he had gone perhaps two miles when he realized the significance of those two police cars parked that close to the Hilliard house. He'd been right: the cops were wise. But the triumph wouldn't come. He'd been right, but what about Glenn back there? What was going to happen now to that girl?

Funny, though — now that he was away from her, what happened to her didn't seem so important. There was never anything he could have done anyway about what Glenn planned after he had the money. The girl was going along in the car then to make the escape look natural and to act as a shield.

Only a few cars approached or passed now, in the late night. He rolled down the window at his elbow. The sharp, cold air felt fine. But underneath the sensation of freedom, there was a feeling of uncertainty stirring. Back at the house, Hank had had a definite plan. Now he couldn't remember exactly what it was. Something about heading west, then doubling back to the Chicago road that would be comparatively free farther north. He could be in Chicago by morning.

He glanced at the gauges. There was less than half a tank of gas. And no money. Only the few coins he'd fished out of that desk drawer in the den. That meant he'd have to pull a job — on his own.

This thought, together with the idea of a strange big city like Chicago where he knew no one, made him go weak clear through.

THE whole house was dark now. It was after 11. In Ralphie's room, Dan flipped on a lamp. He heard his son stir on the bed, and watched him sit up.

Rebellion curled and twisted in Dan. He couldn't do it. They were demanding too much. Was it ever going to stop? So much was happening now, and so fast, that he had not even had time to disentangle its meaning or its threat: Chuck Wright, the parked police cars, the clash between Robish and Glenn, Hank Griffin's departure alone, the uneasy and suspicious realliance between Griffin and Robish. Now this.

Ralphie stared up at his father as Dan closed the door. "That Miss Swift," Ralphie said, shaking his head. "Teaches fifth grade, but what a dope. Thought I was playing a game."

"Thank the Lord she did, Ralphie," Dan said, not moving.

Ralphie caught a hint of threat, and he frowned.

But he was no more amazed at his father's presence than Dan was. Dan could not do what he had been commanded to do. That command from Glenn Griffin was an attempt to reassert his control after his brother walked out, and an attempt to placate Robish. *Junior had to get smart again, see.* Glenn Griffin had explained downstairs. *While you was out, his teacher comes to call. Just passing by, she says, and wondering about the kid's health 'cause he missed school today. I'm in the den and your wife, she handles things clever. The teacher don't suspect a thing. Then Ralphie comes down and gives her a book to take back to school. I'm going nuts but what can I do? Then an hour later maybe, she calls up. She's found a note in the book, see. She says she don't believe a word of it. But she thought the brat's mother ought to know the silly kind of games her son plays. You're going up there now, Hilliard, and you're going to make Junior understand we ain't playing games. You give him a lacing, Pop, or I'll let Robish do it for you.*

"Ralphie," Dan said now, "wasn't last night bad enough? Next time they'll shoot somebody." His voice rose to a cry. "Ralphie, do you want them to shoot your mother?"

"No, no. All I wrote was that we needed help. I said we were prisoners. Aren't we?"

"Ralphie," Dan shouted, "do you want your mother to be killed? Can't you understand? Aren't you old enough?" Dan grabbed Ralphie's arms and began to shake him.

"Ralphie," he pleaded in a harsh whisper as the violence of his shaking increased, "Ralphie, listen to me, start crying! *Please!* You've got to cry now! Ralphie! *Start crying!*"

But the body was stiff between his hands. Dan let go then, stood up, thinking of the delight Robish would find in what he was doing with such pain and reluctance; he lifted his hand, brought it down across the small face, and he heard the sound, saw the eyes pop open, and went instantly sick and empty.

The tears came then, and the astonishment and hurt that he had expected. Ralphie was crying, loud; Dan listened with mingled self-loathing and relief. Then he caught his son to him as he kneeled and felt the boy's hot tears against his own cheek.

"Cry, son," he was whispering softly, "go on and cry."

And in the words he recognized his own longing, the pent-up frustration and anger. He was holding Ralphie to him, close, wishing he dared give himself over to his own fierce hunger for tears, for any release whatever from the pressures building dangerously in his aching body.

IN THE morning you'll have the answer, Chuck Wright was telling himself as he drove aimlessly in his father's convertible. In the morning you'll get the answer from Cindy herself and you won't take any more run-around.

You must have passed this same corner at least ten times, he thought vaguely, but his mind was not on his driving. Why had Mr. Hilliard lied about being a drunkard? You didn't swallow that story, of course, especially after you saw him go plunging homeward without going into the liquor store at all. And he no longer staggered then; he walked fast and steady, like a man in a desperate hurry.

Desperate. There's the word. Cindy and Mr. Hilliard: they acted like desperate people. But desperate about what? Why?

At this point, he caught a red glare in his rear-view mirror. There was no siren blast but a dark prowl car eased alongside him, edged him to the curb, in silence. The red light went off. Chuck Wright, frowning, sat waiting.

JESSE WEBB was glad for any excuse for action. Helen Lamar had apparently dropped out of existence in or near Columbus, Ohio. And while Jesse had one certain piece of knowledge now — that Griffin was in or near the city, or had been around noon today when the anonymous letter was written — the knowledge added up to very little until someone made a move. He was hoping that the report he had just received meant that someone had made a move.

"Bring him in as soon as he gets here," he instructed a uniformed trooper. "And keep those patrol cars out of sight best you can."

He said to Tom Winston, "What's so suspicious, Tom? A guy's driving a convertible in the neighborhood. Is that against the law?"

"Why should he drive round and round in all kinds of circles?" Tom Winston asked. "Here? Tonight? It's worth asking. Here he is, Jess."

Jesse Webb looked up into a young face: mid-twenties, questioning but unfrightened eyes, maybe a little defiant. Tweed topcoat, expensive; no hat.

"Having a good time?" Jesse inquired laconically.

"I don't follow."

"Been drinking?"

"No."

"Let's have your driver's license."

Without hesitation, the young man took his license from his wallet, laid it in front of Jesse.

"Charles Wright," Jesse read aloud. "Business?"

"Attorney. Hepburn and Higgins. Guaranty Building."

"Anything else?"

"Anything else what?"

In a swift and unreasonable wave of irritation, Jesse Webb stood up. "Look, Mr. Wright, let's not be cagey. I reckon you can't get in any trouble unless you got something to hide. What have you been up to the last hour? Play ball."

"I'll play ball, Deputy," Charles Wright said then, "but I ought to know what this is all about."

Jesse Webb's voice was hoarse now. "Three rats broke out of the federal pen in Terre Haute yesterday morning. Don't you read the papers, man? Don't you listen to the radio?" As Charles Wright shook his head, Jesse caught a certain quick alertness in the gray eyes. "Well, we have reason to believe these men are in town. The fact is, Mr. Wright, they might be in this neighborhood you were cruising around, maybe in one of the houses around there." He stopped then, certain that a change had taken place on the face before him. "What's up, kid?" he asked curtly.

"Nothing."

"Damn it, don't lie to me!" Jesse barked. "Your face looks like I just kicked you!"

"Well, I just never—thought of anything like that. It just happens that my girl friend lives around there, that's all. And I got the crazy idea just now, when you said—"

"What's her name, Wright?"

There was a slight pause that Jesse Webb didn't like.

"Her name's Allen," Charles Wright said. Then, and very firmly and convincingly, "Constance Allen. But I saw her go into her house just a little while ago. I'm sure she's all right."

"You *saw* her go in? You brought her home?"

"Well, no. Y'see, that's the pitch. I might as well tell the truth. She was out with another guy tonight. That's why I've been hanging around. It's just one of those things. I guess I ought to be ashamed. Being jealous, I mean."

"What's her address, Mr. Wright?" Jesse asked wearily.

"I don't know the exact number," Charles Wright said. "But she works in our office downtown, and of course I know the house. It's on Oxford."

"Okay," Jesse said slowly, heaving a sigh. "Go on home now, kid, and go to sleep. Forget this happened, hear? Forget it."

Charles Wright turned to the door, but the Deputy's voice stopped him.

"One more thing, Mr. Wright. I want you to read this letter and then think about the way the guy who wrote it feels. Maybe then you won't be tempted to talk this up anywhere."

Jesse Webb watched the younger man read the letter and he saw going through Charles Wright the same feelings that he himself had experienced when he read those pitiful words.

"I guess it'd be pretty dangerous to try to close in, wouldn't it, Deputy?"

"Dangerous for those scum," Jesse Webb said grimly.

"I was thinking of—" But Charles Wright didn't finish; he turned on his heel and opened the door.

"The boy's got a good question there, Jess," Tom Winston said. "What *do* you have in mind? If they were nice and cozy in that Allen house on Oxford Street, let's say."

"We're not at that point yet," said Jesse. "Let's take a look at that map. Did you get the rest of the names filled in?"

"Most of them are there. But you can't be sure, Jess. We haven't had time to do all the cross-checking we should. No directory's up to the minute, Jess."

"Oxford Street. Here we are."

They studied it together, heads bent over the table. Finally Jesse stood up. "I don't see any Allen on Oxford, Tom," he said, very slowly.

"No, but — "

"Now, Tom, you've got something to do. Find out where that kid lives, who his girl friend really is, where she lives. If nothing breaks around here by morning, I might want to talk to young Mr. Wright again."

Behind the wheel again, Chuck Wright kept telling himself: You've got the whole picture now and it's much worse than anything you dreamed of.

He drove south to his father's house, parked the convertible in the garage. He was remembering, as he climbed into his small black car, the way he'd lied to the police with the same instinctual cleverness and cunning that had prompted Mr. Hilliard to invent that story of his drunkenness.

Now he backed into the street, fully intending to drive downtown to his club. Then he brought the car to a halt, hearing again Cindy's words, *Do you have a gun, Chuck?* He jumped out of the car, walked into his parents' house and up to the attic. Only Mattie, the maid, was at home and she stood by, watching, question marks all over her old face. Chuck came down in about ten minutes. It had taken him that long to find the rather odd-shaped Japanese automatic he had brought home from the Orient, a war souvenir. When he climbed back into the car, he had the gun in his hip pocket, loaded.

Chuck headed south, away from the Hilliards' home. Take it slow now, he was warning himself. Cindy doesn't want the police to know. Mr. Hilliard is desperate that no one know. No one will thank you if you try to play hero here and something goes haywire.

But Cindy is in that house.

He tramped on the gas and the car shot forward, going nowhere, aimless.

The police should be told. He was not doing the proper or legal thing in working against the police. But the police is not one man, a predictable human being; the police includes all sorts of human beings. Take that lanky deputy. *Dangerous for those scum,* he had growled venomously. No thought of the Hilliards. His job was to capture or kill those three wanted men. Probably the man was bucking for a promotion.

He finally brought the car to a halt in front of the club. He went inside, picked up the evening papers at the desk, took the elevator to his room. In the *Times* he found pictures of the three escaped convicts. A poisonous bitterness rose in him as he studied their faces. Then, in one sudden violent motion of his hand, his fist crashed into the floor lamp, sent it spinning across the room, against the far wall. The bulb exploded. The room was plunged into darkness. He stood panting, legs apart, the savage violence still unspent in him.

That's it, he told himself harshly, smash up the furniture. Go to pieces. That'll help a lot.

Chuck was thinking of Dan Hilliard and he was beginning to breathe more steadily. The picture of Mr. Hilliard brought a slow, but expanding respect—and with it, something quite different. That something was shame. He remembered the way he had looked upon Mr. Hilliard and his life — conventional, dull, empty.

A man doesn't fight like that for an empty life. He fights for what is precious to him, the way you are going to fight, by doing nothing, for someone who is precious to you.

You are not going to do a thing, Chuck. Nothing.

He took the gun from his pocket and placed it on top of the bureau in the dark.

You are going to be calm and forget any ideas about going near that house until those men have gone.

Without turning on the overhead lights, Chuck began to empty his pockets. He came across a foreign object. He examined it with his fingers for a full minute before he recognized it. It was the key to the rear door of the Hilliards' house. He held it tight in his wet palm.

Was there some way in which he could make use of it?

Hank Griffin, unaware of it, was driving a car without license tags. Several hours ago Dan Hilliard had removed them from Cindy's coupé and placed them on the gray sedan. They were now at the bottom of the river. Hank was on the western edge of the city, heading toward the main east-west highway, U. S. 40. He had caught sight of a clock back there, reading 1:45. His thoughts now had one direction: to get in touch with Glenn. He had to reach a telephone. There was one place, and only one, that he could think of: an all-night restaurant. Where were the all-night joints? On the highways. So he was sticking to his original plan, to get out of town. Only this time, instead of cutting back to the Chicago road, he would call Glenn. He would warn him. He would suggest that Glenn meet him, that they go to Chicago and then send for Helen Lamar.

After Hank made his call, all his worries would be over. Let Glenn dope it all out. A surge of joy lifted in him now, pushing back the early-morning chill.

He made a right turn on the highway, heading west. A huge truck charged past, then nosed off the highway to the right. Hank had to whip the wheel over hard to avoid hitting the rear end of the trailer, and he was 20 yards beyond the diner before he realized the reason for the truck's stopping. He had almost passed the phone. He jammed on the brakes, pulled the coupé onto the shoulder of the road and climbed out.

The air, raw and windy, struck him full across the face. He walked across the parking area, up three steps, into the metal-gleaming interior.

Almost at once, he saw the black phone attached to the tile wall near a side door in the rear. Hank went to the phone, looked up Daniel Hilliard in the directory. He hated looking up names. The alphabet confused him. His nerves were jumping. He shouldn't be here now, anyway.

He had the number now. He dialed slowly, his eyes on the numbers, one by one. Then the phone rang, and he heard the voice at the other end of the line — Hilliard's. He spoke sharply, "I'm calling Mr. James," remembering the name Glenn had told Helen Lamar to use.

Then it was that he caught the flash of dark blue in the doorway of the diner, across the shine of counter. He recognized the wide-brimmed hat and his eyes dropped down the uniform. The trooper was young, and he was leaning across, speaking to the counterman, as Hank heard his brother's voice on the other end of the line, low and hard:

"Hello? Hello? Who is it?"

"Hank," he said, but he had gone stiff and helpless, and the word was a whisper.

It was all he said, because the blue moved around the corner of the counter toward him. Hank replaced the earpiece and took one step, waiting, remembering in a flash that it was a murder charge this time, and that meant the chair. The broad bony face blurred before his eyes, and he dropped his hand carelessly into his pocket.

"That your black coupé out there, mister?" a twanging voice asked, not unpleasantly. "You know you don't have any license plates on her?"

Already, though, Hank's hand was moving, and too late, with the gun in mid-air, he realized that there was no cause for him to fire. The trooper hadn't recognized him. But by then the trigger was snapping and the explosion thundered in the small room. The trooper bent forward, his head twisting sideways.

With the acrid smell of the gunpowder slapping back at him, Hank fired once again, missing, the bullet smashing into the plate-glass window. Then he whirled, lunged out the side door and ran.

The cold air took his breath. He saw a parked truck, made for it, expecting each instant to feel a bullet against his spine. Behind the body of the truck, he stopped, crouching. The coupé was in the opposite direction, beyond the diner. There was a flat, fenced field, but no cover, in front of him.

Glenn, his mind cried. *Glenn, what now?*

A spotlight flicked on in front of the diner, roamed uncertainly over the truck. Another trooper in a car! Hank began to curse. Vaguely he knew that they'd close in if he continued to stand here, but he was thinking, with shock, of the face of the man he had

just shot and he was remembering Glenn's words: *"They'll have you back in stir in less'n an hour."*

Then a bullet struck the earth by his foot. They were firing at his legs, firing under the truck.

Glenn!

Wildly, then, he turned and ran. He had no idea in what direction he was going, but he was afraid of the flatness of field beyond the fence and he could only think of crossing the highway, finding cover on the other side. Even then, though, he knew that he was not going to make it. Despair slowed his working legs. His shoes hit the pavement as a bullet whined past his shoulder, and he knew the blinding blast of the spotlight was on him as he half stumbled, half ran to the middle of the highway. He felt the lance of pain then; it leaped scalding up his leg from his calf and he stopped, without going down.

Then he saw the truck charging along the highway, the world-sweeping glare of lights. Rooted there, and with the pain stabbing upward to his brain, he heard the roar of motor, the hiss of air brakes. He stood upright, frozen in the blast of horn, as the fender brushed safely past at an angle. Then the spotlight beam caught the solid mass of silver-colored trailer that swung flatly at him as cab and trailer buckled. Everything then was intense and terrible and in detail. He knew every second of it, saw it all, realized its meaning, his mind feebly whimpering that it should not be so. The blinding, glimmering wall of trailer took forever to reach him, its sidewise progress slowed by the rubbery protest of gripping tires.

Then it was upon him, and the moment of death itself brought amazement: it had happened — and to him.

CHAPTER 6

AT ABOUT 2:15 in the morning, Chuck Wright was roused by a knock on the door. He stood up, padded in bare feet across the small bedroom and flipped on the overhead lights before he opened the door. He stood looking into the face of Deputy Sheriff Jesse Webb.

"I couldn't sleep, Mr. Wright," Jesse drawled, and stepped in; his glance did not miss a thing, including the broken lamp and the fact that Chuck still wore shirt and trousers, not pajamas.

Jesse sat down on the edge of the bed. "We're slow, Mr. Wright, but in time we get it. You could save us time. And my hunch is those people up there only got a certain amount of time to spare. You know what people I refer to?"

Chuck Wright said, "No. You think I should?"

"I know you *do,*" Jesse said with slow disgust. "Stop stalling, Wright. You're a lawyer; you know you can't cribbage around with the police like this. Listen to me. There's no one named Allen lives on Oxford. If you don't start talking now, I'm gonna slap a charge against you and you can get that law firm to go to work for you. But before they can do anything, I'm going to get the name of those folks one way or the other, badge or no badge."

"Stop rubbing your knuckles, Deputy," Chuck Wright said easily, but not angrily. "I don't bully."

Jesse Webb stood up, strolled over to the bureau, picked up the Japanese automatic, gave it a thorough examination, even checking the clip. Then he simply stared at Chuck Wright, waiting.

"I've got a permit," Chuck said at last.

"Permit be hanged!" Jesse Webb barked. "What'd you have in mind for this, Wright? And don't take me around any more curves!"

"I don't want to have to use it," Chuck said then, slowly.

Jesse Webb lifted his brows once. Then he said, almost too casually: "What's her name?"

"Maybe it's my own family," Chuck said, stalling.

Jesse Webb smashed his right fist into his left palm. "Your folks came home an hour ago from the Meridian Hills Country Club, and you were in their house earlier. Now let's have it. What's her name?"

Chuck Wright took a deep breath. "All right, Deputy. You've got it right—so far. But I'm not going to give you the name, and I'll tell you why. They've gone to a lot of trouble—Lord knows how much—to keep this from getting to the police."

"What do you think I'm going to do when I find out, blow up the house to get those rats?"

"What *will* you do?" Chuck Wright asked.

The question riled Jesse Webb, because of his own uncertainty. "I'll be ready for them, that's what."

This brought Chuck Wright up sharply against his basic fear. "There can't be any shooting when they go, either. You read that letter."

Jesse Webb shouted, "I know that, too!"

"But there might be. You can't control that completely, can you, Deputy? State Police, FBI, the city cops—one guy, just one man, might be tempted to try to pick one of them off when they come out." He took hold of the deputy's arm with both hands.

"There can't be any bloodshed because it won't be just those vermin who get it. You know who'll be killed, don't you?"

After that, there was a long silence. The tall man removed Chuck's hands, but without annoyance. Shaking his head, he said in a soft, almost gentle manner, "There's going to be blood, boy. You better get that straight right now. Glenn Griffin's not going to take anybody along for a ride and then just drop 'em off and thanks for the pleasant company. So when the time comes, we're going to get as many of those three as possible without sacrificing anyone else. What else can we do, boy?"

"I couldn't make that decision for *them*. I can't tell you, Deputy. I'm sorry."

Jesse turned abruptly away. "Okay, kid. I honestly don't know what I'd do if I was in your shoes. But I'm in mine, and I got a job. So that's the way it is. If I make a mistake – "

The ringing of the telephone cut across his words. Without so much as a glance at Chuck, Jesse picked it up. "H'lo." Then: "Speaking." The tall man listened, his eyes swinging slowly to rest on Chuck. "Dead?" Again he listened. "What about the trooper?" He nodded automatically. "Fifteen minutes, Tom."

Chuck's voice had frozen in his throat.

"Put on your shoes, boy. I'm going to show you the kind of filth you're letting this girl of yours take chances with." As Chuck drew on his shoes, Jesse continued: "It may be good news, kid. One of 'em's dead."

DEAD seemed to Chuck Wright an inadequate word when applied to the thing at which he stared, along with Deputy Webb, only 18 minutes later. He was sick. Hot, flushed and faint. He turned away, took a few uncertain steps along the edge of the highway.

"You sure it's him?" Jesse Webb was asking.

"It's the young one all right, Jess," the fat deputy said.

Another voice caused Chuck to turn, the voice of a man in State Police uniform. His voice was hard: "MacKenzie didn't even know the slob had a gun."

Jesse Webb prowled away, inclining his head slightly toward

the fat man. "What about the car? Who does it belong to? Where'd he get it?"

As Chuck turned and walked slowly along the highway, making his way toward the car parked at an odd angle on the shoulder of the road, he heard behind him: "It's gonna take some time to trace the car 'cause there are no plates on her. I've roused Bonham out of bed, though, to start work on the motor serial. That'll take forever. Then there's the gun – *if* it's registered at all, that is. Nothing else in the car to help. Only it looks like it might belong to a woman. Few hairpins – "

Chuck, with the man's voice fading behind him, was five yards from the coupé. The sight of it reached him with the impact of a blow. He had no idea how long he stood there, limp and suddenly cold again.

"Well, kid?" Jesse Webb's voice asked near his ear. "You know who that belongs to? Save us a lot of time."

But Chuck only shook his head. Sirens, spotlights, tear gas and a machine gun set up on the Hilliard lawn? No thanks.

He turned and walked back to the shadowy circle of spectators, found a man whose cap he had noticed earlier. "Your cab here? You want a fare?"

"Yes, sir," the taxi driver said. "A man's stomach can only take so much."

Chuck climbed into the back seat, gave the driver the address of his club. He had the key to the back door of the Hilliard house hard in his palm. An idea had returned to him, an idea he'd had when he first learned what was happening to the Hilliards. Perhaps there *was* something he could do.

Jesse Webb had, in the last few hours, almost forgotten whatever personal reasons he might once have imagined important in this case. What concerned him now was the plight of that family, the man who wrote that letter. As yet, he hadn't even reached the question of what Hank Griffin's actions tonight might mean in relation to those people and to the other two convicts. Jesse would get to that, though. He was working his way to the name of the family in the most laborious and roundabout manner.

Before he could believe it, however, the long wait for essential information was over. He looked up from the counter of the highway diner and saw Tom Winston half turning from the phone, motioning to him with one beefy hand. They went outside, using the door through which Hank Griffin had plunged just before his death. "The gun," Tom said. "Griffin's little black automatic. It's registered in the name of Hilliard. Daniel C. Hilliard."

That was all there was to it. After all those hours, it was as simple as that. Jesse's mind did not have to go over, one by one, the names of the people who had written checks to Mr. Patterson yesterday morning. The name *Eleanor Hilliard* leaped sharp and clear to the foreground of his thoughts. He had it all, and there was in him no particular triumph. Only a slow, cold something stirring far down inside.

He began giving instructions, in a low and controlled voice.

Forty-five minutes later — it was almost four o'clock — Jesse Webb, driving a dark-brown car, the appearance of which could not be associated with the police, was approaching the Hilliard house from the west on Kessler Boulevard. In a very short time now, he would have a complete report on Daniel C. Hilliard and family, but he could already judge a few things for himself: good income, excellent neighborhood, not upper-crust but middle-class comfortable.

Four patrol cars had been alerted, their positions shifted to cover the exit routes from the Hilliard house. But they had no specific instructions yet as to what to do in the event Griffin and Robish attempted to escape with any member of the Hilliard family.

Slowing down, Jesse held the car to a steady pace as he passed the house. It was rather large, set off by itself, flat fields to the west of it, and two or three vacant and wooded lots to the east. The windows were dark. In the driveway, there was a recent-model blue sedan with its nose pointed toward the street.

Then he was passing the woods, coming abreast of the closest house. Walling, his memory reminded him, Ralph Walling. Across the boulevard from the Hilliards there was only an expanse of meadow.

They chose well, he said to himself in grim silence, wishing that he had more time to study the exact locations of the porches, garage, doors. But he had a fairly accurate picture now. At the first street he made a left turn, remembering from the map that it was not an ordinary block here; there was no cross street or road behind the Hilliard house — that is, north of it — for perhaps a quarter of a mile. It was this area behind the house in which he was particularly interested as he turned left again on the graveled back road that paralleled the boulevard.

If a man made his way through the dense woods in the rear of the Hilliard property and, if he could approach the house unseen from behind, especially in the heavy darkness now . . .

Jesse's first job was to find a place for a lookout, a place where a man could keep watch on the Hilliard house. This was what he was working on when he caught sight of a gleam in the woods which caused him to come to a halt. When he walked back to investigate with his flashlight, he found a low-slung foreign sports car, run in off the little road but not quite concealed.

The glove compartment contained a book of instructions, a few packages of cigarettes, a bottle opener. He picked up from the seat and examined a small cardboard box, which was empty. On the lid there were three Oriental-looking symbols in a vertical line; they meant nothing to him. He was about to replace the box when it occurred to him to smell it. The odor was distinct: the smell of gunpowder. And then he remembered the odd-shaped automatic on the bureau in Chuck Wright's room at his club.

He fixed the license number in his mind and drove swiftly to the restaurant where Tom Winston and the others were waiting.

TIME seemed to stand still now for Chuck Wright. He lay on his back, not wishing, even in darkness, to expose his head more often than necessary around the corner of the Hilliard garage. While nothing moved in or near the house, he could not see well enough to know whether either man was keeping watch out the rear windows.

Twenty minutes ago, when he had seen the blue sedan in the driveway, he had known that the two other men were still in the house. Before he dared make any move at all now, he had to know in which rooms they were staying — and he would probably have to wait till morning to find that out.

His idea was to slip in through the rear door, using the key that Cindy had accidentally left in his hand the night before last. Once inside, the small back hall gave him access to the downstairs area of the house; the rear stairway offered a way to the second floor; and the steps leading to the basement provided a place for him to conceal himself if necessary.

That deputy, Webb, had convinced him that Glenn Griffin would not leave the house without taking every precaution for himself; this was the meaning of Mr. Hilliard's letter, too. Very soon now, Chuck guessed, the police would have the name, the address, everything. If they did start to move in, somebody had to be inside that house to see that nothing happened to the Hilliards.

Chuck examined his watch: 4:17. In two hours, the sky would begin to whiten. Then another two and a half hours before Cindy and her father would leave for work. Would they let them leave the house today?

The thought of the Hilliards in there now moved him strangely. It was the first time in his life that outrage and compassion had made him feel a part of something. He felt involved now, one of them.

It came to him at this most unlikely time that he had never really felt a part of his parents' life. He didn't blame them, but he recognized his loss for the first time and began to understand that the fast driving, the foot-loose girls, the general rebellion, had all been feeble attempts to conceal his aloneness from himself.

Strength grew in him, the solid, knowing determination of a man who knew that he was not going to let anything happen to the people he loved. He was going to see to it that nothing happened to Cindy or to any of these people who, by his own secret and mystifying adoption, had become his family.

By six o'clock Jesse Webb was ready for anything. It had been determined, with Carson, the FBI man, making the decision, that they were not to shoot if Griffin and Robish came out of that house with any member of the Hilliard family. They were to hold fire and wait. The State Police had insisted vehemently that this was stupid because the killers would not let their hostages live anyway.

But the decision had been made, and now all precautions had to be taken. Given a chance, the police had to be ready to capture or kill the fugitives.

Jesse mounted a ladder on the east side of the Wallings' house and climbed carefully, in the first light, over the peak of roof while Tom Winston and Carson explained to the startled people inside what was taking place. From the front corner of roof he ascertained that a man placed here could command a view of the Hilliard residence, including that length of driveway that lay between the blue sedan and the boulevard. From higher, it might be possible to see more.

An hour later, therefore, one state trooper and one man from Jesse's office, in the coverall uniforms of an established television dealer, were waiting for their signal to appear at the Walling home to set up a television antenna on the roof.

At 7:50, in the attic of the Wallings' home where a police radio apparatus was being assembled, Jesse Webb received word that the license on the small foreign sports car back there in the woods had been issued to Charles K. Wright, Jr. Thinking then of his wife, Kathleen, who was probably waking up at his mother's house, far across town, never really threatened, Jesse understood young Wright, his reluctance to talk and also the impulse that had now brought him back to this area.

Jesse paced the attic, smoking. He hadn't shaved. He felt tired and on edge. It was almost 8:10, and he was still mulling over a report he had received several hours ago from the telephone company. In the two days since the three had escaped, one long-distance telephone call had been received at the Hilliard home. This had been a person-to-person call, collect, to a Mr. James from a Mrs. Dixon. It had been placed from a pay station in Circleville, Ohio — which was 26 miles south of Columbus, where Helen Lamar's trail had been lost. Undoubtedly, Helen Lamar had bought a car, traveled south, called Glenn Griffin and made arrangements.

Then, at 3:22 this morning, barely an hour after Hank Griffin was killed, someone at the Hilliard number had placed a person-to-person call to a Mrs. Dixon in Cincinnati, Ohio. Did Glenn Griffin want to make sure that Helen Lamar was carrying through with her part of some scheme? Whatever the answer to that, Jesse Webb now had hopes that the FBI and the Cincinnati police would soon have Helen Lamar under arrest.

He stomped down the attic stairs of the Wallings' house, then down another flight and into the kitchen. Tom Winston pushed in from outside and leaned against the table. "A man and a red-headed girl just left the house, Jess. They're walking toward the bus stop. The man looks worse than you do—which is saying something. The girl's a beauty and she looks sore at the world."

"Dan Hilliard and Cynthia," put in Mrs. Walling.

"Cocky, aren't they?" said Jesse. "Letting 'em out of that house even now. That leaves the wife and the little boy, huh?"

Chuck Wright also witnessed the departure of Dan and Cindy. *She's* not in there now, he said to himself, with a lifting in his chest. The sight of Cindy's slender figure sent a warmth charging through him. Now, he thought, if you can get both of those guys to the front of the house for half a minute or so . . .

At the end of the bus ride downtown, Dan Hilliard alighted from the rear door and held his hand out for Cindy. She stepped down to the sidewalk, then rose up on her toes, and Dan was astonished to feel her lips on his. He was aware that several heads turned, grinning, and he found that, instead of being embarrassed, he was grateful. Grateful and humble and shot clear through with the despair that had been growing in him all night.

Dan bought a paper and walked along the familiar streets in the direction of his office, trying to look at everything with an unemotional eye. As 9:30 and mail time moved slowly closer, he knew that panic was his enemy. The plan he had devised in those sleepless hours last night now seemed a figment of his sickened imagination. The scheme was a form of blackmail, really. In those last frantic minutes after the money was in hand and Glenn Griffin was ready to leave the house, Dan intended to use the idea. *"Look, Griffin,"* he would say, *"you had better take me, and only me, in*

that car because I'm the one who can set the police on the man you're paying to kill that policeman." Would the grin flicker, fade? *"I know both the killer's name and the name of the policeman now, Griffin. You let them both slip out last night. And if you take anyone but me on this ride, I'll put the police on the killer, and then all your sticking around here will have been for nothing."* What would Griffin do then?

Dan turned into the department store. The killer-to-be was named Flick, the man to whom Cindy was to deliver $3000 of the money coming in the 9:30 mail. The policeman, whom Griffin was set on murdering in this manner, was named Webb.

But, as he rode up on the elevator, Dan was disturbed by the coolness of his own thinking. In view of the altered facts of the day, it didn't seem to make good sense. Yesterday, the threat might have forced Glenn Griffin to do as Dan insisted. But today the calm intelligence was gone from the young man. He appeared to be cracking up. His brooding wildness this morning threatened to become more unpredictable than Robish's.

Dan was at his desk now. He was recalling the way Glenn Griffin had snatched the phone from his hands last night – it must have been two o'clock – and the way he had spoken into it: *"Hello, hello, who is it?"* But there had been no answer and, as Glenn Griffin replaced the phone, Dan had realized fully that he was, from that point on, dealing with a very different young man.

There was also that other telephone call last night, placed by Glenn Griffin to someone in Cincinnati. After the conversation Glenn had shouted from the hall to the den: *"Hey, Robish! She's still there. She's waiting. There's someone won't let a man down."*

Twenty-one minutes after nine.

Dan's eyes fell on the morning paper in the pocket of his topcoat. He reached for it, flipped it open and looked directly into the face of young Hank Griffin. Over the photograph were the words:

FUGITIVE KILLED: TROOPER WOUNDED
IN GUN BATTLE

There was a knock on the door; then Dan Hilliard's secretary said, "Letter for you, Mr. Hilliard. Special Delivery." She broke off, frowning. "Mr. Hilliard, if you ask me, you're catching the flu. Why don't you go home to bed?"

"I'll be leaving for a while," Dan said, accepting the envelope, which was surprisingly light in weight. "After I've taken care of some business at the bank, I'm going home."

The door closed gently and Dan remembered one more fact about Glenn Griffin, one that explained the others: he had spent much of the night with his ear close to the radio. Glenn Griffin knew what had happened to his brother. And it was this knowledge that had turned him into the hysterical stranger who was beyond reason.

Dan slit open the envelope and counted five one-thousand-dollar bills and one five-hundred-dollar bill.

He slid three of the one-thousand-dollar bills into a plain white envelope from his drawer, carefully placed both envelopes in his breast pocket.

ELEANOR was upstairs with Ralphie, at 9:30, acutely aware of the time. While she played rummy with the boy, she could hear what was said below. There was the steady hum of the radio, and then Glenn Griffin's voice: "Robish. Stick to the window but listen. There's a couple of guys up on the roof of the house next door. They're working on one of those television things."

"Then what you crying about?"

"Who's crying? You just can't tell, that's all. You had more sense, you'd know that."

"Me, I got more sense'n you think, Griffin," Robish replied from the distance. "No gun, but a lot of brains."

"That supposed to mean something?"

"Means," Robish called, "that your kid brother got his last night 'cause he got scared, that's all. You been gettin' jumpier ever since."

Above, Eleanor sensed that, in this brief and broken exchange, she had heard the command shift from Glenn Griffin to Robish. It was the Griffin boy who was nervous this morning, Robish who remained calm and sure of himself.

DAN HILLIARD, at this point, was handing Cindy an envelope containing $3000. They were in the corridor of the building in which she worked.

"Careful now," he said quietly, his eyes holding hers.

Then he walked down the stairs, and at ten minutes to ten he entered his bank. He carried an empty brief case. He spoke to a teller who had served him for ten years.

The teller complied without question, and Mr. Hilliard left the bank with his brief case bulging with small bills. Three minutes later, a fat deputy from the Sheriff's office asked the teller, through the grilled window, to put those large bills aside until he received further instructions.

LESS than five minutes later, Tom Winston was speaking by radio from his office to an FBI agent, not Carson but a new man who had appeared this morning, in the cold attic of the Wallings' residence. This agent, whose name was Merck, went downstairs and outside and motioned to Deputy Sheriff Jesse Webb from the lawn.

Jesse was on the topmost rung of a high ladder placed against the front of the structure and in clear view of the windows in the Hilliard house; the ladder was much taller than the highest peak of the Wallings' roof, and Jesse, wearing a yellow coverall with printing across the back, seemed to be measuring the upright antenna and giving instructions to two assistants who stood off to one side.

Actually, Jesse was studying the Hilliard house and garage — he could see it all from this vantage point — and in this way was working off some of the tension that was eating in him steadily. He was thinking, too, of the long-range rifles with telescopic sights and of the binoculars that must be kept out of sight.

He descended the ladder and walked into the side door of the Wallings' house with the man Merck, nodding as he listened. In the side hall he tore off the coverall and reached for his trench coat, aware of the eyes upon him from the dining room where three troopers and Carson sat in a huddle. But what Jesse Webb was considering was not the information just received — although the money angle explained why the two men were staying in the house — but a movement he had seen behind the Hilliard garage while he stood on that ladder. He hadn't dared use the binoculars then, but he had his own idea as to what that movement was. And he was not sure there was anything he could do about it.

SHORTLY after 8:30 Chuck Wright had become aware of the activity atop the Wallings' house — long before Glenn Griffin had noticed it. Chuck knew that it was very likely that the police had found out and were setting up a way to attack. It wouldn't take that Webb long, he admitted grudgingly.

Now, at six minutes after ten, stiff with waiting, he was bristling with impatience. He had been hoping that, if one of the two men in the house spotted the activity on that roof beyond the trees, the man who was at the rear window would go to the front of the house to investigate. This had not happened. Chuck Wright decided that he would have to create a diversion that would leave the rear of the house unguarded for the space of time it would take him to get into the back hall.

He was prodded, too, by the certainty that Cindy would return to the house. Perhaps that's what they were waiting for in there. If so, and if those police were planning to close in, Chuck intended to be inside, with his gun. He left behind all hesitation and doubt.

But where was Cindy now? And what was she doing?

IT WAS a long, narrow room with a bar along one side, booths along the other. There was a raw-whisky smell about it that added to Cindy's sickening apprehension. She crossed to sit in the first booth, to sit very straight there with her hands on the table, her eyes fixed. Presently a waitress appeared at her elbow, and Cindy ordered an old-fashioned, the thought of it stirring the nausea in her. She looked at her wrist watch. 10:29.

She could only think of the man who was to meet her here at 10:30. She knew what the man wanted; in a sense, she was committing a murder. Certainly, she was aiding in the crime. But what else could she do?

The anger was still in Cindy Hilliard, and it rose chokingly as she watched the little man who entered now, glanced carelessly around, his dim and very pale eyes sliding over her. Cindy knew that she could not control the contempt and disgust in her glare, but the little man who approached frightened her.

"Mind if I sit down, miss?" he asked.

Cindy felt her head shaking, inviting him to do what he did next: slide into the space opposite her, across the table.

"You know my name, miss?" he asked.

Again she shook her head. She did not know it, or want to know it. She wanted to get away from him, to get back to her father's office, to get into the taxi with him and return to the house, as they had been told to do. She couldn't quite believe, though, that this innocuous-looking man could be a paid killer. He looked and spoke more like a salesman or a bill collector.

He pointed to her glass. "You're not going to drink that?"

"No."

"Thanks, miss."

He drank delicately, almost smiling, but his depthless, pale-blue eyes remained on her. "I'm a messenger," the man said then. "You have something for me to deliver?"

She knew that he was lying, that those same hands now resting flatly and without nerves on the table would pull the trigger, killing another man. She opened her purse, drew out the white envelope. The man took it, nodding, placed it in his pocket without so much as glancing into it.

Then an enormous shadow fell across the table, and she looked up. She saw the man across from her glance up, saw those unnaturally faded eyes meet those of the big man standing there.

"What you got in your pocket, Flick?" the big man asked. "What'd the lady give you?"

"A letter, Sergeant," the one named Flick replied.

"Come along to the station," the detective said. "And you can hand over the envelope, Flick."

The astonishment in Cindy broke then, and rage took over. *This can't be. They can't do this! They're ruining everything now!* She stood up. "You can't — " she began.

The big man only looked at her out of very dark but not unfriendly eyes. "I'm only following orders, miss. If you've done nothing, they won't hold you long."

"Am I under arrest?" Cindy asked.

"Not unless you refuse to come to the station like a nice girl."

Tears came to Cindy Hilliard, tears for the first time since it had begun. It was over now for her. But what would happen to the others?

By now Dan Hilliard was back in his office, waiting for Cindy. When the door opened, he stood at once, knowing it was his daughter, that it could be no one else. But the man who entered was very tall, with bloodshot eyes and a slow but definite manner as he crossed to stand in front of Dan. The man flipped back his coat and Dan caught a quick glimpse of badge, of leather holster, of gun butt.

Very slowly then, Dan sank back.

"Morning, Mr. Hilliard," the man said. "I'm Deputy Sheriff Webb. I received your letter."

Dan threw back his head, stunned, thinking: This is the very thing you've fought against. It can't go like this now, now with the money in your pocket. "I don't know what you're talking about, Deputy."

It appeared then that Jesse Webb lost his temper. He pulled his hands out of his pockets and rested on them, with the palms flat against the top of Dan Hilliard's desk, the lean body hunched forward. "Look," he said in a hoarse, cracked voice. "Look, Mr. Hilliard, I wouldn't be here if I didn't have it, hear? It's taken a long time. I started from scratch, but I'm here, and we don't have time to waste, do we, Mr. Hilliard? So let's have the rest of it now, straight, from the beginning. Then we can decide what we're going to do about it."

It was going on 11 o'clock! You can't wait all day for something to happen, Chuck. He was crouched now behind the shrubbery at the corner of the garage, concentrating on the head that appeared, was gone, then inevitably reappeared behind the transparent curtain in Mr. Hilliard's den.

You've got to create your own diversion, he told himself.

He had selected and then rejected various methods before he finally hit upon a way that could be explained, perhaps by Mrs. Hilliard inside, as a perfectly natural occurrence. After all, dead branches often dropped onto roofs.

He picked up a two-foot length of dead bough, drew back his arm and let go. The branch looped up over the roof, cleared the top by inches and dropped out of sight. Then Chuck waited, listening. The sound came – first a thud, then a scudding as the broken bough tumbled and bounced down the far pitch of roof. Chuck's eyes were on the window. The transparent curtains flew back; he saw a square block of unshaven face appear, the eyes darting about. Then the curtains swished down and the head disappeared completely.

It was his chance. He had to take it, knowing as he ran that a bullet might stop him. He reached the porch, slipped the key into the lock. Deep in the house, he heard two men's voices, then a woman's. He edged the door open. There was a small sharp crack of sound. He closed it behind him.

The back hall was dim, very small. He was beginning to breathe heavily now, as he heard footsteps coming to the rear. Chuck, moving very slowly in the semidarkness of the basement stairs, crept down one step at a time.

Above, from the direction of Mr. Hilliard's den, the heavy steps halted and a deep voice said, "All clear here, Griffin."

Farther away, a lighter one called, "Okay. We take the woman's word for it. This time."

Chuck rested against the musty-smelling wall, trying to quiet his breathing. The Japanese automatic had already begun to feel natural in his right hand.

CHAPTER 7

DAN HILLIARD gave Jesse Webb the facts in five minutes. Webb interrupted only once, to question Dan closely about his daughter, Cynthia, and exactly where she had gone.

At the end of his explanation, Dan said, "Flick is going to kill you, Deputy, for the $3000 my daughter's giving him now."

"So that's the way he was doing it," Jesse said, rubbing a hand over his shadowed, unshaven face.

"We had no choice, Webb."

"Who said you did?" The deputy sounded angry. "We'll take care of Flick, Mr. Hilliard. If your daughter went to him, he'll be picked up. There's a city detective following her right now."

Dan stood up, his knees caving. "You fool," he cried. "You idiot!"

"All right, all right, Hilliard. Take a swing at me. How did I know? I was trying to protect your girl."

Dan Hilliard looked ashamed of the violence. "I've been waiting for her, that's all. It's late. Those fellows are going to get anxious, Webb. You know what that means." He was climbing into his coat. "I have to get back up there now. Without her, I suppose." He pulled his hat down, low and hard.

"She'll be all right, Hilliard. I swear she'll – "

"Swear," Dan said in a low ironic whisper. "What can you swear to? That they won't somehow get word that their man Flick has been picked up? That they won't jump to the idea that I caused that? Or Cindy? Can you swear they won't shoot my wife or my son, thinking I double-crossed them? Swear! What can you swear to?"

"To this, Hilliard. That if there's one less Hilliard in that house, there's one less innocent person might be killed in the next hour!"

Dan moved to the door. "Thanks, Webb. I'm sorry I blew up."

Jesse Webb cleared his throat. "If there's any way to get them to come out alone, of course, on the run – " But he broke off. "You want a lift?" he asked briskly.

"I'm supposed to take a taxi."

"Oh." Then: "How about a gun?"

Dan gave his head a negative twist.

"Good luck, Mr. Hilliard," Jesse Webb said.

And then, after a pause, Dan said, "I've changed my mind. About the gun."

"You want one?"

"Yes."

Jesse Webb handed over the .38 from his shoulder holster. The gun was heavy in Dan Hilliard's grasp. He fumbled with it a moment, finally breaking the gun; he shook the steel-jacketed bullets into his big palm.

"Are you crazy, Hilliard?" Jesse Webb demanded.

"Possibly. Only a crazy man'd go into that house with an empty gun, wouldn't he? Griffin doesn't think I'm crazy. That's a very, very long shot, but I don't have any short ones in sight. Do you?"

Jesse Webb shook his head and, as Dan Hilliard crossed to the door, the deputy said, "One more thing. A young fellow named Wright, Charles K. Wright – "

"Yes?"

"I can't be sure, but there's a strong chance that he's hiding near your house somewhere."

"Good Lord," Dan Hilliard breathed, stunned.

"As I say, I don't know. I thought I saw movements behind

the garage this morning. I just thought maybe you ought to have the whole picture."

"Thanks, Deputy," Dan Hilliard said, with all the weight showing in his heavy shoulders as he disappeared.

"The poor guy," Jesse Webb muttered, but with a kind of reverence that shone in his eyes.

UNDER the basement stairs, Chuck Wright was trying to make his own decision. When do you go upstairs, Chuck? His watch read 11:30.

By now, he gathered, the young-voiced man toward the front of the house — that would be Glenn Griffin — had expected to receive a telephone call from some man. At any rate, his voice was shaking now in a way that Chuck didn't like at all.

"Didn't that gal give him the dough? What's happening? Robish, what you figure's happening? Why don't he call like he promised?"

"I don't know the guy," Robish replied from the den. "I'd a-done it for you, Griffin. Give me a gun."

Why did the man refer to a gun in that way? Did it mean that there was only one gun up there?

Take it easy now, Chuck told himself. You can handle them both if they have only one gun, but you can't be sure what would happen to Mrs. Hilliard or the little boy if you tried it.

All at once, he heard Glenn Griffin again. *"Where's Hilliard? Why ain't he back here?"* Chuck realized from Griffin's desperate tone of voice that he had better wait no longer.

In the back hall, he heard, beyond the door leading into the den, the older man moving about. Chuck kept his gun on that door while he backed slowly up the rear stairway, one step at a time. In this way he moved until he felt safe to turn and continue up.

The upstairs portion of the house was not familiar to him. He crept down the hall, a floor board squeaking occasionally. He came to the open door of the front bedroom, across the hall and stair well from the one in which he judged Mrs. Hilliard was staying with the boy.

He backed into the bedroom, recognizing it as Cindy's. With the gun held in front of him, he used his other arm to search behind him. His hand found a door, then a knob. He edged the door open very slowly and stepped back into the closet. Even when he was inside the closet, he kept his eyes and the gun on the hall door.

He had not been there for more than ten minutes when he heard that frightening voice from below: "Here they come, Robish. There's a taxi stopping out front."

FROM the top of the Wallings' home, Jesse Webb had seen the taxi approaching from some distance. He wore again the yellow coverall. He was conscious, with his stomach twisting, of the men deployed on the edge of the woods below, of the patrol cars down the street in both directions. When he spotted the taxi, Jesse glanced to make sure that the rifle was within reach. He called down and could feel the alertness come into the others.

Dan Hilliard stood with his back to the house, paying the driver. Then, with no hesitation whatever, he walked toward his own side door and disappeared.

The longing to know what was happening in that house at this moment made Jesse grip the rungs of the ladder. What were they doing? The girl wasn't with Hilliard. He had the money, but he also had that empty gun. *What was going on in there?*

"Here they come, Robish. There's a taxi stopping out front." Chuck Wright wondered then if he had waited too long. He heard Mrs. Hilliard's mumbled instructions to Ralphie; then he heard that bedroom door open and close and the lock turn. Chuck stepped to the hall door, listening to the swift, muffled flutter of Mrs. Hilliard's footsteps descending the stairs.

They, Griffin had said. That would be Hilliard and Cindy. Cindy, too. He stepped, with extreme caution, to the banister.

Down below, the high-pitched voice: "Where's the redhead, Hilliard?"

Struck with disbelief, Chuck took a breath, held it. He couldn't hear Mr. Hilliard's low-voiced reply. It didn't seem possible, but

Cindy was not in the house. Chuck tried to dry his palms on his trouser legs and then took a firmer grasp on the automatic.

"He's lying," Robish said. "It's a trick."

"The dough's all here," Griffin announced. "Too late for tricks now, Pop." And some of the lighthearted excitement returned to his tone. "I don't like the way you're staring at me. Lay off, see. Put your hands up. *Up!* Let's see what you're carrying."

Chuck Wright, straining, listened. Not yet, he told himself.

DAN HILLIARD felt Glenn Griffin's gun probing cruelly along his sore ribs while the other hand went through his pockets. He didn't flinch when, with a gleam of rage in his anxious eyes, Griffin stood back, the deputy's .38 in his hand.

"You rat," Glenn Griffin said then, and the tone made Dan Hilliard wince inside with an ironic satisfaction. In his astonishment and anger, Griffin was not examining the gun.

Dan saw the gun going up then, swinging high and sideways; he heard Eleanor's stifled shriek at his side; then he felt the muzzle across his cheekbone. A tooth began to throb. He could feel the muscles of his face leaping.

"*Say* something!" Glenn Griffin shouted. "Don't just stand there! What'd you expect to do with this thing?"

Still Dan didn't answer; he felt the blood along the cheek, and he felt Eleanor against him.

"Give me that," Robish said, stepping in, "and let's blow. You got the dough. What're we waiting for?"

But the gun Robish wrenched from Glenn's hand was not the one Dan had brought into the house. Robish held the loaded gun.

"Griffin, snap out of it!" Robish bellowed. "We gotta move!"

IN THE hallway above, having heard the ugly smash of metal against human flesh, Chuck Wright had to grip the banister to keep himself from plunging down the stairs. The gun's on Mr. Hilliard; you can't move.

At the same time he felt caught in the grip of his own helplessness. No matter what he did, one of those guns — for there were two now — would be turned on one of the Hilliards.

"Get the kid," Griffin said. "Hilliard, the kid and your old lady are going for a ride. Any objections?"

"Yes," Mr. Hilliard said, and Glenn Griffin laughed shortly. But he listened, too, as Mr. Hilliard explained why, in a low murmur, which Chuck Wright could not make out. Then Mr. Hilliard's voice rose a notch: "If you don't want that hired killer nabbed, you'd better take me. Only me."

"Listen who's telling us what," Robish snarled.

"Wait a minute, Robish," Griffin said. "Maybe — "

"Nothing doing! What do I care what happens to your cop? It's my skin now. We're wasting time. Those woods out there might be full of Feds for all we know. I'm moving. The kid and the woman!"

Chuck Wright realized then that Robish was lumbering toward the stairway. He wheeled, stepping into Cindy's room, across the hall from the locked door. He brought the Japanese automatic up and stood flattened against the inside wall of the room.

Now? Now, when his back's to you and he's trying the door? One of them now, and fast, and take your chances with the one downstairs?

But they're not your chances, Chuck. They're Mr. Hilliard's. And his wife's. The helplessness was a dead weight in him. He heard Robish's low mutter of rage and then, behind it, in the bedroom, the faint but definite voice of the child crying.

Then Robish stopped. Chuck took one chance. He eased his head around the doorframe, took a look at the enormous body facing the closed door with indecision.

What are you waiting for? All you have to do is tighten your finger, pull that trigger, but be careful now to aim high because of the boy beyond. What are you waiting for, Chuck?

He heard from below a few more words: "Thought we could make a deal, did you, Pop? You're getting pretty brave, ain't you?" Then the tone dropped, changed: "Maybe you better tell me what's happened to Flick then, Pop. Why he didn't call me this morning. You better tell me now, Pop, 'cause pretty soon you're not going to be talking, see?"

Chuck Wright was not prepared for what happened then. He

watched Robish step back, the shoulders still heaving, and he saw him lift his foot.

Although the jolt of the kick shook the whole frame of the man, the lock held, the hinges held. Behind the door, the boy's sobs stuttered off into whimpers. Spitting an oath then, Robish stepped back and kicked again. This time the wood cracked like the report of a rifle. The violence of the sound seemed to stir the big man, and then he was kicking again and again, a low laugh exploding deep within him, and the wood splintered and shredded and broke with deafening reverberations through the house.

"Robish!" Griffin shouted from below. "Robish, you fool! No noise! No racket!"

The last words were spoken as Glenn Griffin himself tore up the stairs. He appeared before Chuck Wright could draw himself back, but Griffin did not see him because he kept screeching at Robish in that high-pitched and terrible voice. "You want the whole neighborhood down on us? No noise, you dumb slob!"

Now Chuck was safe behind the doorframe. But he couldn't wait. The men, both of them, were upstairs. It was the break he'd been hoping for and, now that it had come, he wasted no time whatever. He thought, as he shoved his head around the door, that he heard the front door open and close. The incredibility of it held him rigid there a moment before he fired.

It may have been that split second of time that defeated him. He saw Glenn Griffin's gun coming up at him, and he swung his own gun to the right and fired, expecting to hear the explosion from Griffin's gun but feeling only the jolt along his own arm. He saw Glenn Griffin dropping down on the stairs. Then Chuck saw the spurt from Robish's hand, saw it even in the sunlight, and he fired once again himself, at the big man, knowing that he had missed this time. The reason came to him then as he heard his own gun clattering to the floor and felt, with surprise, the impact of the bullet against his chest. As yet, even when the first wave of blackness broke over him, there was no pain.

Then, slumped down inside the room, wondering a little at the wetness around his chest, he heard—from an echoing distance—what he took to be footsteps descending the stairs.

Then the burning came, and the black wave broke over him and carried him down.

Robish plunged down the stairs, tripping over Glenn Griffin but not falling, muttering fiercely. Dan Hilliard waited, knowing that his impulse of a few seconds before had saved Eleanor but that Robish would kill him and that Ralphie was still upstairs.

When Glenn Griffin had rushed up the stairs, Dan Hilliard had seen his chance, and he had unlocked and opened the front door; without a word, he had pushed Eleanor through it. She was no sooner outside than the three shots exploded above, and she had paused instinctively, breathing one word: "Ralphie." Dan had shouted at her in the echoing thunder: "It's not Ralphie, it's not Ralphie! *Run!*" The very savagery of his reassurance had sent her running but, when Dan himself had closed the door and started toward the stairs, he had been sure that one of those shots had killed his son. The sight of Glenn Griffin slumping slowly down on the stairs above had stopped him, held him in the hall; he expected to see the figure slide down the steps, but instead it was Robish who stepped over the fallen man and came lunging down like a great maddened bear.

Finally, he made out a few of the words that Robish muttered to him: ". . . wise guy . . . got the cops . . . double cross . . . rat . . ."

Dan listened, not understanding the words. What had the police to do with what had happened up there?

Then he heard a voice, from above, a tentative but uninjured voice: "Dad? Dad?"

"Stay there, Ralphie," Dan called. "It's all right!"

"All right," Robish echoed hollowly. "You sneaked a copper in — " The words seemed to give him impetus; Dan saw the idea seep upward in the man, finally reach those opaque eyes. Robish charged to the front door, flung it open heedlessly, driven by fear and rage.

"Any more of you out there?" Robish bawled into the cold air. "I got one of you upstairs! Who wants it next?"

Seeing the man in the half-open door, senseless in the grip of his own terror, Dan Hilliard edged closer.

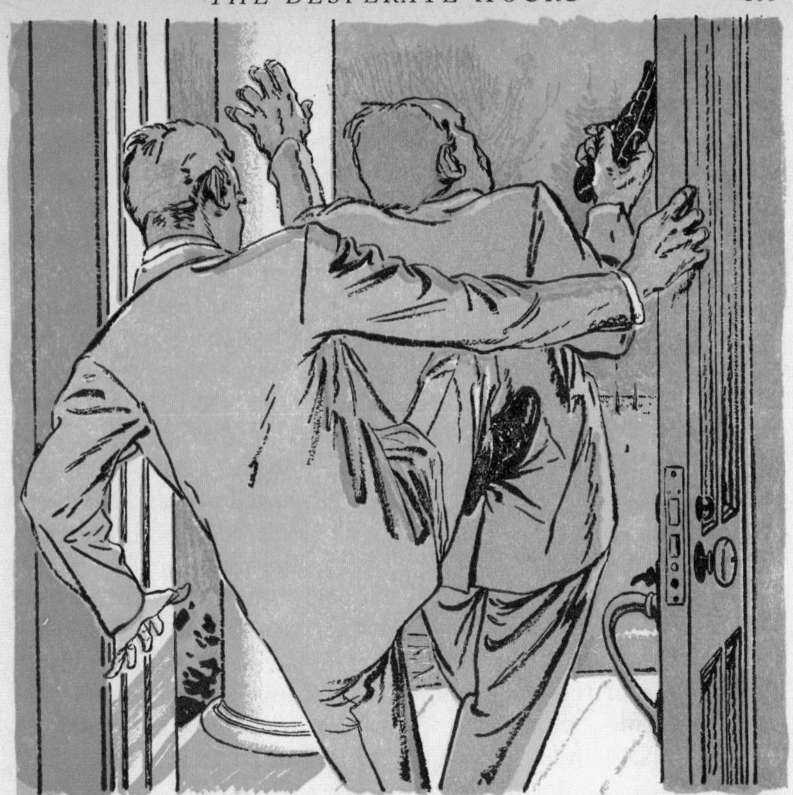

Robish bellowed: "I still got Hilliard and the kid! They're alive!"

Those words roused in Dan a savage fury. He was very close to the man's back.

In one sudden movement then, he grabbed the door, whipped it wide-open, lifted his foot and plunged it into the man's spine. All the coiled rage in him drove his leg, and it sent the hulk of body across the porch — a few spraddled-legged steps at first, then a headlong plunge off the steps onto the grass.

Robish rolled as he struck the ground, lifting the gun. The explosion thundered up and down the street, but the bullet dug into the solid wood of the closed door that Dan Hilliard had snapped shut and locked.

Dan turned then from the door and started up the stairs. Halfway up he stopped, stunned.

Glenn Griffin no longer lay on the stairway.

When Jesse Webb saw a woman emerge from the front door of the Hilliard house, he stiffened, lifting his hand automatically to give the signal that the men below had been expecting. But the woman was alone, hesitating on the porch a moment, and Jesse did not bring his hand down in the prearranged signal. There was that moment of suspense and then three shots rumbled in rapid succession, muffled in the Hilliard house but clearly discernible even at that distance. He saw the woman turn from the house then and begin to run toward the safety of the trees.

After a few seconds that seemed an eternity to Jesse Webb, a hollow shout from the direction of the Hilliard front door galvanized him. Jesse couldn't make out the words, whatever they were. Then a brawny man with a huge head came charging out the Hilliards' front door as though propelled from behind. He fell twisting onto the grass, and Jesse Webb reached for the rifle. In the second he turned, he heard another shot, and he saw the black glitter in the man's hand as he lumbered, trying to run, toward the blue sedan.

Jesse Webb clamped his lean jaws together. Whatever the shooting inside the house had meant, there was still the chance that Griffin was still alive. What would happen to Hilliard and the boy if Griffin were startled now, if he realized the police were outside, if he had that other gun . . . ? But the other gun was empty. Robish had fired. The gun in the house, then, was Jesse Webb's own .38 and Hilliard himself had taken the bullets from it.

"Tom," Jesse Webb said, the rifle still along his arm, "hold fire. Robish is leaving in the Hilliard car. He's armed. Get him three or four blocks from the house. No closer. But get him."

There was no way out for Robish now. They had him.

What held Jesse Webb, what kept him from giving the signal to close in, was the one other unknown element: what had become of Charles Wright and that funny automatic of his? It was Jesse Webb's hunch that that gun was also in the Hilliard house.

If Hilliard wanted him, he would call—if he was still alive.

Jesse looked down for a moment to see Carson leading Mrs. Hilliard from the woods into the Wallings' house. She was not crying. Jesse Webb had already begun to suspect that it was Dan Hilliard who had pushed the woman from the house. What that meant, he didn't know. But he decided, arbitrarily, to give Hilliard another five minutes. He would wait at least until Carson had Mrs. Hilliard's report of what was happening in there.

DAN HILLIARD mounted the stairs, his tread heavy and determined, hearing the motor of his car grinding over outside. As he reached the head of the stairway, where Glenn Griffin had been lying a few moments before, he saw a streak of blood on the carpet. He paused.

But only briefly because, while he heard Griffin's voice on his right, behind the smashed door—"In here, Hilliard"—he saw something in the door of Cindy's room that drew him there instead. He looked down into the gray face of Chuck Wright. His whirling mind took in the dark stain on the floor, the lifeless-looking body, the odd-shaped gun. In one fluid movement, Dan Hilliard picked up the automatic and turned to cross the hall.

He knew what he was going to do now. Before the police came in, before anything else, he was going to empty this gun into Glenn Griffin. But the thought of Ralphie in that room made Dan slip the gun into his coat pocket, with his hand closed over it.

He stepped into the room. Ralphie was huddled in one corner, and behind him stood Glenn Griffin, his dark, unnaturally bright eyes fixed glassily on Dan. But Dan was looking at the icy-white and frozen terror on the face of his son.

It would not be so easy. The boy's eyes returned in sickened fascination to the gun that Glenn Griffin kept fixed on him. The gun was empty, but still it was not going to be so simple.

"Get me out of here, Pop," Griffin said. The insolence was gone. "That copper nicked me. You got more of 'em outside?"

Dan saw the blood-edged furrow along the side of Glenn Griffin's scalp, and he realized that Chuck Wright's first shot had stunned but not seriously wounded the convict.

"Ralphie," Dan said quietly. "Ralphie, look at me. Listen."

"No time now, no time!" Glenn Griffin cried, licking his lips, and he moved the gun closer to the boy's head.

Dan Hilliard became aware of something else then, and worked around it. He couldn't startle Griffin into bringing that gun down on the boy's skull.

"Son," Dan said slowly, very low and definite, "listen to me. Nothing's going to happen to you. That man is not going to shoot you. Do you hear me?" Ralphie nodded, but uncertainty appeared in his eyes. Dan's heart twisted. "He's not going to shoot you, Ralphie, because — "

"Lay off, Hilliard! You don't lay off, I'll get it over with. You got to get me out of here, see!" The frantic note was clear.

Dan ignored him, concentrating on his son. "Ralphie, that man's gun is not loaded."

He was studying his son's face. "Do you believe me?"

Then, very slowly, the boy nodded his head.

"What's going on here?" Griffin shrilled. "Hilliard, you deaf?"

Dan said, as slowly as before: "Ralph, I want you to do whatever I say now."

"Stop the talk!" Griffin yelled. "My head hurts. I got to — " He broke off, and somewhere in his reeling mind a suspicion took root. He lowered his voice. "You wouldn't a-come in here with a empty — "

That moment of self-doubt was what Dan had been playing for. "Ralphie!" he barked suddenly. "Run!"

The shout brought the boy out of the corner in one bound before Griffin could move.

"Get downstairs and outside!" Dan Hilliard shouted.

And then he saw Glenn Griffin lifting the gun, swinging it after the boy. Dan had to break his first impulse with a great effort of will. He kept the automatic in his pocket even when he heard the empty gun clicking. He heard Ralphie on the stairs, skittering down. The boy was gone.

Dan watched the dazed horror in the face across the room; he saw the white teeth bared; he heard the faint boylike cry in the back of the young man's throat as he brought the deputy sheriff's gun up to point directly at Dan Hilliard. Dan heard the clicks, over and over. It was then that he brought the automatic from his coat pocket.

Whatever Glenn Griffin saw on Dan Hilliard's face then — the pitiless eyes, the set of jaw — whatever it was, it caused him to back into the corner, his tongue darting wetly from between his lips. His eyes dropped, but they appeared not to see, not quite to comprehend the meaning of that gun in the white-knuckled hand that moved closer.

Glenn Griffin was sliding down against the wall. His mouth opened and closed and opened again, working loosely, but no sound came. He pleaded with fluttering hands.

The grotesque pantomime sickened Dan Hilliard. He lowered the gun slowly. He didn't have the right to kill this — this scum.

"Get out," he said softly. He felt dirty all over, as though some of the slime had wiped off on him somehow. "Get out of my house," he said, but still quietly.

Then he heard the scrabbling, as Glenn Griffin, whimpering, clawed his way across the bed, staggered toward the hall; Dan heard the quick drum of steps on the stairway and the opening of the front door. Dan tossed the automatic to the floor. He had almost murdered a man.

He threw open the window. "Webb!" he shouted. "Get a doctor and ambulance, fast!" Then he whirled about and strode swiftly toward his daughter's bedroom where Chuck Wright lay unconscious. Dan was bending down when he heard two shots outside.

JESSE WEBB lowered the rifle. The slender, dancerlike figure on the Hilliard lawn lay quite still now.

Two minutes before, Jesse had received the report that Robish had smashed up the blue sedan and the police had pulled him from the wreckage, badly injured, but alive. Alive until after the trial, Jesse thought grimly. It's all over.

But he was remembering, as he climbed slowly down the ladder, the way he had lifted the rifle when he saw that figure emerge from the Hilliard house. Griffin had been running at full tilt, arms raised, hands working convulsively, the mouth shouting indistinguishable words. Had those words been a plea for mercy? Did Jesse remember then that other time when, after using a gun himself, Griffin had thrown it to the pavement and demanded the privilege of giving himself up? Or was Jesse concentrating only on fixing the man dead-center in the crossbars of the rifle sight? He had fired, feeling only the recoil of the rifle, seeing the figure stop, twist, sink to one knee on the grass, remain balanced there until the second bullet reached him.

He made his way into the Wallings' house, hearing the siren wails in the distance, and sank into a deep chair alongside the telephone. He could already hear the soft note of relief in Kathleen's voice. And he could imagine, too, the grim, curt satisfaction in Uncle Frank's voice when he phoned him later.

But Jesse Webb did not share the satisfaction. Another feeling, almost disgust, was in him, and strong. Not because he'd killed a man; he no longer looked upon Glenn Griffin as a man in that sense. The feeling was in him because life should not be so. And then, as he picked up the phone, he was glad for the feeling. It set him apart from men like Griffin and Robish, who also killed. He still clung to a hope that someday it would not be necessary to settle matters in this manner. Until then, he had a job and, in the last two days, he had done it.

Everyone, including Eleanor, had insisted that Dan stay home. Cindy was at the hospital with Chuck and there was certainly nothing more Dan could do now. He needed rest and his swollen jaw looked terrible. But here he was in the waiting room and Eleanor was beside him on the wicker couch.

Jesse Webb came in, removed his hat, and stood there, a trifle awkward. "The kid'll be out of here in two weeks," he drawled. "Your daughter's in the room with him, Mr. Hilliard. She just apologized to me about carrying the money to Flick. Not that she could have done anything different. I guess that's all. Now will you go home?"

Dan stood up. "If the boy's conscious, I'd like to see him."

A little crookedly, Jesse was grinning down at Dan Hilliard. "I want to say something."

"Yes?"

"Something about — you ever want a job, sir, just look me up." It was not what he'd intended to say. It didn't even come close, but it was the best Jesse could manage.

Dan Hilliard was smiling, too, and his eyes made Jesse forget the lopsided shape of the face before him. The eyes were blue now, just like the daughter's, but there was a warmth in them, a knowingness, that it might take the girl a lifetime to acquire.

"The same to you," Dan Hilliard said, and he offered the deputy his hand. "You're stealing my thunder, though. That's my work — handing out jobs."

"Room 402, sir," Jesse said, releasing Dan's hand. "And you get some sleep, hear?" He said that last a trifle more gruffly than he'd intended.

He watched Dan Hilliard moving down the corridor. It's a funny thing, Jesse was thinking, how you never seem to say what's in you. He was thinking of a word, and even the word itself sounded odd in his mind. Magnificence. That was the word. You'd never think of applying it to people like Dan Hilliard and his wife. But it applied.

In Room 402 Dan found a young, full-bodied man stretched out flat on a bed with a very white sheet drawn up to his blunt-looking chin. Beyond the man was his daughter, Cindy.

The young man's head turned slowly as Dan entered, and the gray eyes opened wider.

Dan stepped to the bed.

"You tell him, Dad," Cindy said. "Wasn't he foolish? I was nearly crazy in that police station, thinking he might be in the house, too. Tell the man, Dad, so he'll learn not to be such a reckless fool."

Dan fought down a smile. He noticed the bright spots of color high on his daughter's cheeks.

"You were a reckless fool, Chuck," Dan said. "It came in handy."

Chuck Wright looked very pale. "I couldn't do anything else, I guess." His voice was weak.

Dan cleared his throat. "I know the feeling," he said brusquely.

He turned to the door. "Don't let her rag you, son. Make her invite you to Thanksgiving dinner. I understand you'll be out of here by then."

Dan Hilliard closed the door behind him, struck again by the radiance that he had caught in his daughter's face. He started down the hall. Had he said what he came all this way to say to Chuck Wright? Probably not. There were things you didn't say, that's all. But there were things you knew, without saying.

He reached his wife; she was alone now. She stood up and took his arm. "You," she said, in that same bullying way of her daughter back there, "you're going to bed now. You're going to sleep for three solid days, Dan. I mean it, too."

They went down in the tiny elevator and then through the stone-and-marble entrance hall of the hospital.

In the sunlight that poured down on the wide steps outside, Ralph Hilliard was surrounded by three men who looked like newspaper reporters to Dan. One carried a camera. Ralph stopped talking when he saw his parents, and he waited for them, very adult for his ten years. Then, out of the corner of his mouth, he said to the three men: "Only if you tell him I said so, I'll sue you for libel."

Dan didn't inquire what his son had told the reporters; Eleanor said nothing. After the picture had been taken and they were in the taxi, she turned her face to Dan, kissed him full on the lips, and held him like that for a long time. Ralph Hilliard, embarrassed, stared out the window.

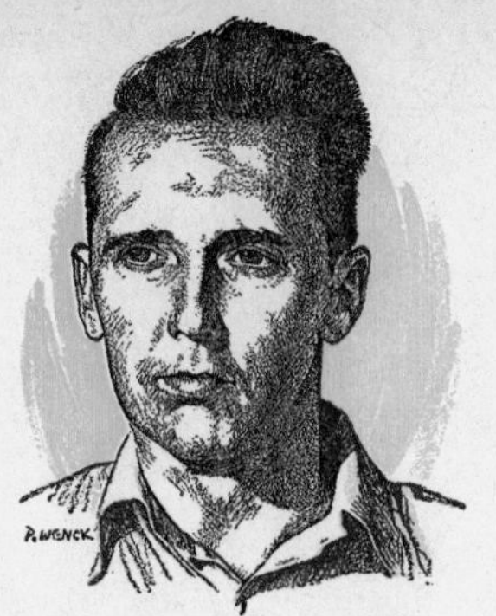

Joseph Hayes

Although *The Desperate Hours* is his first novel, Joseph Hayes has been writing for more than ten years. His short stories are familiar to readers of *Woman's Home Companion, The American Magazine* and *Redbook,* and his scripts are frequently seen on major television programs.

With his wife, Marrijane, whom he married when they were students at Indiana University, Hayes has written 18 published plays, the latest of which, *The Girl from Boston,* was winner of the 1953 Arts of Theatre Award. He is preparing a dramatization of *The Desperate Hours* for Broadway production next season.

Mr. Hayes lives with his wife and two young sons, Gregory and Jason, in Brookfield Center, Conn.

Karl Godwin

General DEAN'S Story

A condensation of the book by

MAJOR GENERAL WILLIAM F. DEAN

As told to William L. Worden

When Major General William F. Dean and I sat down to put his experiences into book form, I was equipped with a tape recorder, various maps, and materials for writing down quickly the things he told me before I should forget them.

General Dean, on the other hand, was equipped with nothing whatever but an astonishing and almost frightening ability to recall every single thing that had happened in three years: places, dates, Korean names, temperatures, house plans, anecdotes, military details, bits of Communist theory and practice.

It may be heresy for a writer to admit it, but the fact is, General Dean wrote this book himself by speaking it. The writing consisted mainly of removing from the tape-recorder report the pauses, occasional repetitions, and sounds of rattling maps which interrupted or slowed the fascinating telling.

On only one point did we have a serious disagreement. William Frishe Dean is an almost painfully honest man. I'm quite sure that he has stood off from himself in judgment, and weighed his own conduct as a general, a fugitive, and a prisoner. The result is his considered and definite decision: he does *not* think General Dean is either a great commander or a true hero.

I think he is.

William L. Worden

CHAPTER 1

On the hot and dusty morning of July 20, 1950, gunfire knit a shrinking border around the city of Taejon, in South Korea. I am no longer a young man, and I awoke very early, although I'd been short of sleep for almost a month. I awoke to the sound of firing, and to the odors no one ever escapes in Korea: rice-paddy muck and mud walls, fertilizer and filth and, mixed with them now, the acrid after-odor of cordite from the artillery, and the heavier odor of thatched-roofed houses slowly burning.

I had hoped we could hang onto a line northwest of Taejon until more help arrived, and now I had to face the fact that we could not hold it long enough against North Korean infantry and tanks. The doom of Taejon was all too evident to the lost and weary soldiers now struggling through it, and to me.

Falling back is a sorry business. It's bone-wearying and bloody for the soldier, frustrating for the commander. An infantry officer must send men into places from which he knows they are not likely to come out. This is never easy, but it's an especially soul-searing business when you're fighting a delaying action, and the only thing you can buy with other men's lives is a little more time. Sometimes I wonder now, when so many people are so kind to me, whether they realize they are being kind to a man who has issued such orders in two wars, and to many, many men.

I had arrived in Korea with the 24th Division on July 3, three days after the Korean War broke out. The situation when I reached Taejon was already fairly obvious. South Koreans, including police officers and some military, were streaming south ahead of the Communists, down the traditional Korean invasion route — the main highways between Suwon, Taejon, Taegu and Pusan. (See map.) South Korean Army headquarters were torn by internal strife, with everyone shouting "Communist" at each other; and my efforts to encourage an ROK stand were lost in a fog of excuses. Our own U. S. forces were still small and there is no denying, besides, that war was a nasty shock to men who had been barracks soldiers in Japan, where living was soft and easy and training had not been too tough. In spite of determined stands by the "Gimlets" (the 21st Regiment) and the "Chicks" (the 19th or "Rock of Chickamauga" Regiment) it became obvious by July 20 that the fall of Taejon was a matter of hours. The situation was so fluid that I had no way of knowing whether we even had a solid line remaining northwest of the city.

In view of these circumstances, I moved my divisional command post farther east to Yongdong and stayed behind in Taejon myself, working out of the 34th regimental command post, located in a schoolroom. My reasons for staying were simple, although I spent a great deal of time later trying to second-guess myself about them. I felt that I could do my job better — make the hour-to-hour decisions necessary — if I stayed in close contact with what was happening, and it was actually easier to get a message or a command through toward the rear than toward the front.

None of which changes the fact that I was forward of my own headquarters on the night of July 19.

Let me make a couple of things clear: I'm not trying to alibi my mistakes, and I'm not a hero. In the fighting, I made some terrible mistakes, and I've kicked myself a thousand times for them. I lost ground I shouldn't have lost; undoubtedly I lost men who should be alive today. I'm not proud of that record, and I'm under no delusions that our delaying action at that time was any masterly campaign. Better men could have done the job better than I did. I am confident that I could do it better next time.*

---

* (General Dean modestly does not mention the high tributes paid to the delaying action he led in Korea. "We desperately needed the six days between July 12 and 18," General MacArthur said later. "General Dean and his men won them for us.")

In any case, I was in Taejon on the morning of July 20 when Lieutenant Clarke, my aide, relayed a report that North Korean tanks had been seen in Taejon itself, although the battle line was still presumed to be well north and west.

This was the sort of report with which the whole division was thoroughly familiar by this time — and of which every man in it was deathly sick. For the moment, there was no general officer's work to be done at headquarters, so we decided to go tank hunting — Clarke, Jimmy Kim, my Korean interpreter, and I. We couldn't do anything at the moment about the war in general. But perhaps we *could* do something about a couple of tanks.

The first three tanks we found had already been knocked out; the next two simply turned and escaped — we didn't have the weapons there to stop them. Some people who escaped from Taejon that day reported that they had last seen me firing a pistol at a tank. Well, they did, but I'm not proud of it. As those two tanks turned around, I banged away at them uselessly with a .45. But that was plain rage and frustration — just Dean losing his temper again and doing something foolish. All I could do, after that display of disgust, was go back to the command post and call for an air strike on the fleeing machines, if the planes could find them.

Presently, we received another, even more surprising, tank report. A lone enemy tank, without visible infantry support, had calmly rumbled through the town from the wrong direction, going up toward the battle line. It passed near the command post, not firing or being fired on, waddled all the way up to the front line, then calmly turned around and came back again, still not firing. Passing the schoolhouse command post a second time, that tanker must have seen more Americans milling around a building than he'd ever seen before, but he just kept going.

We decided to chase this tank, too, and managed to locate a bazooka man and his ammunition carrier. We finally found the strange tank, parked at an intersection of streets lined by Korean store buildings, perhaps half a mile south of headquarters. When we approached — after going through one set of stores, across a courtyard and into some stores only a few yards from the tank —

rifle fire hit around us. The tankers had some infantry protection now, and these riflemen had seen us.

We withdrew through the stores and tried again at a different spot, but again the rifles found us. On the third attempt, we moved directly behind the building nearest the tank. To get upstairs from the courtyard, I had to chin myself on a window ledge, then clamber in. Moving very quietly, the bazooka man and I entered a plastered room, about seven by eight feet. Very cautiously, I slipped up to the window and looked around the side of it with one eye — directly into the muzzle of the tank's cannon, not a dozen feet away. I could have spit down the barrel.

I signaled to the bazooka man and pointed to a spot just at the base of the cannon, where the turret and tank body joined. The bazooka went off beside my ear.

Plaster cascaded from the ceiling onto our heads and shoulders. Fumes from the blast filled the room and concussion shook the whole building. From the tank came the most horrible screaming I'd ever heard (although I heard its equal later and under different circumstances) but the tank still was not on fire. I don't think I'm normally a brutal man, but I had only one thought. I think I said, "Hit them again," and pointed to another spot at the side of the turret. The bazooka fired and more plaster cascaded, exposing the cornstalks to which most Korean plaster is stuck. A third time the bazooka fired, and the screaming stopped while smoke rose from the tank. It was very quiet in the street.

THIS WAS a day in which time got lost. Although I hardly had been conscious of any lapse of hours since early morning, it was almost evening when we came back to the command post for the last time, and I issued my orders for the evacuation of Taejon.

Just about dusk, light tanks from the 1st Cavalry Division came up from the rear, and we organized a column of vehicles — the first of the regimental headquarters — to start out under their protection. But only moments after they left the schoolhouse, we heard them in a fire fight near the center of town.

Shortly afterward it was time for us to go, too. We organized the remaining headquarters vehicles into a rough column and started out toward the east. As we pulled through the city we ran into the tail of our previous column, which had been ambushed. Some trucks were on fire, others slewed across a narrow street where buildings on both sides were flaming for a block or more.

We drove through, careening between the stalled trucks. It

was a solid line of fire, an inferno that seared us in spite of our speed. A block farther on, my jeep and an escort jeep roared past an intersection, and Clarke, riding with me, said we had missed our turn for Yongdong. But rifle fire still poured from buildings on both sides, and turning around was out of the question. So we bored down the road in the general direction of Kumsan, while snipers still chewed at us from both sides of the road.

The fire blocked us again and again. At one spot, a truck lay partially on its side. We stopped, and I ran over. The driver was dead, but under the truck were two men. One said, "We might as well surrender. There isn't any use in this." There were some walking wounded here, too, so I filled my jeep with them and motioned to it and to the escort vehicle to go on. Then I started talking to the men under the truck. A Communist silhouetted himself on top of a hill, so I grabbed an M1 rifle and fired. I hate to admit I'm no great shakes with an M1, and I don't know whether I hit him. But he did drop, and the two men under the truck crawled out to join me.

Then an artillery half-track rumbled up. I think that was the most heavily loaded vehicle I ever saw. So many men were in it already that we couldn't get in—we just hung on to it. We rumbled ahead and presently caught up with my two jeeps, which were stopped. The road made a slight S bend here, and on it the Communists had set up a roadblock. We were under such heavy fire that we had to hit the ditch.

I asked Clarke to make an informal muster, and he counted 17 Americans in the ditch. We started crawling through a bean or sweet-potato field to the bank of a little river. There we lay in a circle and waited for full dark. The group had only a few canteens (neither Clarke nor I carried one) and even fewer arms. I had no weapon and Clarke, who had been hit in the shoulder, insisted that I take his pistol. He said, "I can't use it, anyhow."

Finally, we crossed the river and started climbing the steep slope of a mountain. It was rough going, and I was leading. Clarke worked his way up to me and said, "We have a badly wounded man behind us."

Clarke and I went back to help. Two soldiers were already

carrying the man and, at the first opportunity, Clarke used his first-aid kit to bind the man's leg wounds, although his own shoulder wound had not been treated.

This was a sandy soil, very loose, and it was rough to carry a man between two others. I said, "Hell, get this man up on my shoulders. I can carry him more easily that way, by myself."

But Dean always forgets how old he is. That carry didn't last long. The wounded man was too heavy for me, and in a minute or two I was almost falling on my face. We went back to the two-man carry; and, even then, it seemed to me my turn came around every five minutes.

The party ahead was moving too fast, simply because they couldn't tell where we were. The wounded man was delirious now, drank all available water and called for more. During one of the rest stops, I thought I heard water running, off to one side in the dark. I started off in that direction. The next thing I knew, I was running down a slope so steep that I could not stop.

Then I plunged forward and fell.

When I came to, in the ravine, I had no idea how long I'd been knocked out and at first didn't realize I had a gash on my head. When I tried to rise, I found I also had a broken shoulder. My abdomen, where I had recently had an operation, hurt fearfully, and I was dazed and groggy. I looked at my watch and thought it said 12:30 a.m. — but I now believe it must have been much later. I could see that I was down in a dry creek bed, with very steep sides. All I could think of was, "What's happened to those people up on the hill?"

(Much later, I learned that Clarke had figured that I was looking for stragglers. He waited two hours, and then was forced to go on as dawn was coming. He brought his party successfully back to the U. S. lines two days later.)

I don't think I had walked more than 20 yards from the rest of the party, but I couldn't tell how far I'd run down the bank or rolled in my fall; even today, I simply don't know how it all happened. I do know that I now heard water again, and I needed it badly. I crawled along the dry stream bottom and finally found a little water oozing out of some rocks. I scooped out a hollow with my hands, stuck my face in the dirty puddle and drank. Then I started crawling up the hillside but passed out again. When I came to, I was lying on my side—and an eight- or ten-man North Korean patrol was no more than ten yards from me. There was now a faint glow over the eastern hills, but they failed to see me and kept right on going, scrambling up the steep incline like so many mountain goats, right in the same direction I had been going.

I thought "Oh-oh, this is the end of Clarke and the others." That was the lowest moment I've ever had in my life. But there was absolutely nothing I could do about it.

When the North Koreans had passed, I crawled back to the trickle of water and drank again, and then hid in some bushes nearby. I stayed there all day, still about half-conscious. I could hear trucks over on the highway we'd left, and some firing.

At dusk, I started out again, scrambling up the hill. My shoulder was useless, but I got to the top of the hill and staggered along the ridge, seeing no sign of anyone else. Then the ridge suddenly ended in a sheer cliff. There was a trail zigzagging down, but it was extremely steep and walking hurt me; it was especially hard to get to my feet after I'd been sitting or lying down to rest. The trail led down to a sort of shelf on the side of the mountain, and then down to another; it was murder trying to make the steep ten-foot inclines between. I had got down to the foot of the second incline when rain started to pour down in torrents, and I was almost overcome by the desire for something to drink. I found a big flat rock and lay down beside it. I stretched my handkerchief out on the rock in the rain. When it would get soaked with water, I'd squeeze it out into my mouth, a few drops at a time. I think I spent most of the night doing that.

I was still lying there in the morning when I heard a noise, like something coming down the same path I'd used. I got around behind the rock and pulled my pistol, but the man who lurched into view was an American. I called to him, "Who are you? What outfit are you from?"

He jumped when he heard me but sighed with relief when

—— *General Dean's Route* ▪▪▪▪▪ *Cease-Fire Line*

he saw that I, too, was an American. He said, "I'm Lieutenant Stanley Tabor — from the Nineteenth Infantry. Who are you?"

I said, "I'm the S.O.B. who's the cause of all this trouble."

Tabor had been cut off in the retreat and had started walking south. We went on again that morning, Tabor carrying his carbine and I with the pistol. I've enjoyed walking all my life and normally can outwalk many young people. But not this day. I had to keep stopping for rest because of the pain. After each rest, Tabor would help me to my feet and we'd make a few more yards.

I kept saying, "You go on ahead. One person can get through a lot quicker, and I'm stove-up." But he'd always refuse to leave me.

About one o'clock that day, we found the highway again, but every time we'd try to cross it we would see vehicles or soldiers of the Inmun Gun (North Korean term for the Communist "People's Army"). So we kept on going south through the brush. That afternoon, we stumbled into a tent, put up beside a stream by a mother and two teen-age sons, refugees from Taejon. None of them could speak English, but they gave us some rice and made us understand we should stay out of sight under the canvas until dark. We got the idea that a lot of North Koreans were in the area.

Both of us got some sleep; but when we asked the family to guide us toward my headquarters at Yongdong, they made us understand that this town, too, had been captured by the Inmun Gun.

Now we were really in a bad spot. We would have to swing south, then cut to the east below the main invasion route to Taegu.

That evening we started south again. We didn't make much time. I guess my various injuries had affected my mind because the next days are more or less a blank. I know we had no food and that we did keep going, but the rest is just a haze of weariness, trying to get to my feet and failing without help, and stumbling along one trail after another. Tabor must have kept us both going by will power, because I don't remember having any.

At last we reached a small town. We stumbled into it, and within a few minutes the whole population was around us. We asked for food, and someone brought us water with some kind of uncooked grain ground up in it, and gave each of us two raw eggs. Two men in the crowd spoke some English and the people seemed friendly, so I offered the men a million *hwan* (then about $1100) to guide us to Taegu. Even when Koreans speak English well, they often confuse figures so I drew the number in the dirt.

We should have noticed that the man who spoke the best English had disappeared, but we didn't. The one who spoke less well said, "Okay, okay, come with me." He led us to a house where we promptly went to sleep on the floor.

Several hours later—it must have been early in the morning—we heard a rifle shot just outside the house. At the sound, our little Korean went out the door like a rabbit out of a box. He was simply gone, without any preliminaries.

Outside, a voice called in perfect English, "Come out, Americans! Come out! We will not kill you. We are members of the People's Army. Come out, Americans!"

Tabor said, "This is it," and reached for his carbine.

I said, "Get your boots on. Hurry." We left by another door, away from the rifle shot, and jumped into some high weeds right beside the house. "I'll lead," I said as we started crawling up a little hill in the dark. "With the carbine, you can cover me better than I can cover you with a pistol." I also said, "I'm not going to surrender, Tabor. There won't be any surrender for me."

"That's the way I feel, too," he said.

There were more shots. They heard us in the weeds and shot at the noise. So we reversed our course and went right back through the village, which was in pandemonium, everybody in the street and yelling. We went right past those Korean civilians—and none of them did anything. At the other edge of town, we came out in a rice paddy. These paddies are divided into cells, perhaps thirty feet across, with high dikes between. The water was about four inches deep and the rice stuck up another four or five inches.

We dived into the rice and the water, crawling on our bellies, using our elbows to inch us forward in the old infantry fashion. Two soldiers were across the paddy on a dike, but they did not see us at first. I led out in the crawling, crossing one cell, then scooting over a dike and into the next, while the soldiers continued to search from a parallel dike.

We crossed three of these cells, with the intervening dikes. Tabor was still with me. Then I went over another dike and crawled some more but, when I looked back, Tabor was not behind me.

I crawled to the edge of the paddy, and called "Tabor! Tabor!" The only answer was from one of the Communist soldiers on a nearby dike. He fired at the sound of my voice. I clung to the ground and waited quite a long time, then called, "Tabor! Tabor!" once more. Again, shots were my answer. After half an hour, I crawled back to look over into the last paddy cell we had crossed together; but Tabor wasn't there, either.

I wasn't to see another American for three years.

CHAPTER 2

I HAVE never figured out what could have happened to Tabor that morning. It's difficult to keep going in a straight line when you're crawling with head down, and the paddy cells were oddly shaped. He may have changed direction, losing sight of me, or he may have dropped into a drainage or fertilizer hole.

I learned in 1953 that he was brought into a prisoner-of-war stockade at Taejon on August 4, 1950, and finally died, from malnutrition and pneumonia. I'm still heartsick about him. My recommendation that he be awarded a Silver Star for his disregard of his personal safety in staying with me was made after my return to this country.

It was almost full daylight when I gave up my search for Tabor, and my advantage over the Communists hunting me was gone. I felt like a sheep-stealing dog, but I had to go on. I crawled along the path beside the stream and finally found some foxholes, evidently dug by Communists for a roadside ambush, and crawled down into one.

No sooner had I dropped into the foxhole than I saw a farmer carrying a little girl, about three years old, on his back. He definitely saw me, so there was no point in trying to hide. I got out of the hole and made signs. The word *pop,* made with a sharper sound than in English, means rice in Korean. I said, *"pop,"* and placed a hand on my stomach.

It worked. He made signs that I was to get back down in the hole and stay there. In about an hour he came back with a big bowl of rice. After I had my fill, I tore off the North Korean part of a map I had in my pocket (not being at all interested in North Korea then) and wrapped what was left of the rice in it.

Then I crouched in the foxhole and took out my pistol. I spent the day stripping it down, cleaning it as best I could of the mud and water it had picked up. That pistol was important to me. I had just twelve rounds of ammunition for it: eleven for knocking out Communists and one for knocking out Dean. I figured this last was essential. Even if I could have stomached the idea personally, I couldn't afford to surrender because of my rank. The Communists would be sure to capitalize on the surrender of a general, just as we had in Europe. This was not going to happen to Dean — not if bullet number twelve could prevent it.

I stayed in the foxhole all that day. Toward evening, the farmer came back with more rice. When I showed him the rice I'd saved, he grimaced and threw it away. When you want to keep cooked rice, you wrap it in a cloth so that it can "breathe." Wrapped in a tight paper, it sours. I was to learn a lot about rice, and that was the first lesson.

After dark, I left the foxhole and started walking south again. I kicked myself for being without a compass. Traveling only at night, I could not use the sun effectively to check my direction; and most nights the stars were obscured. I think I made almost a complete circle during the next three nights.

But I did feel better. I could stand up by myself now; and my dysentery was gone. In fact, my elimination came to a complete stop for 32 days. I thought I was a medical curiosity but, when I told my story years later in a Tokyo hospital, Army doctors said anything under a hundred days was nothing to brag about.

On the night of what I think was August 1, I was on a ridge, approaching what I think must have been the town of Kumsan. In the early evening I passed some women working in the fields. As I went by, I noticed that a little boy of about nine left them and was following me. I went over a rise and slipped into some bushes, sure that I had eluded him. After some time I came out again and reached a hill overlooking the town. I picked out a house detached from the others and decided that when dark came I would go there and ask for food. I had not eaten since the farmer gave me rice on July 25 or 26.

But just as I got to my feet again to go down and try my panhandling, a youth carrying a rifle came out of this same house and started running up the hill like mad. Then at least three more youths ran out of other houses farther down the street, all heading more or less away from me. I hunched down in the bushes and was just about to congratulate myself on my hiding place when I heard a rustling behind me—and here was this nine-year-old, pointing down at me and trying to signal to the men. He wasn't more than a couple of yards from me.

I lunged at him, and I'm afraid I really cussed him out. He turned and ran; and I crawled out of there fast and went the other way. There was shooting all around me, and bullets clipped the bushes above my head. Somebody yelled as if he'd been hit, but Dean was on his way.

When I'd come to Korea I had hoped I soon would be a grandfather, but I didn't feel grandfatherly then. If I could, I'd have wrung that moth-eaten little buzzard's neck.

By the next night, hunger was beginning to be a vital problem. I spotted another village and worked down toward it cautiously; but at least ten big North Korean tanks began rumbling through it as I watched. This was obviously a main highway, and no place for me.

I was now getting better at sleeping by daylight and traveling by night, but I still wasn't making much progress. The ridge trails were such slow going that I began to get down on the roads more often. If it was light when I approached a village, I'd leave the road and circle around it through the hills.

But about three nights after my experience with the small boy, I started walking in the early evening and saw a village ahead, and this time I was overconfident and stayed on the road.

Then I met another little boy. This one was five or six years old. As soon as he saw me he turned tail and ran back to the village, screaming as if his end had come.

Well, I knew what that would mean. Instead of turning off the road, I hurried after him, almost running myself. Close by the first houses, I jumped off the road into a ditch and a bunch of weeds.

Sure enough, here came all the males in town. I noticed one rifle and a burp gun; other men had bamboo spears. They followed the little boy back along the road to the point where he had seen me, and I could see the little devil pointing out the exact spot.

Fortunately for me, this town was huddled between a hill and some kafir (maize) fields. I crawled through the fields to a stream and walked along its bed until I was well past the town. Then I came back up on the road. The last I saw of that place, the men were still beating through the weeds with their guns and spears, and all the women were standing out on the main street waiting for somebody to bring me in.

I still didn't like little boys, Korean variety.

Thereafter, whenever I came on a village in the middle of the night, I just walked right through it. Even when it was pitch-black I had no trouble knowing the village was there. You can always smell a Korean town before you see it. You can always recognize the police stations, too, because they're all built alike: a big stone wall around a compound, double wooden gates at the front, and a 20-foot tower, like a silo, somewhere inside. Usually, I just ignored them. But one dark night someone yelled a word that must have meant "halt," just as I passed the gates of the town jailhouse. He scared me half to death and made me mad, too—at myself for being careless and at him for being alive. I was so flustered that I did a foolish thing. I whirled and yanked out my pistol and walked right into him. He was just a youngster, armed with a rifle that had a long thin Russian-type bayonet on it. I shoved my pistol right in his guts, hard, and backed him right into the gate.

Just as he got inside the gate, I turned and walked very fast in the same direction I had been going. It was only a few yards to the corner of this jailhouse compound. Here I turned to the left, ran all the way around the compound and came back to the road on the side from which I had come originally. I waited there to see what would happen.

Inside the compound there was a lot of yelling as soon as the guard recovered enough to give the alarm, and a whole squad of men poured out into the road and headed the way the guard had seen me go. As soon as I saw the direction they were taking, I walked back up the main road on which I had entered the town, and took another road in the general direction I wanted.

By this time my equipment was getting in very bad shape. I was wearing an oversized, cumbersome pair of coveralls. My combat boots were the worse for wear, and one chafed the top of my foot badly. I had a watch that didn't work; a fountain pen that did; a pair of reading glasses; the remainder of my map of Korea; \$40 in U.S. Korean-occupation scrip which nobody wanted; and the pistol. I had no rain gear. When it rained, I got wet. And it did rain, repeatedly and with fervor.

My hunger was becoming dangerous, but there was nowhere to get food. I began to be afraid to go into the villages, for I could see that the Communists had already organized the whole area. Men were at work in big gangs, mostly on the roads; and old Japanese or Russian rifles and burp guns had been given to a few youths in each town, who were just itching for a chance to fire them.

I even had to pick my daylight hiding places well away from villages. During the day, brush- and weed-gathering parties worked the untilled areas around the towns. Few Koreans can afford wood to burn in their homes, and they use brambles and grass for cooking fuel and to make smudge fires against the mosquitoes in the evenings. Each village at nightfall looks as if it is on fire, a little Pittsburgh under its own pall of smoke.

One morning I stopped to take a bath in a stream too close to a village and, when I got out, women already were coming down to the river to wash clothes. I had to crawl into some bushes not more than 50 yards from them and I didn't dare to sleep, fearing that children wandering away from their mothers might find me. If they did, I wanted to be awake to know it.

I got through the day all right; but that evening one woman, carrying a pile of clothes on her head, came up a path not more than four feet from me. As she passed, she looked right at me. If I had a face like hers, I could make a million dollars playing poker. Not a muscle twitched. She just looked and kept on walking.

I was still trying to decide whether she could possibly have failed to see me when my question was answered by the arrival of two young men who came from the direction in which she had gone. Again there was no use in trying to hide, so I asked for food, going through the *"pop"*-plus-stomach-gesture routine once more.

They answered "Okay," and made signs for me to stay down.

I thought, "Boy, I'm in luck again." I could just taste the rice which would be along in a minute. But instead, I heard a terrific commotion and rifle shots started coming over my head.

My two chums had brought out the home-guard force in force. Men gathered around my hiding place in a big half circle, and I could hear them starting to close in toward me. I faded back up the stream, beside a fill. Luckily for me, every time a man in the half circle would take a few steps forward to a new position, he'd yell like mad to let everybody know where he was. Once a man yelled just as I was about to crawl toward the very spot where he stood. I waited, and presently he went on past me.

It was just dumbness on their part, but the fact is I slipped through the circle. They were still yelling and closing in, but I wasn't there any more. I just got out on the road and walked away, not stopping to say good-bye.

I made good time that night, walking about 20 miles. When I didn't have anything else to think about, I'd go back to my worrying. I was desperate to get back to our lines, though I knew my information — that there were far more Communists on the south flank than anybody thought — would be too late to do any good. I just wanted to get back into the fight.

Then, too, I worried a lot about my aides, sure in my mind that they were dead by this time, their young families fatherless because of me. I worried about those families and my own. Sometimes I prayed for people I knew or thought were dead in the war. These were actual prayers, repeated many times.

But when I dreamed, it was mostly about food.

One night, I decided to quit fooling around, trying to follow roads or trails. I'd go right over the mountains to the east. I told myself, "Damn it, you're walking in circles. Go straight east until you hit the railroad, then follow it south — no matter how tough it is."

Well, that sounds good but, when you start crossing some of Korea, it's awfully rough. The mountains average only a couple of thousand feet in height, but they come right up off sea level, so you have to climb every inch of every mountain.

A constant problem up on the ridges was water. Once I wasted a whole day going down to the foot of a ridge to get a drink. For food, I tried kafir stalks, and grass, both of which made me throw up. As I grew weaker, my stomach regurgitated even water.

On August 19 I finally located a house far from any village. I spotted it in the night, flopped down in a path about 200 yards away and slept.

In the morning I was awakened by a man carrying a little girl on his back. I asked for food — and this time my luck was in. He led me back to the house and the whole family came out to greet me. The man turned out to be the eldest of four brothers who shared the house with their families. They brought food out to me right in the yard — rice and pork fat. (I don't know what happens to the lean part of pigs in rural Korea; the only part ever served is the fat.) I ate it ravenously.

With signs I then told the brothers that I wished to stay there four days. I was terribly weak, but I said to myself, "Just give me four days of rest, and I'll make it."

They led me to a lean-to against the back of the house, and I lay down on the mud floor. I stayed only five minutes. Then I had to crawl to the door and throw up everything I'd eaten. I had had no food for almost a month except for berries and a few raw potatoes I found in a field; I guess the pork fat was too much for a stomach ignored so long.

At noon the family gave me more rice and some *kemchee* (fermented cabbage, with garlic). Again I threw it up. All of them were quite concerned about me. I tried to indicate by signs that I wanted some eggs. The family misunderstood (the most fortunate misunderstanding on record) and instead killed a chicken. The result was some wonderful chicken soup, which I kept down. And the next day I kept down three meals of rice, roasted corn and potatoes.

From the beginning I could tell that the second brother wasn't enthusiastic about having me there. In a combination of Korean and sign language he kept talking about the Inmun Gun, and appeared very much surprised when I indicated that I had no desire to see it; perhaps he had thought I was a Russian. He became increasingly nervous. I gave my watch, my billfold (minus an insert with my identification in it) and my fountain pen to the men of the family to try to buy the remainder of my four days of food and rest, but that evening the bad news came. The elder brother, still kindly, nevertheless told me I would have to go. Evidently he was afraid that they'd all be shot if the Communists found me there, and perhaps he was right. I didn't feel that any of these people loved the Inmun Gun especially, but they undoubtedly were afraid of it. The elder brother gave me four ears of parched corn and some rice wrapped in a cloth and led me out on a path about half a mile from the house. There he left me. I could tell he felt I wasn't going to make it back to our own lines. His look said, "You poor mutt, you're finished."

But I thought, "Well, you sad character, you just don't *know*. I'm going to surprise you. I *am* going to make it."

It was a black night and I'd taken only a few steps before I stepped into a hole and fell on my face. I managed to get about 50 yards farther, then just dropped down in the trail and went to sleep. I wasn't especially low in my mind, just tired.

In the morning, the second brother and one of the younger ones, out to gather wood, found me still there, and they weren't at all happy about the fact that I still was only half a mile from their house. They led me another half a mile along the trail to make absolutely sure I was headed right—and going away.

I went on alone again. Strengthened by rest and food, I walked all through the daylight hours of August 23, ate my parched corn, and felt so good that I walked all night, too. I found an orchard and filled my pockets with peaches, rested a while, then took off again, walking all the afternoon of August 24. That evening I hit a main highway. I think I made 20 or 25 miles that night, and the only interruptions were when I had to hide out now and then to let groups of homebound highway workers pass me.

But again I walked too long. The next day, daylight caught me just opposite another village. I went off the road and up into some brush under chestnut trees, from which I could see the village, less than half a mile away.

While I rested under the chestnut trees, my spirits were rising. I decided that I could walk the hundred and twenty miles I figured to Pusan in ten days on the strength my two-day rest had given me. And there was one new, wonderfully reassuring factor. Away over to the east I could hear the rumble of artillery—definitely guns, not bombing. I had not heard this since we'd left Taejon, so it was like hearing from an old friend.

"I'm on my way back," I thought. "I'm going to make it."

That afternoon an old man and some boys came through the chestnut grove to cut brush, and they saw me. Once again I worked my system, asking for food. The old man smiled as if we were long-time friends and gestured toward the village. I rose and boldly marched down the highway to the first house, where a man was in the back yard making straw shoes. I made signs for food and got vigorous and friendly affirmative nods. The woman of the house brought out rice, with garlic beads as a side dish. It was delicious. I ate all I was given and asked for more to wrap in my handkerchief.

I left there about five o'clock, but had gone only a short distance along the highway when a short little Korean passed me, hiking along as if he were going to a fire. He got about 20 feet ahead, then suddenly stopped, waited for me to catch up, and walked along beside me without saying a word. I asked him the route to Taegu and other towns and, when we sat down to rest at a bridge, he picked up some rocks and in the dust marked the routes to Taegu, Pusan and Chonju. Although he spoke no English we managed to understand each other, and I made him the same offer I'd made before—a million *hwan* to guide me to Taegu.

He intimated that I shouldn't worry, everything would be okay—he would take me right past the Inmun Gun. I don't know how I got all that without any English, but I did, or so I thought.

Farther down the road we came to a river where, to ford the stream, I had to take off my coveralls. I should have suspected something then, for he offered to carry my pistol for me. I didn't let him.

When we reached the far bank and I had dressed again, we climbed the bank—and there was trouble waiting for us. A village came right to the river at this point, and waiting for us was practically the full manpower of the village, ten or fifteen men in native clothes and all armed with clubs or spears. The man in front, carrying a club, had an especially ferocious expression on his face and motioned to me to go back, but I didn't want to undress and cross that river a second time. I pulled my pistol from the holster and pointed it at them. As I walked toward them, making threatening motions with the pistol, the whole group backed up slowly.

Meanwhile, the little Korean by my side kept jabbering to them, and I thought, "He's fast-talking them." The whole gang let us go through the town.

But before we had gone more than a fraction of a mile, a second Korean caught up with us. I realize now that this was the character who had been at the head of the village mob, but at the time I failed to recognize him without his club. Han, the man who was guiding me, made me understand that this new chum was "okay, okay." We three walked down the road together until we reached a bend.

Han said suddenly, "Inmun Gun!" and signaled to me to get down. I jumped into some bushes beside the road, holding my pistol ready.

Han went on ahead but came back in a few minutes, saying, "Okay, okay."

"This boy is all right," I thought.

We went ahead and, around the bend, found 50 or 100 South Korean civilians filling holes in the road, all working fast, although I saw nobody with guns keeping them at it. We walked right past, and no one interfered with us.

When we came to another bend a little farther on, we went through the same routine—the Inmun Gun! warning, Dean jumping into the bushes with his pistol, then an okay and another stroll right past a working party. This time I noticed two men with rifles, and there was an uncomfortable feeling along my spine when we turned our backs to them. But again nothing happened.

I thought, "This Han is a pretty good boy."

When we started again we went only a short distance, then turned into a house beside the road. I understood that Han wanted to stop there for food, but inside they served us only sake, with a plate of garlic beads. I took one tiny glass of the liquor, and the people in the house and Han urged me to take more. I thought, "What are these people trying to do? Get me drunk?" But I still wasn't suspicious.

A third man joined us in the house, and walked along with us when we left. At the next bend we did the Inmun Gun! routine a third time; this time for a small town. We walked right through the town, but just as we got on the other side there was some yelling behind us. I got out of sight while Han and his second friend went to the rear. Then Han called something to the fellow who had stayed with me (Little Ferocious, who had led the village gang), and he motioned me to come out. I did, once more putting my pistol back in the holster, then sitting down on the edge of the road.

All of a sudden, around a corner from the village came about 15 men, and somebody fired a rifle over our heads. I reached for my pistol and got my hand on it, but the little devil sitting beside me grabbed my wrist with both his hands.

I struggled to my feet, with him still hanging on, but I couldn't get the gun out. We fell in the dirt and rolled around in the road, but the gang was already on top of us. They were all yelling, and I suppose they were telling me to surrender, but I kept on fighting with this fellow who had a hold on my arm, and trying to kick somebody where he'd never forget it. I remember thinking, "This is an ignominious way to have your lights put out, but this is it."

Then several of them grabbed me and began twisting my arms, and that shoulder of mine really hurt. But no physical pain hurt so much as the thought, "Well, these miserable devils have you as a prisoner."

They tied both hands behind me so tightly that the circulation was cut off, then jerked me to my feet. I tried to run. I wanted them to shoot me. But I was so weak that I made only a yard or so before somebody shoved me from behind and I fell on my face again. They all laughed.

They pulled me up again, but I couldn't walk. My shoulder hurt too much, and those bonds on my hands. So they finally took the ropes off, and we all marched to the police station. Han was standing there beside the door, looking pleased with himself, and so were the other two who I had thought were helping me. I did wish I could have one last kick at a couple of them, but there was no chance. In the station, they took away my identification tags, an immunization register and some snapshots of my son and daughter. While they were searching me, I noticed a calendar with Arabic numerals on a wall. I pointed to it, and one of the men put his finger on the figure 25. It was August 25, my wedding anniversary.

Three years later, Han Doo Kyoo, aged 40, and Choi Chong Bong, 24, were arrested by South Korean police as my betrayers. They had received the equivalent of five dollars for turning me in to the Commies. Although the prosecutor had asked only five-year prison terms for them, the judge sentenced Choi to death and Han to life imprisonment. I had previously written to President Rhee, asking clemency for the two men if they were convicted, but the trial judge declared the court had not received any official notice of my request. Their defense statements indicated that they had intended to take me through to U.N. lines, but ran into so much trouble that they decided to turn me in to prevent my death in a hopeless fight. I'm simply not in a position to guess whether this might have been true; but I did not feel their punishment would accomplish anything.

CHAPTER 3

I SPENT that night at the police station in Sangjon-Myon in a cage—literally. It was about four feet long and the same height but built like the letter L. I could sit in one position in it, with my knees drawn up slightly, but could not lie down or stand up. This was nothing they had dreamed up especially for my benefit; I suppose they ordinarily kept the town drunk in it on his bad nights.

I made one horrible mistake that night: I took off my combat boots. One had chafed my foot until my instep was infected; also, they smelled awful. I made signs to the guards that I'd like to have them set outside to air. This suggestion was greeted with startled enthusiasm. If those people had spoken perfect English, they couldn't have said more plainly, "Boots? Oh, my goodness, that's something we overlooked." They took them out of the cage and somebody else had them on within five minutes.

Shortly after dawn, a guard brought me breakfast — rice, soup and *kemchee* — and I demanded my boots. Instead, somebody brought me a pair of Korean rubber shoes — not mates, and with holes in the soles the size of pancakes. When I tried to walk, they came off. I made noises of complaint, so finally one fellow folded newspapers to make insoles, then brought some straw rope and tied the shoes to my feet.

Then I was marched under guard a short distance to a military headquarters in the town of Chinan. There a cheerful young captain was already busily cleaning the pistol I had never had a chance to use. He ordered up food for me — a bowl of boiled pork fat. After my walk I ate this like candy, and the captain was so pleased that he sent out for a bag of ginger cookies, which he paid for himself. I ate these, too, and the young captain was as pleased as a child who succeeds in getting a puppy to eat.

Two women in uniform also were in the house. One of them was some sort of political instructor: she held a class for the soldiers at headquarters. I was pleased, in a backward sort of way, when an air-raid alarm — they used a series of rifle shots and a bell — interrupted the instruction and everybody had to run for cover in doorways.

I was moved twice during the day, to different buildings in Chinan, but otherwise ignored until about seven o'clock in the evening, when I was taken out to a truck packed with 37 Korean civilian prisoners, mostly men. I was pushed toward the center of the mob, and there I wedged myself down. I put my feet out in front of me, and that was a bad mistake. People sat on my feet and insteps, others on my legs and knees. Knees jabbed into my back and ribs, which still ached, and pushed against my broken shoulder.

Three or four guards clung to the sides of the truck, with one foot in and one out. None of the prisoners showed any emotion whatever. As we started out I saw a road sign in English: "Chonju — 78 miles."

But we still weren't fully loaded. About ten miles out of Chinan the truck stopped beside a rice paddy, and a line of about 40 men with their wrists bound, and roped together, climbed right in on top of the rest of us.

The truck ground ahead again but, fortunately for us, faltered and stalled on a hill, and the guards had to take off some of that last chain gang. With the remainder, we bumped on into Chonju, arriving in the middle of the night, just as a flight of our bombers unloaded on one end of the town near the railroad tracks.

We were ordered out of the truck in front of the police station when the bombing started, and I was hustled under the archway of a school or church in one of the mission compounds. When my guard finally brought me back, past a mission hospital, we met townspeople carrying two litters with a woman and a child on them.

We were taken to the provincial penitentiary — ironically, I remembered having inspected it when I was military governor of Korea — and I was led off by myself to a 20-man cell. It had a nice smooth floor and 20 little wooden pillows lined up along one side. The guards locked the door, and I picked out a pillow.

As a policeman back in Berkeley, California, many years before, I'd watched people taken off to cells. But this was the first time in my life that I'd been on the other end of the story. I slept fitfully, listening to the U.N. bombers overhead.

In the morning a guard shoved a little tin bowl of rice into my cell, but just as I was about to eat it he indicated I should thrust it outside again, and some grass soup was poured over it, the most sickening stuff I've ever tasted. Hungry as I was, I could only pick at it. Then a guard handed in a pencil and a printed form, which asked my name, rank, organization, what my orders were, where I'd landed in Korea — and where was Syngman Rhee?

They already had my identification tags, so there was no point in trying to hide my identity. I put down my name and rank —

and as for orders, I wrote: "To assist the Republic of Korea in repelling the aggressors from the North." I knew full well that under the Geneva Convention on prisoners of war, I didn't have to answer any such questions. But I figured the answer would make the Communists mad — and I wanted to do just that.

After about an hour guards came and took me to the office of the commandant, a rather handsome but unshaven man, wearing North Korean Army blue breeches and black boots, but a civilian coat. He had the only green eyes I've ever seen in a Korean; somehow they reminded me of a tiger's eyes. However, he was friendly and apologetic for having put an officer in a cell. Then he also asked a question: Where was Syngman Rhee?

This was question number one of some thousands asked me, and it made no more sense than most of them. Always, question and long-winded harangue went right together. Now the commandant went right on, "Your family and your countrymen are concerned about you. You must go on the radio and tell them that you are being well treated, and also tell your people that there is no use in continuing the war. Tell them the people of South Korea have welcomed us as their brothers. You must do this to save the lives of your countrymen."

There was much more of this. I said I didn't know where Syngman Rhee was and that I wouldn't go on the radio; that nobody would believe any such a statement even if I did make it. I don't remember my exact answers to some of his questions, but I gave him quite a speech.

He said, "If you were released, would you continue to fight us?"

I said, "Yes. I know I can do better next time."

He didn't care for that. Finally he said, "General, you're a brave man, but you're very ignorant politically."

That ended the political part of the discussion and, after a bath and shave, I was provided with some patched but clean clothes, and posed for some careful "before-and-after" pictures. Then I was taken to a cottage where there was a U.S. army cot — and where even the inside plumbing worked. But I was called back to the commandant's office that afternoon.

This time five or six Communist reporters were present. They shot a whole series of questions at me: "Why do the Americans bomb innocent women and children?" "Why do they bomb children in swimming?" "Why do they bomb farmers along the highways and kill their cattle?" I answered all these questions by saying that Americans never knowingly harm women, children or noncombatants; but this didn't even slow up the flow of questions. The next was, "Why do Americans prey on schoolhouses and churches?"

I said, "A church or a schoolhouse is struck only when it is evident from the air that the Inmun Gun is using it as an army installation, especially a command post. The Inmun Gun brings military operations right in among civilians."

My principal questioner at once said, "We won't discuss that any more."

The interview ended with several of the reporters giving me lectures about what was wrong with United States policy. I think even the interpreter was a little bored.

After that interview, I thought, "At last, word will get out that I'm a prisoner, and my family's fears will be eased." But though the interview was printed, nothing was picked up at this time, even by Communist newspapers outside Korea.

Back in the cottage, that cot looked wonderful. I headed toward it as soon as I could. This, I thought, would be the night's sleep I had been dreaming about for so many days.

But I was restless and, every time I turned over, the cot squeaked. Every time the cot squeaked the guards would bellow at me. I suppose they thought I was trying to escape. Then, in the middle of the night, my dysentery started up again. The first time or two I had to get up I had an argument with the guard, but he finally got the idea. I would simply holler *"benjo"* (Japanese for toilet). Any Korean above the age of 16 understands Japanese, although some of them pretend that they cannot: it was a required language all the time the Japanese controlled the peninsula.

There was more questioning the next day, this time by a stout major general of the Inmun Gun who sat behind the warden's desk while a youngster with a submachine gun stayed in the room to guard him. The commandant and the interpreter also were there, but the general did the talking. I think the other two must have been as tired of the same old questions as I was: Would I go on the radio to broadcast? Why were the Americans here? Why were nonmilitary targets bombed? The only thing he left out was Syngman Rhee, and I felt I probably should have reminded him to ask that, too.

Neither of us could be sure that the interpreter was getting everything straight. This was evident when he asked me about the bombing of civilians.

I said, "We're not in the business of bombing civilians—we're too busy working on military targets."

I don't know how that was interpreted, but it infuriated the young guard. He snarled and jumped forward, pointing his submachine gun at me. I laughed and asked the general, "What's the matter with him? Does he want to shoot me?"

The general spoke to him in Korean and ordered him out of the room. To me, he said, "The guard is very young. He is greatly disturbed by the barbarities which your army has committed against his countrymen."

I still wonder what the interpreter told them in Korean.

I said, "As long as we're talking, there's something I want to get off my chest. You people are not following the tenets of the Geneva Convention. Of all the men who captured me and shot at me with arms while I was being pursued in the hills, only one wore an arm band, let alone a uniform. You're fighting this war with men dressed in civilian clothes, so far as I can see."

The general didn't deign to answer this.

During this interview, I was amused to discover that our American names and numbers confuse the enemy almost as much as the many Korean Rhees and Paks and Kims confuse us. Many questions concerned happenings on the east coast of Korea or involved Negro troop units. Finally I realized that this general had me confused with Major General William Keane of the 25th Infantry Division, and was hopelessly fouled up between the 24th Infantry Regiment, part of that command, and the 24th Infantry Division, which I commanded. I didn't bother to straighten him out.

That day my dysentery grew worse, and the next morning a doctor came to see me. He felt my stomach and listened to my breathing, but spent most of his time giving my chest a thorough thumping — although personally I doubted that the seat of dysentery was to be found in the chest. He left some medicine but, whatever it was, it did me no good.

In the evening the prison commandant showed up, and let me know that I was to be on my way again. I was given a tight-fitting American fatigue jacket. When I pointed to my feet and the old Korean rubber shoes, the commandant looked all around — and the unluckiest guard in the prison was right where the boss could see him. This fellow had big feet for a Korean, and was wearing G.I. shoes. They were the most odoriferous shoes I've ever approached, but I could just cram my feet into them. Then I was ordered into a truck with three guards and an officer. All the prison officials came out to bid me good-bye, like old friends. It was quite a farewell.

We drove north into Taejon and, when we arrived, I savored one thing: the fact that six knocked-out tanks still stood there.

I was taken out to an old mission schoolhouse near the Taejon airport and spent the day sitting in the office of a man who apparently was the local commandant. Nobody bothered me, and I was supposed to rest and perhaps to sleep, but found it difficult while sitting in a chair. I was not happy to notice that the furniture had very familiar markings — the 24th Division Medical Battalion.

One thing amazed me. An enlisted guard stayed in the room all the time; and, whenever the officer would leave, the guard would promptly go through his desk, riffle papers, and calmly help himself to the officer's cigarettes. Even when the officer was in the room, and made the mistake of laying a package of cigarettes on his desk, the guard would calmly help himself, just as he might do from his best buddy's supply. I found out as time went on that this was a regular practice in the Inmun Gun. Maybe it's part of their Communist theory that private property is wrong.

That night I started north again, with new guards, in a captured 24th Division jeep. In it I learned, for the first time, another odd thing about the Inmun Gun: that the driver of a vehicle is its undisputed boss, no matter who's riding with him. An officer is just like any other passenger.

This particular driver reminded me of a drugstore sheik of the 1920's. His long, lank hair hung down to his chin when it was in disarray. To get it out of his eyes while driving, he'd throw back his head, whirl it from side to side, and let the hair fall more or less into place — all this, of course, while he continued to push the jeep at top speed. Somehow, he managed to stay on the road until we reached the suburbs of Suwon, where he whirled his head once too often. We hit the ditch, bounced over the debris of a wrecked tank (it sounded as if we had hit a mine), and blew all four tires. We finished the night by walking a couple of miles into town.

After breakfast at a hotel, the officer went away by himself, and I guess my two guards decided it was too much trouble to watch me all morning. They took me down to another building where at least thirty Korean prisoners, all civilians, were wedged into one eight-by-ten room. I was put in with them, to sit cross-legged like the silent others.

Almost immediately, a young boy near me, 14 years old at most, spoke to me softly in English. He told me that some peacetime American officer at Ascom City, between Seoul and Inchon, had befriended him as an orphan and had sent him to school for a year in Texas; I think in Austin. He said the officer had not been able to adopt him but had provided the year's schooling as the next best thing.

He was an intelligent-looking youngster, dressed in American schoolboy clothes. Now he was a political prisoner. I started to ask him more questions, but the guard came to the door and growled at him; and afterward the youngster whispered to me, "Don't talk to me. There are snoopers in here and they've told on me. I'll catch it now."

I managed to slip the youngster some hard candy I had acquired, but I had no chance to do anything else. My own guards returned, the escort officer with them, and the expression on their faces announced plainly that they had been chewed out for putting me in with the Koreans at all. The youngster from Texas did not change expression when I left. The last thing he had said was that he expected to be shot. He hoped that they would do it quickly, without torture.

THE Battle of Ideas—the most important part, to me, of my captivity—began with my arrival in Chonju and that original suggestion that I should broadcast on the Communist radio, and did not end until the Communists had given me up completely. This long debate between us gave me important clues to the workings of the official Communist mind.

One of the things I noticed first was that they were much more anxious to have me say what they wanted me to say than to extract any really new or useful information. Pressure on me was greatest to agree to perfectly obvious falsities: that we had exploited the people of South Korea or that General Douglas MacArthur had ordered Syngman Rhee to start the war. On questions of real significance—like our defense plans for Japan—they gave up when met with baldfaced lies or simple refusal to answer.

I also noticed that the questioning failed completely to evaluate known facts. It just went on and on, over and over the same lines, even when the answers could not possibly have made any difference. In September of 1950, for instance, they hammered at me day after day to learn prewar plans of the South Korean Army, which by this time were thoroughly out-of-date. There was also an almost pathological insistence on getting something signed. I would not broadcast on the radio, therefore I must sign a paper *saying* that I would not go on the radio. I would not sign a proposed letter, then I must sign a letter saying *why* I would not sign a letter. This could not have been solely for the sake of the signature, to be transferred later to vastly different documents: they had my signature on literally dozens of documents captured at Seoul. Rather, I think that this was a business of a minor functionary feeling that he must take back *something* to show his superiors after an attempt to question Dean. Any old signature would do.

Another Communist tactic is the planned mixture of the real

with the fanciful. A questioning may start on topics so absurd or unimportant that even the person being interrogated gets bored with them — and then switch to something quite important when his guard is presumed to be down. Or the prisoner is threatened with cold or starvation, and suffers both. Or he is told that, unless he coöperates, something will happen to his family in the United States.

But the most important characteristic I discovered in the Red mind is inflexibility. They never give up; they never change even the most absurd propaganda line once they are committed to it. Possibly nobody below the top rank dares to change, and the top rank is too difficult for anyone else to influence.

This verbal Battle of Ideas between my Communist captors and me continued everywhere we stopped. After a doctor had thumped my chest again at Suwon, I was moved north to Seoul, crossing the Han river on the same hand-operated ferry which elements of the Seventh Division were to use a month later to reach the burning city. I was taken to the police-department building, where a major general told me to sleep on a table, which I did with the greatest of ease. In the morning, I had a remarkable meal — steak, three eggs, French-fried potatoes and eight (count them) small loaves of bread; also a can of evaporated milk, which guards insisted that I drink undiluted. I ate everything but the bread — of the eight, I was able to get down only a loaf and a half, secreting the other half loaf in my pockets. Guards took away the remaining six. Then, for the next several hours, I was kept busy regretting how much I'd eaten.

Very soon, another group of newspapermen with notebooks came in and questioning began again. These men were mostly interested in my experiences since capture. I said quite a lot about that terrible truck ride between Chinan and Chonju, but I could have saved my breath. The minute the story became unpleasant, the general simply forbade the press to write it down.

That afternoon another major general showed up to question me, mostly about military matters. I suddenly developed a very bad memory, but when he asked about the strength of the 24th Division, I decided to take a little wind out of his sails. The North

Koreans were so cocky about having pushed us back that I knocked three or four thousand off our actual strength. The general pulled out one of our tables of organization and began reading off unit sizes, but I stopped him. "That table is only for war," I said. "We didn't expect a war, so we came understrength."

I thought I was getting along quite well with all this when he threw me a real curve. He said, "Did you personally explain to your men why they are fighting?"

That was a telling point, because I hadn't. I had done so in Europe and in Japan, but here in Korea I just hadn't gotten around to any explanations except to officers and headquarters groups. That question really hurt me, and I hated like sin to have to look that buzzard in the eye and say, "Of course I did."

After this interrogation, there was apparently a plan to start deferring more to my rank. When I was sent on north again from Seoul that same day, this deference consisted of placing a wobbly kitchen chair in the exact center of a truck. I was ordered to sit on this, and a six-man guard, armed with four submachine guns and two rifles, found seats on the floor all around me. An officer sat with the driver.

Once again the driver of the truck was the boss. He was a most un-Korean type of Korean: he acted as if women were human. He stopped to pick up a girl hitchhiker even though the English-speaking officer beside him obviously was opposed to the idea. This time, my guards apparently were men going home on leave. On the way they sang, and it seemed to me that all the songs were political. There was the Inmun Gun marching air, and another about Kim Sung Soo, one of South Korea's outstanding leaders, which was like a hate song, or perhaps even unprintable. Another, sung with the same inflection, and undoubtedly a hate song, was "E-Syngman." Koreans usually reverse the order of names, placing the family designation first. And a single character may be translated Rhee, Dee (or Di), or just as E. There was also a song extolling Stalin.

The driver loved to sing, too, and each time he joined in he would lift his head to bay out the choruses toward the stars — and take his eyes completely off the road.

We finally crossed the Imjin River and stopped just south of the 38th parallel in a town which I believe was Paekchon, parking in front of a police station while the escort officer went inside. I shall never forget that town. All the time we sat there someone was screaming inside the jail. It was screaming even worse than that I had heard coming from the tank we had hit at Taejon, and it kept on monotonously. Someone was being cruelly tortured; and whatever they were doing to him continued intermittently all the time we were there.

Finally we went on again. The men continued their singing, and the driver went on flirting with ditches every time he raised his head to give voice. This even affected the uncommunicative officer. I said that I thought they must have searched for a week to find such a rotten driver, and the officer agreed. They had succeeded, he said, in finding the worst driver in Seoul.

As we were dropping down into a long valley, the driver finally lifted his head too far and ran us off the road into a rice paddy. The truck turned over. But this was a vehicle without a top, like most of them in North Korea, and we were all thrown clear. We walked seven or eight miles to a town I was told was named Oreo, although I've never been able to locate it on a map.

I was taken to a hotel there, but there was so much curiosity about me that in the afternoon the officer took me down to the center of town so everybody could have a look. Nobody threw anything, or even jeered. They only stared, like people looking at a monkey in a zoo. I must have been ahead of the infamous prisoner marches which later covered more or less this same route.

During the day someone repaired the truck and, that night, we drove on to Pyongyang, where I was put in a western-style house with two rooms. I had a cot here, too, but had to sleep with the lights on and a guard always present.

CHAPTER 4

AT PYONGYANG, I met two men I have every reason to remember. The first was an interpreter, a pleasant Korean in civilian clothes. He did not give me his name, Lee Kyu Hyun, until later, and then he asked me never to use it, as he was under orders not to tell it to me. He had been a professor of literature at Kim Il Sung University, but had been drafted by the Inmun Gun to translate captured documents. Later I was told that the North Koreans had captured many secret documents, both from our Embassy in Seoul and the headquarters of the Korean Military Advisory Group.

Lee expressed great surprise about me. He had been told that I was a tough, rugged individual who liked only outdoor sports — an uncultured type. He was amazed when I asked for something to read and also amazed that I cared for music or painting. He could not understand how in the world anyone who believed in "culture" could also be a professional soldier.

Lee soon began to bring me reading matter — a Communist novel, written in English, and the July issue of a Soviet magazine, *News*. The latter contained stories of strikes in Japan and articles criticizing the United Nations for interfering in Korea.

I read anything they'd let me read; I wanted to find out what modern Communism was all about. I had studied Marxism when it was still taught at the University of California as a political-science course, but the North Koreans' ideas about "Leninism" were all new to me. Not one officer in a thousand in our Army — and, if anything, an even smaller percentage of civilians in the United States — has any idea of what the Reds mean and you can't fight them intelligently unless you do know what they mean. In the United States we cannot afford to be so ignorant.

In one of my first conversations with Lee I repeated a frequent request I had made to be taken to a prisoner-of-war camp. I remember his answer very well. He said, "Oh, the men in your camps are very happy, very merry! Very cheerful! They are whistling and singing and cracking jokes all the time." But he did not say anything about taking me to join them.

Of two interpreters I finally had, I liked Lee the less, but I think I may have done him an injustice. At Pyongyang and Sunan, he shouted at me when my interrogators shouted, ranted when they ranted, but this may have been only to impress the North Korean officers. For Lee went to Pyongyang on October 10 — this I learned much later—and surrendered to American troops when they took the city nine days later. Under interrogation he told a straight story of his experiences with me and gave American officials the first detailed word that I was alive.

On September 6, I met the other man I shall always remember—for very different reasons. He was a colonel named Kim. Even today, I could pick Kim out of any crowd. I know the way he fumes when he is angry; the unctuous approach he uses when he's trying to wheedle; the manner in which spittle foams out of his mouth when he's threatening—yet I find it difficult to describe him. But I'll be able to reach out a beckoning finger when I see him again—and I'll be waiting for that day. Not that he was unpleasant at first. Quite the contrary. He was kindly, interested in my welfare—and left me a thick folder of alleged statements by American prisoners of war. These concerned a resolution, said to have been approved at a mass meeting of prisoners, calling for American troops to cease fighting. Some 800 typed signatures were attached, many of them names of officers and men I knew.

Kim's request was simple: I should sign the petition and go on the radio to tell the people of the United States that we should stop fighting. He said, "Now I'll give you time to think this over."

The next morning we moved again, because of the increased bombing of Pyongyang, to the village of Sunan.

A doctor had visited me at Pyongyang and had given my chest the usual good thumping; but my dysentery was growing worse and I was fast growing weaker. I normally weigh about 210 pounds, but was down to about 110 when captured and had gained little, if any, since then. But when the very polite and kindly Colonel Kim came back to see me, a day or so later, he insisted that I take a walk with him. I tried, but simply could not keep going after 50 or 100 yards. So we stopped at a point from which we could look down over a valley; and while we sat there he gave me a lecture on the virtues of Communism.

He wondered if I had not noticed a vast difference between South and North Korea. I told him that the farmhouses in North Korea looked much poorer to me and that I thought the people lacked comforts which farmers in South Korea took as a matter of course. That didn't please him at all. He pointed out a housing project being constructed near Sunan as an example of what Communism was doing for the people. He also said that North Korea actually wasn't a true Communist state, because people could still own their own homes and there was sanctity of private property: farmers merely paid one fourth of their crops in taxes. But all large industries and public utilities such as railroads were owned by the state; women had full equality with men; and industrial workers had priority at state-operated food stations. I should, he said, realize how wonderful all of this really was. It was a long, exhaustive lecture, and I was exhausted.

We finally went back to the village for lunch. It was delicious—there was even boiled beef. After lunch the colonel asked if I had signed the petition asking our people to stop fighting. When I said that I had not, I could see he thought he had wasted his boiled beef.

About September 10 Colonel Kim came back again; and this time all he wanted was my signature on two long written statements, one to the effect that we were making a mistake by fighting in Korea, the other attacking Syngman Rhee. The colonel made himself exceptionally clear. "If you sign these," he said, "you'll go to a prisoner-of-war camp immediately—and you won't be tortured." He didn't shout or scream, but he wasn't the kindly friend he had been previously—except for a few minutes, when he suddenly asked whether I liked to drink.

I said, "No. I seldom drink hard liquor. I do like a little sherry wine before dinner, but that's usually all."

This confused him a little, but he wasn't stopped entirely. "Then," he said, "all you have to do is to sign these statements, and you'll be taken to a nice house in the country and have an easy, pleasant life there until the war is over. Also, there will be plenty of fine sherry wine to drink."

He embroidered that house-in-the-country picture quite a lot, but I think he was a little troubled because he couldn't stock the cellar with Scotch or vodka.

For two more days the colonel stayed with me, alternately

dangling in front of me this hope for a lazy country life with a bottle of sherry, then shifting over to the war crimes of the United Nations — mostly, the bombing of schools and churches.

Here I must explain something. During the next three years I had a true worm's-eye view of our air war. I was in no position to evaluate the effects of bombing as a whole; I knew only the effect of bombing on a few people, with whom I had direct contact. So when I say that bombers missed or hit an apparent target, or that bombing increased hatred for the United States, no criticism of aerial warfare is meant.

For three years those jets and bombers in the skies were my only link with my country. There was no sweeter sight to me than the vapor trail of a Sabre, no sound lovelier than the solid *whuummp!* of a salvo of bombs. Those were my people working, and I cheered them, every one.

At Sunan, however, it did seem to me that there was a good deal of bombing wasted on roads when I could still hear switch engines chuffing up and down on the undamaged railroad.

During this time I was very weak and bed was still the greatest thing in the world to me. My cares seemed to drop away if I could get back to my cot and sleep. But about 11:30 one night Colonel Kim stormed in and said, "I want you to sign this request to stop bombing our innocent villages."

I said, "Nobody will believe it if I sign anything like that. If I could get back to my own people, however, I certainly would advise them to concentrate more on military targets. I'm sure those are the orders, but sometimes there are errors."

He kept insisting that I sign a statement. I was very tired and sick, but I don't intend to alibi — I merely got what seemed like a brilliant idea at the time. I said, "No, I won't sign a statement, but I *will* write a letter to General Walker."

I guess that letter from Sunan was a silly thing, but I did write it. I wrote along these lines:

> Dear General Walker: Unfortunately I was captured on the 25th of August. It was a physical capture. I was overpowered on my attempt to get back through the lines. [I did want both

General Walker and my own son to know that I had *not* surrendered.] I've been well treated but I'm anything but happy at being a prisoner of war. I urge that you impress upon the Air the necessity to confine our air attacks to military targets.

William F. Dean.

I don't think I ever would have written this letter if I had been fully awake. Later, I reviled myself for having written it. I only hoped that General Walker would understand that I wanted more and better bombing, not less of it. But so far as I can learn, the Reds never did anything with the letter.

One of the most difficult problems for a prisoner is that of maintaining his judgment. You have no one on whom to test your ideas before turning them into decisions. A thought which normally you would discard as soon as you saw that it affected listeners adversely, balloons in your mind until you are sure it must be exceptionally clever.

Kim was there almost every day after that, and the mask of friendliness was gone. Paraphrased, what he had to say, again and again, was: "I've got you now. I'm going to discredit you. You signed one thing, so you might as well sign anything I put in front of you. I've never lost on a man yet, and I've had them tougher than you." Often this harangue was delivered just after he'd shaken me awake in the middle of the night.

I signed only one thing more for him, however, and again I thought that I was being cute. Kim had been after me about the alleged hatred of South Koreans for Americans and wanted me to sign a statement that we should withdraw from the peninsula. I said that I wouldn't sign that, but I would write one similar to it. As nearly as I can remember I worded it, in part:

> Many South Koreans through fear have outwardly manifested hostility to all Americans; and if we drive only to the 38th parallel, it will be only a matter of time until we have the same problem again, because the seeds of Communism have been planted in the South. . . .

Again I attached my signature — and with it, an invisible hope that anyone on our side who read it would see that I was urging our people to come north of the parallel, not to stop at it.

Colonel Kim was pleased with the statement at first. He went away carrying it like a treasure. But a couple of days later he was back, fuming mad. I guess he had showed it to somebody who understood English well enough to see what I was trying to do.

On the night of September 14 he got me out of bed again and ordered me taken back to Security Police headquarters at Pyongyang. There I was taken to an enormous room where a lieutenant general was seated at a massive table. (I believe he was Lieutenant General Pang Ha Sae, head of the North Korean Security Forces.) The general invited me to sit down. He said he understood that I had refused to "coöperate" but he was sure that I would "coöperate" with him. He wanted to know three things: What were American intentions in the Far East? What secret weapons did we possess? What was the plan of maneuver for U.S. Forces in Korea?

There was a special reason for that last question. The tide of war was turning, and U.S. Marines and soldiers were either landing at Inchon or steaming toward it in the amphibious assault that broke the back of the North Korean Army in 1950.

I told the general that I didn't have any of this information, but succeeded only in bringing on a harangue. The gist was that I was completely at their mercy, they were going to try me as a war criminal for things I had done as military governor in 1948, nobody would know what had happened to me because the American newspapers and radio already had reported me as dead, and they had "trained operators" who would make me talk, whether I wanted to or not.

Finally, he said that he would give me a few minutes to think things over. I was taken to an anteroom and given a cup of tea. I was so tired I went to sleep sitting there. Lee said I snored.

After a few minutes I was awakened and led in to see the general again. When I said I had not changed my mind about talking he was angry. He said, "You won't talk?"

"No."

"Then you must sign a statement saying *why* you won't talk."

I said that would be all right with me. On a paper I wrote:

> Fortunately I do not know the information you seek. But even if I did, I would not give it to you, because by so doing I would be a traitor to my country. So help me God. William F. Dean.

Once again, my signature seemed to get the general off some sort of hook, and he let me go back to Sunan, where another doctor came to see me. After the usual chest thumping, he put me on a diet of *chook:* rice, cooked until it is soft and gummy.

On the night of September 16 the delightful Colonel Kim returned with three other officers. They set up a table in the room where the guards were sleeping and for hours pored over papers. Colonel Kim came into my room once to tell me, "Well, tomorrow we're going to interrogate you. I have trained assistants who are going to get what we want to know."

I thought the next day might be tough, so I went to bed and got some sleep. They started about nine o'clock in the morning, with three interrogators working in shifts: two lieutenant colonels, Choi and Hong, and a Major Kim, just to confuse the name situation. A second interpreter, Tal, came along to spell Lee.

The interrogation took place in my room. I sat on a straight chair—handmade by somebody who hated the human race—facing a table, with one of the interrogators on the other side. The interpreter sat at one side, and a guard usually stood, holding his submachine gun. When Colonel Kim would come in now and then to see how they were getting along, he'd loll in an easy chair. The room was icy—the temperature was about 33°—and the Koreans all wore heavy overcoats. I started out in my summer suit and sock-footed; my infected left foot had not been treated and was now the size of a small balloon. I had no padding left on my hipbones and, when that homemade chair became unbearable, I would sit on both hands, which also swelled to twice their normal size.

Lieutenant Colonel Choi began the interrogation, using a prepared list of inquiries, mostly about military matters, while I developed a convenient lack of memory. What secret weapons did we have? Were we going to use the atom bomb? The questions went on and on. I was tempted to manufacture a few secret weapons just for his benefit, but resisted. The trouble with that sort of lying is that we might actually have some of the things I dreamed up. I could have created some dillies out of my imagination.

After four hours, we stopped a few minutes for lunch, and then Colonel Hong, a big, well-built Korean, took over. I learned from his questions that he had been in Seoul, helping to organize strikes, when I was military governor. He boasted that he had never been to high school, but he knew the Communist Manifesto by heart and could quote the Geneva Convention by paragraph.

It was never a matter of more than technical interest in North Korea, but the Geneva Convention sets up definite rules for the treatment of prisoners — adequate food, clothing, and reasonable care. A prisoner may be questioned legally only about his name, rank and serial number. Officers, says the Convention, shall be treated with due regard for their rank and age. Where possible, orderlies shall be provided for officers who normally would have them in their own armies, and the holding power is required to provide advances against military pay. Needless to say, I never saw anything like pay, orderly service, or treatment corresponding to my age and rank.

When I protested that I could not be questioned except about my name, rank and serial number, Hong quoted paragraph such-and-such, stating that in special cases prisoners could be required to give further information. I was a special case, he said, because I was a war criminal, owing to my acts as military governor.

Hong's questioning went through every event in Korea from World War II until the Korean War started, but at last we had 20 or 30 minutes for supper. In the evening Major Kim took over. He concentrated on questions concerning the economics of South Korea, and then spent hours telling me about the defects of capitalism, and the ills of the United States.

Finally I said, "Have you ever *been* to the United States?"

He said he had not.

I said, "And you're trying to tell me about things I was born and raised with!"

He jumped up. "I'll have you know," he said, "that I was a professor of economics at Kim Il Sung University. I got my doctor's degree by writing on the United States."

Perhaps I would have been more impressed if my hands hadn't hurt so much from sitting on them.

Major Kim kept it up for his full four hours but finally he, too, wilted, and Lieutenant Colonel Choi came back, fresh as a daisy, with questions about the air war. He obviously thought I was the most stupid general officer he'd ever encountered. Finally, I said, "Well, you were lucky: you were fighting the second team when the war started. But we'll have the first string in presently – perhaps we do now. All American generals are not as dumb as I am. You just happened to catch the dumbest."

I got Hong's attentions again in the middle of the night, then the special ministrations of Colonel Kim, who reprimanded me for a full hour for not "coöperating." While he talked my teeth were chattering, and this seemed to annoy him. He said, "What are you making your teeth go that way for? Are you cold?"

I said, "Yes, I'm a little chilly."

"This isn't cold," he said. "Take off your coat! Take off your shirt! Take off your trousers and your undershirt! I'll show you what it means to be cold."

I ended up in my shorts. The temperature was still 33°.

Then Choi went back to work. After an hour, during which Colonel Kim departed, Choi also was annoyed by my teeth chattering, because he said, "You may put on your undershirt." I could see the pattern now. Choi was to be the kind friend during this endurance contest, while Colonel Kim (who had already shouted too much to pretend to be kind now) would play the part of the meanie. It's an old police-interrogation technique.

The undershirt felt wonderful, and I was allowed to keep it on until Kim returned an hour or so later. Then I went back to shorts-only once more. I didn't get the T shirt again during the entire questioning.

There were breaks for meals – when I got nothing but *chook,* which left my mouth filled with white flakes, like alkali – but the Choi-Hong-Kim, Kim-Choi-Hong-Kim succession never stopped for 68 hours. The only other breaks I got were when I'd yell *"Benjo,"* and run for the latrine outside the church. A guard always went with me, to see that I didn't loiter; and usually they

lived right up to their orders. One enlisted man was a little kinder than the others and, when he was along, I could steal a few seconds outside to stop and pick up fallen chestnuts. I ate them on the spot.

Then Colonel Kim called a halt. He used the last hour himself to give me information: I was a dog and a robber, "and," he said, "I'm going to treat you like a dog." He ordered the guards to take away my cot and medicine and washing privileges. He said, "You can have one blanket and sleep over there in the corner on the floor. You'd better think things over. It's getting colder. If you fail to coöperate, we not only won't give you any clothes, we'll keep you outdoors."

He threatened, too, to have my tongue cut out. I said, "Go ahead and cut it out. Then you won't be able to make me talk." After that I heard nothing more of that particular threat.

I had no trouble getting to sleep on the smooth boards of the floor. I had had 68 hours of questioning, during which a guard would yell at me or kick me with his bare foot if I dozed in the straight chair. I slept most of that day and that night, rolling off the bare floor onto the rug when the guard wasn't watching.

The next morning at eight, here came the boys again. Hong was the lead-off man, and Exhibit A was an alleged captured South Korean government report on severe suppression measures taken against guerrillas and Communists in 1949. What was my conclusion about that?

I didn't have any. I had been in Japan that year.

Finally, we got onto the national elections of 1948 when I was military governor of South Korea. That was the only free, secret-ballot election in Korea in 4000 years, and I was proud of the way it had been handled. I had organized local committees, made speeches telling the people of the importance of voting, and sent out more than 1000 people to inspect the different voting areas. Instances of violence that occurred were due, I felt, almost entirely to the Communists, who were ready to do anything to prevent the organization of the new government as later they were willing to start a war to prevent its functioning.

Oddly enough, in the middle of a session in which I was being called a robber and a running dog of Wall Street, one of my interrogators — Hong, I think — paid me a sudden compliment.

"One thing we have to admit about you," he said, "is that you never violated Korean womanhood. You're a thief and a murderer, but you never had a concubine." Apparently their prewar intelligence system in Seoul had interested itself in all sorts of details.

As the interrogation continued, I began to notice a few amusing things. One was a sure way to make any interviewer hit the ceiling. Many of these questions actually were long harangues, and the only real query was at the end: "What is your conclusion?"

I'd just say, "I have no conclusion," and the interrogator would blow his top. He'd worked a long time over that statement, and he hated to waste it for just one measly little four-word answer.

The questioning did not go on steadily. There were periods of an hour or two when the interrogators were out of the room, but they didn't do me much good. My hands were swollen to ham size, my hipbones were like two boils, and sitting down at all was continuous misery; but I still had to sit there as if being questioned. If I nodded, the guard would shout or kick me with his bare feet. And in these silence periods I always had trouble in getting the guard to allow me to go to the toilet. I'd say *"Benjo,"* but frequently he would shake his head in a negative. I'd just go out anyhow. That left him no choice but to come with me or shoot me, and I guess he'd have been in the soup if he shot me — though I was sure they were going to shoot me eventually anyway.

Colonel Kim now came back to take an active hand. He tried to get our defense plans for Japan out of me for two or three hours, yelling, storming, and asking the same questions over and over. While he was at it, I just sat there. Once he screamed, "You're sleeping with your eyes open!"

After Kim got through that time, he said he was getting tired and, if I didn't start coöperating soon, they'd take measures to see that I did. The other three interrogators were tired, too, so they let me go back to sleep on the floor — without my blanket. I was keeping track, just for my own satisfaction, and this time they had not done so well: it had taken me only 44 hours to wear out four of them. I slept on the floor most of the day and was looking forward to another night's rest. I felt I wasn't in too much trouble yet. During one attack in Europe, in 1944, I worked four days without sleep, and I knew I could do that well again. I thought, "If they go over five or six days, I'll probably just go to sleep in spite of them."

I did not get that night's rest. About 9 p.m. I was awakened. Nobody said we were going to dance again, but I got the general idea. Major Kim came on stage, then Hong, then Choi, but they all showed signs of running out of questions, and I was left alone for hours, just sitting in that uncomfortable chair and being kept awake by the guard's toe. Whenever they'd think up a new question or one more way to ask an old one, one of them would come in and work on me for a while.

In this manner we passed the night, the next day and most of the next night — 32 hours. About the second midnight, Colonel Kim took over once more, for what was to be the last interrogation. He was in a standing-up, table-pounding mood, talking about the murder of innocents by our aircraft when I broke in, "I've seen atrocities committed by your troops worse than anything you've mentioned. I've seen our men captured, then murdered in cold blood while they had their hands tied behind them, at Chochiwon. And I talked to a lieutenant who saw your men drive prisoners ahead of them, to try to get others to surrender — then shoot them when we opened fire to repel an attack."

This so infuriated Colonel Kim that he yelled, "Close your eyes! I'm going to spit in your face."

I ought to have said, "Spit, you creep, and I'll knock you on your ____." But I just wasn't up to it physically. I said, "Close my eyes? Go on and spit! You've been spitting in my eyes for the last half hour."

I don't know how the interpreter told him that, but it must have been accurate. I thought Kim was going to have apoplexy.

He said, "All right, this is the end. We're going to torture you."

CHAPTER 5

COLONEL KIM leaned back. "Do you know," he asked, "how we torture people?"

I said, "No."

He described a process in which water is forced either into the mouth or the rectum, under pressure. The latter, he said, "forces everything in you, everything, to come out through your mouth. It's very sickening."

I said, "The shape I'm in, that'll kill me quickly. That sounds good to me." He had been fuming, but now he spluttered.

"Sometimes," he said, "we drive bamboo splinters up under the fingernails and then set fire to them."

The setting fire didn't sound too bad to me, but that business of driving the splinters hurt just thinking about it. I laughed at him, but perhaps the laughter was a little forced.

"Also," he said, "we have electrical treatments. The building where we use these, our laboratory, is just a mile from here, and in the morning we'll take you there."

It was almost morning.

He said, "You know your own people think you're dead, so we can do anything to you we want to do. Under torture you'll probably die but not too fast for you to give me the information I want — in detail. Do you want to write a last message?"

I said, "No."

He said, "Then you must sign a statement that you do not want to write a last message."

I said, "Okay. I'll write a last letter to my family."

He gave me paper and a pencil, and I wrote:

> Dear Mildred, June and Bill: I was physically captured on 25 August and have been a prisoner of war ever since. I did not surrender but was physically overpowered. . . . I am terribly ill and do not think that I will live much longer. . . . June, do not delay in making your mother a grandmother. Bill, remember that integrity is the most important thing of all. Let that always be your aim. Mildred, remember that for 24 years you have made me very, very happy.

That was all.

When it was translated, Colonel Kim said, "Why do you say that you are so ill? Why don't you tell them we're going to kill you?"

I swear too much, but perhaps this time it was justified. I said, "Why, you dumb bastard! I know you'd never send out any letter which said that. I didn't write that for your benefit. I wrote that so my family would know I was dead, and what I was thinking about. Now you can kill me and it'll never be held against you. I've stated that if I die, it's by natural causes."

He just looked at me. Finally, he said, "All right. In the morning, we go to the laboratory," and he stomped out.

Remarkably, a guard had brought back my blanket. I rolled up in it in the corner and after a little while scooted over on the rug, where it was a tiny bit warmer.

One guard always walked a post outside the building and another was always in my room, each of them armed with a regular submachine gun with a circular ammunition drum. Through cracks in the partition between my room and the guards' room I had noticed that an extra gun always sat in a corner between the wall of the building and the partition, on the side opposite me. The guards all slept on the floor but, when no officer was present, they frequently flopped down on one of two big overstuffed chairs I was never allowed to use. Sometimes they dozed.

This morning while I was lying on the floor I thought, "If they take me up to that torture building today, I'm so weak that I might tell them something before I die. I've got to get that gun."

This was not a new idea. I'd planned that, when I was strong enough, I would get it, somehow, for an escape attempt. But at this time I couldn't have made a hundred yards even if nobody interfered with me. I thought, "I've got to knock myself off, and fast, before they torture me." The trouble was, you see, I *did* know the defense plans for Japan.

The guard in my room slumped down in the comfortable chair and obligingly went to sleep almost immediately. That left the 20 guards in the other room. If they all went to breakfast in the cookshack and the guard on duty didn't waken, the time would be ripe.

About 5:30 a.m. they all trooped out. Colonel Kim, Choi, Major Kim and Hong all slept in the cookshack — or so I thought. The interpreters were in their own room, with the door shut. When the guards left, I slid quietly out of my blanket and started crawling. I thought, "When I get the gun, I'll fire one short burst out of the window in the general direction of the cookshack. If old Colonel Kim's on the ball, he'll come fogging out of there to see what it's all about. The second burst will get him. Then I'll stick the muzzle in my mouth and finish the job — but I'll have Kim's company when I go. I wouldn't want to miss that."

I crawled to the door between the two rooms, rounded the partition and reached the corner, passing close to my former cot, but not being able to see on top of it from my crawling position.

I got the gun in my hands and came up to a kneeling position. I tried to pull the bolt back, but it jammed and I must have made

some noise. There was a bellow behind me. From the cot, the 180-pound Colonel Hong swung down and rushed me. Instead of sleeping on the floor of the cookshack where he belonged, like a good member of the proletariat, this big capitalist-thinking character had grabbed an opportunity to sleep on a soft mattress.

I swung the gun. There was no time for Colonel Kim now, but I could still get Hong. Hong was a brave man. He charged right into the barrel of that gun — and the damned thing wouldn't fire.

Hong hit me from the front, my room guard from one side. Then there were Koreans all over me; I don't know where in the world they all came from. In seconds it was finished, and I was being marched back into my own room. I was seated in the straight chair when Lee, the interpreter, came in, his face blanched. He said, "Why, General, you would have killed *me!*"

I said, "No, Lee, I didn't want to kill you. I wanted to get that son-of-a-gun, Kim, and myself. They said they were going to torture me this morning."

Lee hadn't been there when Colonel Kim was ranting. He said, "Oh, they didn't say that. They will never torture you. General, you must never take your own life. There's always hope. But I'm very much afraid you would have killed me, General."

I never saw Colonel Kim again. Perhaps he was somehow disgraced by my suicide attempt (that would have been *too* bad); perhaps he simply gave me up as hopeless. I do hope he didn't drop dead. He and I have a few things I still want to discuss, and I'd hate to think that there won't be another chance.

They left me sitting in the chair until midmorning. Guards took the drawstring out of my shorts — the only clothing I had on — and removed from the room everything else with which I might conceivably have harmed myself: string, knife and fork, everything. Thereafter I ate with a spoon, which was removed immediately after I laid it down.

In the evening Choi came in once more, and his attitude had changed. "Colonel Kim has gone," he said. "I'm going to have charge of you. You're a sick man and we must make you well."

My cot, sheets and blanket were brought back into my room, and I was allowed to sleep or get up as I chose. My clothes were also brought back. The next morning another doctor came to see me, left some more medicine and gave my chest another resounding thumping. The only explanation I can give for this standard procedure by all Korean doctors is that they see so much tuberculosis, they just automatically assume any patient must have it.

Choi was a changed man from then on, kindly and friendly. But on October 1 he said, "As a personal favor, will you write a letter for me? I'm leaving tomorrow night, and I'm supposed to get some information from you. Will you write what you think you did well when you were military governor of South Korea? Also, your personal opinion of Syngman Rhee? If you do this, I assure you that you'll go to a prisoner-of-war camp right away."

I wrote two notes for Choi. In the first I said that I was proud of our record in Korea, in agriculture, the rehabilitation of cotton and silk mills, the production of paper, the building up of railroad and shipping lines. About President Rhee I wrote: "I feel that he is a devoted patriot and lover of his country. . . . Everything he does, he feels is in the best interests of his country."

These notes satisfied Choi, who departed the same day.

So did I, about 10 p.m., in such a hurry the guards wouldn't even let me rescue my extra pair of shorts from the laundry line.

Our vehicle was a small truck. Besides a couple of iron safes, it carried the interpreter, Tal, a lieutenant, the driver, and three guards — U Eun Chur, Pack Chun Bong and De Soon Yur — of whom I was to see a great deal.

We moved north with convoy after convoy of other trucks, all running at night and all in a hurry. Nothing had been said to me about any change in the military situation, but anyone could tell that this was a retreating army, getting out fast.

It was not far to Huichon, about 100 miles, but we were 13 hours getting there. And on that cold night I was struck by the actual tenderness of the three guards, especially U Eun Chur, the senior sergeant, in trying to keep me warm by holding a blanket over me.

In Huichon that next day I slept in a Korean hotel, on the floor; and for most of a thousand nights thereafter I continued to sleep on floors — sometimes on concrete or clay with flues imbedded in it, and hot to the touch; occasionally on matting over wood, the typical Japanese-style floor; much of the time on hard-packed dirt.

The outstanding single characteristic of most Korean country-town hotels and ordinary Korean homes is that they have *no* furniture. I mean that literally. The Japanese run to pint-sized tables and low-slung lacquered cabinets, and the Chinese love screens and carved chests. The average Korean does without any furniture whatever.

The typical North Korean house is a two-room structure with a kitchen. One room, about four by eight feet, is built below ground level, and one whole side of it is taken up by a sort of covered fireplace, open on the room side but topped with a flat clay or concrete cover, broken by three holes for cooking pots.

Flues from the fireplace lead under the raised floors of the other two rooms, each about eight feet square, before the smoke escapes through the chimney. The kitchen is equipped only with rice bowls and a stone water jar, in addition to the three cooking pots — one for rice, one for soup and the third for water. Walls are mud, reinforced with cornstalks; the roof is carefully thatched, the inside sometimes covered with paper — and in between live big Norway rats. There may be a window or two in these houses, but rarely any glass.

The Korean *ondols,* a system of heating flues built under the floor, always surprise Westerners: they seem so modern. But surprise wears off, and the vagaries of the *ondol* begin to wear on your nerves. Very few draw properly, and often more smoke drifts in from the kitchen of a Korean house than goes under the floor to create heat. Each floor has a hot streak in it — sometimes so hot you can't sit on it comfortably — while the rest is cold.

I had been repeatedly promised by this time that I would be taken to a POW camp where I could perform my duty of seeing to the proper treatment of the prisoners. Instead, I was merely moved, in Huichon, from the hotel to a "Korean-Japanese house" — that is, a house with one *ondol*-heated room, and one with no heat but with *tatami* mats on the floor. This room could have been heated by the charcoal-burning device called a *hibachi* or by a stove, but I saw few of either of these in North Korea.

Tal seemed to be in charge now and he bought food with a lavish hand — chicken, hog liver, beef heart, eggs and greens, in addition to the inevitable rice. But we had no beverage (nor do most North Koreans) except *swoong-yoong* — water boiled in the rice cooking pot after the rice has been removed but before the pot has been scraped. This is full of browned rice fragments and has a pleasant flavor. A bowl of this, taken with great slurpings of enjoyment, is the typical ending of a good Korean meal.

We stayed in Huichon ten days, and I had about decided that life as a prisoner was not going to be too bad. The interpreter let me sun-bathe on a porch and a doctor gave my chest another thumping, lanced my infected foot, heretofore untreated, and sent me some medicine which cured it quickly.

Then a major visited us, and in his wake came two of the restrictive orders that I was to get to know so well. Apparently the guard had complained about the fact that I didn't sleep well at night; also that people might see me (now a constant fear of theirs) when I was sun-bathing. Orders were issued that since I couldn't sleep well at night I must not lie down at all during the day. I was ordered off the porch and even forbidden to stand up inside the house except for emergencies. Both these orders were enforced for more than 18 months.

During the daylight hours that week I noticed that one or two United Nations light aircraft were almost constantly above us, as if on patrol; and during my last day at Huichon an air strike plunged down on the railroad area. That evening I heard a call which was to come frequently: *"Pahli, pahli, pahli!"* The rough translation is, "Hurry, hurry, hurry!" I packed up (which consisted of rolling my blankets) and, in the same truck that had brought us to Huichon, some civilians, my guards, a major and I joined a heavy jam of northbound traffic. This was a retreat, fast becoming a rout. At midnight we headed for the mountains to the north.

Our truck was a very high vehicle, open-topped, loaded with luggage as well as the assorted human cargo. The cold was bitter, and I wrapped blankets around my back to keep warm. Halfway up a very steep mountain grade, with a 200-foot drop to the right, we stopped, blocked by a traffic jam ahead. The major, the driver and one guard walked ahead to investigate the delay. I decided to rearrange my blankets around my shoulders, and stepped on the front seat of the truck, some seven feet from the ground. Then I yanked at the blankets behind me—and jerked my own feet right out from under me.

I pitched forward, could not free my hands, and landed on my head in the gravel. I rolled and went over the top of the cliff, grabbing for anything—and one scrub tree was just where I needed it. I hung on, and the tree held. When I looked up, I was about six feet from the top. A river was far below me.

There was yelling and screaming above and, in a moment, U Eun Chur and the major both leaned over the brink. U reached

down, and I scrambled partially up with his help. When the major reached down I assumed that he, too, would help me but, to my amazement, he began slapping me around the head.

I swore at him, really sharply, and it seemed to help, even though he didn't understand English. He stopped slapping me and gave me a hand until I got back on the road. My head was bleeding, and I wanted to kill that major with my bare hands. But I just wasn't strong enough to try it.

Since no one spoke English, I had to wait until the interpreter rejoined us days later, to find out what in the world that major thought he was doing. The interpreter explained, "He just lost his head and was very sorry. He thought you were trying to commit suicide, and he would have been severely punished if anything had happened to you."

This was October 13 and, along the way toward the Yalu, I could see that the war was moving north almost as fast as we were. In a long valley leading toward Kanggye, a provincial capital, several villages were on fire. Thousands of civilians walked north along the highway; and from byways came whole cadres of unarmed youths, marching in military formation under the charge of a soldier or two, carrying pistols. It looked like a mass mobilization of every male beween 14 and 50.

The escort major grunted in satisfaction every time we passed one of these groups but, when he saw the smoking villages, his curses were quite clear, even though in Korean.

We reached Choesin-dong, a suburb of Manpo, that day. (Manpo, an industrial town, lies on the Yalu River, the border between North Korea and Manchuria.) In Choesin-dong we were shown to one of the filthiest one-room houses I'd ever seen.

After four days we moved to a house in Manpo proper. Sergeant U went into town and spent most of the day trying to buy some rice. Finally, he came back with a 25-pound sack of it, and some garlic and pork fat. When we finished that, guards spent hours each day trying to buy food. After a time, it was so hard to get that we went down to two meals a day. Rice and a vegetable soup without meat stock formed our diet, with Chinese cabbage tops as a sort of salad. Once in a while, we had a few ounces of meat or chicken — cut into small chunks, boiled until all the flavor was gone, then liberally laced with red pepper.

In the Manpo house, four of us slept in one eight-foot-square room while a fifth always squatted on guard duty. But the house had a window from which I was permitted to look because it was so situated that no one could see me. From it, I noted that a Russian civilian family was living across the street, including a man who must have been important, because he had a Korean company-grade officer as driver of his jeep. I also saw three Russian officers strutting around the street.

Two North Korean lieutenants and one captain shared the Manpo house with us. I judged that all of them had recently been in Seoul, for they kept repeating the name. Each had loot of some sort — U.S. .45s, cigarettes, six bottles of penicillin, which they gleefully displayed to one another.

A couple of days later, a woman lieutenant—the same girl who had held political classes in Chinan—joined our little party and moved in with the captain. This should not be interpreted as anything more than a necessary arrangement. The North Korean Army seemed devoid of sex. I have no explanation for their apparent lack of interest. There was none of the calendar art which goes along with most armies (even the Japanese), and there was apparently no talk about sex.

The lady lieutenant brought with her a collection of American silk dresses, cosmetics, and a bottle of fine French perfume, of which she was especially proud. The moment she left the house one of the enlisted men went through her luggage like a terrier until he found the perfume. He poured fully half the bottle on his head as you might use hair tonic. The place smelled like seven beauty parlors.

I could tell in many ways that things were now going badly for the Reds in the war. An English-speaking Korean came to the house briefly. He waited until a moment when he could not be overheard, then whispered to me, "Could you walk seventy-eight miles?"

I knew precisely what he had in mind, and that he was thinking of his own fate as much as mine. "Seventy-eight miles? I can do that on my head. I can crawl that far." This might have been just boasting, because I still was very weak.

He was the one who finally shook his head. "It's very cold," he said. "Much snow." While I protested, trying to help him screw up his courage, he talked himself right out of the idea, and the opportunity to escape never came so close again.

ON WHAT turned out to be the night before we left Manpo, I was taken to a more isolated house. There our party included my guards, two lieutenants and a captain and an English-speaking civilian, a happy group in an eight-foot-square room. A girl cook, who turned out to be a sergeant, moved right in with the rest of us. It was still possible to lie down, but we rolled over either in concert or not at all.

The *"pahli, pahli, pahli"* call came once more the next morning. In a tearing rush my guards and I set out for a government building a few blocks away. Trucks were parked in a courtyard and we got into one of them, after acquiring a new captain as tour-party director.

There must be a million Kims in Korea, but the Captain Kim who now had me in charge was a churlish, English-speaking lad, whose standard answer to any question was, "It's immaterial." I asked him where he had learned English, and he admitted that he had gone to school in Kokura, Japan. Thereafter, I got no information. I asked his rank. He said that was immaterial. So was his name, and he did not care, he said, if I chose to call him merely, "Hey, you." He was a very pleasant fellow.

We drove to the Yalu River, and the captain showed a pass to guards on a pontoon bridge. Thousands of people were lined up on the Korean side, waiting to cross, but our pass got us through the mob, and on the west side of the river I noticed immediate differences. Here were vendors with whole cartloads of meat, more than I'd seen in months, and other vendors hawked a sort of corn fluff as a delicacy. Mule-drawn vehicles were common.

I asked Captain Kim if this was the first time he had been in Manchuria and got a straight lie for an answer. "This isn't Manchuria," he said. "This is a Chinese section of Korea, like your Chinese section of San Francisco."

I said, "Then what was that river we crossed?" The captain didn't answer. My transportation into a neutral country again violated the Geneva Convention, but I was in no mood to protest. "This," I thought, "is good. My chances for getting away are at least triple what they were in Korea."

We drove a few miles to a town, which must have been Chian, and stopped in a sort of hotel. We passed through a kitchen where a mule was walking around and around, turning a press that squeezed out those lovely corn fluffs, and that night we had an excellent Chinese dinner, with pork, gravy, rice and meat-stock soup. But the Koreans didn't *like* this wonderful food. The next day they set up elaborate arrangements for getting Korean food — the usual watery soup, rice and no meat — from some other place. I had to sit there and smell those wonderful Chinese dishes being cooked in the next room without being able to get any of them. However, I had to pass through the kitchen several times during the night. Each time I slipped over to the press, grabbed a handful of corn fluff, and stuffed it into my mouth. I felt like a small boy sticking a finger into the icing of his mother's cake.

Four of us, plus one waking guard, were crammed at night onto a shelf six feet by six. (I think the hotel had been a stable, and we were in a stall.) There wasn't much room, and the captain turned out to be a pinwheel sleeper. All night long that bird pivoted on his head, kicking first one of us, then the others in rotation as he spun around, without even waking up. The only person not miserable was the duty guard watching us, who was thoroughly entertained.

We stayed in Chian until the night of October 30, with me sleeping or sitting the whole time on the shelf. The Korean reasoning in taking me to Manchuria can only be surmised, but to me the most logical explanation is that they intended to use my rank as a bargaining point in whatever peace negotiations might occur. The moment their military situation improved I was hauled back east across the river.

That trip, made in a jeep in the midst of a snow and sleet storm, was bitterly cold. I was crowded into the middle of the back seat, and one of the guard's suitcases, with very rough corners, kept bouncing against my shins. This was more painful than it sounds, and I finally said, "Stop the jeep."

Captain Kim said, "What's the matter?" But when I told him, he said, "That's immaterial."

I said, "The hell it's immaterial! Stop this jeep right now." And I pulled back my fist as if I were going to hit him.

When I think about it now, I can see that almost every time I tried a real bluff it worked — shoving the sentry when I was a fugitive, trying to kill Colonel Kim, now threatening to hit the captain, who could have mowed me down with one hand, in my condition. I got the jeep stopped and that suitcase off my shins.

As we drove back into Manpo, the snow and sleet continued. At a corner, I glanced up a side street. Men were marching there in the snow, their heads bent, their gait that of the very weary. I saw them only for a moment, and then we had gone past. Though I looked back frantically I never got another glimpse of those other American prisoners, plodding through the night. Nor — though I was constantly on the lookout — did I ever see a sign of a POW camp in North Korea.

I was taken to a different house in Manpo this time. Its latrine facilities were unusual. The approach was over a raised catwalk, hazardous with ice, and the facilities themselves were directly above the pigpen, a sort of raised perch visible from all directions and open to the winter winds of Manchuria.

I stayed in Manpo, in various houses, until January 12, 1951. It was bitterly cold and the food steadily deteriorated. I sat on the floor, crawled on the floor and slept on the floor. Much of the time no interpreter was present. Planes bombed the area, but with less and less frequency. I guessed at the course of the war by the numbers of Chinese troops I could see occasionally. (As I learned later, the Chinese entry into the war had by this time changed its whole character. U. S. Marines and soldiers had to fight their way south from the Yalu River on the east coast, finally evacuating their battered units from Hamhung on December 24, 1950. Meanwhile, in the west, the Eighth Army was driven back rapidly, losing Seoul on January 4, 1951.)

Once Lieutenant Colonel Choi, of the Sunan interrogation team, came to see me, with more questions to be asked through Tal. He asked one giveaway question: Was it true that we were landing two Japanese divisions in Korea?

I told him that I had no information on this, but I was struck by the expression of outright terror which crossed Choi's face. Hatred of the Japanese is beyond belief in Korea, but so is fear of the small soldiers from the islands.

Except for Choi's visit, my days were alike. I lived with an every-50-minutes kidney trouble which had replaced my dysentery. I sat with my back against a mud-plaster wall and refought many times the 20-day campaign before my separation from my division. I worried about my family and their finances. And over and over again, as we ate our rice, I planned a dinner to be served on my first night of freedom. It would include prime ribs, an artichoke, a small baked potato with cheese on it and a good-sized hunk of butter, quick-frozen peas, a big helping of head lettuce with French dressing, ice cream and a huge cup of black coffee.

Thinking about food helped to keep me warm. So did massaging my bare toes. No one wears shoes in a Korean house, and I discovered that my feet seemed to keep warmer without socks, though the temperature inside hovered around zero.

I was permitted to wash once a day and worked out a system so that I could get a partial sponge bath out of a single basin of warm water by using a handkerchief as a washcloth. But it was complicated by the fact that the washcloth, when I laid it down beside the pan of water, always froze before I could pick it up again. I had no idea water could freeze that fast.

Most of the time I simply watched the Koreans, which wasn't hard, because ten of us sometimes were living in one eight-by-eight room. De Soon Yur, the most kindly of the trio of regular guards, was exceptionally odd in appearance. Above the waist he was built like a middleweight, but his legs were those of a 12-year-old child. He looked as if he had been mismatched at the belt. He also had the shortest fingers I've seen on a grown man, but he could do incredible things with them: he could even thread a needle in the dark. De was one of the few guards who did not later leave to become an officer; Captain Oh told me that this was because he preferred to stay with me.

U Eun Chur, the senior sergeant, was an old army man, and an authority on Communist doctrine. Pack, the youngest and the brightest of the trio, was notable because the girl cook so transparently thought he was wonderful. She shared her cover with him when we slept and gave him money when she finally left. But, in spite of her perfectly obvious interest, Pack never did anything about it except to carry her luggage to the railroad station on the final day of her stay.

Captain Kim departed early in November and, after that, U was in charge. One man always watched me, at least one was always away trying to buy food, and all of the soldiers spent a great deal of time studying Communist doctrine. *The History of the Communist Party in the Soviet Union* was their principal text, and they appeared to be memorizing it, as children might study a primer. U held almost nightly review sessions, and each man was called on to recite.

Generally, these people treated me kindly—within the framework of the restrictive rules. I ate what they ate. I was equipped no more poorly than the others. They had no thread, no nails, very little cloth of any kind, few needles and no leather. They unraveled old knit clothing to make new things, laboriously twisting the thin yarn strands together by hand in order to make thicker skeins. They resoled shoes with slices of rubber and fabric cut from old truck tires.

Socks in Korea are not darned but patched. The guards all patched their own until patches were on top of patches, and I learned to do the same with mine. But I never tried what I saw—one guard patching another's socks while they still were on the feet. The whole process looked hazardous to me.

Once, while I was watching U, he must have misread my interest as scorn, because he suddenly held up a sock as if he were going to throw it away and yelled, "American! American!" I was sure he resented the fact that he had to patch that sock, whereas an American soldier would merely toss it away. But he had misunderstood my expression. I was just wondering how in the world you could ever get any American, soldier or civilian, to be half that frugal.

None of these soldiers ever had any time off, and none received more than an occasional letter. The only variety in their diet or mine was a very rare helping of soybeans, roasted, or, as a special treat, a bowl of *noo-roong-gee,* which is the browned rice that clings to the sides of the cooking pot and tastes vaguely like toast.

Our girl sergeant-cook, E Sun Koom, was always kind to me. She washed my clothes without complaint and sewed cotton batting between my two blankets when the cold became so unbearable that I couldn't sleep. Only one thing about her annoyed me. Each day, after breakfast, she would wash outdoors, then return to our room with her hair damp, sit cross-legged on the floor facing the dim light, and take out a rather elaborate toilet

kit, which included a bottle of pink hair cream, a popular American brand, to pour on her hair. Then she'd comb, and glycerine would fly off the comb into my face as I sat behind her. I wasn't allowed to move, so all I could do was duck or put up my hands as shields. The guard on duty always had a real nice laugh.

When E Sun Koom left us, I wanted to give her some token of appreciation for her kindness. Everyone seemed short of buttons and they continually stole them from each other. So I pulled the six ornamental buttons off my suit coat and gave them to her. Several days later I saw Pack sewing them on his own clothes.

Many of the things I resented at first in my captivity became less important in my mind as I watched these Koreans dealing with each other. I think they are generally less unkind than completely inconsiderate. They would grab things from each other without a word of apology; or, if a roomful of men were sleeping and the guard on duty felt like singing, he would burst into loud voice—and nobody complained. At Sunan I had resented the guards' habit of kicking me with their bare feet to keep me awake. But that is their way of dealing with each other — the kick is a good method of getting attention, nothing more.

As 1950 ended, air raids around Manpo were lessening, while the number of night trains pulling out toward the south increased. Antiaircraft fire also was increasing in our area, including some obviously from heavy guns. Evidences of disaster for the enemy, which I had seen only weeks before, had vanished almost entirely.

On January 12 I heard the familiar *"pahli, pahli, pahli."* Once more I put on all the clothes I had, rolled my blankets and prepared to move — this time more than 100 miles south again. On the way, U covered my head with a blanket every few minutes, just as we approached some spot where bombing had done important damage. He acted as if he were trying to keep me warm, which annoyed me thoroughly.

It was an uncomfortable ride, cold and crowded. We spent the first night in a house where a farm family moved over to let seven more people sleep. But sleep didn't come to me. The temperature outside was six below zero, the house was terribly cracked, and the biting wind swept through. I noted with astonishment that the farm family had only light clothing and one big cover of some sort, under which they all slept. A little boy, three or four years old, was naked when he stepped over us to go out once during the sub-zero night; except for the runny nose common to virtually all small children in Korea, he showed no ill effects when he came back in and snuggled under the common family coverlet.

Again, as when coming north, we traveled only at night, and the second night was much worse than the first. My position on the truck was even more jammed, I could not get the truck to stop when I asked, and I was thoroughly embarrassed. When we did stop again, at dawn and near Huichon, my feet were freezing. When I tried to walk a few dozen yards to a house I fell repeatedly. At breakfast the *kemchee* was frozen in the rice bowls.

That night when we were ready to start I had a terrible time with my shoes. Outdoors, I couldn't get them on at all; but a captain objected violently when I wanted to bring them inside.

After 20 or 25 minutes of tugging I finally stuffed my feet into them — and we were off on another wild, nightmare ride, first through the ruins of Huichon, then past the site of a recent battle. Villages through which we passed were in shambles.

At a road intersection, an officer stopped us with orders that I was to be taken off the truck. The night was very cold and the ground icy. I fell again and again. My guards were disgusted with me and bawled me out in Korean. Angrily, I shouted back at them that if they had let me exercise I would have been able to stay up now. I cussed them out and they cussed me out, but neither side knew what the other was saying.

We went on, walking and falling, for more than a mile, and at last reached a house used as some sort of office. And here was Captain Kim, the boss of my Manchuria junket, whom I never had learned to love. He was delighted to tell me some news: United Nations troops, he said, had been decisively defeated. He said, "We have many airplanes now and it is only a matter of a few days until there will be no more Americans on the Korean peninsula. Your own press and radio proclaim that this is another Dunkirk. What do you think?"

I told him that if the situation even approached his description, the American people really would get angry — and then he'd better begin to worry.

He left the building. I've never seen him since.

CHAPTER 6

I EXPECTED to resume the trip to Seoul any moment, but I was ignored until the next evening when we walked to another small village near Sunan. We had no food until, in the evening, Sergeant U returned from a junket with some pork fat and *dough*. *Dough* — pronounced just as it reads — is a cake of ground rice, steamed over boiling water. It tastes precisely like flour and water, and for a long time I thought that's what it was. The Koreans consider it a first-class delicacy.

This was the beginning of my worst year — a year of two houses, two caves, many flies, malaria, inadequate food, a succession of odd guards and terrific boredom — all within a three-mile radius. I had difficulty in remembering who or where I was, and in maintaining any sort of sanity.

For some months, in the little two-room house near Sunan, I lived in a room less than eight by four feet, with no light except what filtered through a paper window or came around or over a 66-inch-high partition.

The general orders continued: no standing, no lying down in the daytime. I slept with a guard sitting in the doorway where he could watch me constantly, and with my head always toward the door; but after great argument — and the guards' inconvenience in stepping on my head a couple of times when they wanted equipment stored in my room — I finally was permitted to shift ends, so that the light by which the guard was studying Communist theory would not be directly in my eyes.

When the guard on duty dozed or read, I managed to get in a few exercises. I had to be careful, though, not to raise my hands above the partition, or someone in the outer room would yell.

Somewhat later I got permission to walk for ten minutes a day — inside my own little room. I counted off this space carefully and one day, when a guard let the time run over a little, I managed to get in 2500 yards of walking by taking four steps in one direction, then four in the other, on a diagonal.

At first I was required to sit in the guards' room all day, but this became too crowded — there were finally seven guards in one eight-by-eight room — so my required seating was in the doorway between the two rooms. When they were especially afraid that people coming to the door of the house might see me, I had to sit in the dark end of my own little closet. I had nothing to read, but could not have read in any event. There wasn't enough light. Once, I managed to make a calendar, with a pencil which I hid in my summer clothing, but it was soon discovered and taken away from me, and U really bawled me out. I couldn't understand his Korean but had no trouble with the tone. Thereafter, I scratched the date in the dirt under my sleeping mat each morning. I kept track of the days for almost a year and, when I had a chance to check, my date was correct.

This village was apparently the center of a Chinese staging area. Troops were around us all the time, and I could hear frequent firing of American machine guns and M1 rifles on a range nearby, while mule-drawn transport frequently creaked along outside. Quite often I could hear Chinese women soldiers, who laughed a great deal, talking to the Koreans outside the house.

After a severe spell of illness in the spring, my morale hit a new low, and I realized I had to get something to think about. So I started working simple algebraic problems in my head and playing mental anagrams — how many different words can be made out of the letters in the name Sacramento? San Francisco? Having no paper, I kept score in my head and obtained simply fantastic totals. Then I tried working on squares and square roots of numbers in my mind. I memorized the squares of numbers from 1 to 100. Then I began hunting for fast systems of squaring. For example, the squares of numbers between 10 and 20 have the same right-hand digits as those between 60 and 70, and the relationship follows through. So the square of 40 is 1600; the square of 41 is 1681, and the square of 42 is 1764 — and the square of 90 is 8100, the square of 91 is 8221, and the square of 92 is 8464.

If you are not interested in mathematics, this sort of thing may drive you to pounding your head against the nearest wall; but, believe me, it kept me *from* beating my head against one. I finally rationed myself to squaring 500 numbers a day, so I always had something to do the next day.

U Eun Chur was still in charge of me. He always wavered in his attitude toward me, worrying terribly when I was sick — mostly, perhaps, because of his responsibility for me — but in virtually the next breath restricting my activities even further. The top in restrictions came one day when he caught me counting to myself. My hands were swollen from disuse and beriberi, as were my feet, so I had worked out a cross-finger exercise, which consisted of pressing the thumb and the forefinger together five times, hard, then the thumb and the second finger five times, and so on across both hands. By then I knew better than to let the guards see me doing anything unusual, so I did this exercise with my hand hidden by my side while I sat with my back against the wall. But as U Eun Chur passed me once, he saw my lips moving. Immediately he said in Korean, "What are you doing?" and made me understand by mimicking my lip movements.

I said, "Counting—*il, ee, sahm, sah, oh.*"

He scowled, and there was no mistaking his negative. I must not, he indicated, count without permission.

I'm still of two minds about U. He enforced every restrictive rule to the letter and made up new ones of his own. But he was a fine soldier and scrupulously fair. I admired the way he drilled his squad, made them study their propaganda, and divided the work. He became a second lieutenant and left us in May.

During my lowest moments at this time, I was bothered by a clairvoyant obsession: that both Lieutenant General Walton Walker, of the Eighth Army, and Colonel "Hank" Hampton, my close personal friend, had been killed. I'm positive that no one had mentioned either name to me for months, but I was just as sure as if I had read the news somewhere. I even had dates—early November for Colonel Hampton and early January for General Walker. In midsummer I learned that I had been right about General Walker's death, although wrong about the time and, after I was released, I found that Colonel Hampton had indeed been killed at Suwon in the autumn. I have no explanation.

De Soon Yur, who was always kind to me, took over as chief guard when U left. But I had several severe illnesses including (I think) hepatitis, and life became even less pleasant as U.N. bombers increased their raids in the long spring days. We spent a lot of time in a stinking air-raid trench outside the house.

I objected to the trench on various grounds, among them the fact that going to it interfered with my newest game—killing flies. I had done a little strictly amateur fly-killing the previous autumn; now I got serious about it. In April 1951 the first of the season's fly crop appeared, and I started batting at them with my palm and keeping mental track of strikes and hits. I ended May with an even 300 flies killed and a batting average just over .300. Then, in mid-June, De presented me with a fly swatter he had manufactured from a willow branch and an old half sole. My average immediately took a terrific jump to .760. I was studying flies and think I eventually might have batted .850. The trick is never to try to swat a fly when he's standing still. Wait until he starts walking, or lifts his front feet to wash. Then you bust him, because he can't take off without shifting position first.

The guards were interested but insisted that I couldn't count my score unless I produced each corpus delicti. So I carefully saved each deceased fly during the day, then crawled over — a dignified procedure — to present them at night. A guard would then lend me a pencil to put down my total kill and batting average for the day. My all-time top, in 1953, was a 522-fly day; my grand total came to 40,671. Anyone who wants to challenge my swatting record will have to show me the flies.

My illnesses left me even weaker as time went on and again put off my half-formed escape plans. Even when I went into the kitchen, my legs would sometimes collapse; and a couple of times I passed out completely, just trying to walk. A doctor was called to see me — and at least he knew exactly where to press my abdomen so that it hurt the most. He ruined my opinion of his diagnostic ability, however, with one question. Had I, he wondered, ever had a venereal disease? I was happy to tell him I had not. When I showed him my feet, still swollen and as painful as if they had just been frostbitten, he was not in the least interested. So I went barefoot because I no longer could get my socks on.

Major Kim, with an interpreter, Captain Oh Ki Man, came to ask me more questions several times. Then, on July 17, De Soon Yur announced with obvious pride that we were going to move to a "trenchee" — he had picked up the word from my designation of the air-raid shelter. That night we moved up a steep hill directly behind the house to a covered trench six feet wide, about fourteen feet long, and barely high enough for a man to stand beneath a dirt-and-log roof. It was entered through a right angle at one end, and the floor was three feet below the doorsill. Five-foot bunks for two guards were in the main tunnel and, at the far end, a bay had been dug back into the hill. This five-by-six-foot haven was all for me. Three and a half feet of the width were occupied by a wooden bench, my sleeping couch by night, my sitting room by day.

The cave, De assured me, would protect us against *bihanggi* (airplanes) and flies. Although the summer outside was boiling hot, the cave was dank, full of mosquitoes, chilly and completely airless. I put on my heavy underwear and winter clothing to keep warm. Rain such as I've seen only in Korea started as soon as we moved in. The sky just bucketed. The roof leaked, and guards dug ditches in a fruitless effort to drain the water off the floor.

Robbed of my fly-killing pastime, I spent my time looking at the rock walls, which contained mica, quartz, and, I'm sure, a few flecks of gold, and massaging my sore feet. My dysentery was back, so I was a little more miserable than before. After two weeks of this, a guard shook me awake in the middle of the night. I put on my clothes and stepped down from my wooden bench into water already almost waist-deep. It had covered the guards' bunks, a little lower than my own, and still was rising. We splashed the length of the tunnel and, in pouring rain, sloshed back down the hill to our village house.

The rain kept right on after we got back. The air-raid trench filled and overflowed into the kitchen, and clouds of mosquitoes had a wonderful time.

When a woman was hired as cook, things grew bad for me because the guards were adamant that she must never see me. This meant that I spent even more time in my lightless closet, unable even to run up my fly-killing score for fear she might hear the swatting. I don't know how they explained the extra rice bowl.

On August 4, I began to run a fever with a typical malarial four-day cycle, which left me sleepless and half out of my head. I was gradually going insane from the sound of a clock which hung in the guards' room where I could not see it. I swear this Korean clock made a special dull sound, dih-dah, rather than a normal tick-tock; and I beat my brains out trying to figure the time from the sound. I couldn't get enough water to drink and was becoming more and more delirious. Finally, I scratched a note, "Quinine or atabrine," and De went off to see a *weesah* (doctor).

To my delight, De came back in only a few hours with five big yellow atabrine pills, which gave me almost immediate relief. U. S. Army doctors later told me this may have saved my life, for atabrine is a treatment for dysentery as well as for malaria.

Later that summer, after a second attack of malaria and more atabrine, I was moved back to the cave, now larger and better ventilated. Food, too, was improving, in fits and starts. Once I was given a whole pound of butter (which I put in my soup, a spoonful per bowl, in place of meat stock) and four cans of Soviet-supplied evaporated milk, which I shared with the guards. They didn't care for butter.

In October 1951, we left the cave for good and moved to a concrete house about seven and a half by twelve feet, stuck right into the side of a hill, the roof camouflaged with dirt. It had been built especially for me and even had two glazed windows — just too small to put my head through.

The new house was clean, but the sod-covered roof proved a special attraction for North Korean rats. These characters proceeded with all speed to dig tunnels for themselves under the sod, then kept on burrowing down toward the heat of the room. Terrible engineers, those rats. They dug so deep that only a thin skin of paper and dirt was between them and the open room below, and their tunnels took in water from the upper ends. The result was that the roof leaked — water much of the time, rats now and then. At least five times, a wildly flailing rat landed on my face while I was asleep.

Each time this happened the whole house went into pandemonium while the guards held a wild and woolly rat hunt, trying to stab the rat with a pencil, dagger or bayonet. Four or five men would be in my tiny room at once, all stabbing. By the time they finally got the rat, the room looked as if it had been bombed.

THEN, quite suddenly, on December 19, 1951, Dean's prison life changed for good. The first indication was another visit from Major Kim and the interpreter, Captain Oh. For once they posed no new questions about the course of the war. Instead Kim said, "Wouldn't you like to write a letter to your wife? You don't want your family to worry."

I felt something strange in this, but I said only that I'd written a letter a year before and Choi had promised to mail it.

Both of them said, "Oh? We didn't know about that." They insisted that I write another anyhow — and do it that night. Kim provided a pen and paper and seated me on the floor at a wobbly little table in the larger room of the house. The house was wired for electricity, but our bombers had been busy on the transmission lines, so we had only an oil can with a wick in it for light.

I had hardly had a writing implement in my hand for 16 months, and I was horrified at my own script. My N's looked like M's, and my M's like nothing legible. I struggled through a letter to Mildred, then tried to read it, but I couldn't even make it out myself, so I rewrote it twice more. Oh started to translate it, but stopped at once because I had started: "This is a red-letter day in my life. I have just been told that I can have a pencil, and that I can write to you — "

That part about a pencil wouldn't pass, Major Kim said. I did the whole letter over, foolishly not insisting that they read all of it first. So the next version also was turned down, this time because I had written, farther down: "I haven't seen a fellow American since July 1950."

Version number five finally was approved, well after midnight, and I had to make only two copies of another letter, to my daughter. When I simply was too tired to write any more, the two officers left, carrying my letters and some photos taken at Pyongyang shortly after my capture, signed by me to show that they were genuine. The letters were turned over to U.S. representatives as the first letters in the original exchange of prisoner mail, on December 20 or 21. But before they were given to our people the texts were furnished to the Communist press.

I slept very little that night, I was so excited about having a pencil. And in the morning I had another visitor — a major general, no less, named Lee. With him was my old chum, Lieutenant Colonel Choi. This gave me an opportunity for which I'd been waiting, and I let Choi have it. One of the first things I said to the general was, "This is the man who told me that I could wash twice a day, and I've never been permitted to do it. Why?" I was getting adept at their own type of phraseology. "This is the man who was going to take up with higher authority my request to go to a POW camp. What does higher authority say?" And so forth.

The general was making a big act out of being friendly, so I really poured it on old Choi. Choi squirmed. He said, "That must have been Colonel Kim who was responsible." I never learned what, if anything, General Lee did to Choi, but he himself was demoted later for having failed to visit me and for my general treatment. When I learned this, it looked to me as if they were making old General Lee a goat for a general prisoner-of-war policy they now wished to repudiate.

But this day everything was just dandy. The general didn't approve of the thin cotton pad on my bed, so it was replaced by one much thicker. He ordered a sheet for me, so an aide brought in a strip of cotton cloth about twenty inches wide and seven and a half feet long; I never figured out what to do with it. To replace my summer-weight suit, the aide produced a pin-striped woolen, made in Eastern Germany.

Finally General Lee suggested that I have a drink with him. The aide brought in a half pound of butter in a tin, sliced bread, dried devilfish, black fish eggs and sake. We sat down, and the general launched into a long statement, the gist of which was that we couldn't possibly win in Korea.

I didn't do much talking, because I was too busy eating that wonderful food. I don't care for sake, but I drank two small cups of that, too. When I had finished, the general indicated that I could keep what remained—butter and sake. But after he left I learned that I had misunderstood him. He meant that I could have the sake; the aide came back and got the rest of the butter.

Early the next morning, December 21, Captain Oh was back. Would I state that I had not been beaten? He said, "The general may be punished unless you do this for him."

I suppose that I'm a sucker for people who ask favors, but I was grateful to De Soon Yur, if not to the general. I mentioned De's kindness as my guard, and demanded again that I be taken to a POW camp so that I could see how other prisoners were being treated.

That evening I began to understand the reason for all the hoorah of the previous few hours. A whole group of newspapermen arrived, all but one either Chinese or Korean. At the head of the group was an Occidental. He strolled across the room, which wasn't much of a stroll, grinned widely and held out his hand.

He said, "Hello, General Dean. I'm Wilfred Burchett, the correspondent for *Ce Soir,* a French left-wing newspaper."

I shook hands and said: "Are you American or British?"

He said, "I'm an Australian, and I've come to get your story of how you were captured."

I could hardly take my eyes off Burchett, a fellow Caucasian. You have no idea how important that can be after a year and a half. I felt like throwing my arms around him. We all sat down to an interview which lasted till dawn.

On that and subsequent meetings I came to know a little more about Wilfred Burchett but never arrived at any real explanation either for his choice of the Communist side in this war or for his kindness to me.

The basic details of his story are simple. Burchett worked for British newspapers prior to World War II, then became known to many American war correspondents, as well as to Army and Navy officers, when he represented a London newspaper in the Pacific war theater, working almost entirely with United States troops and naval units. His reputation for competence was high; and newspapermen who worked with him then have told me since that they knew of no special political leanings he had at that time. But as that war ended, the little Australian with the receding hairline somehow seemed to get out of gear with the free world. He was in Europe for some years, changed employers a time or two, was divorced from his British wife — then changed sides entirely. He arrived in Korea during the early part of the North Korean movement to the south but sent no dispatches that aroused world interest until he suddenly appeared with Communist negotiators in the truce talks.

His first visit to me had been so exciting, because of the news he brought and the about-face in my treatment, that I had not thought too much about why he was there, though I noticed his use of Communist terminology: "stubbornness of the Americans" or "failure of The United Nations," and the repeated references to

Kim Il Sung as "the Supreme Commander." Yet he did a straight reporting job, talking to me, and tried to sell me no propaganda. I remember him as a kindly man, cut off from his own people for the sake of strange beliefs.

CHAPTER 7

THE FINAL 20 months of my captivity in North Korea were in sharp contrast to the first 16. Truce negotiations were about to begin and my interview with Burchett and the other Communist newsmen got through the Iron Curtain, so that my family finally had word that I was a prisoner and alive. Less than a fortnight after the interview, Captain Oh brought me copies of three telegrams, delivered via the Communists at the truce talks and passed north to me. My mother had wired, "It's a miracle"; my wife, "It seems like a dream"; and my daughter, "You have a husky grandson, born March 24, 1951."

My treatment now notably improved. I was again allowed to read and write, and petty restrictions, like not being able to stand or to lie down in the daytime, gradually vanished. Captain Oh and my guards began to celebrate everything from Inmun Gun Day to my wife's birthday (which I had mentioned to Oh). It got so that I dreaded the sight of a bottle of Bulgarian vodka or sake. Burchett and other correspondents stopped by frequently and asked about my treatment. In fact, I went from the status of being ignored to being feted, in one big jump, and I never quite got used to it. Nor can I give any explanation of why my treatment improved so much, that of other prisoners very little or not at all. I may actually have been, as my captors claimed, the only American in the exclusive custody of the Koreans.

I hate the thought — and always will — that I was well treated while other soldiers suffered, and there is little satisfaction in the fact that I didn't know about — and couldn't do anything about — the others. So while the welcome I received when I finally got home was wonderful, in some ways it was hard to take. I wish those thousands of other soldiers could have shared it much more than they did.

Some of my new privileges, of course, turned out to be delusive. All during my captivity I had wanted to play a sort of Chinese chess called *chang-kee,* very popular with my guards; but I was seldom allowed to. Now, during an interview, a photographer wanted pictures of me playing *chang-kee.* The guards produced a board and I thought I might get more chance to play it — but the board was taken away right after the picture. For another picture, a bench was brought in for me to sit on. I enjoyed every minute of this, not having seen anything resembling a chair for a year and a half; but as soon as the photos were finished, the bench, too, disappeared.

But other things were better as 1952 went on. We got some fish now — a sort of small herring normally used as fertilizer in Korea; and, in the spring, the root of the Chinese bellflower, *tow-raw-gee* — so liked by Koreans that they have a song: *"Tow-raw-gee,* why do you grow so far up in the mountains?"

One day, Captain Oh told me that from now on I would have the food Korean generals got, including polished instead of unpolished rice.

I asked him, "Do your generals eat better than enlisted men?"

"Yes," he said, "they must eat better to fulfill their greater responsibilities."

After that, I got polished rice much of the time, and an occasional egg, broken raw over my rice. My interest in these disappeared the day I broke one neatly — and out onto my rice dropped a fully formed chicken.

In spite of better treatment, I was both bored and depressed when summer came, by a succession of illnesses and the lack of action. One day — I must be vague on details to avoid hurting people who helped me in North Korea and are still there — I began to get suggestions that perhaps I was in the wrong army. I could have a division in the Inmun Gun — or perhaps even command a corps. But I soon spoiled this offer. When someone asked me what I intended to do "for the sake of peace" when I got home, I said, "I'll try to build up the military unit to which I am assigned in such a manner that it will impress any would-be aggressors." After that, no more was said about a corps in the Communist Army.

The war was not bothering people around me that summer. Food continued to improve and everyone seemed relaxed. I saw Communist jets overhead more than I saw our own and once, in August, I saw one of our own planes knocked down while the Koreans around me cheered. Then, one day, U.N. aircraft made a terrific attack on nearby Pyongyang, with hundreds of bombers and a regular umbrella of jets. There was no question we had control of the air. I heard no cheering, except what I was doing, quietly, myself.

In February 1953, we took the route north again to Kanggye, where we spent the next six months.

During my afternoon walks, I now noticed more and more U.N. planes above, usually jets. I followed them with satisfaction — and my guards watched them for bacteriological bombs. The North Koreans had started their great defensive campaign against these nonexistent bombs with a national inoculation campaign the previous February. Everybody — soldiers and civilians alike — had received four separate inoculations and revaccination. They were monster shots — worse than any I've received in our own army — and all of North Korea had fever and sore arms. Then, in May of 1952, Captain Oh showed me a copy of an alleged confession of germ warfare by a U.S. pilot. I asked him if there had been any more cholera, typhoid or malaria than usual in North Korea.

He said, "No, but only because of our national inoculation. We were ready for the germ bombs when they came."

Germ bombing was a big hoax, dictated from above, but it was certainly sold to the North Korean people. The civilian population became so inflamed that a downed U.N. airman had virtually no chance of getting away.

On June 16 we moved south once more, traveling in daylight. I was amazed at the gangs of Chinese I saw, usually wearing shorts and jerseys, working on the railroads. Others were tilling the fields. Apparently they just moved in with the Korean country families, who worked side by side with them, in perfect harmony so far as I could see.

Captain Oh told me later that if a Chinese soldier misbehaves with a North Korean woman he is shot immediately. He said,

"They have much stronger discipline in that respect than we have, and the conduct of our men toward women is much better than that of your troops. When we were retreating we lost many of our women soldiers because they were ashamed to take off their clothes to cross rivers; but the Chinese women soldiers think nothing of it, and the men behave."

When we got back to the village near Sunan, Captain Oh told me that only one question remained at issue in the armistice talks, and they surely would be completed in two or three days. "General," he said, "you'll soon be going home. Within thirty days you'll be seeing your loved ones."

Peace came suddenly on July 27 — and was marked by a wild celebration in which hundreds of thousands of rounds of ammunition were wasted at Pyongyang. The very night of the cease-fire, trains began running in and out of Pyongyang, thousands of people suddenly surged out of the hills, leaving their caves and scattered shanties to pour back into the valleys, to their bomb-ruined homes.

As for myself, I was informed of one more move — to Kaesong. The guards I had known for so long were left behind, and I felt as if I were parting from long-time friends. We stopped in Pyongyang, where Captain Oh turned me over to a lieutenant colonel. The last I saw of Oh, he was standing on a corner, waiting for one of the rickety buses which had just started to run again in that demolished capital.

It was September 4 when we finally took the road from Kaesong to Panmunjon. On the outskirts of Kaesong, we ran along a column of trucks standing beside the road. Some of the gaunt Americans crowded into them recognized me and began to yell — those wonderful Yankee voices hollering, "Hey, General Dean! We didn't know we were waiting for you!"

At the head of the column we stopped, and the Korean escort got out. An English-speaking Chinese officer and a Chinese guard with a submachine gun got in. There were a few more minutes to wait — long enough to think briefly of three long years and the men I had known during them: Colonel Kim, whom I want very much to meet again, under different circumstances, when I might have a few questions to ask him, and Choi, the man who disliked admitting his own orders but was terrified by the very thought of the Japanese. I thought of Lee and Tal, the scholarly interpreters; and of a couple of men who risked their lives for me and probably saved mine but must not be mentioned because they still are in North Korea. Most of all, I thought of De Soon Yur, with his short legs and stubby, wonderfully efficient fingers. I wish that he could visit me in the United States so that he could see with his own eyes just what we have. It is possible for men to be enemies and friends at the same time, and we were.

Presently the column of trucks with our jeep at its head moved south toward Panmunjon, past piles of American clothing—which would have been precious anywhere in North Korea—thrown away in the neutral zone by Communist repatriated prisoners as they rode north. We passed several northbound truckloads of these men, nearly naked, shouting and screaming and waving tiny little North Korean flags like so many truckloads of monkeys.

We passed an American military policeman, standing at an intersection with his parked jeep, his boots, helmet and equipment shining and immaculate. Behind me, the Americans in the trucks set up a concerted shouting; but for once no soldier taunted an MP. They were too glad to see him.

We pulled up to the exchange point, and immediately a big American colonel stepped to the side of the jeep and saluted me. He said, "Welcome back, General Dean. Will you step out, sir?"

The Chinese officer spluttered, "No, not till his name is called."

The colonel swung toward the Chinese, and suddenly looked twice his size. I don't doubt that he had been tried beyond endurance by this same Chinese before. He said, "Your authority is finished, right here. We'll take over, right now." As he spoke, he took a step toward the Chinese.

I could see that this might develop into something highly unpleasant—and there were truckloads of men waiting behind me.

I said, "Never mind, Colonel. Let them call off the names. A few more minutes won't matter now."

Nor did they.

MP

In my last hours as a captive, I had tried to add up the results of my three years in North Korea, and to assess what, if anything, I had learned from them.

For one thing, I had had an opportunity to know the North Koreans themselves — the farm hands and soldiers, cooks and prison guards, the people who make Communism possible. I grew to know them as I never could have in a lifetime as an uncaptured general. I learned their character: many-sided, kind and cruel, inventive, clever, stupid, resilient, unpredictable. I saw their fear of responsibility, which will let them walk around a person dying in the street without giving aid, so they won't be personally responsible. I discovered how hard it is to understand their surface reactions: Han, the man who turned me in to the Communists, for instance, smiled at me afterward as if he had done me a big favor. I saw their courage when I learned — quite by accident — that Major Kim, Captain Oh and De Soon Yur had all lost their families in the war during the very time that I knew them, but they had never bothered to mention the loss to me. Major Kim's reaction was typical: he remained friendly to me and shrugged at his misfortune. He said only, "That is war."

Perhaps I'm naturally naïve, but the most important discovery of all to me in Korea was that the ordinary Communists who guarded me and lived with me really *believed* that they were following a route toward a better life for themselves and their children. Sitting on the dirt floors of their cold houses they pored, hour after hour, over the works of Stalin and Engels: the devil's mixture of fact and fancy, half-truth and lie that is beautifully prepared for people with thousands of years of hunger and backbreaking toil in their background, with cold, sickness and death as constant companions.

It's easy for us to say about these North Koreans, "Oh, but they're so badly mistaken." It is not so easy to explain to men of limited experience just why their ideology must fail. We can't convince them with fine words. We must show them something better — like our free election of 1948 in South Korea, which the Communists tried so hard to discredit.

I think the worst moment I had in North Korea was with a

slow-brained guard named Kim Ki Mon. One day, he drew a map of Korea in the dirt. He said: "Chosen (Korean) house, okay?"

I said, "Yes, Chosen house."

He said, "Not American house. But Americans in Chosen house. Why?"

You and I know the complicated answer to that, but we must make men like Kim Ki Mon understand it, too. For all Asia we must have that answer, simply told.

Each of us needs to know exactly what we are fighting, in Korea or anywhere else. An army can be a show window for democracy only if every man in it is convinced that he personally represents the ideals that make a world free.

Every individual in our armies abroad must realize that our whole country is judged by his behavior. Terrific harm can be done by mere thoughtlessness. Through all my conversations with Koreans who had chosen Communism, after seeing something of our government in South Korea, ran one refrain: they resented being called "gooks" and the slighting references to their race and color more than they resented any of our policies, or even the sight of foreigners riding in big cars while they and their families had to walk.

When I was governor, a Korean newspaper called me "the general who walks" because of my habit of walking to the office and nosing around the streets of Seoul. Before I left Korea in 1953, I vowed that if I were governor again I would walk even more — and so would a lot of other Americans in the government. And use of the term "gook" or its equivalents would be an offense for military punishment.

If I were to take one of my guards, a convinced Communist, De Soon Yur, to the United States, I'm not sure I'd bother to show him legislatures at work or even courts in which the accused has a chance for justice. I'd take him to an American supermarket and walk him past a hundred-foot meat counter. I'd like him to see the milking machines in a modern dairy, Kansas wheat elevators, an Iowa wheat field and a big knitting mill. I'm not sure the *processes* of democracy would impress De Soon Yur, who is a practical man.

But if I could show the *products* of democracy to him, I might unmake a Communist fast. What we need for Korea is something to compare favorably to the Communist promises of a hectare of land without excessive rent, and rice without too much millet in it.

In other words, I believe we must present a better world than the Communists. We must have an answer simple enough for the dullest to understand. And we must each of us really *know* the things for which we fight.

If I learned anything in captivity, these were the lessons. They may almost have been worth the three years.

William F. Dean

WILLIAM F. DEAN first came under the spell of the Army when, at the age of five, he was taken to see cadets and soldiers drilling at the St. Louis Exposition of 1904. He sought admission to West Point while he was in high school in Carlyle, Ill., but was unsuccessful. During World War I he tried to enlist, but he was under age. His mother refused consent. Finally, when the Dean family moved West, the future general took student military training at the University of California and won his Regular Army commission after graduation.

After the usual slow peacetime rise through the ranks, Dean found himself fretting in a Washington staff job during World War II. He kept requesting a combat assignment, however, and eventually assumed command of the 44th Infantry Division, which he led through France and Germany. In 1947, he was chosen for the delicate job of Military Governor of South Korea. *General Dean's Story* details his adventures during the Korean War. Today, General Dean is Deputy Commander of the Sixth Army.

* * * * * *

A well-known journalist and war correspondent, William F. Worden is the author of 91 articles and 54 short stories. His World War II experience in the Pacific, from the Aleutians to New Guinea, and his postwar job as *The Saturday Evening Post* correspondent in Japan, gave him helpful background when he began to put General Dean's memoirs on paper. Mr. Worden is a special lecturer at the University of Washington and Associated Press correspondent for the Pacific Coast area.

Illustrations by HARRY BECKHOFF

MR. HOBBS' VACATION

A condensation from the book by

EDWARD STREETER

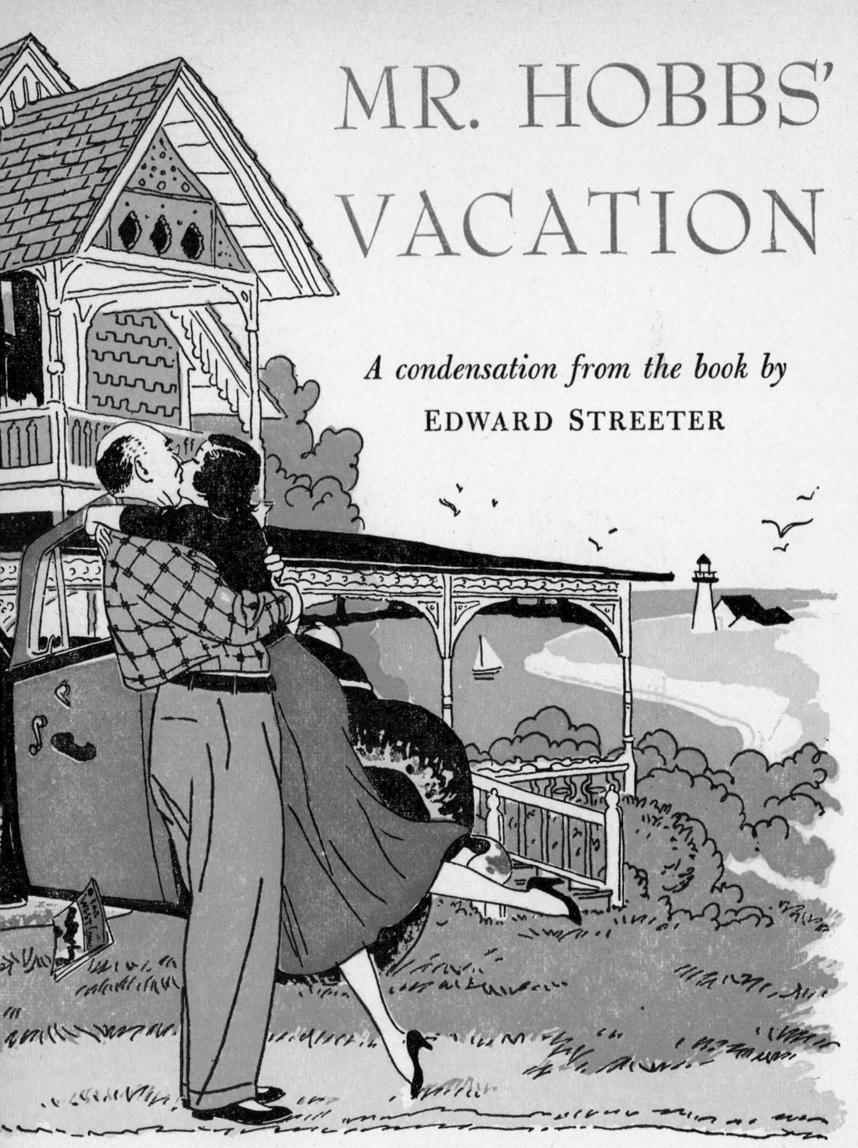

ALL YEAR long Mr. Roger Hobbs looked forward to his vacation. He would relax on the beach, catch up on his neglected reading in the evenings — and, of course, enjoy his visiting children and grandchildren.

It didn't take him long at Gray Gables to realize that while you can have one sort of vacation or the other, you can't have both — not with three families and three generations under the same roof. Grandfathers, he learned, are seen (and billed) but not heard.

Once again, as in *Father of the Bride,* Edward Streeter charts the amusing frustrations of an American male who is wax in the hands of his womenfolk.

THE island village of Rock Harbor basked sleepily in the May sunshine. Only a few people moved about, only a few automobiles stood beside the high curbs of the main street. In the harbor, only a few fishermen's skiffs swung lazily at their moorings and the pleasure boats were missing. But hundreds of miles away a series of conferences was being held, the results of which were to have a direct impact on many a Rock Harbor citizen.

Mr. and Mrs. Roger Hobbs of Cleveland were wrestling grimly with the problem of selecting a place in which to spend Mr. Hobbs' vacation — a place which would be satisfactory to all the members of his large family and reasonably acceptable to him.

Mrs. Hobbs declared that she was willing to go anywhere at all as long as her beloved children were around her. She was grandchild-happy. Much as she loved her children, she would have sacrificed them with a whoop to get her hands on her three grandchildren for one precious month. For weeks she had been phoning and writing her married daughters to pin them down.

She had visualized a rambling summer cottage on the New England coast, where the swimming was good, where there would be young people for her daughter Kate, a sophomore at Smith, and where the grandchildren could roll around under her delighted eyes.

She heard about a house that was just made-to-order for them from her friend Retta Nickerson.

"It's not expensive," she reported to Mr. Hobbs, "because, from what Retta said, I guess it's not one of the *newest* houses. It's about eight miles outside Rock Harbor so that you could mix into things or not, just as you felt like. It would be fun for Kate and heavenly for the grandchildren — and just what *you* want. . . ."

"In what way?" asked Mr. Hobbs. But he knew the matter had been decided.

"It's called Gray Gables," said Mrs. Hobbs.

"DIDN'T that sign say Rock Harbor?" asked Mrs. Hobbs. She swung the car down the road to the left. "I do hope the place is as nice as Retta said it was going to be."

"For what we're paying for it," said Mr. Hobbs, "it ought to be a castle. Fool idea anyway, renting a house we've never seen in a place we've never been to."

There was a short silence. "This must be it," said Mrs. Hobbs. "The real estate man said the fourth house on the left."

"I'm afraid you're right," said Mr. Hobbs.

A plump, freckled face, which still reflected the merry innocence of youth but gave indication of a more earthy beauty in the offing, emerged from the bundles and boxes in the rear of the car. "Good Lord, Pop," Kate said. "Don't tell me we're going to live in this wilderness. I thought we came here to have some *fun.*"

It was a rambling, two-story, gray-shingled house, surrounded on three sides by a deep porch above which rose an amazing series of bays and gables joined by scrollwork. To Mr. Hobbs, it was reminiscent of an abandoned hotel — long-abandoned, for sinister reasons. Below, he made out the blurred outlines of a sandy cove protected by jagged rocks. The door creaked as Mrs. Hobbs and Kate disappeared into the house. Mr. Hobbs followed, feeling as if he were entering a vast tomb.

He was in a large room, the walls and ceiling lined with boarding stained a dark brown. In the center was a table littered with last year's magazines, its legs connected with basketwork. Scattered about were several armchairs, all from the same basket factory. They had a sprung look as if they had been frozen in the act of collapsing. In a corner, a pile of green wooden chairs had been nested. A chintz-covered sofa, at one end of which some heavy body had created a kind of bucket seat, completed the furnishings.

Mr. Hobbs pushed open a swinging door in the back of the

living room. "There is no water," he said from the kitchen.

"The real estate man said he'd left directions on the mantelpiece for starting the pump," Mrs. Hobbs reminded him.

He found the paper and sat down to read it.

> The pump is very simple and should start easy. Open the petcock on top of the cylinder. Pour in two teaspoonfulls of gasolene (white — don't use no red). Remove rear plug in head of pump and prime with pint of water. Shut off valve to pressure tanks. Open overflow valve. Adjust set screw clockwise 1½ turns. Press down hard on foot starter. If engine don't start first time keep on jamming down on foot starter then adjust set screw counterclockwise as engine warms. Open butterfly valve. Close overflow valve. Open valve to pressure tank. When pressure gauge reaches 50 lbs. turn off by pressing screw driver against spark plug and engine head else you'll blow out the tank.

"I don't like to hurry you, dear," said Mrs. Hobbs, "but couldn't you read that tomorrow? I'd like to get that pump going as quickly as possible so we can get some hot water."

Mr. Hobbs turned the paper over and over like a man in a daze. "Water," he said. "Hot water. I don't know what the devil this guy's talking about. I don't even know where the pump *is.* I couldn't see to do anything if I found it. I wouldn't know what to do if I could see. Tomorrow I'll get some bright young fellow from M.I.T. to come down and make a study of this thing."

THAT NIGHT Mr. Hobbs lay very still in his narrow iron bed that sagged like a hammock. He thought of his comfortable bed at home, of his tiled bathroom where the water leaped forth from the faucets at any desired temperature. Things were not working out quite as he had planned.

But he looked forward to the arrival, in a week or so, of his two married daughters and their families. Then everything would fall into the groove. As he thought of the happy hours he would spend with his grandchildren, a warm glow of anticipation permeated his being. There would be walks on lonely beaches, collecting shells, telling stories to eager, upturned faces. There would be long evenings of talk when he would have an opportunity to know his sons-in-law better.

It was one of the disappointments of his life that the girls had not settled down comfortably in their home town. Susan, his intelligent, easygoing oldest daughter, had unaccountably fallen in love with Stewart Carver, an engineer whose ideal of a home was a place within walking distance of whatever huge and mussy building project he happened to be working on. They moved from one dreary dam site to another with their two children, a springer spaniel and five barrels of unopened wedding presents.

Jane, who had the kind of beauty that made strong men grip the edges of tables when they beheld her, had lost her heart to Byron Dangerfield Grant, a tall, gangly young man who taught economics at a university in Indiana. She considered his mildly socialistic ideas on economics divinely inspired. When Mr. Hobbs, who was a hardheaded businessman, suggested the Kremlin as a more likely source, she was prepared to fight him to the death. The arrival of Byron, Jr., had filled her cup of happiness.

Mr. Hobbs looked forward to reliving his early married days through a second generation. There was an image in his mind of himself and Susan's four-year-old, Peter, rambling over the countryside, hand in hand; exploring, observing, learning, one from the other. Not that he did not love his other two grandchildren tenderly. But Peewee Carver was only a little over a year old and Byron Grant, Jr., was now completing his sixth month in the world. Like most males, Mr. Hobbs' affection for beings that could neither walk nor talk very well was more of a tribute to their parents than to their personalities.

IT MIGHT be said that Mr. Hobbs and family were now, after a week on the island, officially accepted as members of the Rock Harbor Summer Colony. Mrs. Hobbs had gone to school with Mrs. Archer Gabrielson, the pivot around which the community revolved, and she gave a cocktail party to introduce the Hobbses to their fellow Colonists. Mr. Hobbs told Mrs. Hobbs that under no circumstances would he let himself in for any such rat race.

He didn't propose to get tangled up in this kind of twa-ti-twa.

Having asserted his individuality, he tried on three possible costumes, chose one which later proved to be 100-percent wrong, found on arrival that he didn't know anybody just as he had foretold, tried to make up for this deficiency by drinking several Martinis in quick succession, and eventually agreed to rent a sailboat from a man whose name was either McHugh or McAdoo and to join the Rock Harbor Yacht Club. When he arrived home, he realized that he hadn't asked the cost of either.

As Mrs. Hobbs said, however, if one came to a place like Rock Harbor one really should be a part of it.

THE Yacht Club pier served as a hitching rail for a long row of dinghies. Out in the harbor, bobbing violently at their moorings, were the sailboats, including Mr. Hobbs' Spatterbox, *Dashaway*.

With Mrs. Hobbs and Kate he surveyed his property gloomily. Unfortunately, at that miserable party Mr. McHugh (or McAdoo) had asked him if he was a sailorman. He had indicated, with becoming modesty, that he knew a bit about such matters, which had eventually led him to give McHugh-McAdoo and a group of others a blow-by-blow account of the time he had been in the Bermuda race.

It had been a fatal mistake. When they were leaving, Mr. Hobbs had suggested that McHugh-McAdoo take him for a trial run the next morning in *Dashaway,* to show him the ropes.

"Nonsense," McHugh-McAdoo had roared. "You're an old Bermuda man. You don't need me. You've been used to big stuff. You're going to get quite a kick out of *Dashaway."*

Mr. Hobbs had said he was sure he would and, at the moment, had believed it. Now, as he watched *Dashaway's* mast swinging crazily among a grove of other thrashing spars, he began to have doubts of his sanity.

Kate was tugging at his coat. "Come on, Pops. Let's go."

"Yes, Rog. Let's go for a ride in it."

"First of all, you don't 'go for a ride' in a boat," said Mr. Hobbs. "You 'go for a sail.' And secondly, you don't take a little racing shell like that out in a gale like this."

They looked disappointed. At that moment two little girls with pigtails, accompanied by a fat boy, came noisily down the pier. While the Hobbses watched, they threw a sailbag into one of the dinghies, dropped casually into it, cast off and rowed out to one of the boats. In a few minutes their little craft, heeling far over, slipped through the fleet into the open harbor.

"Well," said Mr. Hobbs. "We'd better be going back."

"Listen, Pops. If those little girls can go out, *we* can."

They went back to the clubhouse and got their bag of sails and a pair of oars. Mr. Hobbs felt physically sick as they lowered themselves into the dinghy.

The trip out to *Dashaway* was a nightmare. The dinghy had apparently been built for small children. Three full-size people weighed it down almost to the water line. What had looked like sparkling wavelets from the pier suddenly became a menacing sea which slapped viciously against the sides of the tiny craft and hurled water over Mrs. Hobbs' ankles.

"Rog, couldn't you row so that all the waves don't come inside? I don't want to ruin these shoes."

Mr. Hobbs glanced over his shoulder. The *Dashaway* was only a few feet from them, tugging at its mooring line like a trapped animal and rocking violently back and forth.

Mr. Hobbs looked despairingly at Mrs. Hobbs sitting calmly in the rear of the dinghy with her hands over her shoes. Wouldn't someone put a stop to this suicidal expedition?

"This is fun," said Mrs. Hobbs. She removed her shoes and tossed them gaily into *Dashaway's* cockpit.

Mr. Hobbs could never remember how they managed to transfer from the tossing dinghy to the tossing sailboat. It was one of those feats of the sea that he associated with the movies and adventure novels rather than with industrialists from Cleveland.

He straddled the centerboard box and shook the sails out of the bag. "Now," he said, in what he hoped was a casual tone, "if someone will hand me the main halyard . . ."

"The what?" Mrs. Hobbs said.

"The rope you tie onto the top of the sail to hoist it up."

"Why didn't you say so, dear? Where on earth do they keep it?"

DA

A ganglion of ropes was slapping angrily against the mast. Shielding his eyes, Mr. Hobbs looked up at the masthead which was behaving like an inverted pendulum. He was immediately forced to clutch the edge of the deck until the dizziness left him.

By tugging gently on each rope, he eventually discovered one with a free end. He unhooked it and inched his way cautiously back to the cockpit. The halyard somehow slipped away from him and flew out into space, only to come flailing back past his head with the next roll of the boat.

"Gracious," said Mrs. Hobbs, "shouldn't that rope be tied up?"

"Catch hold of it," said Mr. Hobbs, "and hold it till I'm ready for it." He devoted his attention to the pile of canvas at his feet. He handed the jib to Kate. "You put that on," he said.

"How?"

"Darling, you've got to work it out. Don't be helpless."

He passed the edges of the mainsail through his fingers until he came to a corner. That might be the top. He continued along the edge. Another corner. *That* could be the top. Good Lord, another corner. Why didn't they mark the thing "Back," "Front" and "Top." Maybe it didn't make any difference which you used.

A dinghy passed containing two little girls who waved at *Dashaway*. "Nice breeze," they called. Mr. Hobbs watched them with astonishment as they leaped casually aboard the next boat and went about the business of putting on the sail.

Ah, that was it! The top was the corner with the black number sewn just below it. Of course. And the part that went along the mast had those little zipper things. He worked in frantic haste, lest his models sail away and leave him helpless once more. Somehow or other the sails were on and up, slatting savagely as if resenting such amateur handling.

One of the little girls in the next boat cast off the mooring line. Their boat's sails filled and it went dancing across *Dashaway's* bow. "Race?" called the little girl at the tiller.

"You bet," shouted Mr. Hobbs. "Meet you out there." He tried to make his voice sound hearty and jovial, but it came out high-pitched and strained. Calm, Hobbs. In emergencies the leader must be calm.

"Now," he said, "tie the dinghy to the mooring can." He felt immensely pleased with himself as Kate carried out this order.

"You're wonderful," said Mrs. Hobbs admiringly.

"Cast off," he said nonchalantly. It was the nonchalance of an actor saying "So long" to his pals in the big battle scene as he steps from his cozy dugout into a rain of shellfire.

Kate's voice came back to him on the wind. "I can't untie this slimy rope from the tin can."

"Don't untie it for gosh sake," he shouted. "Throw the tin can over with the rope."

He heard the splash of the can buoy. Instead of veering off gracefully to the left as the other boat had done, *Dashaway's* sails continued to slat as it drifted downwind, threatening to swamp the dinghy. "We're skidding," said Mrs. Hobbs.

It was true. *Dashaway* was going sideways through the water almost as fast as it went forward.

"Pops, you're going to hit that boat off to the left if you don't stop drifting."

Drifting! It came to him suddenly. "The centerboard," he screamed. "Will *somebody* drop the centerboard! I can't do everything."

"Don't yell at me, please," said Mrs. Hobbs. "Just tell me quietly what to do."

"The center — " began Mr. Hobbs. "Listen, Peggy. Undo that rope just under your right hand. Then let the board down slow — "

Mrs. Hobbs screamed as the rope tore through her hands and then let it go. The knot at the end hit the slot in the centerboard with a thud that shook the boat.

"Is that what you wanted?" asked Mrs. Hobbs. "It felt to me as if the bottom fell out. The thing almost took my hand off."

Mr. Hobbs' clenched teeth caused the muscles in his jaw to protrude. *Dashaway* had stopped going sideways, but it was now tearing through the water like a torpedo, pointed at four of its bobbing sister boats. In one of them two young men stopped putting on their sails to watch.

"Why don't you go around those boats?" asked Mrs. Hobbs. "Gracious' sake, Rog, we almost hit them."

Beneath the sail Mr. Hobbs caught a glimpse of the pale, gaping faces of the two youths as *Dashaway* flashed past their stern. Then the little boat was miraculously through the fleet with nothing ahead but the dancing waters of the bay.

Kate came back to get out of the spray. "Gosh, Pops, I didn't know you could sail like that. I wouldn't have had the nerve to go through that mess of boats."

"Your father sailed in a Bermuda race, dear," said Mrs. Hobbs. "I have perfect confidence in him."

Mr. Hobbs did not hear. His mind was elsewhere. They were headed straight for the open sea. Nothing to worry about. He threw back his head and enjoyed the movement of the wind in his hair, the same wind that had played in the hair of Magellan and Sir Francis Drake. Kate lay stretched out on the forward deck. Mrs. Hobbs sat on the floor of the cockpit, her face glowing with excitement and pleasure.

A half hour passed. Suddenly Mr. Hobbs' grip on the tiller tightened. The unpleasant thought had just occurred that sooner or later he must go back, his goal no longer the open ocean but a tiny white buoy bobbing in the center of a score of boats.

At the thought of dashing into that melee and picking up his mooring in this gale, panic seized him. Rather than endure that humiliation under the critical eyes of a lot of little fat girls in pigtails, he would turn when the time came, head straight for shore and make a crash landing on the rocks. Or would it be better to keep on going, straight out to sea, and eventually get picked up by a passing freighter?

Steady. Think it through, boy. What would Magellan and Drake have done?

At least it would be prudent to practice coming about while he had plenty of room for error.

"Hard alee," he said.

"What did you say?" asked Mrs. Hobbs.

"We're coming about."

"What do I do?"

"Nothing."

She settled back contentedly in her corner. The boat swung

to port and she slid away from the centerboard box and fetched up against the side of the cockpit. "Rog, for goodness' sake, look what you've done. I don't get any sun or anything. Can't you tip it back the way it was?"

Mr. Hobbs sailed on, unheeding. His mind had become a great chart on which he was plotting the steps necessary to bring his loved ones safely back to that can buoy. If ever he made it, he swore silently that he would never detach *Dashaway* from it again.

He headed for Rock Harbor, the wind on his starboard beam. A few hundred yards away the mast tops of the Spatterbox fleet were just to leeward. He hadn't realized how fast they were tearing through the water until the little white hulls gave him something against which to measure his speed.

He rehearsed the plan which he had worked out so carefully. He was to run past the fleet as he was now until he came abreast of the mooring can. Then he was to let the sail out as far as it would go and at the same time make a right angle turn and let *Dashaway* come up to the mooring on its momentum. Next he must drop the mainsail while Kate hooked the can with the boat hook. Now they were among the boats. Their boom scraped the shrouds of one. They missed another by inches. Then they were abreast of the mooring.

"Ready with the boat hook, Kate."

"I don't see how you do it," said Mrs. Hobbs.

His chest swelled with pride at the compliment as he shot *Dashaway* into the wind with a flourish. Kate lay in the bow, straining toward the can with the boat hook.

Dashaway went slower and slower and came to a stop a few feet away from the mooring. Then like a playful terrier it turned to the right and went flying across the rope connecting the dinghy to the can. He felt the rope go under the boat and apparently catch on the centerboard. They came to a straining halt with the dinghy glued to their right side and the mooring can to their left.

"What a funny thing," said Mrs. Hobbs.

"Let down the mainsail," roared Mr. Hobbs. No one paid the slightest attention. He leaped for the halyard and loosed it from the cleat, but the force of the breeze held the sail rigidly in place.

Then he had an inspiration. If he pulled up the centerboard, the rope would slide along the bottom of the boat and they would be free. Shoving Mrs. Hobbs' cringing body to one side, he pulled it up. *Dashaway* lurched forward a few feet, then stuck again.

Kate had come aft and was peering over the stern. "The rope's caught between the stern and the rudder," she said. "I can see it."

"Never again," cried Mr. Hobbs dramatically. "Never again will I come out with a gang that knows nothing whatsoever about sailing. This ends it, I tell you. I'm getting rid of the boat — "

Kate had taken off her shoes and stockings. Pushing her father gently aside, she lowered herself over the stern. Straddling the rudder she began to work the rope down with her feet. In a few moments they were free.

Dashaway immediately came up into the wind like a colt which gets tired of eluding its pursuers. Mr. Hobbs had forgotten to make the halyard fast, as a result of which the sail fell over their heads in voluminous folds. They were drifting downwind on one of the boats. It was occupied by the two little girls who had wanted to race. They stopped putting the cover on their sails and watched the approach of *Dashaway* with open mouths.

Mr. Hobbs had tasted the dregs of the cup.

"WILL you help me get these things out of the car?" called Mrs. Hobbs.

Mr. Hobbs sat up on the couch swing and peered sleepily over the veranda rail. The rear of the sedan was piled to the roof with cartons and packages.

"Good Lord," said Mr. Hobbs.

"Don't get excited, Roger. The children will be here in a few days, and I had to get an indoor drier and a Bathinette and a stroller and a playpen. . . ."

"Just why do we have to buy a playpen? We pay an outlandish price for this house just because there are acres of land around it for the children. Then the first thing we do is drop them in a playpen. Those things cost money. Do you think I'm a maharaja or something?"

"Don't be sarcastic," said Mrs. Hobbs. "I had to lay in a lot of baby food, too." Mrs. Hobbs was burrowing among the packages in the rear of the car. "Isn't that stupid, Rog? I left the life belts and the curtains at Terrey's store."

"The life belts and the what?"

"Just some inexpensive curtains for the children's rooms. They have Mother Goose pictures on them. You'll have to drive back and get them for me."

At Elwell Terrey's General Store, Miss Haskell, the ageless clerk, met him just inside the door. "Good morning," she said. "Mrs. Hobbs left two packages. Wait a minute and I'll get them."

He strolled into the toy department and was examining a circular rubber swimming pool when she returned.

"Those swimming pools are nice for those that have the money," she told him. "They've put a terrible price on them."

"How much are they?"

"I really hate to mention it. Twenty-four sixty. I see you looking at those big rubber horses. Those are nice, too, if you've got the price — handy for the children if they get out beyond their depth and can't swim. We've got a fine line of velocipedes, too. Don't know where you're going to ride them around here but the kids go for them."

An hour later Miss Haskell and Mr. Terrey accompanied Mr. Hobbs to his car. Each carried a double armful of merchandise.

"You're sure going to be a popular grandpa," said Mr. Terrey.

The sound of an alarm clock jarred Mr. Hobbs out of a deep sleep. He knew immediately that this was an unusual day but, for the moment, he could not recall what was to make it so. It was only 6:30. He could hear Mrs. Hobbs splashing in the bathroom.

Of course! This was the day the Carvers arrived on the island. But they weren't due until the 12:30 boat.

"What's the idea of getting up in the middle of the night?" he called.

"Because there are about ten thousand things to be done before they get here, that's why."

He swung his feet to the floor. Outside, the ocean was brilliant in the sunshine. It was a good day to be alive and, once dressed and fully awake, he went about his chores lightheartedly.

"Please don't dawdle over your coffee," said Mrs. Hobbs. "The living room has to be cleaned up. It's all cluttered with your papers and letters and things."

"Why should a man destroy his private papers just because his grandchildren are coming?" grumbled Mr. Hobbs.

He stuffed the offending papers into a drawer. Then he wandered onto the porch. On a table lay the canvas case containing his surf-casting rod, and a tackle box. He picked them up and with an uneasy glance toward the house started down the steps.

"Roger Hobbs, where are you going?"

He stopped, feeling like a guilty schoolboy. "There didn't seem to be anything else to do around here so I thought I'd just go out to the beach for a few minutes," he said apologetically.

"Once you set foot on that beach you're perfectly irresponsible. You'll never be back in time to meet the boat."

"Good Lord, Peggy, the boat doesn't get in for hours. I promise I'll be back at half past eleven."

Mr. Hobbs loved the lonely five-mile stretch of sand where he and a few neighbors fished. Although it was by far the best beach on the island, for some reason the land behind it had never been developed. The great dunes gave way to bayberry thickets and these in turn merged into scrub pine, uncut by path or track. On each sandy point, colonies of sea gulls drowsed in the August sun. Among the seaweed the sandpipers scurried excitedly, running forward with twinkling legs, stopping to peck, then rushing frantically to the next morsel. In the dry seaweed the sand fleas jumped restlessly like bubbles rising from the surface of champagne. Mr. Hobbs didn't catch anything that morning, but, given a lonely beach and a high blue sky, it really didn't matter.

He walked back to the car and reached into his tackle box for his wrist watch. The children were pulling in on the twelve-thirty boat. He looked at his watch. It was a quarter to one.

Mr. Hobbs was in the doghouse.

He didn't need to be told officially. The emptiness and immaculate neatness of Gray Gables pronounced its silent verdict. The old house seemed to say reproachfully, "At least there was *someone* here who didn't forget."

He noticed a piece of paper pinned to the mantel and took it down apprehensively. It had been scrawled by Mrs. Hobbs in what must have been a moment of emotional tension.

> I was never so mad in my life. First you go off fishing and then you forget to come home, leaving me without a car. Mary Ogden is taking me to the boat. For pity's sake, if it ever occurs to you to come home, see that there's plenty of hot water and *don't use the clean towels.*

Mr. Hobbs sighed remorsefully.

He went out to the kitchen to find something to eat. The icebox was crammed with mysterious objects, wrapped neatly in wax paper. He shut the door without further exploration and made a sandwich of peanut butter moistened with catsup. He despised both, but they were the only ingredients which he felt safe in using at the moment.

He went upstairs to wash and check the hot-water heater; then he walked down to the pump house. Might as well fill the tanks and be on the safe side. The pump house was his undisputed domain. Just to look out over the water, across the tops of the bayberry bushes, made him feel better immediately.

He sat down on a broken box and let his mind wander over the weeks which lay ahead. It was curious how the relationship of everything seemed to shift the moment grandchildren came on the scene. Susan and Jane, for instance, suddenly ceased to be his "children" and became his "married daughters." With motherhood they had acquired new insights, a new wisdom which made them almost strangers. Mr. Hobbs found himself slightly afraid of them.

He had noted a change in Peggy, also. She was probably living the days of her early married life over again through her grandchildren. The difference was that this was a vicarious experience which she could go through alone and unaided.

Mr. Hobbs rose impatiently. In a few minutes he'd be feeling sorry for himself. The forgotten grandfather! Nuts! He walked rapidly up the hill. As he reached the top, the Ogdens' car turned into the drive, followed by a mud-encrusted station wagon.

The latter vehicle was piled to the roof with suitcases and cartons between which odd bits of clothing and gear had been stuffed like mortar until a semisolid mass had been created. Young Peter Carver hung from one of the middle windows; Peewee sat on a hanging seat between her parents. As the car came to a halt she began to scream.

The front door of the station wagon flew open. Susan and a large springer spaniel came bounding out together. Susan threw herself into her father's arms. "Pops!"

He kissed her. "Darling, you're wonderful. Gosh, I'm glad to see you."

"You've certainly been a big help," said Mrs. Hobbs. His happiness faded like a mirage. He shook hands with his big son-in-law.

"Gracious," said Mrs. Hobbs, "I didn't know you were bringing the dog." The springer, who had been running in circles and barking furiously, suddenly threw himself on Mrs. Hobbs with joyful yelps.

"Of *course,* Mother. That's Rumpus. We never go *anywhere* without Rumpus. Peter, don't you see Bompa? Get out and give him a big bear hug."

"I don't want to," said Peter, moving to the other side of the station wagon. "I don't like this place. I want to go home."

"But Peter, darling, this is Bompa that you've talked about so much. Don't you like Bompa?"

"No." Peter stuck his fists in his eyes and began to howl.

"He's tired," said Susan.

"Of course he is—poor little thing. For heaven's sake, Roger, help Stewart unload the car."

"They'll be all right when they get some food in them and have a nap," Susan said. "I'll take Peewee and Peter and leave you and Stew to handle the junk, Pops."

She pulled Peewee out of the hanging seat and entered the house, followed by Mrs. Hobbs dragging Peter. Mrs. Ogden waved to no one in particular and drove away. Mr. Hobbs joined his son-in-law at the back of the station wagon, feeling awkward.

"Well, Stew," he said heartily. "Good to see you."

"Good to see *you,* sir." That was it. This constant use of the word "sir." How could you ever be at ease with someone who was always calling you "sir"?

"Have a hard trip?"

"Oh no, sir. Only four nights on the road. Peter always throws up a good deal the first day out, then he settles into the groove. He's a good little traveler."

"I see," said Mr. Hobbs. He was dismayed to find that they had reached the end of their conversational rope in forty seconds flat with ten days to go. A mountain of baggage was beginning to accumulate on the driveway.

"Stew." It was Susan at the front door. "Will you bring in the carton with the children's things?"

Stewart Carver selected a bulging carton. "Excuse me, sir. I'll be right back."

Methodically and grimly, Mr. Hobbs unloaded the dusty contents of the station wagon, down to the last broken plastic toy. The result lay about him on the driveway and lawn. Stewart did not return. Mr. Hobbs picked up two suitcases and carried them up to the second floor. Then he went back for another load.

Slowly, like the builders of the Pyramids, he toiled upward with his burdens. No one told him what went where, so he piled everything in a huge mound at the head of the stairs.

With each trip he felt his strength ebbing, his heart pounding faster. Each time the thought occurred to him that this might be his last load. He wondered how it would feel. "Suddenly Mr. Hobbs' face turned ashen-white. He spun around and pitched headlong down the steep stairs to lie unnoticed at the bottom."

The vision upset him so that he did not attempt to bring up the smaller packages and loose things but merely piled them in the immaculate living room wherever he could find a place.

SEVERAL hours later Mr. Hobbs stood before the living-room table agitating a shakerful of Martinis. He stood because there was no place to sit down. Every table and chair was covered with half-opened packages and the floor was littered with cartons, paper, toys, clothes, sneakers, battered picture books and other oddments of family life. Susan sat curled up on the sofa, her bare feet protruding from the edges of a striped beach skirt. Mr. Hobbs decided she must have Moslem blood in her. She had never been able to keep a pair of shoes on her feet once she crossed a threshold and apparently she did not own a pair of stockings.

She was watching Peter with loving eyes. He was engaged in removing objects from the tables and hurling them to the floor.

"Look," said Mr. Hobbs, as a heavy glass ash tray went down with a crash. "This stuff isn't mine. I have to pay for the pieces. Lay off it, Peter. *Hey!"* He caught a tottering lamp.

Peter reached for a cigarette box. Mr. Hobbs approached him menacingly. "Now, look here, young fellow. I told you to lay off that. And when I tell you something I mean it. I don't want you to touch *anything-on-those-tables*. Do you understand?"

For a moment Peter stared at Mr. Hobbs in astonishment. Then his face became contorted and he ran sobbing to his mother.

"For goodness' sake, Roger," said Mrs. Hobbs.

Susan looked troubled. "I hate to say this, Pops, 'cause of course it's your house, but Stew and I don't believe in that sort of thing. We never say 'no' to the children. Psychologists agree it's the only way to bring up kids without neuroses. If they're doing something you don't want them to do, substitute something else. These ash trays and things we'll just pile up on the mantel."

She began to remove objects from the table. The fire irons came down with a crash around Peewee.

Susan pulled her out from under them. "That's all right. She's not hurt. Just scared. Here, dear, you can play with them now."

Mr. Hobbs refilled his glass and drank it off quickly.

"EVERYBODY go on to bed," said Mr. Hobbs. "I'll put this stuff in the kitchen, then I'll take Rumpus out. I need a breath of air."

He carried half a dozen empty ginger-ale bottles and several glasses into the kitchen. By the time he had washed the glasses and put them away everyone had disappeared.

Everyone, that is, except Rumpus, who lay on the sofa, his nose between his paws, his eyes following Mr. Hobbs suspiciously.

"Come on, boy," said Mr. Hobbs in his best coaxing voice. Rumpus did not remove his nose from his paws and continued to stare coldly. "Up we come, boy," said Mr. Hobbs in his heartiest Boy Scout manner. He approached with outstretched hand. Rumpus gave out a low, businesslike growl.

Mr. Hobbs pulled the fire tongs from under a chair where Peewee had cached them. "Get off that sofa, you miserable cur," he said in a choked voice. Rumpus glanced at the upraised fire tongs, slid off the sofa and under it. Mr. Hobbs turned off the lights.

Susan's voice called down to him through her closed door. "Pops, you didn't forget to take Rumpus out?"

"No," said Mr. Hobbs. "Good night, Bunny."

It was a long time since he had called her that.

"Good night, Pops."

LIFE at Gray Gables had entered a new phase. The Grants had arrived two days after the Carvers — beautiful Jane, her far-from-beautiful husband, their six-months-old son, Byron, Jr., who seemed doomed to look like his father, and Merrylegs, a melancholy cocker. With the arrival of the second wave, the kitchen had become the hub around which the life of the Hobbs family revolved. It had not been built to accommodate large groups. Kitchen engineers would have described it as having a low congestion point. It was a scene of turmoil from early morning until late at night — swarming with people who shoved and pushed and obtained what they wanted by reaching over the bent bodies of others.

Feeding ten people was bad enough but, in this instance, each age group ate on a different time schedule. While one meal was being eaten, preparations for another were under way. The endlessness of it all was most depressing to Mr. Hobbs. To make things more complicated Jane kept taking over the entire stove periodically for the sterilizing of bottles.

For weeks Mrs. Hobbs had been reminding Mr. Hobbs that,

with such a big household, organization was everything. She had told him that she proposed to get up each morning a little before the others and put the coffee on. Why, Mr. Hobbs wanted to know, couldn't one of the children get up and make the coffee? Because, Mrs. Hobbs had said, they needed the rest. Why they needed it, Mr. Hobbs had never been able to discover.

In any event, if he would please let her run these matters it would be much simpler. She and one of the girls would cook breakfast. Everyone else would sit quietly at the table and there would be no confusion.

It was a good idea. The only hitch was that it did not work. Susan and Jane were engrossed with the feeding of their young. Stewart and Byron were too full of early morning cheerio (and much too hungry) to wait for anyone to cook for them. The little kitchen quickly became a milling bedlam. People popped bread into the oven and went away, other people pulled out the cinders, popped in fresh bread and went away, dogs sniffed in garbage pails and were ejected yelping through the back door, children were trampled underfoot—and, like bubbles through the basic uproar, rose a stream of unnoted remarks. "Mother, isn't there any more Brillo?" "Will *somebody* watch my egg?" "Good heavens, the toast." "Hasn't *anyone* seen Peter's bib?"

Mr. Hobbs found it most unrestful.

He was the only one who obeyed instructions and sat quietly at the table. Eventually, one of the girls placed his coffee and eggs before him. That was a satisfying thing about daughters. They had an instinctive maternal feeling for fathers.

Peter and Peewee were placed at the opposite end of the table from Mr. Hobbs although why Susan troubled to put them there he could not understand. Neither of them ate anything. He had been brought up on the myth that children were always hungry, but apparently the modern generation took no nourishment until it was well along in years.

Susan kept Peewee supplied with table silver, ash trays, broken toys, kitchen utensils, assorted stones and sea shells. Peewee tested each object by crashing it against the tray of her high chair after which, if it failed to break, she threw it to the floor in disgust.

Occasionally Susan introduced a bit of toast or bacon into the picture. These Peewee consigned to the floor immediately.

"I should think she'd get more of a kick out of the glass and china. They break easier," suggested Mr. Hobbs. At that moment Peewee managed to get her hands on the egg timer. She raised it high above her head, enjoying to the full the blissful instant before total demolition.

"Stop that," yelled Mr. Hobbs, springing from his chair. "That's the egg timer." Peewee eyed him with amazement as he snatched it away. Then her face contorted and she began to howl.

"Dad, what in the world are you doing to her? Oh, you poor little dear! Did naughty Bompa scare you to death?"

Mrs. Hobbs called in from the sink. "For pity's sake, Roger. What *are* you trying to do to the child?"

"She was trying to smash the egg timer," mumbled Mr. Hobbs, but Susan picked Peewee up and was walking with her up and down the living room. He had already been forgotten.

Peter was also on a hunger strike. With hands clenching the seat of his chair, he scowled at Mr. Hobbs over an untouched plate of bacon and eggs, a full glass of milk and a glass of orange juice, which he had partially disposed of through spillage. Mr. Hobbs controlled himself as long as possible. Eventually he came to the breaking point. "Listen, Susan. Are you going to sit there and watch that child starve himself to death? I haven't seen him eat for two days."

Peter's eyes brightened with anticipation. The lines of his mouth curved downward more sharply. Mrs. Hobbs, her ears always alerted for trouble, called from the kitchen. "Now Roger, don't *you* get into that. Let Susan bring up her children *her* way."

"All I want to do," said Mr. Hobbs, "is keep them from starving to death on the premises." Susan, unperturbed, removed the uneaten eggs, the untasted milk and orange juice and carried them into the kitchen. An expression of pain came into Mr. Hobbs' face as he heard the eggs being scraped into the garbage pail.

Peter slid from his chair and stood beside his grandfather. "Take off my bib," he demanded.

The sound of the wasted eggs was still in Mr. Hobbs' ears. "Look here, young fellow, you say 'please' to me when you want me to do something. And let me tell you something else. Eggs and bacon and milk cost money. Don't you know there are millions of boys in this world that would give their shirts for that breakfast? You'd eat it if you were *my* child, by gosh. You'd eat it or you'd go to your room and stay there."

"Pops, will you *please!*" It was too late. Peter, having finally succeeded in creating the crisis for which he had been yearning, burst into anguished cries.

"As a matter of fact, sir, I think you're absolutely right," said Byron Grant, extinguishing a cigarette in his coffee cup.

"Well, that's *your* opinion," said Stewart Carver, relighting his pipe carefully. "Susan and I just happen to have different ideas."

Jane Grant's modulated voice from the kitchen: "I think I hear Byron, dear. Will you run up and see? I'm doing the formula."

Susan's voice from the porch: "For heaven's sake, Jane, stick to it and get finished before I have to cook Peter's lunch."

"Wasted effort," shouted Mr. Hobbs. "Why cook it? It's easier to throw it away raw."

Before this avalanche of people had descended on him, Mr. Hobbs had made careful plans for handling his end of the household duties. Mrs. Hobbs had said that one thing she couldn't stand was a lot of men bumbling around the kitchen, a sentiment which aroused no opposition from him. And so the chores and the house cleaning had become his responsibility.

He spent an evening drawing up a schedule which he had tacked conspicuously by the kitchen door. Stew Carver was to take care of the pump. That would show how good an engineer he was, thought Mr. Hobbs grimly. Stew was also assigned to the garbage and the bottle and can details. Byron Grant was the emptier of scrap baskets, tender of the incinerator and general grounds keeper. Kate was appointed cleaner of the upstairs quarters.

For himself he retained charge of the living room. The early morning picture was discouraging. Every inch of space was covered by broken toys, incomplete decks of cards, dog-eared magazines, half-finished letters, capless fountain pens, half-empty packages of cigarettes, letters and post cards, pipes, shells, colored stones, books, knitting, mending, photographs and all the rest of the confetti of living.

There was an empty chest of drawers at one end of the room. He allocated a half drawer to each adult. Each morning he collected all the flotsam and sorted it, item by item, into its proper place like a postmaster.

It was regarded by the other adults as an unwarranted infringement of private rights, but the daily miracle of creating order out of confusion brought peace to his soul. He dumped broken toys, shells and stones into the big round wood basket. Peter and Peewee did not regard this as a violation of their privacy. The happiest moment of their day was when Mr. Hobbs had finished his morning cleanup and they could spill the contents of the big basket in an alluring pile on the living-room floor.

Mr. Hobbs' system was well-thought-out but it did not work. Stewart and Byron were full of good will. Their spirit of cooperation was 100 percent. Both of them, however, believed that it was their inalienable privilege to sit on the rail of the porch and smoke after breakfast.

No references to their responsibilities which Mr. Hobbs might make through the windows of the living room were broad enough to dislodge them. Time slipped serenely by while, from the kitchen, complaints about overflowing garbage pails and scrap baskets and declining water pressure became steadily louder.

Eventually, Mr. Hobbs would find himself at the pump house or watching the writhings of burning cartons or relieving his feelings by throwing empty bottles at the rocks.

When his sons-in-law saw him returning from these expeditions they were genuinely distressed. If only he would give them a moment to relax after breakfast all these things would be cared for. This was *his* vacation. He should not be asked to lift a finger. They meant it. They were good boys, his sons-in-law.

He went upstairs to inspect Kate's department. Her bedroom door was still closed. Getting a broom and dust pan from the hall closet, he swept around the edges of the rugs, working quietly so as not to wake her.

Mr. Hobbs had declared fiercely at the beginning of his vacation that his evenings were to be his. He was going to read. All winter long he was either too tired or too busy to open a book. Now he proposed to get his fill of reading.

There was a big, battered, comfortable chair in the living room which Mr. Hobbs had appropriated for his sole use and he would retire to it each evening with a book in his hand. Across the room the Grants and the Carvers would be starting a bridge game and on the other side of the table Mrs. Hobbs was at her never-ending task of knitting. A peaceful hush fell over the house. The scene reminded Mr. Hobbs of a picture in an old *St. Nicholas* magazine.

The spell was short-lived, however, for bridge did not seem to be any deterrent to argument between the Carvers and the Grants. As their talk wandered controversially over the entire field of politics, sociology and international relations, Mr. Hobbs found it difficult to know which side he disagreed with more.

He disliked these interminable arguments over questions to which there could be no answer even if the participants had known what they were talking about. He tried to keep out of them. Inevitably, however, some goad sank so deep that he could no longer endure it in silence — and there he was, in the thick of the fight.

The subjects differed but the pattern remained about the same.

Byron: Did you put on the jack of spades, dear? What I'm trying to say is that all this talk about balanced budgets gives me a pain in the neck. The balanced budget is just as obsolete as the gold standard or the high-wheel bicycle.

Jane: I agree.

"You would," thought Mr. Hobbs.

Susan: You're great ones to talk. You'd balance your budget if you had to starve to do it. Is it my lead?

Jane: That's personal. For pity's sake, don't let's get personal.

"I'll tell you all something," said Mr. Hobbs. "If we keep on..."

Byron: I'm not nearly as concerned with balanced budgets as I am with free speech. We're getting into the same state of mind in this country as the Salem witch-hunters. Is that your ace?

Stewart: Nobody values free speech more than I do but did it ever occur to you, Byron, that responsibility goes with freedom?

Byron: Words! The issue is do we have free speech or don't we! I'll take that trick.

"I'd like to say something on that point," said Mr. Hobbs.

Peter: (From the second floor) Mommie.

Susan: Free speech doesn't give anyone the right to teach my children treason. Yes, dear, Mommie's here.

"Let me tell you something," said Mr. Hobbs. "If I was a college president, I'd fire every . . ."

Peter: Mommie, Mommie, Mommie, Mom . . .

Stewart: For goodness' sake, what's the matter with that child?

Susan: Oh, he just wants ginger ale.

"I never saw a child consume so much ginger ale in my life," said Mr. Hobbs. "This afternoon . . ."

Stewart: No one believes in free speech more than I do, but when you're at war . . .

Jane: That's the kind of a remark that *makes* war.

Susan: I agree with you for once, Jane. What we've got to do in this country is to lead the world into a better way of life by helping those who have less than we have. . . .

"Who's going to pay for it?" Mr. Hobbs shouted.

They stopped playing and looked at him as if he had just emerged through the floor boards.

"*We* are, sir," said Byron. "This *country's* going to pay for it, out of our boundless resources. It's the price of leadership."

"Where are you going to get the money?" Mr. Hobbs cried frantically. "Are you going to keep on running this country into debt till the dollar's not worth a nickel or do you want to keep on raising taxes till we're all doing slave labor? I pay now . . ."

"The trouble with your generation, sir," said Byron, who had an irritating habit of lowering his voice at such moments, "is that you're using outmoded yardsticks for measuring our economy. – Your king, Jane? – You keep measuring wealth in terms of dollars and balanced budgets and national debt. Wealth has nothing to do with dollars. Dollars are only *symbols.* Wealth is the natural resources of a country – the productivity of its factories. . . ."

"The potential of its labor force," muttered Jane absently.

Mr. Hobbs ran his finger under the edge of his collar. His voice trembled slightly. "Listen. If dollars don't mean anything, then there's something cockeyed about this island we're living on. It was dollars that bought that beef tonight that you all gobbled up. Nobody ever handed me any natural resources and I never paid a grocery bill with the potential of a labor force. The trouble with you young fellows is you've got your heads so far in the clouds you can't see the ground. I want to tell you that when I started . . ."

"Roger, Roger," said Mrs. Hobbs. "I don't see why you always get so excited." She held up a half-knitted sweater. "Susan, do you think that's going to be too big for Peter?"

"Looks all right to me, Mother. He'll grow into it, if it is."

"Rubber!" shouted Stewart.

"That was a good rubber," said Jane. "If you'd led your king of spades, Susie, I think you'd have had us on the hook."

"I think I'll go to bed," said Mrs. Hobbs. "The air makes me sleepy. Coming, Rog?"

"I'm going to take the dogs out," said Mr. Hobbs.

The two dogs rushed down the front steps and were swallowed up by the darkness. Crossing the stubbly lawn, Mr. Hobbs picked up the path to the cove. He passed the black form of the pump house and his feet touched the coarse sand of the cove. Here the stars seemed to shine with greater brilliance. At his feet the small waves broke, pushing up the beach with a gentle hiss. He could hear the occasional sniff of the dogs.

He saw the nearness and immensity of the night sky and felt the cool breeze off the quiet water. Tomorrow he would lie in that buoyant water, floating on his back with arms outstretched, and from the beach behind him would come the sound of children's voices and the occasional bark of a dog.

The confusion, the moments of weariness, the petty exasperations, like the bridge-game argument just past, were being washed out of his consciousness. The pictures he would carry home with him at the end of summer were of a different sort — the feel of wet sand under bare feet, the sigh and moan of the southwest wind as it poured through his bedroom window, the lift and fall of seaweed as the incoming tide crept between the rocks, the muted sound of distant surf. And so many little things, things one hardly noticed at the time — the smell of bayberry — fat, white clouds in a summer sky.

These were the pictures he was bringing home, and always in the background were Byron and Peewee and Peter — fat little legs running or staggering across the sand — the sound of their laughter. He was living in what he suddenly realized was an atmosphere of life and vitality, yet he had been thinking of it in his blindness as hopeless confusion.

Mr. Hobbs felt integrated once more. Filled with content, he felt his way back up the path toward the house.

Edward Streeter

To BE a successful banker is difficult enough, but Edward Streeter has also won a reputation as an outstanding humorist. Born in New York City, he worked as a reporter for a few years after graduation from Harvard, then saw service as a lieutenant in World War I. Amid military duties he found time to write the number-one comic hit of that period, *Dere Mable,* which had a sale of 600,000 copies.

After the war he began a career in finance, eventually becoming vice-president of The Bank of New York, a post he still holds. Concurrently he has delighted a host of readers with *Daily Except Sunday, Father of the Bride, Skoal Scandinavia* and, most recently, *Mr. Hobbs' Vacation.* Mr. Streeter lives in New York, is married and has four children.

The Power

Illustrations by Richard Stone

and the Prize

A condensation of the book by

HOWARD SWIGGETT

"The Power and the Prize," copyright 1954 by Howard Swiggett, is published at $3.50 by Ballantine Books, Inc., 404 Fifth Ave., New York 18, N. Y.

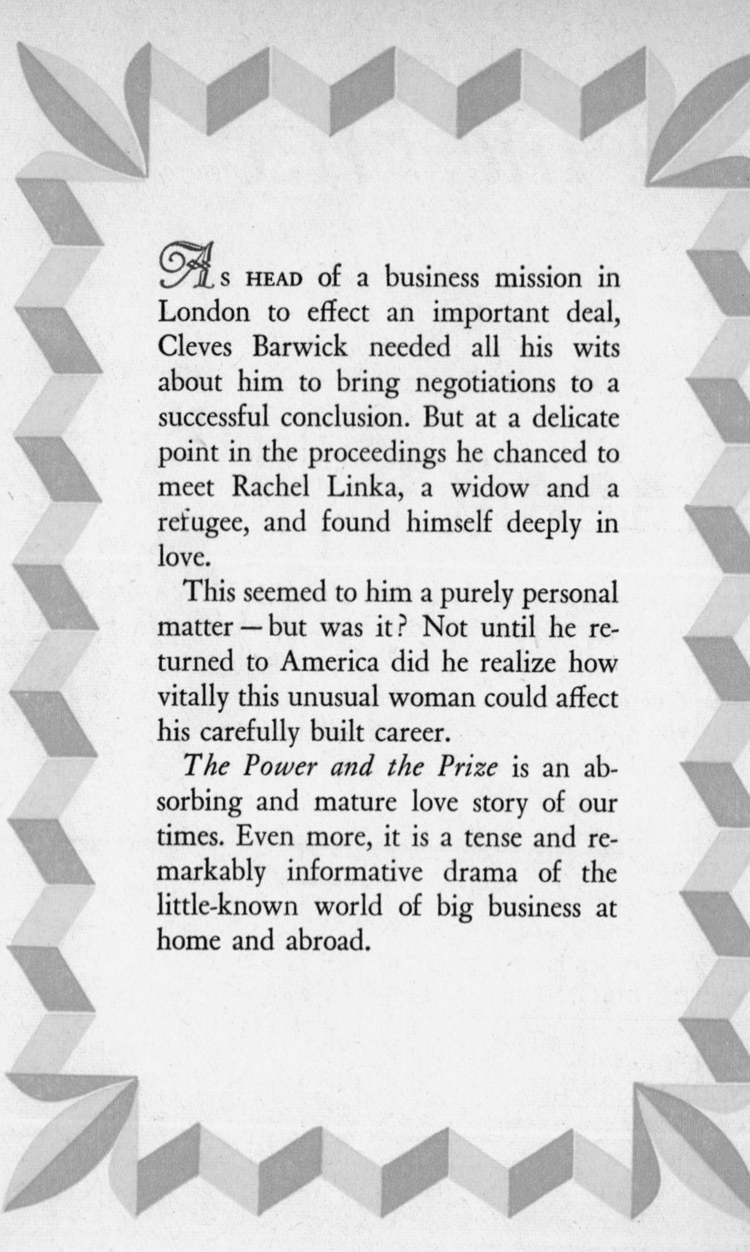

AS HEAD of a business mission in London to effect an important deal, Cleves Barwick needed all his wits about him to bring negotiations to a successful conclusion. But at a delicate point in the proceedings he chanced to meet Rachel Linka, a widow and a refugee, and found himself deeply in love.

This seemed to him a purely personal matter — but was it? Not until he returned to America did he realize how vitally this unusual woman could affect his carefully built career.

The Power and the Prize is an absorbing and mature love story of our times. Even more, it is a tense and remarkably informative drama of the little-known world of big business at home and abroad.

CHAPTER 1

IT WAS vital to each man that the other be kept uncertain of his real intentions. Their lives did not depend on it, but much of what they lived for did.

They got in the rear of the Daimler and both reached to pull the armrest down between them, slumping back like tired runners after their long day's conference, conducted with such reserve under its outward candor.

The car turned west out of Bishopsgate Street, heading for the offices of Dunstanley, Carew (Metals) Ltd. near Horseferry Road. In the heavy Friday-afternoon traffic the chauffeur drove as slowly and carefully as they had talked. Through the steamy car windows London looked forlorn in the October drizzle.

The day had been harder for the American, Barwick, than for Carew. He could not be sure how far to go, what to concede, what to insist upon, until he had talked to his own men. They would tell him whether what Carew had asserted was reality. Yet all day he had had to appear to Carew and his attorneys as though he accepted it fully.

Neither man spoke. Cleves Barwick was 40, Vice-Chairman of Allied Materials Corporation. He wore a soft shirt and a blue double-breasted suit. In the dismal afternoon light his dark face looked cold and a little hard. The habitual tolerance and good humor in it had gone with the strain of the day.

Carew, ten years older, had his Burberry buttoned and his black Homburg set straight on his head. Under its curled brim iron-gray hair showed over his ears. His thin, handsome face was more like a fine actor's than a businessman's.

"I'm exhausted and I know you must be," he said now. "I wish you'd reconsider coming to the country with me. I promise to leave you alone, or I can give you some golf or a little rough shooting. My wife would be delighted. Why don't you do it?"

Barwick wished very much he could accept, but it was impossible in their present relationship. Even if in a few moments his own people reported that the Carew Process was all and more than had been claimed, he could not be the guest of a man in his house and then drive the ruthless bargain which Allied Materials expected of him. All day he had felt a more and more unpleasant sense of guilt about the last-minute surprise condition his Chairman, in New York, had insisted upon.

"Thank you," he said, "but I don't believe I'd better. I've got my two colleagues to look after. We'll have to talk to New York after I've digested this tax data. Perhaps you'll ask me again."

"I shall indeed," Carew replied, and both men reverted to their thoughts.

Dunstanley House, the company offices, faced the Thames. The bustle and busyness in it impressed Barwick the first day he saw

it. Clerks hurried past, carrying invoices and shipping orders. There was the familiar noise of business machines and the same telephone activity as at home. But there was an intangible difference in atmosphere. Perhaps it was the doors that were always closed after you entered "a room." People always knocked, and the man sitting at his "table" took his time about telling them to come in. There was something really private about a private office.

When they reached the building, the lift took them to the top floor. "Find Mr. Barwick's people," Carew told the attendant at the desk. In a moment a door from the inner offices opened, and Everett and Struthers came in. Barwick looked at their impassive faces. Both Carew and he knew that what they would say to him would largely determine the course of their lives for months, and of their companies for years to come.

Carew greeted them casually, opened a door on a small conference room and motioned with a smile for them to use it.

Lester Everett went in first. A stocky man of 50, he had a large, almost hairless head and face and a childlike expression. He was the Chief Engineer of Allied Materials Corporation and one of the outstanding metallurgical engineers in America, highly paid, highly regarded, considered as steady and sensible as the Grand Central clock. Walter Struthers carefully closed the door. He was the Chief Accountant, tall and thin, a little younger, gray hair clipped short to where he was getting bald, steel-rimmed spectacles, many pens and pencils in his coat pocket.

"Well?" Barwick asked. "How was it?"

"Cleves," Everett said in a half whisper, "there is absolutely no doubt about this. They've perfected it, and it works."

"Oh, no!" Barwick said. "Not really."

"Yes, really. Since earliest times metals have been produced from ores by smelting. But with their process and their patent they can make metal powders right at a mine site. We've got to have this whatever it costs. It makes every smelter in the world obsolete."

"I have verified their claims on cost reduction to my own satisfaction," Struthers said quietly. "It cuts copper by forty percent, nickel and cobalt by sixty, probably seventy-five."

"You're absolutely sure that you've seen enough to say this?" Barwick asked them. "You're prepared for me to telephone New York today?"

"Yes."

"Bearing in mind, Walter, that I told the Board that if this were true and, if we got the license, we would step up our net earnings by ten percent?"

"That's conservative."

"How did you make out?" Everett asked.

"All right, but I had to talk mainly in generalities until I heard from you. What actual tonnage are they doing?"

"Five tons a day each of copper and nickel, as they claimed. Now Cleves, there are two other things. First, we've got to keep their engineer, Chutwell, absolutely on our side. I know he's not one of their directors, but on this he could swing it one way or the other. I tell you this because I didn't think you were particularly impressed with him," Everett went on. "Second, we've got to be very careful. We're sure that Pitt-Sempill, that young director of theirs, has somebody from New York down there."

Barwick thought a moment. If there was an active competitor there in a more favorable position, would Carew have asked him for the week-end?

"You're sure this isn't just a selling come-on they've dropped on purpose?" he asked.

"I'm sure," Struthers said, "there's somebody here."

"I see. Well, I'll have just a word with Carew. It's almost noon in New York. Why don't you go to the Savoy and put the call in for six o'clock London time?"

"O.K.," they both said, trying to hide their excitement.

Carew looked up from the letters he was signing. His usually pale face was flushed, and Barwick knew that Chutwell must have already told him how impressed Everett and Struthers had been. His own relief and excitement were so intense that he would have liked to discuss final terms then and there, before whoever the competitor was from New York could see Carew again.

"Well, how did it go?" Carew asked.

"Very well indeed, they seem to think," Barwick replied.

"I was sure it would. Now see here, since it has, why don't you reconsider and come down to the country with me?"

Barwick smiled. "It's very appealing, but I promised to take my teammates around London. And there is a personal matter I'd like to get settled. You remember having cocktails with the Malcolm Tierneys? He's on our board of directors."

Carew's face fell and he put his hand to his forehead in mock theatricality. "Oh dear, I know what you are going to say. That Artists' Refugee Organization Mrs. Tierney is interested in. She asked me to look into it and it completely slipped my mind. But dismiss it from yours. I'll get a full report."

"You do know it then?"

"I don't, no, but when she spoke of it, I knew I had heard of it before, but I couldn't think where. Give me just a moment," Carew said, frowning at the table. "By George, I think it was Chutwell, though why I can't imagine." He rang for his secretary. "Ask Chutwell to come in."

After an interval Chutwell entered. He was a thickset, beefy man of 45 or so, with a cheery, florid face and a cordial manner. His voice and gestures seemed a little finicky and out of keeping with his general John Bull appearance.

"Chutwell," Carew said to him, "did I ever hear you speak of an Artists' Refugee Organization?"

"Well, sir, you may have, though only vaguely."

"Good. Come back in a moment and tell Mr. Barwick all you know about it." When he had gone Carew continued, "Now, if he hasn't what you want, we'll get it somewhere else. Only one other thing: we're not unaware that to a degree Chutwell appears a bit of a thruster, and I want to be quite sure he goes down well with you and your people. I don't mean technically. There he is all that can be asked."

"Oh, they both like him very much."

"Good. Well, that's that, and I'm off. Good night." He went out and Chutwell re-entered.

"Hello," Barwick said. "Some friends of mine are interested in this refugee outfit."

"Yes, sir; what would you like to know?"

"Look," Barwick said, "I wish you wouldn't call me 'sir.' We only do that in the Army."

"That's very nice of you. Actually, Walter and Les both told me not to do it, but in Mr. Carew's room, what I mean to say is — "

"Incidentally, I am delighted at the way you got along with Walter and Lester today. It's going to make it all much easier."

"Oh, yes, we hit it off right away and got down to first names. About your Refugee Organization, Mr. Barwick. Confidentially, I got to know it in a rather odd way. Some friends of ours were here from Brussels and it fell to me to entertain them and, of course, London isn't Paris or even Brussels. I didn't know just what these people would like and I proposed taking them to the theater and giving them a supper later and letting them make their own plans. Isn't that the line you would have taken?"

"Oh, I should think so, yes."

"Well, one of the chaps asked me if we were to be just ourselves for supper and, when I said yes, he said, 'Is that not the way to bore oneself?' French, you know. I hit back and asked him what he suggested. He said, 'My dear old friend, do you not know the Artists' Refugee Organization?' He told me that in that organization were some very rare entertainers. That he knew some of them from Paris and, in short, that I could not do better than to enlist three of them, whose names he gave me, for after the theater. We should then bundle them in motors and toddle up the river for supper. The place he left to me. Well, Barwick, it was a very gay night."

Thinking of Vivian Tierney, it was difficult for Barwick to control his indignation. "I see," he said. "Are you telling me that this sort of thing is all the outfit does?"

"I shouldn't say it was all, but in my view it's what keeps them going. They've got writers and musicians, but, of course, what chance is there in London for them? I mean to say we have our own writers and our English music." Strains of "Pomp and Circumstance" seemed to fill the room.

"I may tell you," Barwick went on, "that a certain amount of American money is being sent over under a very different idea of what's done with it. Do you mind telling me, did you simply ask for the companions you wanted and they did the rest?"

"In substance, yes, though there was a woman at the office there who tried her best to block it. I told her she'd hear more of that and that I wasn't there to be blackguarded. My Belgian friend had told me whom to appeal to, a Mr. Resnikoff, if there were any question, and I did so at once."

"Wait. What was the woman's name?" Barwick asked.

"Uh—Linka, Rachel, I think."

That was the name Vivian Tierney had given him. "And what's her exact position? Secretary?"

"Something of the sort."

"And she was definitely against this?"

"Yes, but Resnikoff was in another room and with him I had no trouble at all. He gave her a very proper dressing-down before me, though in some foreign language."

"This certainly gives me a picture of one side of it I didn't know about. You haven't gathered there's anything political about it, what we call subversive, have you?"

"In the case of this woman," Chutwell said, pursing his lips, "there well may be. She took the regular Communist line in her abuse of me: 'exploitation,' 'money interests,' all that stuff. I put a good deal of it down to jealousy of the good times the other girls were having."

"They're still at 121 Victoria Street?" Barwick asked.

"Oh yes. Now I've told you this much, I'll go a little further." Across Chutwell's beefy face crept a sly smile. "Mr. Carew told me, as he left, that you were not going down to Surrey with him. I wanted to say this to you before, but my American opposites were doubtful about it. Frankly, I feel I may know you better than they do." He was now beaming, flicking the ash from his cigarette with infinite grace. "I am having a little party for your boys tomorrow night, and—mind you, I shall take refusal as a personal affront—you are coming, Cleves. There'll be eight of us, and Sunday morning you can send your friends back in New York a firsthand report on their Refugee Organization. *Voilà, m'sieur.*"

Barwick looked at him carefully. Could Struthers and Everett have known of this proposal and was that what they meant when they said Chutwell must be kept on their side?

"Oh, Mr. Chutwell," he said, "I can't possibly do that. You're very kind. I do appreciate it and I'm delighted that Everett and Struthers are going to have some relaxation. But I've got things I must do and I'm dining somewhere."

"Come along later."

"No, quite impossible. Thanks," Barwick said abruptly, rising.

Chutwell pursed his lips. "You have no objection to the others going?"

"Of course not. What they do Saturday night's no business of mine. Take 'em to Paris. Do what you please. Have fun." He opened the door and asked for his hat.

CHAPTER 2

THROUGH the grapevine, almost 200 people of the Allied Materials Corporation's staff in Rockefeller Center knew that the call was coming through from London. Only a half dozen really knew what it was about but all knew that something "really big" was in the wind which they felt would benefit them personally, if only because the company they worked for was getting still richer and more powerful.

It was the holding and sales company for its 20 mining and production subsidiaries from Minnesota through Missouri to the Gulf and, though it had thousands of stockholders, it was still very much the company of George Salt, its Chairman. In building it up he had been very careful of two things: to have no one on the Board or in the company who would ever have a reason for wanting him "out," and to avoid any possible competition for Barwick.

He was known to be "generous with his associates" money-wise, but very careful of titles. He handled the problems shrewdly. Barwick was Vice-Chairman, but there were no vice-presidents. He liked to tell people: "Down in our little shop there are only a few of us, working along together." It had actually become a matter of pride and prestige with the key men at Allied to have a simple functional title.

Walter Struthers, who anywhere else would have been Vice-President in charge of Finance, was proud to be Chief Accountant, and the brilliant Lester Everett to be not Engineering Vice-President but Chief Engineer. They tended to regard their vice-presidential equals among competitors the way a Marine colonel does a full general in the Nicaraguan Army.

Not all Salt's directors were happy about it, but he made it an issue of rugged simplicity. "Is there anybody in the industry who can give as quick an answer as we can? Whose net's more favorable?"

Well, that was true, one of the directors agreed, but where are we if Barwick breaks a leg? No one ever referred to Salt's approach to 70. You couldn't, in the face of Allied earnings.

As the clock got closer to one, Salt paced his office more and more restlessly. At 66 he was still a splendid figure of a man, ruddy and handsome with thick white hair, his dark-gray flannel suit cut tight enough to show off his fine shoulders and the absence of a bulge at the waist.

When Carew had called on them here in New York three weeks before, Salt had been very much against the proposed deal. "Just another English firm with its hand out," he had said. Nor did he fully understand what sort of setup was being proposed.

In return for a license to use the process, Carew wanted 50 percent of the stock in the licensee company. He also wanted Allied to advance him $10,000,000 to equip and operate a mining concession in West Africa.

The impatience with which Barwick had listened to Salt's objections both startled him and hurt his feelings. He hated to refuse Barwick anything, or even differ with him. In the 20 years since that July day in 1932 when Leonard Ogilvy, one of Allied's directors, had sent in his young brother-in-law, just out of Yale, Salt had come to look on Barwick with the affection of a devoted father. He intended that, in his own good time, Barwick should succeed him.

"Now, Cleves," he had said, "I don't want us at odds over anything, and you may be right about the value of this, but I don't want you stubbing your toe, either. You really don't know that it's as good as you think."

"I know I don't," Barwick told him, "but it won't take long for Everett, Struthers and myself to find out in London. You've always prided yourself on leading the industry in technological advance. Well, you can't pass this up. If Carew is right, we can increase our net on royalties alone by ten percent. It puts us far ahead of any competition."

"Well, can I think about it overnight?" Salt asked.

Barwick smiled. "You certainly may. I didn't mean to harry you so." Although what had once been youthful idolatry of Salt had slowly changed to perception of his overwhelming vanity, his love of being Lord Bountiful and the evasiveness beneath his outward frankness, Barwick's feelings were still affectionate and grateful, though at times impatient.

"I don't know that I understand this West African concession thing," Salt said.

"Well, the mineral deposits are said to be very large. A processing plant can be built there and produce metal powders at fantastically low costs — consider the enormous savings in freight, for one thing. Carew hasn't the capital to do it alone. He wants the loan secured by the concession, and he wants to keep title."

"Certainly the new company — or better yet we — should have the title. It'll be our money."

"I imagine a good deal of personal and national pride is involved," Barwick replied. "It isn't easy for them to come over here and ask for money. I don't see what we want with a lot of West African real estate, and we won't do too badly as it is. It may be best to let them keep some of the prestige. It might be the sort of gesture that makes friends and attracts more business." The last was a passage from the Salt Gospel.

Salt's great head shook violently. "No, no, Cleves, you're wrong there. The British are universally unpopular. Look at the Mau Mau, Hong Kong. No, sir, the concession should go to Allied, and I'll tell you why — and I am disregarding what I'll bet is going to be a whale of a tax advantage. Forget that. This thing is going to need discussion in Washington. They will expect it. Certainly we, looking to the tax position, will want to tell them. Now, how are we going to look saying, 'Oh, about West Africa, we are just doing that for the British who have done so much for us?' "

"It doesn't have to be put that way."

"Well, let's leave it till morning," Salt had said.

By the next morning he had changed his mind, was all out for the deal — but with his original reservations as to title unchanged. In the end Barwick, Struthers and Everett flew to London under restrictions as to bargaining to which Barwick regretted agreeing.

As THE call began, the connection was very bad. All Barwick could hear was Salt bellowing: "Is the title question settled?" Then the static cleared and they could speak and hear as though they were in the same room. Salt chortled: "Hear you fine now. How are you, anyway? How's the weather there?"

"All right. Please listen. We are absolutely satisfied the process is everything they claim. Everett has been all day watching production. There's no question about it."

"If Les is satisfied, I am. I'll back him anywhere."

"I have been with our friend and his attorneys myself on tax structure and the unblocking of sterling. The former is more complex than we thought but not insoluble, but have Henry Dennison's best tax man ready to come if we need him."

"O.K. on that."

"Now, their laboratories and their whole setup are most impressive to Lester and Walter. We think the estimates on the mining and earth-moving equipment Carew gave us are excessive. Are you getting this? They should be checked against the secondhand market."

"I'll attend to it personally. But what about the concession? Is the title question settled?"

"How could we go into that until we were satisfied this thing worked — "

"I know, I know. Don't get touchy. Take your time."

"I start Monday on the deal. Now finally, we are a little bothered about a New York competitor being here and we don't know who it is. We understand he's set to accept any terms they propose. You might find out if any one in particular is known to be in London."

"Well, if they want to do business with somebody else, tell them to go ahead," Salt bellowed.

"Now, George, keep your shirt on. We don't want a slip from overconfidence."

"I agree with that. Any message for your father?"

"Give him my love. Good-bye."

Barwick's suite was on the river side of the Savoy, and it was unusually pleasant and homey in the lamplight: new chintzes on the chairs and sofas, the double wine-colored curtains shutting out the night, a cheery blaze in the fireplace. Struthers got up to make them a drink.

"I wish you could get St. George Chutwell over to New York permanently," Everett said. "We could certainly use him. My, he's a great fellow."

"Well, maybe we can," Barwick replied. "I hear you're dining with him tomorrow night."

Struthers handed them their glasses. "Yes, is that all right? I don't know what he has in mind. He asked Les if he thought you'd like to come."

"I knew you had said you didn't want to get involved socially too early," Everett said.

It is wonderful what a change will do, Barwick thought to himself. Everett had not mentioned even once his very troublesome wife in Montclair and his face was animated and happy. Far from showing a sign of professional jealousy toward another engineer, which he often did at home, he thought Chutwell "a great fellow" and "a bang-up engineer."

"It went O.K. at the top level, didn't it?" Struthers asked. "I've got to hand it to you, the way you carry the ball."

"I said it was largely generalities about taxes and sterling. Tell me more about this competition. Who let it drop?"

"One of the technicians at the laboratory," Everett said. "I was talking to him about the pressure under which oxygen was forced in and he laughed and said to St. George: 'I didn't have questions like this from Mr. Pitt-Sempill's American yesterday.' I pricked up my ears, but St. George looked upset and changed the subject. Well, about an hour later, St. George said to us: 'Now see here, I can't advise you chaps but, if you like this, I can tell you what I'd do in your place. I wouldn't let Mr. Barwick hold out for too much, because there are people who are prepared to go ahead on our terms.' A little later he said to me: 'Les, I told you that, and I dare say I shouldn't have done it, but I want you and me to do this and nobody else.' I said: 'Can't you tell me a little more?' And he said he couldn't."

"He gave no idea of just what he thought I'd be wrong in holding out for?" Barwick asked.

"No, he didn't," Struthers said, "but I had a hunch it was the West African title thing. I wish we had some idea who the competition is. It makes me uneasy."

"Well, at least," Barwick said, "we know enough not to be complacent next week and maybe, if St. George has enough to drink tomorrow night, he'll tell you." He glanced at his watch. "I think I'll have a bath and dine here in my pajamas. I've got some letters to write. Come in to breakfast about eight thirty."

UNLIKE his usual athletic self Barwick felt extremely tired and slightly depressed. The elation he had felt, on hearing that the process was valid and worked, had eased off, mainly because of the position he had let Salt maneuver him into on the concession terms.

He had originally protested that if Allied must have the title, then Carew was entitled to know it at the very beginning of negotiations. But, at the time, Salt had swung around from watching the North River and said, "Absolutely not. I've thought this out. I want that concession. It's our money that's going into it. But," and he had held up a finger, "it's the thing they'll hang onto to the death. We'll get nowhere talking about it until the very end. They're too emotional about that Empire of theirs. But when we've gone along on everything else — give a little, take a little — and you're in London and it looks like signing the next day, and they're getting ready to give you a dinner, then you get a cable saying it must be *our* concession or it's all off. And they'll give in."

Barwick felt guilty about this, for it seemed to him that throughout all the negotiations of the next week Carew was entitled to suppose all the cards were on the table. He also felt irrationally annoyed about having been invited to Chutwell's party, and he wished very much he had not promised Vivian Tierney to get cluttered up with her Refugee Organization. To have to tell Vivian that her devoted work and her own and her friends' money were subsidizing the kind of business Chutwell described would be about as unpleasant a thing as he had ever faced. And if, as Chutwell implied, the Linka woman, Vivian's contact, was in sole opposition, he did not want to be drawn into the matter. Well, the best thing was to get it over with and tell Vivian to wash it out.

"I'd like to go to 121 Victoria Street," he told the chauffeur the next morning. He got in and the car rolled out to the Strand and shabby but mighty London.

No street was shabbier than Victoria and no door more dismal than that of 121. On one side was a small stationer's, on the other a tobacconist's. The Artists' Refugee Organization was on the sixth floor, the porter told Barwick, and the stairs were more reliable than the lift, which ran only to the fifth, anyhow.

Up Barwick walked to the sixth. On one of the doors a painted placard had been tacked, with *Artists' Refugee Organization* written on it in beautiful lettering. Beneath the lettering there were sketches of a singing lesson, a play rehearsal with the actors in a circle of chairs, and a life class in an artist's studio.

He knocked, heard the clink of cup and saucer, a quick step, and a woman opened the door. She was rather tall, or seemed so because she was so slender. She wore a sweater and tweed skirt and around her neck a blue handkerchief was knotted. The door she held open was between her and the window and he could not see her face very clearly.

INQUIRI
ARTISTS REFUGEE
ORGANISATION

"Yes?" she asked. Her voice was low and there was a slight foreign accent even in the monosyllable.

"Good morning," he said. "My name is Barwick. I'm from New York. Mrs. Tierney, who is a friend of mine, is on your board and asked me to look in on you."

She stepped back and he saw her face clearly. He was uncertain as to her age—somewhere between 30 and 40, he thought. Pale and thin, burned away, as it were, to the last fine gold, her face had a sorrow in beauty such as he had never seen. Her black hair was parted on the left side. The low forehead came down to great dark eyes which looked as though they had seen all the world's sufferings. Her mouth was wide, with beautiful lips.

He wanted to stare at her to fix every detail but, for some inexplicable reason, he felt as shy and ill at ease as a schoolboy looking at his feet.

"You look so funny," she said, laughing. "I'm Rachel Linka. Please come in and I will give you a cup of tea."

She poured tea into an old mug and handed it to him with what seemed to him celestial grace.

"I'm still laughing at you," she said. "Why are you frightened?"

"I'm not frightened," he said, thinking he had never seen anyone like her.

"Well, what can I tell you? Would you like to offer me a cigarette?"

"Oh yes, here, please keep them."

"Perhaps I will. They are very expensive, and I am quite ruthless about taking such things. We have had such nice letters from Mrs. Tierney. She seems a very warm sort of person."

"Yes, oh yes, she is. Is the work going well?"

Sorrow came back to her face and eyes. "When you say well," she said slowly, "you must remember that we are dealing mostly with people who have lost hope. They are the sort of people who have the brightest hopes for life—artists. The work would be 'going well' if some were members of a great orchestra, or a repertory theater—or many things like that. Most of us are people to whom music is the reason for life. Not that we expect that, not that we are not thankful for being alive, and for all that people like Mrs. Tierney are doing for us. And certainly not that we are unwilling to be waitresses, dishwashers, anything. Still, I think it cannot be called 'going well' when a woman of artistic talents or a man of musical genius is a dishwasher in a restaurant. But I do not want you to think any of us do not understand reality."

He knew that Vivian's faith, at least in her, had not been misplaced and that he must do something tangible to help her. The thought of her being goaded by Chutwell and that man Resnikoff infuriated him.

"I would like," he said hesitatingly, "to make a contribution now just to show you how I feel about this, if I might. Would a thousand dollars — ?"

"You just suddenly decide to give away a thousand dollars? It must be very nice. But why?"

"Do you analyze the motives of every contributor?" he asked.

"It was quite wrong of me to say that," she said after a moment. "I'm a nasty person in many ways. Here is a pen. We would be very grateful if you gave us any money."

Barwick took a check from his wallet and reached for the pen.

"Now I will get you a report I wrote yesterday," Rachel said. "When you have read it, if you will send me any questions you think Mrs. Tierney will have, I will answer them." He realized he was being dismissed.

"I could read it now," he said as she took it from a drawer and handed it to him.

"Please take it with you. I have a great deal to do."

"Should I see — is it — Mr. Resnikoff?"

"He's our director, yes. If you like, I will ask him to telephone you. Where are you?"

"I am staying at the Savoy, but during the day I'm at Dunstanley, Carew's."

"Oh, no, it isn't possible," she said, dismayed, half-breathless, coming closer to him. He was aware of some fragrance about her, her own, like pink clover after rain. A rage to kiss her struck him. "You can't be — it mustn't be that you are a friend of Mr. Chutwell's."

"I barely know him," he said. "He's one of their engineers."

There was a silence. Her look was one of anger and contempt.

"I would like to — " he began, but she interrupted curtly.

"Will you please go? I have very much to do and I hear people coming now." There were steps outside and two men and a woman came in, panting from the climb. She spoke cheerily to them in German and Barwick felt himself urged invisibly toward the door.

"Miss Linka, do you close at noon today?" he asked.

"It is Mrs. Linka. Four o'clock Saturdays," she replied and turned back to the little man with a violin case who was making them all laugh at something.

A stranger in a strange land, Barwick walked downstairs. "You might drop me somewhere in Charing Cross Road," he told the chauffeur.

As the car left him, he thought he felt symptoms of softening of the brain. He entered Hachard's famous book store, reflecting on the curt indifference of her dismissal of him. He felt like a schoolboy told, "I will never speak to you again, Cleves Barwick, as long as Chutwell is your friend."

Most of us are people to whom music is the reason for life, she had said.

"Where would I find biographies of composers?" he asked a clerk.

"There," the clerk said, pointing down the wall, "where it says Music. You might also try Biography. I'd have a shot at it if I were you."

Barwick looked at him with acute displeasure. Having a shot at it was not what he wanted. In a matter of hours he wanted a complete after-education in music, so that he could talk to and understand Rachel Linka. He felt ashamed that his appreciation was limited to a liking for beautiful sounds, particularly those made by the human voice. He realized how superficial this was. He must seek the Masters. It took him a quarter of an hour to find lives of Bach, Beethoven, Mozart and Schumann which, wrapped in old newspapers but tied with the beautiful English twine, he transported to his rooms at the Savoy.

Taking off his coat and shoes and loosening his tie, he lay on the bed. He examined the books one by one and looked at the pictures—but what had their text or pictures to do with him or with Rachel Linka? There was no reason to suppose she was a musician. She might be an actress or a painter or a scholar, or just a displaced person of intelligence. What business of his was it if she objected to refugees' dining with St. George Chutwell? Personally, he preferred to make his own dates but, if some men didn't, that was their affair. Nor was there any reason for feeling sorry for this woman—not "this woman," but Rachel Linka, a person. She had not been afraid to speak her mind to Chutwell or to him. She knew what she was doing. He must remember what *he* was doing—dealing with Carew. That was all. That was what Salt took for granted. And Vivian Tierney, also.

He began to feel a special and illogical resentment toward poor Everett, now excited as a child about going out to "see life" with Chutwell, to the distress of Rachel Linka. Everett, who a few days before had come to his apartment early in the morning and said he was going to kill himself—and then turned the idea over to him. . . .

CHAPTER 3

EVERETT's telephone call had awakened Barwick the morning after the first meeting with Carew in New York. Over the wire he stammered something about being "desperate" and having to see Barwick at once. It was just seven o'clock. "Is this about Carew?" Barwick asked with a healthy yawn.

"No, Cleves, no."

"Well, come ahead," Barwick told him, hung up and stretched. He got out of bed, shaved, showered, dressed and made some coffee, which he took into the living room. A damp wind from the East River was blowing the curtains. Of all the rooms in New York, he thought this was the best. The north wall was covered with bookshelves. There was a fireplace in the west wall with a seascape over it, and the space between the French windows on the south was crammed with the memorabilia of 20 of his 40 years, photographs of teams and regiment, commissions and citations, men and girls and family, and a Signal Corps shot of Rome as it looked the morning he entered it with the Fifth Army. The room was comfortable, rich, sentimental and masculine.

Everett arrived. It was startling to see his pink face unshaven. His rumpled shirt and tie were obviously yesterday's, and he was not wearing his hearing aid, as was customary, so that Barwick had to shout at him. He knew that Everett, with whom he had worked closely for several years, was married and lived in Upper Montclair, N. J. He knew there were no children, and he had never met Mrs. Everett. And that was all he did know about his close associate's life away from Allied. The story Everett poured out was of an early marriage to a girl from an Ohio river town. She was then blonde and attractive. Now she was coarse, ignorant and "hateful." As his deafness increased, Everett said, she had begun to hate him because of it, shouting at him even when he could hear, humiliating him in public. A normal social life was utterly impossible. She had "taken to drink." Any peace with her was bought with money and more of it.

"What is the immediate crisis?" Barwick asked.

"She's going to Salt, she says, and tell him the story and expose me. She says if Salt won't see her, she'll come in the office and shout it out. Cleves, if she does that, I will kill myself. All I have in the world is Allied. It's my whole life. If you could call her and say you'll see her privately, it might work. It's the last resort."

"I still don't see what she'll have to talk about." The pale, sweating face before him was appalling. Everett wiped it with a messy handkerchief.

"She has one of her relatives staying with us . . . a niece, seventeen . . . we can't get a maid to stay because of Ella's abuse . . . this niece has been doing the work . . . last night, after another tirade from Ella, I went out to the kitchen to speak to Louella a moment . . . the shades were up and I switched the light off . . . I was kissing Louella when Ella caught us." He poured it out as one long sentence.

Mrs. Cody, Barwick's housekeeper, was arriving, and he only nodded and patted Everett's shoulder sympathetically. Plainly, Mrs. Everett must not go to Salt. He could see that clearly, but

he could not visualize Lester Everett kissing her niece. If he had ever thought of him at home, it was to dismiss him as one of those "happily married" men for whom, as Everett had said, Allied was all of their lives.

He thought a moment, looking at Everett's stricken face. "All right, I'll call her," he said. "Now I'll give you some clean clothes and you can have a bath and shave." He asked Everett for his home number and went into his bedroom. When he reached her, Mrs. Everett talked to him largely in semialcoholic giggles, assuring him she had never intended to make trouble. "You take me to lunch some day soon, Mr. Barwick," she cooed. "Or why don't you drop in for a cocktail some night? People have come all the way from Chicago for my old-fashioneds."

While he was trying further to restore Everett with some breakfast after the call, Mrs. Cody said Mr. Salt was on the wire.

"Cleves," he roared, "I'm at the office. Hardly a soul here. I thought you'd certainly be in early. That's why I came. I've had a lot of thoughts on Carew and I see it much more in focus. I tell you it's got very real possibilities. But I can't find Everett anywhere. Got his house. Some girl said he'd left very early and they don't know where he is — "

"It's all right, George," Barwick said soothingly. "He's here. We'll be down in fifteen minutes."

"Grand, hurry along, take your time." Salt hung up.

That day, the rest of Carew's stay and thereafter, Barwick had covered up or substituted for Everett. While it seemed essential that Everett go to London with him, it became evident that he could not go with any peace of mind while his wife was in her present state. If it came to Salt's ears that "one of his key men" was in some "domestic difficulty," he was quite capable of firing him forthwith, so high a value did he put on suitable matrimony among his colleagues.

But all seemed serene until the evening before the day of departure, when Barwick, after some last-minute shopping, went to his father's house on Twelfth Street, to dine.

The Reverend Doctor John Cleves Barwick, retired, answered the door himself with word that Mr. Salt was on the wire. Barwick took up the telephone and said hello.

"I've searched this town for you. I don't care where you go, but I *wish* you'd leave word. I've got to see you at once. Here."

"But I can't come there now. I'm at my father's and I'm dining with him."

"Go, my boy, if you must," his father said in a loud whisper. "Dinner can wait. It's steak."

"I tell you, Cleves — and I apologize for the way I talked — you'll understand why when I tell you. But you must come here, now! It absolutely cannot wait."

"All right," Barwick replied, and hung up. He put his arm

affectionately around his father's shoulder. "I'm very sorry," he said. "I suppose it's the price you pay."

As HE came up the broad curve of the stairs, Barwick could see Salt pacing his paneled library. "Close the door," he said. "Sorry to be this way. Thanks for coming."

Barwick sat down, hoping Salt would.

"I think," Salt began, still standing, "it hit me hardest because I had such absolute faith in you. I wouldn't have believed it possible for you to have covered up anything from me."

"I don't know what you're talking about but, if you'll try to tell me, I'm sure we can clear it up," Barwick said quietly. For the life of him, he could not imagine what was coming.

"You left the office this afternoon without saying where you were going," Salt said. "Naturally you're free to do that, but I would have thought on the afternoon before you left for abroad, I might have been shown the consideration of knowing how to reach you."

Barwick glanced at the clock. "Let's get into this. I take it I wasn't dragged up here for a lesson in office behavior."

"Don't talk that way, Cleves. You and I have got to face some pretty terrible things and we mustn't quarrel with each other. You'd every right to go where you pleased. Unfortunately, you had only been gone ten minutes when that woman arrived."

"What woman? Not — "

"Yes, Everett's wife. Vulgar, common, noisy, half-lit, she came in. Of course there was no one at the reception desk — why, I don't know. She barged into the main office and asked two hundred people where I was. By a miracle, John Lamey was passing, grasped the situation, brought her in to my secretary and shut the door. Miss Tibbetts tried to quiet her and I heard the uproar and came out. The woman shot past me and sat herself down by my desk. I give you my word, I thought she was out to kill and I kept my eye on her handbag. Well, I don't need to tell you what she said. She informed me she had talked to you. You can imagine my feelings. She said you had given her no satisfaction, and that you had pleaded with her not to see me. That it would worry me—as though I were some infirm old dodderer who couldn't face trouble. That's what you must feel about me—"

"Of course it isn't. Everett came to me with the story. If it had happened to you, I wouldn't have expected you to tell me. I hoped it would all boil down and be forgotten. How does it stand?"

"It stands this way. We have admitted to our highest councils a man of whose home life we knew absolutely nothing. Do you know another business of our size in the country that would have let themselves in for that? Do you know what American Brake Shoe does about the wives of its personnel?"

"No, and I don't care. The only question is how this stands."

"Do you realize that Everett is a lecher?"

"No, and he's not. He's evidently had a frightful life with this woman, there was a pretty kid around the house, and he kissed her."

"Do you think for one moment you can trust the engineering judgment of a man like that? To have ever married this blowsy animal has shown a basic lack of judgment that's utterly destroyed any faith I've got in him. I don't care how good an engineer he's pretended to be, he's got his head on the wrong way. I've never felt sure of him."

"That's not so. What did she expect you to do?"

"It's not an expectation. It's a threat. She says it's not only her young niece, it's half the girls in our office. She says we're to give her a job in his office where she can know all he's doing—"

"That's nonsense. Did you gather she'd be home tonight?"

"Yes, she said she would. In case I called her she'd like to start work tomorrow."

"Well, I better go see her, I think."

"But what can you tell her? I pleaded with her."

"Let me telephone while I'm thinking," Barwick said. He rang his father again and asked whether dinner could be a steak sandwich and coffee in his study, that he had to go to Montclair.

"Absolutely, my boy," his father said. "How soon will you be here?"

"Twenty-five minutes."

"It'll be waiting. Medium rare."

Barwick then called the Everett residence and asked the girl who answered if he could speak to Mrs. Everett. When she came to the phone, he said to her: "Mrs. Everett, this is Cleves Barwick again. Do you suppose, if I came out now by car, you could do a great favor for me?"

"Why, sure, Mr. Barwick, and I'll have a nice little old-fashioned, not too little, waiting."

"Well, grand," he said, without telling Salt what she said. He hung up.

"Call me, no matter how late," Salt said. "If it's a question of money, go ahead. Jackson will drive you out."

As he was being driven to Montclair, the most worrying thing was what his father had said when he told him the whole story. "Defense against people like that is difficult. A long process of after-education is required. They know their own weapons — malice, viciousness, utter lack of standards — will not be used against them. When, as with this woman, they can link themselves with morality, they are often invincible for a time, and the fact that in the end it comes to nothing means little to them, if they can have their day."

Barwick's angry impatience mounted during the drive. Here were Salt and he, and a valuable man like Everett, accustomed to the management of large affairs, resourceful and cool in any emergency, operating a business with sales over a quarter of a billion dollars a year, brought down to dealing with a blackmailing psychotic woman, all because they didn't "want trouble."

THE LADY opened the door herself.

"Well, how you do, Mr. Barwick," she said, spacing and accenting each word. "Let me take your hat and set ye doon. Les has gone to the movies. I've got a nice little drink waiting for you and me. You don't have to hurry, do you?"

"It's very good of you to let me come out," he began, and with a shudder took the old-fashioned. He could write a somber sonnet to the unwanted drinks he had had "for business reasons."

"Just taste that," she said with a wink. She looked as he had supposed she would. At one time she must have been a tawny animal, hard for a young man to resist. To his surprise she still gave the feeling of being good-humored and, as they say, her own worst enemy. She wore a peasant blouse with a round low neck and had what appeared to be a Spanish dancer's skirt wrapped around her hips. Her face was ravaged and coarse, and he guessed her to be closer to 50 than 40. She was already slightly tight, her speech slurring occasionally, but the intoxication was still in the amiable stage.

He congratulated her on the drink and they sat down opposite each other. Her diamonds glittered in the light. One foot tapped incessantly.

"Now, what's the favor?" she asked. "I was afraid you were going to scold me for barging in on the Big Chief. My, he's nice. Man of distinction. You're nice, too." She perched the high heel of her slipper on the edge of the sofa.

"Mrs. Everett," he began.

"The name is Ella," she replied. "You know, I should never have gone to the office. If I'd known what the Old Man and you were like, maybe I wouldn't have. I know I promised you, but I couldn't help it. I was sitting here all alone this afternoon, and I got to thinking about that louse, Everett, and what he had done to me, and I knew I had to pay him back — "

Her face seemed to shrink, contorted with rage and hate. "I've had all I can take," she said, draining her glass. "Now, you listen here to me. I didn't have to marry Everett. I could have married anybody, fellows from Cincinnati, Louisville, Chicago — they were all after me, had their own businesses, college fellows. What was Everett? A draftsman, taking correspondence courses, and you bring him East to a big job. We got an apartment in Newark. We hadn't been there two months when he begins to go deaf on me. That was five years ago. What kind of a life do you think I've had since? I never met one single person from the company. I said to him, 'Do they know you got a wife?' He said eastern people weren't sociable, so I sit home. But I keep trying to make it a home. Do you see that break front? Two thousand dollars. I didn't care. I wanted things nice. Then he gets a hearing aid. But when he comes home at night, he turns it off and works at his damn problems. Many a time I said, 'Let's have some friends in.' Nothing doing." She lit a cigarette with a lot of stage business of blowing out the match and dropping it in the ash tray.

"Still and all, I put up with it. Like they say, I live in the future. But I get so I can't stand it here alone, and I ask my niece to come to stay. She's only a kid, seventeen in the fall, scrawny little thing. Well, you know what happened. How would any woman feel? Wouldn't she feel as I did? Well, then you call me up, and I don't know, I'm all heart when I'm appealed to right, and I did tell you I'd forget it. Try to, that is. But today, I was here all alone and I got to feeling worse and worse. I think if Everett can do that in his own home, what's he doing in the office? And then I figure there's just one thing to do. Make them let me work there right alongside of him. I think about it—and I have a couple of drinks to settle me—and then you call up and say you want to ask a favor, and the hell of it is I'm all woman and I melt." With that, she did—into tears.

Barwick thought to himself that when alcoholism was added to loneliness and frustration, it did indeed become a matter of prolonged after-education, as his father had said. He felt enormously sorry for this blowsy woman. He felt sorry for Everett, and he felt very sorry for himself for being involved in it all.

"Now, Mrs. Everett—"

"I told you the name was Ella," she sobbed.

"Ella, as far as the office goes, I am positive there is no other woman in Lester's life. The thing is you've got to help me in something that means a great deal to a great many people. I feel I can ask it because you are the sort of woman you are." He waited until more tears were wiped and the handkerchief replaced.

"What I want to ask is enormously important to the company. I have to ask you to let Lester leave for London with me tomorrow with a clear mind. I'd like to tell you about the thing called the Carew Process that's involved, because you'll understand it." He outlined the elements of it and she listened, hands, head and foot never moving.

"Gosh," she said, "that is big. Is that the sort of thing you work on there? I figured you played cards all day with your secretaries."

Barwick continued. "If Lester's going to be any help to me, you will have to let him forget whatever it is that has been troubling you both. When he gets back, who knows what fresh start you can both make? In many ways Lester is a genius. They're never easy to live with."

"Suppose I say 'yes' and tell the Old Man I'll be good and all, how do you know you can trust me?"

"You give me your word and that ends it."

"I don't see what I get out of it. I'm still stuck here with a bottle and a TV."

"You'd get an inner satisfaction."

"You know," she said slowly, "that could be. You're smart. I like you. I might just happen to do this for you. Try anything once, I guess. I promise. But you can't just walk off now. You've got to stay and tell Everett what's happened. I'll get you and me a little drink first, how's about it?"

"Lester's at the movies?"

"Yep, plenty of time."

"Well, I have a big idea. We'll get him out and tell him."

"You mean page him? Hey, I could go for that. What's the idea?"

"You and I go down in the car. We have them announce that 'Mr. Cleves Barwick's car is waiting and will the patron who knows Mr. Barwick please come out.' Fun or not?"

"Yeah," she said, "fun. Wait'll I get my mink. You're really cute."

AN HOUR later all was serene, except that Everett insisted he must not have to face Mr. Salt at Idlewild the next day. Barwick's patience was at an end.

"Listen," he said, "I've had enough of half-cooked emotions. Be at the airport, and act like a man."

"My feelings — "

"We've all got feelings. Forget it."

CHAPTER 4

WELL, that was the story. Salt had been accustomed to say Everett was one of the two completely happy men he knew. The swift change of attitude from "ready to swear by his judgment" to "always having my doubts about him" never troubled Salt. He was a judge of men. His other completely happy man was John Lamey, who had guided Ella Everett to Miss Tibbetts, his secretary.

Any evidence of avarice or ingratitude, whether by an employe or customer of Allied or some "damn foreign government," led Salt to philosophize aloud on John Lamey.

"There he is, almost my age, and he's kept the books of the Presbyterian Synod of New York for forty years outside my office, wherever I was, and he's never asked for a thing for himself. He has no family except a sister in Indiana. And he's happy. He has no further ambitions than serving. 'They also serve who only stand and wait,' " Salt would say, and invest it with such feeling that avaricious men like his directors would feel a little ashamed of making money and make it a point to shake hands with Lamey and call him "Mr. Lamey."

His alleged happiness became part of the Allied credo. Even Barwick had accepted it until one morning when he had walked to the office through a driving rain. Lamey was already at work, and almost no one else had come in yet. Barwick stopped to speak to him, shaking his dripping hat into the puddle gathering from his clothes. "I never could understand, Mr. Lamey, why the office force howls so about weather like this. Too much city life, I suppose."

Lamey got up respectfully. "It isn't just that, sir," he said in his thin voice. "It's quite hard on many people. It means an extra fifty cents to have your clothes pressed and it may be a problem if you have only one pair of good shoes, and it may mean a doctor and medicines. It isn't always easy to be prepared for a rainy day. The suit that has gotten wet through may be the only one you want to wear to the office."

"I hadn't thought of that," Barwick said. "You're quite right."

Later in the day he said to Salt, "George, you don't forget poor old Lamey with all this inflation, do you? When did you give him a raise last?"

"Oh, Lamey's taken care of," Salt said. "Has what he needs. Doesn't want any more. Nothing to spend it on. He's got a room around on Fifty-third Street in a house that's been converted into offices. He's made an arrangement to get it rent free in return for sitting in the lobby until ten. The fellow is resourceful. Worked it all out by himself."

It was his own life which concerned Barwick most now — and what Rachel Linka might think of him suddenly seemed the most important consideration of all. It was strange that what she had said about music should seem to have so much to do with it. He remembered with amusement how Salt had once reviewed the whole field of music.

"I don't pretend to know music or musicians," he had said, "and I don't want to, but I have looked up some of them and a more worthless lot I never read of, never knew where their next cent was coming from. Take Wagner, borrowing from everybody. Tschaikovsky, cadging money from a woman. Mozart, they don't even know where he's buried. Compare that sort of thing with Charley Ives, class of '98 at New Haven. Charley wanted to compose — well, no objection to that, the way he did it. Learned the insurance business at Mutual Life, formed his own firm, Ives and Myrick, splendid, big agency, and did his composing in his leisure. Now he's got the Henry Hadley Medal and the Pulitzer Prize, and his class and Yale are proud of him. Compare that with some of the so-called 'great' composers. Orderly life. Had a pattern. As you may know, I'm one of twenty-four men who send a box of cigars to Sibelius every month."

Twenty-five years ago Salt had thought of himself as someone like Mr. Justice Holmes, whose "sons" would be a special aristocracy. "I've got a remarkable group of young men around me at Allied," he told people. "I'll put 'em up against those Princeton Tigers of Clarence Dillon's any time. My boys are seven years younger on the average, but they're learning business, not peddling bonds."

There was something touching in his faith in these bewildered young men. And when in November '29, he had finished bailing them out and attending the funeral of one, they slipped gradually away to Washington, to teaching and to Texas. He saw that with uncanny misjudgment he had not picked one winner.

That had been the bad time when it seemed for a while that Salt himself would have to go into the discard. But then Leonard Ogilvy, one of his directors, sent him his young brother-in-law, Cleves Barwick. He was the son of the renowned Presbyterian minister, the Rev. Dr. John Cleves Barwick. That was a good start, Salt decided. The boy's good looks, which were actually only normal health, youth and symmetry, impressed Salt. The depression had brought a lot of scrubby-looking people in, and when Fred Johnson, the company treasurer, said good looks were no recommendation to him, Salt went back to what was still the Law and the Profits to him — 23 Wall Street. "J. P. Morgan, the elder, picked Robert Bacon for his good looks, didn't he? Morgan partner, Secretary of State, Ambassador to France — that's not failure in my book."

Very soon Fred Johnson and the whole organization up and down agreed Mr. Salt had really picked a winner. Barwick went through and up the organization — order department, cashier's, sales, branch offices and management, with everybody pulling for him. It was done by an enormous capacity for work, a combination of tact, modesty and good will, and an extraordinary flair for arousing confidence. He went into the Army in '41, and came out an infantry lieutenant colonel. In '48 Salt lent him to Washington and he was abroad in Paris for a year. In '50 he became Vice-Chairman of the Allied Executive Committee, after having managed the merger with Plant Metals.

Salt, who had always wanted a son like Barwick, showed a joy and pride in him which was most touching. He often wished it were possible for one man to say to another, "I love you like a son." He also wished, pathetically, that Cleves would confide in him more — and that he would get married. If he married and his wife had a son the next year, and they pushed him, why, when he entered Yale, he, Salt, could be there, proud as a grandfather. He'd only be 83. His father lived to 86, sound as the then dollar the day before he dropped dead.

The afternoon Cleves had so severely questioned the ethics and wisdom of the concession condition, Salt had hurried down to see Guy Eliot, president of the Founders Trust Company. He talked at length to Eliot about Cleves' "vision," his balance of mind and his ability to get things done. Those, he said, were Barwick's essential qualities.

George Salt was an important stockholder in the Founders and Allied was a very large depositor in the bank. Eliot knew from previous visits that Salt wanted Barwick on the Founders Board as much as he had once wanted a son to go to Yale.

"Oh, I know Cleves and I like him," Eliot said, "and I think our directors would, or do, and, of course, Mr. Debevoise is eighty-one and has no sons, and I should think it was worth considering. I don't know that I can say any more today, George. But I would like to ask you a question. What's the other side of your wonder boy? After all, he's a human being, though you may not think so. But what's wrong? What's his weakness? Where's he vulnerable? He's what, forty, you pay him somewhere around fifty grand, I suppose — and he's not married, is he?"

"No, he isn't," Salt said.

"Why not? Good-looking, athletic, interesting, sociable — though I did see him reading alone in the University Club the other night. If you say to me, he's too damned selfish to get married, wants it all for himself — well, I don't know, maybe a good quality in a bank director."

"He's not selfish."

"What about women? Friends' wives? Anything of that sort?"

"Oh, no. You've got to remember his career hasn't left him much time."

"Doesn't take much time. Still, I don't press the point, though I am curious. Getting back to this reading at the University Club — our friend isn't by any chance a 'deep thinker,' is he?"

"Oh, certainly not — that is, you know what I mean. Guy, let me put it this way. In a week or so I'm going up to my hunting lodge as I have for many years. I'd rather have Cleves with me than any man I know and I've felt that way since '33, and I've never taken him. Do you want to know why? Because, with all the people we've got, with all our resources and our trained organization, I've never wanted us both to be away from Allied at the same time."

When Salt got back he went into Cleves' office. "By the way, I told you I was talking to Guy Eliot the other day," he began in the tone of boyish embarrassment which he could so effectively use. "I saw him again today. You know how I feel. They will probably make old Debevoise an honorary director, and I think your name will come up and be acted on favorably. You'd like it, wouldn't you?"

He would like it tremendously, Barwick thought to himself.

"Cleves," Salt said a little huskily, "I've only got two wishes for this year — I'd like the Carew business to go through, sure, but what I want is to see you on the Founders Board and married to a nice girl."

Barwick laughed, touched by the older man's obvious emotion. "You fix the first, and I'll look into the other," he said. He knew he was being had and would have to go along on the concession. Salt was often callous, bigoted and evasive but the sum of him had a young and attractive buoyancy, and underneath unquestionably lay a deep affection for Barwick.

A few nights later, at the Malcolm Tierneys' party for Carew, Vivian Tierney had reminded Cleves that Salt's estimate of his essential qualities was by no means everyone's. "You should have heard George Salt raving about you before you came," she said. "He thinks you'll be Secretary of the Treasury in ten years, which brings me to my news. Darling, the Founders Board is all wrapped for you. There!"

"Oh, that's an idea of George's."

"Don't try to look modest. It's wrapped, waiting delivery when you get back from London. And I want to tell you what someone else said. Mal and your loathsome general counsel, Henry Dennison, were having a drink with another man at the University

Club when you passed, and Dennison said to this man: 'You know Barwick, don't you?' And this is what he said: 'George's Crown Prince? Of course I do. He's a fellow of extraordinary ability.' He said you'd go far, very far, because you'd conform to anything that would put you ahead and you had an uncanny sense for what those things were. Can you take this?"

"Yes."

"He said your next move would be to marry an enormously rich woman who'd be at the head of all the good works in New York."

"Did he know her name?"

"He said you'd take fifteen minutes out to have a child."

"Mal and Dennison agreed with all this?"

"Well, you know Mal seldom says anything. He thought it was very uncalled-for, but he said Dennison told the man — and these are his words: 'I see quite another side. Frankly, what has always worried me about George's attachment to Barwick is that I consider Barwick basically superficial. There's a streak of light-mindedness in him I've never trusted.' I hope I haven't hurt your feelings."

"Oh, by no means," Barwick said.

"Because I'm terribly fond of you, as you must know. And I keep wondering whether you are what I think you are, or what these other people think. Which are you? You needn't answer. I wish you luck in all you want, with all my heart. Oh, Mr. Carew, are you having a good time?"

It was almost twenty minutes of three. Barwick grabbed his hat and raincoat and hurried downstairs, and out to the Strand. At 120 paces to the minute he strode along, running across the traffic. He had a sudden terror of being late, of not reaching 121 Victoria Street before four o'clock. He did not remember feeling such urgency even at seventeen. Certainly not since.

It was just 3:30 when he reached Victoria Street. He slowed down and strolled along to 121. The porter was standing in the doorway looking at the rain.

"Is anyone still on the sixth floor?" Barwick asked him.

"The lydy's there. The others're all gone." Barwick started up the stairs.

The door was ajar, and he stepped in. Under the pitiless light of a shadeless bulb, Rachel was putting some things into her purse.

"Oh, it's you," she said. "I hope you haven't come for your check?"

"You know," he said, "I'm a very lighthearted fellow beneath this wet coat. I could make you laugh. I came back to ask you to dine with me tonight. I hope you will. I hope so very much."

"Don't hope too much, because I won't. Now, do you mind going, so I can put the light out?"

He walked outside and stood blocking the staircase. She locked the door. "Mr. Resnikoff has a telephone. I can give you his number and he will be able to suggest someone for you to dine with. Now, may I go downstairs, please?"

They clattered down in file. "Have you another engagement?"

"No."

"Then you refuse because you don't like me?"

"I don't like Americans. I don't like lords of the world of any nation. I don't like people who have whims and write checks for $1000. I don't like businessmen. Please go on down."

"I need to rest," he said. "I walked miles this afternoon. Are you tired?"

"Very."

"Wouldn't you like me to carry you down?" She began to laugh. "You see," he said, "I told you."

"You only make me laugh because you're so pathetic. You haven't the least idea of what to say. Now, go along and don't look so sad. I hate having to console everyone."

"Oh, I am very cheery about it. I was thinking what we'd have to eat. I thought of oysters and pheasant."

"How dull."

"We're coming in for a landing. At what time would you like to dine?"

"If I said yes, where would it be?"

He wanted to say his sitting room at the Savoy. He wanted to be alone with her, to be able to learn what she was like. "I thought

Claridge's," he said, "about eight o'clock or earlier if you can. Where shall I come for you?"

"Have I said I'm coming? Because I am. I will come to Claridge's — no, really, please let it be that way. You had to wrestle with yourself about asking me to come to your rooms, didn't you?"

"I'd thought of it."

"And you didn't think it proper? Please say you didn't think it proper while I count ten."

"I didn't think it proper," he repeated. "What were you going to do if I hadn't said it?"

"Oh, kill you, for not being as 'proper' with me as you are with everyone else."

"How do you know how I am with everyone else? Tell me."

"You're like a proper little boy, *bien levé*."

"Well then, it's settled," he said heartily as they reached the foot of the stairs. "I'll come for you at what time and where?"

"I'll come to Claridge's at seven thirty," she said, "and if you find out you don't want to come, I'll understand and that will be that. Indeed, we will both be free to change our minds."

"But I want to call for you in the rain."

"No," she said curtly, "and that will also be that. I don't want you to call for me."

"Well, I'll take you home now, and we can discuss it."

"No," she said flatly. "You will not take me home. Let me ask what you will wear tonight."

"I'll come as I am, if you like, in a clean shirt."

"You think I wouldn't have anything 'proper' to wear to Claridge's and you don't want to hurt my feelings, is that it? You can say it. You can say 'this is more trouble than it's worth and I will call Resnikoff and get someone for dinner who isn't an unreasonable fool.' "

"You're really marvelous," he said, laughing. "No call to Resnikoff. Claridge's, seven thirty."

"If you have a dinner jacket with you, I would like you to wear it and be very glossy and starchy. Now I run across the street for my bus. Good-bye."

CHAPTER 5

THE THOUGHT of going to her room in Sloane Square to be alone in that rainy day's end, trying to solve the present and the future, seemed to Rachel like going somewhere to die. It had seemed like that many recent evenings. It had seemed like that until almost four o'clock, when the ridiculous Barwick said he had a light heart under his wet coat—and all that nonsense on the stairs. She could not remember a sensible thing he had said, and yet he *looked* so sensible.

On impulse, she got out at Bond Street, just above Piccadilly, and hurried across the sidewalk into a badly lighted shop. Sheet music was in racks on the walls. A few musical instruments were on display. "Good evening, Mrs. Linka," the proprietor said. "Very quiet day."

"Good evening. I'd like to play until a quarter before six. The Bechstein, please, if no one's using it." Stripping off her gloves, she gave him five shillings and he showed her into a "studio."

She felt the need of playing something deeply emotional, but something which would also tax her musicianship to the utmost, even to the absorbing of her emotions. As she struck the first chords, the walls of the small room seemed to her to shift and fold away, as when a scene changes in a theater before the audience's eyes. She began to play Bach's E-flat minor Prelude, playing it through until she had lost and found herself again. London, the Refugee Organization, Barwick, sorrow and suffering, were washed away. She was no longer a troubled person but a pianist concerned with nothing but perfection.

IT WAS raining harder when, at slightly after quarter past seven, she stood outside the Sloane Square flat trying unsuccessfully to stop a taxicab. As she looked into the black, wet night it all seemed quite hopeless. If she had told Barwick where she lived, he would have come for her. His chauffeur would have an umbrella. There was a cab stopping! She called as the passengers got out but a man darted across the street to take it. She suddenly felt very faint and hungry and like crying. A policeman came along, his rubber cape glistening with rain. He looked at her and asked if anything was the matter.

"I can't get a taxi, and I have to be at Claridge's. Could you stop one and ask them to take me along?"

"Sorry, miss, I'm afraid it's quite impossible. Quite contrary to regulations. Best to bide at home tonight. Good evening, miss." It was almost eight and she could not keep back her tears.

Then around the corner a car came crawling with the driver looking out for house numbers. It stopped in front of her and Barwick got out.

"Hello," he said. "All ready?" The chauffeur with an umbrella came around in front of the car. Rachel picked up her skirts and ran beside him past Barwick to get in.

"Claridge's, please," he told the driver. "Well, sorry you've had to wait. It was a little complicated. Time was the limiting factor."

She leaned back, feeling very warm and cared for, while he tucked the rug around her. "I have never heard a more self-satisfied remark," she said.

"Wasn't it? You said this morning that you didn't like businessmen, but you must admit they're competent."

"I'm now to hear about American know-how, I suppose?" she asked, teasingly.

"Yes, wouldn't you like to?"

"I must admit I would. I'm stunned with gratitude and awe."

"Wait'll you see me really in action. Well, I didn't see in this storm how you'd get a taxi without ruining your clothes. But where were you? I went to 121 Victoria Street, but the porter had gone home and all was locked and barred. At that point many men would have given up. Admit?"

"Certainly."

"I almost did, but then I went into the cigarette shop next door. Tobacconists, as you call them in Western Europe, are always mixed up with Underground Movements, and are usually men of a good deal of resource. This proved to be the case. A door in the back of his shop connects with 121 to permit him to use the water tap in the back. I found myself in 121 and climbing the stairs."

"But there was no one up there. When was this?"

"Oh, about seven twenty-five. As you say, there was no one there and the door was locked. Well, it wasn't a very good door and I pushed it in. That wasn't good for the lock, so I left a pound on your desk. Then, as they say, I ransacked the place and found the traditional Black Book with many addresses. So, well, here we are."

"If I had gotten a cab and gone to Claridge's, I should have left there by now," she said.

"There you overlook the thoroughness with which Big Business in America does things. Far from leaving, you would have been given a drink and a message. Three informers, the commissionaire, the head porter and the maître d'hôtel were already in my pay. With a description of you." He took her right hand and kissed it. "Your hand is very strong," he said.

"I played for almost an hour after I left you because I was in a very bad mood and I thought it would help."

"Did it?"

"Something did. I feel like laughing for hours, but I think it's because you're *verrückt,* mad, and I love mad people."

THE CAR drew up at Claridge's and they made an impressive progress past Barwick's secret agents. As they went in for cocktails, he saw her clearly for the first time. She wore a long black-chiffon evening dress and the beauty of her face and head was of a portrait to be seen only in a special light. The sorrows in her eyes had been washed away; she looked happy and self-possessed.

As they sat down, Barwick saw Pitt-Sempill across the room discreetly pointing him out to a dinner party. Rachel saw him, too, and said, "Someone knows you. Does it make any difference to you? Were you uneasy about what I'd wear?"

"Frightfully," he said. "Is that cocktail all right?"

"Mr. Barwick," she said, drinking some of it, "you look very scrubbed, very starched and very nice. I am very glad to be with you, and your blue eyes with your dark face are attractive, which, however, is only a general observation."

Presently the maître d'hôtel bustled up to say that dinner was

served and they went into the dining room past Pitt-Sempill and his party, who stared amiably as Barwick said hello to him.

Paper-thin smoked salmon was waiting. Champagne was chilling. A pheasant was being carved. "This is treason to what I believe in," Rachel said, "but I am so hungry." She tasted the salmon and closed her eyes in bliss.

"Are you a professional pianist?"

"I wanted to be. I have given only two concerts. I'm not really very good any more."

He thought a moment as he ate, nodding vaguely as the champagne was shown him.

"You must talk," she said. "That's what I came for, mostly."

"It's harder to talk to you here. I find being with you makes me tongue-tied."

"What you hope is that I'll tell you the story of my life, isn't that so? You are saying to yourself: 'I've brought this waif here and I'd like to hear the gruesome details and it will be quite an experience.' I'm not very nice, am I?"

"It troubles me that you seem so unhappy under your beautiful exterior."

"I was unhappy all day, and I'm really not now, and I'm sorry I say horrid things to you. I would like to tell you what happened, partially because of Mrs. Tierney and more because I want some-one to know. So could I tell you and then forget it?"

"Of course. I'm honored."

"They may bring the pheasant; I'm not that unhappy. I have been in London three years. I came from Vienna. My husband was killed in the Austrian Resistance in '45. I was in a concen-tration camp. Don't ask about it, it's just for you to know. And that's all I want you to know except what happened today. The reason I was so horrid to you this morning was because of Chut-well. I thought you were going to be like him about our organiza-tion. You see, he and people like him have made it into an 'Enter-tainment Bureau.' It is quite degrading to think what has hap-pened and I have done everything I could to stop it. Perhaps the most terrible part is, as Resnikoff proved to me today, that I am quite wrong. If it were not for these fees, we should have dis-appeared long ago. Most of the patrons are rich and many have made special gifts. Only through them have we been able to carry on our relief on the Continent and bring people to West Germany or here. So you see, I have not been very practical about it. That is why I resigned this afternoon when Resnikoff asked me to." She busied herself with the pheasant without looking at him.

He felt a deep concern for her, an alien, alone, jobless. "What will you do?"

"You needn't look so despondent. Now that I've told you, I feel better. There is something else I can do. Perhaps I'll tell you sometime."

"Tell me now."

"No," she said firmly, but smiled at him. "You Americans think you have all the know-how. We have some in Europe, too. Now I am in a mood for one of your absurd jokes and something in my glass."

She wanted very much to ask him if he was married. What difference did it make? Well, it made this difference. She could not enjoy herself so much if dinner were to be followed by looking at family snapshots. "That's Junior and that's our girl, little Nancy, named for her mother."

Then she saw the dessert. "Oh, how lovely! I'm sure to gain at least a half pound tonight, which will be very nice for me, with winter coming on. I am sorry for all the nasty things I've said to you."

When they had gone into the coffee room he told her that he would probably not be in London much more than the next week. He hoped it would elicit a response, but she merely nodded, sipped her coffee and declined a liqueur. He asked her if she would like to go somewhere to dance, and she said no, politely, that she was very tired.

"What will you do tomorrow?" he asked.

"Well, I shall hope to sleep very late and do some laundry and I have an engagement with some friends after that. Would it displease you if I asked to go home now? And thanked you deeply for having me here?"

"It wouldn't displease me because you do seem very tired and I realize what a strain the day has been. I'm sorry, though." He put her evening wrap around her, and felt an absurd tug at his heart.

"About tomorrow," he said, as they got into the car, "can we have tea and supper somewhere?"

"No, I said I had an engagement."

"Dinner Monday?"

"Why do you want to have dinner Monday? You'll be busy dispensing know-how all day."

"Please don't be so difficult. I must see you."

"Don't have a paroxysm. Yes, all right."

"That's better."

"I only said yes because I was afraid you'd strike me," she said.

"I'll call for you at seven thirty."

The car stopped at her address and Barwick told the chauffeur not to wait, that he wanted to walk. The car went quickly off.

"That's quite wrong of you, you know, because I'm not going to ask you to come in."

"I know it," he said. "I just feel like walking."

"Dinner couldn't have been nicer, you couldn't, the evening couldn't. I am most grateful. Good night," she said, giving him her hand.

"Monday, now," he said firmly and turned away quickly toward Pimlico Road.

"Mr. Barwick," she called after him, and he came quickly back.

"Please don't make trouble for your colleagues and Mr. Chutwell on my account. The blame isn't wholly theirs. I don't know whose it is. It was silly to call you back to say this—but you're so nicely mad I was afraid you might send them back to America tomorrow."

"You are so sweet. I'll spare them," he said, taking her hand.

"There's one you could send back if he belonged to you, and in a ship full of holes," she said, leaning against the open door.

"An American?"

"Of course an American, *and* a businessman, *and* rich. He has been the most intolerable of them all."

"Who was this?"

"His name was Rutkin."

"Stanley Rutkin," he blurted out in spite of himself.

"Yes, then you do know him? He's one of you!"

"He's not one of us, though I know him."

She pulled her hand angrily away. "Go to see him. He's at the Grosvenor. Compare your experiences." The door slammed and he heard her running upstairs.

It was a great piece of luck to learn that Rutkin, head of Metal Alloys, was his competitor. It was typical Barwick luck, the break that favors the fortunate man, Salt would say. He himself would know better, now, how to handle Carew. All very fine, all good business, he thought bitterly. That was what he was in London for, business, not pleasure. He turned, hands dug in his coat pockets, and started for the Savoy.

CHAPTER 6

THE FRAME of mind in which Barwick awoke Sunday morning, if not that of love, had a suspicious and excited exaltation about it. His thought was instantly of Rachel, her slim figure, her wonderful eyes and mouth, her decorum, her insight, her bitterness about the world. Saying nothing mighty or profound, she had yet given the impression of having built up, out of suffering, an independence, an inner integrity, beyond any price. The very intensity of her reaction to his knowing Rutkin was part of it. He realized he must dissociate himself in her mind from Rutkin, not only as a man but as a business rival. He must be very careful not to imply that what she had said gave him a business advantage.

When he had dressed and eaten breakfast, he sat down to write a note.

Dear Mrs. Linka,

I am very grateful to you for the great pleasure your company gave me and hope you are not too tired today.

May I say this about Mr. Rutkin? I know him, as I know several hundred men in business, but, as it happens, I have never been alone with him in my life or seen him except at meetings of the metal industry.

And may I also say I can hardly wait for Monday night?

Sincerely yours,

Cleves Barwick

He rang for a page and told him to have the note delivered at noon. Then he went down the hall to Struthers' door and rapped noisily. Everett, in a bathrobe and pajamas, opened it.

"Walter's not well," he said. "A stomach upset of some sort."

"You look rather frightful yourself," said Barwick, gratified that they were suffering for their gay evening. "I thought you wanted to go sight-seeing." He puffed his pipe.

Everett coughed. Struthers appeared from the bathroom in his pajamas. Barwick had never seen him without his spectacles, never seen him with his hair mussed, or without his "neat business suit" and collar and tie. Shuddering, he made for the bed and pulled the comforter over himself. "Very sorry, I must somehow have had too much last night. You saw my preliminary flow-of-work chart, didn't you?" he asked feebly, closing his eyes.

It was impossible for Barwick to continue his uncharitable attitude toward the poor wretches. "Well," he said, "I'll leave you. I hope you feel better. It passes in time, you know."

"I don't feel very good," Everett said, "but I wouldn't have missed it. It's done something to me. I had no idea women could be that way, such refinement and — oh, I don't know — nothing vulgar."

"I really didn't drink much," Struthers said.

"Oh, that's all right," Barwick said as he left. "You may be interested to know that Stanley Rutkin's in London."

Carew greeted him cheerily on Monday morning and asked at once if he had got what he wanted on the Refugees.

"Oh, yes, thanks. I dropped in and had a talk with them."

"Good. Well, I hope we can be done with the Civil Servants today. I've asked Pitt-Sempill to come along with us to the Treasury people if that's all right with you."

Barwick said it was. It must indicate that Rutkin was not making progress for Pitt-Sempill to leave him.

Late that afternoon the Treasury notified them that, with respect to exchange regulations, there was no objection to either the proposed licensing agreement or the West African concession. Though expecting it, Carew, Pitt-Sempill and Barwick listened with relief at being decontrolled to trade and negotiate on their own as businessmen. But for the first time in his life Barwick did not feel great ardor for battle. In spite of Rutkin, he was still worried about the last-minute ultimatum on the concession, perhaps because ordinarily it was the sort of thing Rutkin would do. He could see Carew, with his appealing manners, saying, "One must feel we could have been told of this originally." He would feel the same way himself, though in such situations in the past he had said imperturbably, "Well, there it is and it's our final word."

What disturbed him, of course, was that it involved Rachel Linka. Every other woman in his life accepted without question the business practices he represented. But he could hear this one's biting, destructive comment, based on absurd concepts: "It must have given you great satisfaction, because you were the stronger and richer, to humiliate these people. Can you wonder that I don't care to have dinner with you?" Well, madness certainly lay at the end of that line of thinking. That, indeed, was having your head on the wrong way. But he could not find a better reason for the distaste with which he looked forward to the next day.

As they left the office, Carew asked, "Shall we be able to go ahead among ourselves in the morning? I don't want to push you."

"Oh, certainly."

"We'll have a revision of our machinery estimates by then," Pitt-Sempill said. "There was a very helpful telegram from your people with revised prices."

"I'm glad of that," Barwick said.

"Assuming that we meet no obstacles we haven't foreseen, Lord Dunstanley is rather anxious to give a very small dinner for you Friday night. He's rounded up some magnates and he hoped that you might speak to them," Carew said. "If you'd like to think about it, tomorrow or Wednesday's plenty of time."

They appeared to wait casually for his answer. While it was in accord with normal business hospitality, he knew it was also a trial balloon. If he said yes quickly, they would understand there were no major obstacles ahead. He could hardly let them assemble a dozen busy men and then propose conditions they themselves would not accept and thereby turn the dinner into a fiasco. On their side it must mean they were through with Rutkin.

He said, "It's very kind of Lord Dunstanley. If it would be all right to let you know tomorrow, may we leave it that way?"

They said of course and when, shortly afterward, they had dropped him at the Savoy and were alone, Pitt-Sempill said, "Well, I judge we're in the clear."

"I'm not quite so sure," Carew said. "I rather judged he had a considerable reservation. I think he would have accepted at once, if he had felt free to."

"Oh, I don't think so," Pitt-Sempill replied. "More likely he had made an engagement for Friday. I saw him dining at Claridge's Saturday night with an extraordinary-looking woman."

"Really?"

"Nothing out of the way, a lady. Well, that's by the bye."

"I have been uneasy since I was in New York," Carew said, "about the concession title. Yet I made our position clear and they appeared to accept it. Too easily, I thought at the time. But surely they would not have come this distance and spent the time and money, and gone this far, if they had had a reservation."

"It doesn't seem so," Pitt-Sempill said. "Oh, I think it's all right. And, of course, there's always our other friend."

Carew sighed deeply.

At seven fifteen Barwick was driven to Sloane Square. His manner was matter-of-fact in spite of his inner excitement. That was new and strange and it troubled him. He wasn't in love, he told himself. He was just going to have dinner with a new and unusual person.

"Here we are, sir," the chauffeur said, whisking out of his seat. "Better weather than we had last time."

Curtains were drawn at all the windows, with slants of light shining through here and there. He struck a match in the vestibule, found Rachel's bell, rang and waited what seemed many minutes, ringing twice again, but there was no answer. Well, she might be playing the piano in Bond Street and have lost herself in the music. No cause to worry.

Then through the clear edge of the frosted glass he saw a young woman coming downstairs. How characteristic of her not to answer the bell. She would say, "Oh, I hoped you'd be gone," and, instead of being annoyed, he would think it very amusing.

He stepped back and the young woman opened the door. She was not Rachel, and she gave a gasp of alarm and hurried past him. He caught the door before it closed and went upstairs, looking at the cards on all the doors until he found Rachel's on the fourth floor back. He knocked and the silence said there was no one there and he knew that no one had intended to be there.

The door could easily be forced and he felt a consuming desire to see her room and her things. Only by the exercise of great self-control could he go back down the stairs. The terrible evocations of masculine doubt and jealousy arose before him. He saw her with another man in some dreadful place, or herself waiting in despair for such a man. But all this was madness. How could it possibly matter if a bitter-tongued stranger, unknown to him 60 hours before, stood him up? "You're a grown man. What's one woman you meet on a trip abroad?" anyone would say.

He waited inside the door, watching the driver standing by the car. At eight o'clock he pocketed his pride and went out to him. "I'd like you to go back to the Savoy and see if there's a note or a message and bring it here," he told the man, who said, "Right, sir," and drove off.

It was almost a quarter of nine before he returned. "There was nothing at all, sir," he said. Barwick could not think of a moment in his life when a disappointment had so affected him.

He ate a grim dinner back at the Savoy. Then he took the books about the composers off the shelf and put them away in a wall cupboard.

At 7:30 in the morning a page woke him to deliver a cable. It was from Salt.

> RUTKIN IS IN LONDON. NONETHELESS DO NOT RECEDE ON OUR CONDITION OR BRING UP UNTIL END. DON'T FEEL TOO DISAPPOINTED IF IT DOES NOT COME OFF. REGARDS AND GOOD WISHES.

As soon as he was dressed he sat down to write a note, and never had his thoughts seemed so thin.

> Dear Mrs. Linka,
>
> I cannot believe there was a misunderstanding about our meeting last night. While I do not want to be a nuisance, I must see you. You must understand that. Will you please give the messenger a reply?

That is the most ineffective letter I have ever read, he said to himself, and signed it *Cleves Barwick* without other closing. He instructed a page to deliver it and wait for a reply. "If I have already left," he said, "put it in a hotel envelope, address it to me and send it to Dunstanley House."

When he left at a quarter before ten, the messenger had not returned from Sloane Square.

It was a sullen, lowering day, with sky and river swollen with rain. In Carew's room the wall lamps were lighted and there was a large vase of russet chrysanthemums, almost as bright as the electric heater, glowing in one corner. "I shall leave it to you to demand tea, coffee, sherry or whisky before you're chilled to the bone," Carew said with a smile. "I suppose it's a pleasant seventy in Rockefeller Center today."

"It's almost certainly not so raw outside," Barwick replied, "but it's very cheery in here. I shall be sorry to leave London. Let me say first what can be no secret to you. Everything that my working party and I have seen here makes us anxious to go ahead at once. We have told New York so most emphatically. I hope we can agree on all details today and at least initial a letter of intention by tonight."

"This is most gratifying," Carew said.

"To review, we are to form a company with five hundred thousand dollars capital to which you will convey the exclusive license. It will license our production subsidiaries and yours at a ten-percent royalty. It may grant sublicenses in the judgment of the board. The right is global. You will nominate and we will employ two of your engineers and two of your accountants at their present salaries plus American living allowances. Movement of them, their families and effects at the new company's expense. Allied will nominate a president and you a vice-president. Allied will provide office space at its present cost."

Carew nodded.

"Now I must come to the point Mr. Salt raised at our first meeting. That is, the primary division of the stock, the shares, in the new company."

"It was to be fifty-fifty," Carew replied.

"I recall your saying that, but we pointed out it was practically a rule with us to have fifty-two percent in any new venture. We think it is common practice and assume it's acceptable."

"I do recall Mr. Salt made some such observation," Carew said, "but took it that a process such as we were offering would be an exception to any rule. Surely we are entitled to an equal partnership. We came directly to you. We saw no one else at the time. I'm afraid it would not go down very well with our people."

Barwick replied: "Whenever the question of absolute control is left open to any doubt, you're simply inviting trouble. You must have had the experience. Decisions which must be taken cannot be taken. After all, we're not going to do anything to the prejudice of a powerful minority. The income difference is trivial."

"On that basis why shouldn't we have the control, since our process is the root of the matter and presumably, with all respect, we know more about it than you do?"

"You, yourselves, have chosen New York as the head office for the process. You have asked us to put up the money and in effect manage the enterprise. Now, surely, nobody in New York's going to do that without control any more than you would in their position. Besides, you'll have three directors to our four. Certainly anyone in his right mind exercising the deciding vote is going to think a long time before he overrides a strong protest from your people. But, as you know, it seldom comes to that. We're not going to have battles."

Carew got up to look out the window. He had, of course, said as much for the record as he needed to. What troubled him was what would follow. Would his hand be strengthened then by a longer contest on this point?

"What about a British chairman?" he asked.

"I think Mr. Salt's seniority, if nothing else, entitles him to that. However, he's sixty-six and on his retirement I should hope you would succeed him."

"That's very good of you," Carew said. "Well, I don't want to seem to haggle about this. Can we say fifty-one percent to you, forty-nine to us, directors four to three?"

"Yes," Barwick said, after the few seconds in which he was

supposed to weigh it. They both felt better after the practice round and, as it moved to finality, Barwick felt himself yielding to the desire to press for profit and advantage.

"Am I correct — " he started to say, when there was a knock on the door and Carew's secretary came in with a letter for Barwick. It was in a Savoy envelope addressed in a man's hand. Inside he could feel a smaller envelope. He put it in his pocket, unwilling to trifle with the issues before him.

" — that we have only West Africa to consider?" he concluded.

"Yes," said Carew. "So I see it. We are certainly prepared to go ahead, and I take it West Africa is merely a matter of personnel and machinery. In fact," he continued, pointing to documents bound with scarlet tape, "the letter of intent is there, ready for our initialing." He smiled. "I wasn't going to have it said that we were not as quick as our American friends."

Well, Barwick thought to himself with some shame, I am about to carry out my assignment. "I must tell you first that I have had a cable today which raises the vital question of the title to the concession."

He could see the blood mount in Carew's thin face and the effort he was making to control himself. "I can't conceive of there being any question about that. Surely it was clear from the start and in its case no demur was made."

"There was always a question in our minds, but we did not feel it necessary to bring up every objection at our first meeting," Barwick said, rubbing out his cigarette.

"But we've had a number of meetings here, and you've suggested nothing of the sort. My dear Barwick, this rather shakes me. What, exactly, are you asking?" There was a note of anger in Carew's voice.

"That the title run free and clear to Allied, which, we realize, entails your supporting it with the government or elsewhere."

"You mean to say the title to Allied — not even to the new company, though even to that we should never agree? No, Mr. Barwick, I don't accept it even for consideration. After all, we're not mendicants, nor fools, nor knaves. I'm sorry, but I take this very badly."

"I have been directed to say this is an indispensable proviso and to act accordingly."

"But how can you? Are we to have nothing? Is our pride, our experience of years around the world, to be thrown out the window? We have asked for a secured loan for the concession. A matter of ordinary business — " Carew was on his feet.

"We have no thought of humiliating anyone, but we shall have to find the money, the machinery, the crews, and take all the risk of its going wrong. A drop in price of the raw materials involved would be a grave matter. It would be a most serious one for you if you were indebted to us at the time."

"I simply cannot understand so important an issue being left to this moment. Can you imagine my position, or our firm's position? We should be the laughingstock of the City. Do you mind my asking whether Mr. Everett and Mr. Struthers know this?"

"I give you my word no one in London except you and me knows it, nor will anyone learn it from me. I'm very sorry that you feel as you do."

"Good heavens, how would you expect me to feel?" Then Carew regained control of himself and went on more quietly. "Look here, there must be some way around this. . . ."

"I'm afraid that, without the title, anything else would be useless," Barwick said.

Carew thought a moment. Then he turned to Barwick with a great deal of dignity. "That is your last word?"

"There never has to be a last word. Whatever you and I may feel, we both have to tell our people. I'll talk to Mr. Salt this afternoon but I am positive he will not recede."

"Well, will you ask him to?"

Barwick shook his head. "No, I agree with him."

There was a long pause until Carew said, "I shan't be able to see Lord Dunstanley until late in the day but, as with you, he will neither agree nor will I ask him to. I'm afraid it's gone badly."

"I'll be at the Savoy, or they'll know where I am," Barwick said, getting up. Carew opened the door for him and told his secretary to be sure the car for Mr. Barwick was ready. "Ask Mr. Pitt-Sempill to be good enough to see me at once."

As soon as the car door closed, Barwick tore open the long envelope, and then the small one inside it. The note, in tall, thin, graceful script, read:

> Dear Mr. Barwick,
>
> I am sorry you were put to so much trouble on my account. I did not want to see you and do not want to now, so please do not try. I hope your stay in London will be pleasant.
>
> *Rachel Linka*

What a day, he thought, and ahead nothing but a talk with Salt. He placed the transatlantic call for two o'clock London time, and made a digest of what he would say. On balance, severe as Salt's decision might be, the new point he himself had made that morning — that the debt would be a grievous one if world prices receded — made it evident that Allied should not recede. What were Carew and his people likely to decide? Rutkin, if he had been dangling and was now turned to, would certainly ask on what point the negotiations with Allied had broken down. But would he say: "Well, if Allied with their resources feel that way, we certainly do." Probably not.

It was after three before he talked to Salt, who began: "Well, all tied up?"

"It's not tied up. On the face of it, it's all off because of the concession."

"I find that sort of attitude very disappointing," Salt said. "Did you tell them so?"

"Look, don't ask me questions like that. If you don't want to leave what I say to me — "

"Good Lord, Cleves, what's gotten into you? Aren't you well? I ask you a simple question. Are you there?"

"Yes, I am here. I wish I weren't. I did my best and I think I was a fool not to insist we have this out to start with."

"Listen, they're just going through the motions. It'll be all right. You got my cable about Rutkin. If he wants it on their basis let him have it. Want me to cable Carew I'm disappointed?"

"Certainly not, and I don't intend Rutkin shall have it."

"All right, all right, just an idea. Cleves, why don't you go out and relax tonight? You've been under a lot of strain. You don't sound like yourself. Anything wrong?"

"No. I imagine I'll hear from them sometime and I think I'll wait it out, but I want it understood that I either have some discretion or I come home," he said truculently.

"Cleves, of course you've got discretion. Do as you please. Give them the earth but stop talking as though you and I were at odds. You're taking all this in a way I've never known you to. Now, call me up tomorrow. I'll be worried about you. Let me know how I can help."

Barwick banged up the telephone, annoyed with himself at having talked like a prima donna with no excuse for it. The fact was that his irritability came from the cutoff by a woman in Sloane Square and he was ashamed of it. Nonetheless, his strong athletic body felt exhausted. And the fact that he had no desire, except to see someone who did not want to see him, was humbling.

He decided to write to her. The thing he must not do was to protest, plead or lament. He must not be woeful. So he wrote:

> My dear Mrs. Linka,
>
> It seems quite unnecessary to have such strong views, particularly as I have gone to great trouble to prepare an agenda of excellent jokes for our next meeting. Therefore I shall be at your door, fourth floor back, at seven o'clock tomorrow evening. I will not force the door but, if you are not there, or refuse to open it, grave reprisals will be taken, the nature of which is under constant study.
>
> With great respect,
>
> *Cleves Barwick*
>
> If you would like me to bring anything, such as a grand piano, please let me know.

He thought a moment and reached for the telephone. "Please get me Maggs Brothers in Grosvenor Square," he said and waited impatiently until a gentle voice answered. "This is Mr. Cleves Barwick," he said. "I am an American staying at the Savoy."

There was no comment and he went on. "As a matter of urgency I should like to get an autographed letter or an original score or part of one by Beethoven, Mozart, Chopin or Schumann. I will pay in dollars. I only mention dollars to facilitate matters."

"Quite; we're always glad of dollars. I'm not sure we have what you want. Certainly not Beethoven or Mozart. However, there is a letter of Chopin's here. Does the text matter?"

"No, not at all."

"I think it's eighty-five pounds, something of the sort."

"Good. May I give you a personal check on my New York bank, or would you like some references?" Barwick asked.

"No, no, your check will be quite satisfactory. Just post it along."

"Then you will get a messenger and send it at once?"

"It's already being taken from its case. Thank you very much, Mr. Barwick."

WHEN it came, Barwick immediately sent it off with the note to Rachel. He did not see how she could fail to laugh and so long as that was the case, all was not lost.

After a solitary dinner in the Grille downstairs there was a telephone call for him. "Carew here," a subdued voice said. "Would it be convenient, Mr. Barwick, for you to be at Lord Dunstanley's house in Eaton Square at eleven in the morning?"

"Yes, entirely."

"The car will fetch you. Thank you very much. Good night."

"Good night, Carew."

CHAPTER 7

BARWICK had met Lord Dunstanley the day of his arrival. He was a great, gaunt, beak-nosed Englishman about Salt's age, topping Barwick by several inches. It was impossible not to like him personally at once, as indeed Barwick did, although he surmised that as a businessman the Chairman was out-of-date. He was almost certainly more fun to be with than the retired admirals and generals some American corporations put into high sinecures.

All Dunstanley's active years had been a preparation for meetings such as the one with Barwick. He had listened to Carew's account of the impasse with not a great deal of surprise. It happened at some point in all large affairs. When Carew finished, he had said quietly, "Well, I had better have a word with Barwick, myself." That was the accepted thing: "the elder statesman," the man of great prestige and long experience of men and affairs, came in and smoothed out the troubles. He could not imagine it would not happen in this case.

"I think we must try it first, of course," Carew had said, "but I doubt very much that it will avail us anything."

"Come, come, these fellows aren't monsters. You've made it clear you think very highly of Barwick, as indeed do I, from what I've seen of him. The Americans are very much like the French. They ask for a great deal more than they expect to get. They like to talk and talk."

"Barwick is not what they call 'a great talker.' I am in no doubt that he has said their last word and that we can take it or leave it. I grant you what has shattered me is their leaving it to this moment. I won't describe it as bad faith, but I should hate to have done it. You realize, of course, that, if Barwick doesn't yield, we are left with Rutkin, who does agree?"

"There must be other people than Rutkin in America."

"There are, but our option on the concession is running out," Carew replied. "Rutkin's not the sort of American I like. Barwick and even Salt are more our sort. But Rutkin may be the coming dominant type. He has acquiesced in everything and there's no doubt about his money. He may feel that the prestige of getting the process is worth so much to him that he doesn't have to haggle. He has apparently been perfectly candid with us, in contrast to Barwick."

"I gather he is not a gentleman," Dunstanley said.

"I'm afraid that's of small consequence," Carew replied. "It is of some consequence that Chutwell considers Everett, Barwick's engineer, indispensable."

"Well, I suppose if worse comes to worst, Everett might be persuaded to join Rutkin."

"I had thought of that and Rutkin brought it up. The Americans treat such things lightly. They blithely say, 'We'll double your salary,' and there it is."

DUNSTANLEY met Barwick at the head of the stairs and said, "Very good of you to come along, Barwick. I had the feeling that away by ourselves we could settle our little difficulties. Now, would you be comfortable in that chair? Cigarettes beside you, or can I offer you a cigar?"

Barwick seated himself and took a cigarette.

"Now tell me," Dunstanley went on, "what is the bee Carew has in his bonnet?"

"Well, sir, it was my unpleasant duty yesterday to tell him our people felt they could not go ahead without sole title to the concession. I wish very much, in view of Carew's feelings, that I did not have to say it or that I brought different word to you today."

"I take it, then, there is no change?" Dunstanley asked. Barwick shook his head and his lordship looked at the toes of his own beautifully polished shoes.

"In taking this position, has it been fully realized that it is more than a matter of pounds, shillings and pence with us? That portion of Africa has been under the Crown for over ninety years. British brains, blood and, I may add, a good deal of humanity and justice, have been expended there. This touches us very deeply. Our flag has come down in many parts of the world in my lifetime, but the reason that is so is because we have ceaselessly scattered abroad the ideas of independence and human freedom. Now must you men, our friends, take this away from us, also? I must ask you to think of that."

"We have thought about it from every angle," Barwick said regretfully. "But the issue is not political nor national. It is the fact that we have to find and risk a very large sum of money and will not do so except as our own venture."

"We have been brought very low, it appears," Dunstanley said wearily, sitting down in a deep chair with his long horseman's legs stretched out. It struck him that this was something new. For the first time in his life he felt the threads slipping away from him. Not by an eyelash had this man, his son's age, yielded anything. He felt a sudden and intense distaste for the whole business. Why should he have to decide between a man like Rutkin, who was not a gentleman, and one like Barwick, who was but was also a Shylock?

"What should be done?" he asked hopelessly. "Without any derogation of your position, should I see Mr. Salt? Surely you cannot want us to turn elsewhere. Or is that what you leave us to do?"

"I have every hope it will not be necessary," Barwick said.

"It would not go begging," Dunstanley said. "But why, over this one point, should it be necessary?" As he said it he looked very old, very tired.

The mantel clock struck the half hour and he was on his feet like a boxer. "I wonder if you will excuse me," he said. "Our Choral Society rehearses at twelve fifteen and I shall just have time to get there." With all the excitement of an undergraduate going to his first football practice, he bustled Barwick out to the hall and down the stairs, humming in a fine baritone "Thanks Be to God, He Laveth the Thirsty Land." Barwick remembered it from his father's church.

"I dare say we'll manage this somehow and I shall be seeing you very shortly," his lordship said as they got in their cars.

Barwick wished he knew whether Carew had simply let Dunstanley play his part or whether, faced with finality, he was moving in another direction. It was all very well to issue this ultimatum. If it was refused, Allied had lost something they would always regret. In short, they must not lose. What seemed to Barwick the thing to do was to get Carew to New York, away from London, with its mighty past. But sound though the idea was, he was dismayed to think of leaving London and Sloane Square.

Carew was not at his office and Barwick left a note.

My dear Carew,

I have talked to Lord Dunstanley and, while neither of us was able to change his position, the meeting was not without value. I should like to suggest that we leave everything as it stands for twenty-four hours, and talk again tomorrow afternoon. If this is satisfactory perhaps your secretary will leave word at the Savoy.

Yours sincerely,

Cleves Barwick

About three o'clock the secretary telephoned to say Mr. Carew was glad of the suggestion and quite agreed. Thereupon Barwick placed a call for Salt for ten thirty New York time, leaving him with an empty hour ahead. It was interrupted halfway through by the arrival of Everett and Struthers, who were "reporting in" from the works at Dagenham with Chutwell. Even Struthers was enthusiastic about what the "technical boys" had shown him.

Now they were off to a lecture at the Institution of Electrical Engineers. "I'll join you after one word with Mr. Barwick," Chutwell said, as the Americans went to their rooms to leave their things. "You get what you wanted on that Refugee crowd, all right?" he asked Cleves.

"Oh, yes, thank you."

"Well, what you may not know and may want to know is that the woman there—you remember I told you about her?"

"Yes," Barwick said.

"The fact is that she's been found redundant, as they used to say after the war, and she's out. It will be a different place and there'll be much less call on the States for aid. From what my friends have told me, this woman's a sham and a fraud."

Barwick stared at him, marking the spot where he would like to begin taking him apart. What a terrible guy you are, he thought.

"Do you know, Chutwell," he said, "I don't believe I'd say that sort of thing, if I were you."

"Oh, I'm not one to bandy a woman's name. No offense intended, just thought you ought to know."

"I see. Well, now I know, so run along to your lecture and be damned quick about it." The last six words he said to himself.

He talked to Salt a few moments later, telling him the situation and that he saw no indication that their friends would change their position.

"Why not tell them they have forty-eight hours to accept?"

asked Henry Dennison, talking on an extension in Salt's office.

"Because I don't consider that business," Barwick replied. He could hear Salt telling Dennison he agreed with Cleves. "My idea is to get our friend and his chief engineer to come back to New York with me — "

"I like that, Cleves," Salt said. "You feeling better today?"

"Oh, fine. If I can get him to New York, he would not have to concede in front of all his people. Of course, I don't know that he'll come."

"What have you learned about Rutkin?" Dennison asked.

"Only that he's here. By inference I know our friend saw him after we broke off. If they had gotten very far, I would not have been asked to see their chairman this morning."

"All right, Cleves. You go ahead on your own lines. That all right with you, Henry?" he concluded to Dennison.

"Frankly, I don't know," Dennison said in his precise voice. "I had expected Cleves would put us more in the picture."

"Oh, he can't do that," Salt said. "This costs money. We've run up a terrific bill, as it is. I don't like this calling up people all over the world on a straight business matter. Then, Cleves, we will see you shortly. Anything you need?"

"No, thanks. G'bye," Barwick said. He felt much relieved. He was sure, in the end, they would get the process and, as it stood, he was free for the moment for his own business in Sloane Square.

WHEN later he went out to his car, he noticed a man standing by the Inquiries Desk, and he had the impression the chief page was telling the man who he was. As he got out at Rachel's address, he noticed a taxi which had been behind them slow down and then drive off. But he thought nothing of it.

He went into the vestibule, rang a basement bell at random and, when the door buzzed open, he climbed the stairs and knocked on Rachel's door. There was silence. Then he knocked again and the voice he wanted to hear asked, "Mr. Barwick?"

"Yes."

"Please go away. I don't care to see you. I am deeply offended at your sending me that Chopin letter."

"Why, don't you like to read other people's letters?"

"Mr. Barwick, this does not make me laugh."

"Will you come out to a quiet dinner in Shepherd's Bush?"

"Of course not."

"May I come in and have some of your dinner?"

"You may not come in. I will not come out."

"Do you know, that's exactly the way I talk to people. We're very much alike." She made no answer, waiting to see what he would say. After a time his silence began to worry her. "Are you still there?" she asked.

"Oh, yes. I'm quite happy. Doing a little plotting, long-term planning, that sort of thing. Don't worry about me. By the way, this door's very badly hung. I can see you very well, you know. Lift your chin a little. Good. My, those slacks are becoming."

He could see her get up in a fury and step out of his line of vision. *"Unverschämter Astlochgucker,"* she sputtered.

"I see you now in the mirror."

"Thank heaven, I'm dressed," she said.

"Oh, if you weren't, I shouldn't think of looking. After all, we Americans respect womanhood. You know you wouldn't have to change to go to Shepherd's Bush. Just come as you are. After all, it's only to say good-bye."

"What do you mean?" she blurted out.

"I am going back to New York."

"When?"

"Day after tomorrow, probably."

"I'm looking for the Chopin letter. Wait a moment."

"Is it Chopin or his music you don't like?"

"It's you and your intolerable use of money to have your way. I will not play games with you any longer." She unlocked and opened the door a mite, with him leaning against it. "I trust you not to try to come in," she said. "Now, good-bye. Dreadful as you are, I wish you good things, fun and games in New York. How they must miss you there! Does your wife ever get tired of games?"

"I am not and never have been married," he replied.

The relief with which she heard it made her really angry. It was intolerable to have it make such a difference to her.

"If you will please come to dinner with me," he said, "I promise to be serious. I can be."

"Oh, no, don't be. That would be awful. Your only attraction is that you're crazy. I haven't any interest in you at all except to wonder how long they'll let you go around by yourself."

"It's only a matter of time, of course. They might pick me up tomorrow. What was that you called me?"

"Shameless *Astlochgucker*. Peeping Tom."

"I see. Well, I'll wait on the stairs while you get your coat."

"Am I getting my coat? I thought I was giving you the letter, and you were leaving."

"No, that was changed."

She shook her head. "It is I who am crazy. Wait downstairs, please."

He did, in a far greater quandary than he felt about Carew. He had no clear idea of what he wanted to say to her. Looked at objectively, this could hardly be love he felt. Infatuation? Well, if so, at a flood close to love.

He let his mind range over the last 20 years. He had not married in the early 1930's because of the depression. He had not married as war broke out because it wasn't fair to come back maimed or marred. He had not married afterward because—but these statements were all nonsense. The reason why he had not married was that he had never felt as he did now. There was no scale of comparison for this breathless, illogical excitement. It was new as the morning and mysterious as the night sky.

At dinner, in spite of himself, he talked ponderously. She listened attentively with an amused look in her dark eyes. "Why are you suddenly so changed?" she asked. "It's very informative, very cultural, I must say, but don't try so hard. I quite agree that Western Civilization is menaced. So I have found it for some years. Now answer my question."

He laughed. "I suppose I am concerned about leaving London and wondering what you will do."

"Oh, you mustn't worry about that. I've decided. I am going back to the world's oldest profession. It's illegal, the police bother you, but you can easily make enough to live on, and I happen to have a flair for it."

He felt cold sweat all over him, and an actual nausea he could scarcely control. "Don't say such a thing," he said. "How can you?" He wiped his face with his handkerchief.

"Are you ill?" she asked.

"Ill? How do you suppose I feel?"

She reached out her hand and put it on his. "Dear Mr. Barwick, please. I had no idea of upsetting you at our good-bye dinner, or I wouldn't have said it. But I don't see — oh, dear God, I do see! What do you think the world's oldest profession is?"

"Must I say it?"

"No, no, no, no — it isn't that. Oh, you *are* nice. *Money-changing* is the world's oldest profession. It's just as I said: it's illegal, the police bother you, but it does serve a purpose. I feel like crying. Is it so bad for you?"

"No," he gasped. "It's all right."

"Now I *am* crying," she said.

He handed her his clean handkerchief and they sat in silence for a moment before she asked him why he had felt so overcome.

"You must realize," he said, "that even in this short time I have come to feel very deeply about you. If I seemed to make it all a jest, it was because I wanted to hear you laugh, because the sorrow in your face saddened me. Because I suppose I'm in love with you. You may not believe or understand it."

"Why shouldn't I? How do you think I have felt since the moment you came in and looked so ridiculous? Why do you suppose I've been so horrid to you? Why did it matter to me that you might be someone like Chutwell or Rutkin? But we mustn't think this is love. I am new to you, you to me. And in your case what seems to you love is many other things — curiosity, novelty, adventure, perhaps even just diversion. Few men are happy when alone."

"Does all this apply to you?"

"Yes, I suppose it does, except that I am by nature difficult, hateful and impossible, and you make me want not to be — because you're crazy," she concluded with a smile.

"I have to go back to America in a few days," he said. "Will you have dinner with me tomorrow night?"

"Yes."

"I am involved with these people all day," he said apologetically.

"I know. Suppose I would only see you during the day?"

He hesitated. It was the first question of true or false between them. It shook him to realize that he could never speak anything but the truth to her.

"I hope," he said slowly, "you will not say it but, if you do, they will have to wait."

"I won't say it. I know about business. I'm sorry I asked you. I would like for us not to say any more tonight, please — because it is all very confusing to me."

"You'd like to go?"

"Please."

As the car turned into Sloane Street, he said to her, "May I kiss you?"

"Of course," she replied, turning to him.

They said good night on the sidewalk. He was to call for her any time after six the next night.

CHAPTER 8

At breakfast the next morning he told Everett and Struthers in confidence that he was going to ask Carew to return to New York for what he expected to be the closing. Everett's cherubic face fell and Barwick said, "If he agrees, I want him to bring Chutwell along, of course." Everett looked relieved.

"Anything gone wrong?" Struthers asked.

"No, nothing unexpected, and not really wrong. I'm not being mysterious but Carew asked me to let the issue remain between him and me."

"When would we go?" Struthers asked.

"Saturday, I think."

"I think I'll go write the wife before I go to the office, if that's O.K."

Everett made no move to go and said nothing until they were

alone, when he asked: "How would it be if I stayed over and came on next week with St. George?"

"As far as I'm concerned it's all right. I'll have to ask Carew."

"Cleves, try to fix it for me, will you? I don't see how I can ever go back to Montclair. I might as well tell you, St. George introduced me to someone — her name is Berta — I don't suppose you can understand."

"Yes, I can understand," Barwick said.

"She really likes to talk about chemistry and metallurgy. You know what I'd like to do is start all over. The Carew process is new, she's new — leave everything else. Ella could have all the money. I'd even assign my pension rights to her. I don't know poetry but I remember a line somewhere that says what I feel when I think of going back. 'Shades of the prison house begin to close,' that's all I remember. Please don't say anything about this to Walter. He was along when I met this girl."

"I won't. Does Chutwell know how you feel?"

"No, it's a funny thing. I don't want even St. George to know yet. He left before we really got to talking. He doesn't know I've seen her since. What do you advise me to do?"

"I don't think anyone can advise you. I think your friends will help you do whatever seems best for all concerned. I have no objection to your staying over, if Carew agrees. We'll see what we can do." Barwick watched him go off comforted. Not even Allied was now all of life for Everett, he realized.

He decided to telephone Carew at once. "Will you come to lunch with me in my sitting room?" he asked heartily. "I have a new idea and I will appreciate your coming."

"Why yes, I'd like to," Carew said. "What time?"

"Is one thirty too late for you?"

"Suits me very well. See you then. Many thanks."

"What I want to suggest is," he told Carew, as they were finishing their chops, "that I return to New York in a day or so, but that you come over early next week, and let us see whether we can't reach a satisfactory compromise. I can't hold out any firm hopes of a change in our position, but — "

"It ought not to be beyond the wit of man to settle it. I agree with you," Carew said. "I *will* come over next week, probably with Pitt-Sempill along, prepared to do anything within reason to meet your wishes. But we shall consider that we are free to talk to anyone else we choose to in New York about it."

"I see," Barwick said. "May I ask whether talks have already begun?"

Carew pushed his plate away. "To a degree, yes."

Barwick got up to ring for the waiter. If he protested or asked for an option of, say, a week, he both weakened his position and possibly implied that Allied would yield. It was obviously best to accept with a show of confident indifference. "I think that's perfectly fair," he said to Carew.

By the time Carew left, it had been arranged that Chutwell would come over with Everett, and they had reached a new level of goodfellowship. To Barwick's relief, Dunstanley's dinner for the magnates was not referred to.

At five minutes past six he climbed the stairs again to Rachel's. *Unverschämt,* he peered at the crack in the door. It had been neatly filled with cardboard. He knocked and again there was that chilling silence, followed, though, by the sound of someone moving, and Rachel's voice asking who it was.

"Cleves," he said. "Has the day seemed like a year?"

"Yes, two, but listen, I am just in my bath. So please wait downstairs. I'll hurry all I can."

Even to his impatience, the waiting was brief. He heard her door slammed and locked and her steps running downstairs. Coat was over her arm, red toque in her hand, and she had on a gray woolen dress with big buttons down the front.

"Oh, such a rush. I am only half-dry, and so out-of-breath," she said, kissing him quickly and handing him her coat.

"Darling, you are lovely," he said as she put on the tiny scarlet hat. "If you will, we can have dinner in my sitting room. Please say you will. There's even a coal fire."

"Just for the fire, I will," she said. "Am I not being nice? What about your colleagues? Will we see them?"

"They're staying with Chutwell for the night, not that it matters."

"Well, I have myself a job of work beginning next Monday with a Greek currency speculator who got his start by outwitting vultures around Port Said. Now, how much do you disapprove?"

"Well, quite a bit, because I don't want you arrested," he said.

In the bright hall of the Savoy, he felt a pang at how frail she looked, and at the self-possession with which she waited while he took his key and two letters.

The table was laid by the fire in his sitting room, and the waiter had just brought in a small bowl of flowers.

"I'll put my things away and see my face in a good light and a good mirror for once," she said, as he told the waiter to bring cocktails. She came out in a moment smiling and let him kiss her again for an instant before she pushed him away. "Read your letters," she said, wandering around the room.

"They're from my father and my sister."

"How many of you are there?"

"That's all, except my sister's three young children."

"There were six of us. I don't know what happened to three of them. I have one brother."

"Where is he?"

"In Israel. You do understand I'm Jewish?" she asked casually.

"Of course."

The waiter came in carrying a shaker and salver with stemmed glasses and canapés.

"I'll ring when we are ready," Barwick told him. "You can eat steak, I hope?" he said to Rachel.

"I certainly hope so, too," she said, sitting in a deep chair by the fire. Barwick bent over and kissed her.

"You smell like pink clover. I noticed it at 121 the moment I spoke to you. What is it, you?"

"Must be, nothing else. Please sit down over there. No, a little farther away. Good. What day and hour exactly are you going?"

"Saturday morning."

She finished her cocktail and held her glass out to him. "I'd rather not talk about it until we are all through dinner."

They dined slowly and well, with relative calm. She elicited a good deal of autobiography from him, but gave almost none herself. When the table had been rolled away, Barwick pushed the chairs arm-to-arm before the fire. "I should like to make a brief statement," he said.

The time had come. She supposed she knew what he was going to ask. He got up and moved restlessly around the room.

"I don't know why this is so hard to tell you," he said.

"Because you're so proper, I suppose."

"I do not feel as I may appear to," he said a little helplessly. "I don't go around saying these things."

"What things? You haven't said anything."

"That whether or not you believe it, I am in love with you."

"What a pity," she said, though scarcely able to speak. "A day or so in New York and you'll be quite recovered."

He seated himself on the arm of her chair. "You're the most wonderful person I have ever seen, your beauty, everything about you, the way you talk, your music. Do you think I'm frightful?"

"No, not frightful, oh my dear one, I love you too, why did this have to be?"

He kissed her, lifting her slim body close to him. "I want to marry you," he said against her lips. "Will you marry me?"

She pushed him away gently, rose and patted his cheek lightly. "Of course not."

"You said you loved me. Why not?"

"I will try to tell you in a moment," she said. She went to lean against the mantel. "You say you love me and want to marry me and this is a great honor for any woman, of course, and particularly for a refugee whom you have known six days. If you loved and really wanted to marry me, I probably should also feel honored. But I can't feel very much so about infatuation — "

"How can you say that? You said you loved me. This isn't infatuation. This is true love, love forever."

"I am trying to explain to you how ridiculous it is. Let us suppose that I love you — that's merely an assumption of the moment — and will marry you. *That very instant* you will face the question of how you are going to explain me. To your father, your sister,

your friends in New York, Lord Dunstanley, Mr. Carew—and, worst of all, that Chutwell."

"I don't have to explain anything to anyone."

"But you will. And I would not like being explained. You would find that the person whom you are infatuated with would become hateful and impossible. Now I'm afraid if I stay any longer, we'll just laugh and be sensible about it. I am not, in another way, insensible. I shall never forget my mad American and shall always think of him with tenderness. You see that I'm right, don't you; so may I go?"

"Certainly," he amazed her by saying. "I'll get your coat."

"Thank you for being so sensible," she said sadly. "I was afraid you'd be more difficult."

He brought her coat and helped her on with it. In the taxi they were both silent, preoccupied with their thoughts. At her house he unlocked the vestibule door for her and stepped inside. "In such matters it is most important to avoid the morose," he said, putting his arm around her. "Therefore, I'll say no more, except good night. But I shall be here on the stroke of six tomorrow. Will you be here or will it be necessary to scour the city? Either way you prefer."

"You really go Saturday morning?"

"At ten."

"Then I will be here to say farewell, a long farewell." She kissed him, pressed closer an instant and then went upstairs without looking back.

Though in great stress of mind and heart, Barwick could not but give himself high marks on his conduct of the last half hour. Viewed either as warfare or business, he had been able to adhere to sound fundamentals. There had been no panic, no loss of sight of the prime objective, even though when he had first said he wished "to make a brief statement," he had not realized it would end with "marry you." What had happened? The words had come with the ease of light. As Vivian Tierney had implied, he had never felt like risking all for love, but now — with fire and flood in his heart, the memory of her mouth, and her slim frame in his arms — risk or cost concerned him less than the valleys of the moon.

PROMPTLY at six the next evening he knocked on her door. She opened it, wearing a checked apron over her dress, and stepped aside. The tiny room was lit by two shaded candles on a small table with a white cloth and a tiny bowl of flowers. Two glasses and a pint of champagne were waiting.

"I love you, love you," she said in his arms. "I love you so much I have let you in. It's my room's world *première!* You will have to sit on the couch, unless you mind very much. I have our supper — not what I've recently become accustomed to, but enough — if you would like to have it here."

They laughed and talked and kissed, looked at her little possessions, listened to recordings, supped late, and merrily washed dishes in the bathroom and then had coffee.

"I went to the Embassy," he said, "but I couldn't learn whether, if you come to New York on a visitor's visa and are married, you have to leave and come in again under a quota. But I will know all about it almost as soon as I'm in New York."

"Oh," she said, "this is something new. This isn't what we talked about last night. I thought I explained."

"Oh, I didn't pay any attention to that farfetched explanation. My mind was elsewhere – on arrangements for your living until you come over. Now, what I have done is to see a man named Hopkins I know at the Guaranty Trust, and I cut your signature off that first absurd letter of yours and he has it, and an account in your name. All you have to do is to go in and sign some stuff sometime. Here's his card."

"But this makes me absolutely furious. I told you it was out of the question and I will not be kept. You spoil everything – money, money. You think you can have your way about everything because you're rich."

He smiled cheerily and finally she began to laugh in spite of herself. "What next?" she asked.

"I don't know just the ritual about this, but would you sit down beside me?" He took a tiny leather box from his pocket and handed it to her. "It is yours. I hope you like it."

She looked at him in astonishment. "Is this a ring?" she asked slowly.

"Yes. I would like to put it on your finger myself."

Tears came to her eyes. "Something has put a spell on you. You *are* out of your mind. I can't take this. I can't face everything that would follow when you really knew me. We are worlds apart in everything that will matter later – "

"That's nonsense," he said. "You say you love me. My general competence will cope with the rest. In a week or ten days you'll be in New York."

"But, everything else aside, I don't want to go to New York. I hate America."

"Oh, when you see it, that'll all disappear. Twenty-five eating places in Rockefeller Center alone – that should impress you. Gross area of almost six million square feet, Toscanini's orchestra and ice shows in season. What more can you want?"

"I want you to treat me as a mature woman of the world."

"My dearest," he said, taking her in his arms, "I will treat you as friend, comrade, guardian, lover, all my life. I only talk this way because leaving you at all tears my heart out. Put the ring away if you don't want to look at it now. Say you love me again."

"I do."

"Good. Say that you will come to America to marry me within a matter of days."

"I cannot promise. I must think for us both, because you don't really think," she said.

"Here is my house address and telephone number, and here is the office's. Write to me at the office. Now, what sort of a passport have you got?"

"I have one issued in Vienna by the International Refugee Organization after I got out of Regensburg."

"You're an Austrian citizen?"

"Yes, but stateless when I got the passport."

"Do you know how the Austrian quota stands?"

"Oh, full for years to come."

"I see; well, that's all right. Never liked easy problems. Do nothing about the visa until you hear from me."

"You know, I'm very sure I can't get a visa and so all this has no reality anyhow. Promise to telegraph me from New York as soon as you see this differently, as you will, of course."

"Oh, sure."

He drove to the Northholt airport with Everett, Struthers and Chutwell early the next morning. As they went in to weigh their baggage, Everett held Barwick back.

"Cleves, about Ella. I don't know how she's going to take this delay. In the end, it doesn't make any difference, but I'm scared of any outbreak that might spoil my new start. I really want to stay in England—shuttle back and forth. Will you call her up for me and cable if everything's all right?"

Oh Lord, that again, Barwick thought. Yet if he didn't, who knew what she might do? "Yes, I will," he said, covering his annoyance as much as possible.

"You're not sore at me, are you, Cleves?"

"No, no," he said wearily.

Chutwell managed to have the last word. "Good-bye, sir. I take it I need not report further to you regarding 121 Victoria Street." He gave the impression that, while he knew enough to "keep his place," there was a chip very near the edge of his square shoulder.

CHAPTER 9

SALT was very glad to find Mrs. Struthers at Idlewild, Sunday morning. What a contrast she was to that dreadful Everett woman — pretty, nice manners and attentive. Saw right away what the country was coming to with this flood of immigrants flying in. The cacophony of shrill foreign voices jabbering at each other made him furious. Israeli rabbis with beards; pale, fat men from that Athens plane bundled up in mufflers and horse blankets on this fine mild morning, their wives wrapped in furs, smelling of the perfume he was sure they had slapped on instead of washing.

"Their ways are not our ways, Mrs. Struthers," he told her. "There, there they come. They both look tired." He moved around the fence to block all traffic while he greeted Barwick, shook hands with Struthers and turned him over to his wife.

"Cleves, you look tired. We get this thing settled, I want you to go off for a month."

Barwick and he got into his car. What a relief to have him back. "Now here's the schedule," he said. "I'll drop you at your apartment to have a bath, and the car'll come for you to bring you to lunch. Your father's coming, and your sister and brother-in-law. Well, how is everything? I can tell you this. Rutkin's back with his tail between his legs. Dennison's coming in about four to talk. I'm not interfering with your plans, am I?"

"No, far from it. Very nice of you to have the family up."

The drive along the parkway with the harbor waters rolling under the west wind, and the towers of New York suddenly breaking into view under the high blue sky, stirred Barwick. This was the New World indeed after the rain and chill of London. He must make Rachel feel about it as he did.

From the apartment he sent her a long cable and, before bathing, inspected the whole place. The grand piano could go in the living room by the east windows. His bedroom would be done over, made feminine and pretty — and conjugal with a double bed. That was almost all that was going to be needed. He would keep Mrs. Cody on as long as necessary, pension her off if Rachel did not like her. Money might be the moral menace Rachel thought it was, but it had great advantages.

LUNCHEON was as pleasant a family affair as could be imagined. Even Mrs. Salt had a little color in her faded cheeks, as though for once her husband had not absorbed all the oxygen in the room. When they went up to the drawing room for coffee, Barbara drew Barwick over to a window. "Cleves," she demanded, "tell Sister what's caused the change in you? You look slightly spiritualized, and that famous powerful mind seems to wander. You don't pay attention. You're not — you know — by any chance? Some English flower, all gold and ivory? I'd be so glad, so tell."

He laughed. "No, no, no English flower. Ears still full of the engines on the plane."

Len Ogilvy, his brother-in-law, came to join them. "I think you can put your mind at rest about the Founders, Cleves," he said. "It's all very neat."

"Oh, that's good," Barwick answered vaguely.

"He doesn't really care, Len. Something's happened to our brother."

They all laughed, and Barbara asked her father if he was up to walking in the park with his grandchildren.

Henry Dennison arrived after four, when the others had gone. When Barwick had filled them in on details, Dennison came at once to the point.

"What compromise is there which will satisfy both sides? In other words, what have you got in mind, Cleves?"

"Well, first we must remember that they are looking for a compromise, too, and may very well bring one. I don't see that we need to have ours all ready the moment they come in — "

"We certainly can't go in unprepared," Dennison said.

NITED STATES
CUSTOMS
ADMITTANCE

"Henry's right there, Cleves," Salt broke in.

"No, but we can wait it out a while. I think very often the perception of the moment is a lot better than a long preparation. As Carew makes his case, he's shrewd enough to see that he's being given a hearing—and very possibly he may say to himself: 'Well, I have done my best, and I can't do any more.' "

"Let me understand you, Cleves," Dennison said. "You proposed bringing them back to New York without any clear-cut idea of what was to be said?"

"Yes, I should say so," Barwick answered. "But I also made it clear that in my judgment, away from London, Carew was very likely to concede."

"Well, of course, it's not my way of doing things," Dennison said. "I'm afraid I don't place much reliance on intuitions. We may be sure Stanley Rutkin will have a new proposal worked out to the last detail. When you decided to bring them back here, I certainly supposed there was a definite plan."

"There is. They're not going to land, demand an answer and walk off if they don't get it. They're accustomed to taking time. The more they see of Rutkin, the better. They'll like him less all the time," Cleves replied confidently.

"We can't usefully say any more today, I suppose," Dennison said, "but I don't like it. When are they coming?"

"Toward the end of the week," Barwick said.

"What about having them to dinner at the Union Club," Salt said. "Henry, Guy Eliot of the Founders, you and the boys, and how many of them?"

"Three. Carew, Pitt-Sempill and Chutwell. I think it's very good. Let's do it before we talk," Barwick said.

"I feel all right about this, Henry," Salt said. "I think I'll be in a position to swing it either way." It was a phrase with which Salt often closed a meeting, and its fatuous arrogance had never annoyed Barwick more.

At Rockefeller Center in the morning, the elevator shot into the sixties like a jet, bounced on its air cushion, and Barwick stepped out to the heavily carpeted reception room of Allied Materials Corporation. He went along the corridor of private offices, stopping at the open doors to speak to various people. All were plainly glad to see him. At his own door he said "Hi" to young Mrs. Donaldson, his secretary, and skimmed his hat to her. She caught it and hung it up with a grin.

"I'll be with you in a minute," he said, going on to Salt's corner office. Neither Salt nor Miss Tibbetts had arrived but John Lamey got up to speak to him and Barwick wished he had brought him something from London. There was something terribly pathetic about his shabby gentility, his fresh but frayed shirt and collar, his patched but polished shoes. And something incongruous about seeing it in premises representing so much wealth.

Returning to his own soundproofed, carpeted office, he found his big desk as bare as when he had left except for a small pile of unopened letters. Mrs. Donaldson had no disasters to announce and no complaints of her own. She gave him a list of personal calls and those he was to return.

Left alone, he called Ella Everett in Montclair.

"Oh, I'm perfectly fine," she said. "How you been?"

"Fine."

"I got like a reprieve, didn't I? I hope he don't hurry back. I'm sort of busy now. Call me again, hear?"

Well, Barwick thought, nothing to trouble us there. He then called a lawyer friend to ask if he knew any firms specializing in immigration questions. He got a name and set out to see them. It was his nature to feel sure he always knew, given the facts, what decision to take but, as he went down in the elevator, he was not altogether sure it was right to have said nothing about Rachel to his father, his sister, or to Salt.

THE next morning at the office Mrs. Donaldson came in with an open cablegram. "They're coming," she said. It was from Carew, giving flight number and arrival time on Friday.

"Make hotel reservations for them, please. I'll meet them at the airport."

"Shall I tell Mrs. Everett?"

"Oh, I suppose so. And take this note to Mrs. Tierney:

'Dear Vivian,

'I saw your people in Victoria Street and found no reason to suppose there was anything subversive at work. At the same time there has been a change of personnel and possibly it would be best to hold off until it is clearer what they are going to do. One of the London people we have been dealing with will be here over the week-end and knows them. I'll let you know what he has to say.

'Best to Malcolm and you.' "

He had an appointment with Farragut, the lawyer whom he had asked to look into Rachel's visa, and he took the subway downtown.

"Well, I think we have good news for you," Farragut told him. "There seems to be no reason why Mrs. Linka cannot secure a visitor's visa to come here, always assuming there is no security difficulty, of which you seemed sure yesterday. That would probably allow a stay of six months, though in practice the immigration people often bring it down to three. Therefore, she ought to go with her IRO passport to the Embassy in London at once."

"And how quickly would she have it?"

"No real delay. Ninety days, I should say."

"But I can't wait ninety days. She has to be here next week. Whom should I see?"

"Depends on whom you know. But I think I'd advise not being precipitate. Too much influence can backfire. You are not, I should judge, able to say categorically that Mrs. Linka has never belonged to any organization coming under the McCarran Act —and, of course, I don't suppose we know at all about her husband."

"I told you he was killed in the Austrian Resistance."

"Well, there you are. May well have been a Red. Did you ask her?"

"No, I didn't."

"It would certainly be preferable to have the complete story of her life. Everyone she's known well, how she happened to know them — names, dates, places. *Then,* we go full steam ahead."

"Do you mean to tell me," Barwick asked angrily, "that this

country is at a point where the Government judges whether a man of my position and antecedents, commander of a fighting regiment, two Purple Hearts, is capable of selecting a wife who doesn't plan to overthrow the Government?"

"What you say is naturally in your favor, but you appear to be overlooking the crucial point, which I supposed you understood. It is simply this: An applicant for a visitor's visa must establish that he or she is coming to the United States for a temporary purpose and is able and intends, upon the conclusion of the temporary stay, either to return to the foreign country of residence or proceed to another foreign country. It then follows that if she comes here for the purpose of marriage and with the intention of remaining, she cannot do so under a visitor's visa but must await a quota-immigrant visa. I must advise you that an attempt to rush a security investigation simply invites trouble."

"Why didn't you make this clear to start with? Never mind, skip it. Would you please have your secretary phone mine? I'm catching the eleven o'clock plane to Washington. Send your bill to my office. Thank you."

On the short, swift flight he began to realize that Washington was the seat of a federal government representing all the people and not an aid society anxious to do him a favor. The important men he had known during the last administration were now gone. The impetuous trip had been made without any plan and he wondered if his head really was on the right way.

There was, of course, his classmate, Howard Carruthers, now at the Assistant Secretary career-man level in the State Department. They had been "close friends" in college but, in the 15-odd years since then, they had scarcely seen each other. It would be almost easier to go to a stranger than to Howie, but Barwick decided to try.

Carruthers was out when Barwick reached his office and he waited a restless hour for him. He entered at last with a great padlocked brief case, said, "Hi, Cleves," as though they had seen each other before lunch, and put the brief case in a safe. He was a rather short, well-built, well-dressed man, with an air of fatigued but amiable patience toward the world.

He took Barwick into his fine inner office with a not displeasing air of satisfied importance. "Well," he asked, "what trouble brings you here? Are you a distressed person?"

"Have you got time to listen to me?"

"You forget I'm a public servant. That's what we do. Try to make your story as harrowing as possible, but don't tell me it's unique. They all are."

"Howie, I'm trying to get married. The lady is an Austrian citizen living in London with an IRO passport. She's beyond words, Howie, absolutely exquisite."

"They all are, the little darlings. What's holding you up?"

"You and your laws."

"The executive branch of the Government does not make the laws. All you do is go to London and marry her and as the wife of an American citizen she acquires nonquota status and you come back."

"But I don't want to be married in a foreign country, that is — "

"Now don't let your patriotism run away with you. You can alternatively wait until Britain becomes the forty-ninth or fiftieth state. You'll be a nice old man and they'll wheel you up to the altar."

"What I meant was I can't go back to London at once, and I want to marry her this week or early next. Can you fix it?"

"Nope."

"You mean there's no alternative to going to London."

"That's right, Brother Lochinvar."

Barwick gritted his teeth. Why had he ever asked Carew to New York?

"Boy, it certainly hits you middle-aged Bennies hard, doesn't it? Tell me something more about her."

Barwick brightened up. "She's perfectly beautiful, a musician, was in a concentration camp. Her name is Mrs. Rachel Linka. Her husband was killed in the Austrian Resistance."

"Have you known her long?"

"Not very long, no."

"Now control yourself while I ask this question. Is there any possible degree of Communist affiliation, past or present?"

"To my knowledge, no."

Carruthers rubbed his nose. "And you consider you would know if there were?"

"I am positive I would."

"Could you truthfully say to me that you cannot go to London because of important business here?"

"Most decidedly," Barwick replied, and gave him a brief account of the Carew negotiations.

"There is no way she can come here unmarried freely to stay. There is a possibility that a visitor's visa could be expedited, but only on the grounds of her intention to return to England or, and this is very important, go to another foreign country. Canada is a foreign country. Now whether, if she were here, it might occur to both of you to go to Canada and get married, I have no way of knowing. I'm not a mind reader. But if I had a letter from your Chairman saying that Allied won't be able to pay any taxes this year unless you stick in New York, I might show that letter around. I could say, 'Here's an indispensable man with a war record a yard long and a romantic interest that's being frustrated by red tape. Let's give him a break and expedite a visitor's visa for his light of love.' Now remember," Carruthers cautioned, "this is all your idea. I have said nothing." He put out his hand. "Congratulations. Don't get your hopes up. Can I tell Diddy? The poor girl pines for romance."

"Sure, tell her. Here is Rachel's name and address. I never can thank you enough."

Carruthers took the slip of paper. "My boy, your government has a paternal interest in all large taxpayers."

Barwick drove to the airport through the beautiful city with its autumn leaves falling everywhere and its early lamplighting time making it a little mournful, a little nostalgic, but filling him with a sense of relief and exaltation. He decided to cable Rachel as soon as he was back in New York. Since she didn't have a telephone of her own, he would ask her to name a place and time where he might call her; and he determined to make a formal announcement of his wedding plans to Salt and his family the next day.

SALT blew into Barwick's office at ten, ruddy and breezy. "You're the very devil," he said with an affectionate pat on the shoulder. "Why didn't you tell me you were going to Washington? But it's just as well you were away." Salt paused, grinning all over. "Go ahead, ask me why."

Barwick grinned back. Salt was never more boyishly attractive than when he had a big surprise up his sleeve.

"Why?" he demanded enthusiastically.

"Oh, you'll see, my boy, you'll see. You think nothing gets done without you around. Now, Vice-Chairman, you will come to your Chairman's office at exactly ten twenty-five." He left like a happy conspirator.

At 10:25, Barwick knocked respectfully on Salt's door, opened it and said, "Vice-Chairman reporting, sir."

"All right, Vice-Chairman, come with me." He led Barwick down the aisle to a storeroom door beside which an electrician was waiting. Salt unlocked the door and opened it on utter blackness. "I'll tell you when I want the lights. You know which one first?"

"Yes, sir," the electrician said.

"Now, Cleves, you're going to see how a trained organization does things. O.K., Number One lights."

There was a click and on a large table the lights came on outside a model of a processing plant somewhere in West Africa. It was perfect to the last technical detail and even to the American flag blowing in a trade wind over the building. There was even the simulated whirr of the agitators.

"Number Two lights," Salt ordered.

On the next table lights came on to reveal the paved streets and trim bungalows of the European compound. "You see those screens? They're not copper, not for that climate. They're Monel metal. Do we know our West Africa or don't we?"

"Oh, that's a wonderful detail. Good boy."

"Go ahead, put all the lights on," Salt said. "Look at this."

Miniature bulldozers were tearing their way through a jungle to a mine site. Back of them concrete mixers and road rollers were already paving their track and 20-ton Macks were unloading men and tools. The unroofed plant itself was on the next table and they went through it in detail, Salt indicating the puppet native laborers and European technicians with his pointer.

"Cleves, don't you think this will show Carew why we must have the concession? Did they have anything like it?"

"They didn't. I think it's overwhelming. I don't know anyone else who could have applied such imagination and technical skill so quickly."

Back in Salt's office he felt very well about everything. Those models were extraordinary. They effectively disposed, by their miniature mass, of all Carew's objections which were not sentimental. And, like most fortunate men, Barwick had a secret hunch that when one thing went well, all went well.

"I told you we were keeping busy here, didn't I?" Salt said, very pleased with himself. "Now tell me what the Treasury said."

"I went down to Washington on a personal matter I'd like to tell you about," Barwick replied. "I am going to be married if the lady will have me."

"Why, Cleves, what a perfectly marvelous piece of news! Washington girl? Anyone I know? This is superb. Your father must be almost as pleased as I am. I can hardly wait to tell Guy Eliot. Now what's her name, how old is she and did her father go to Yale?" Salt demanded, beaming at him.

"I met her in London."

"An English girl; well, that's all right. Now don't make me ask questions. Begin at the beginning."

"Her name is Rachel Linka. She's a refugee from Austria living in London. Her husband was killed in the war. I am trying to get a visa for her to come here and I've got to get a letter signed by you to support it. I saw Howie Carruthers yesterday."

Salt stared at him in incredulous amazement. "You're not asking me to believe you've gone to London, met a refugee and in a week asked her to marry you?" he exclaimed. "What kind of name is Linka?"

"Jewish, I assume, like Warburg, or Seligman or Einstein."

"That's quite unnecessary. I'm not an anti-Semite."

"Well, you take an extraordinary tone about this. To use your words, 'you're not asking me to believe' you're not going to congratulate me? I'm bothered about her visa and I expect help."

Salt looked out the window, tapping his fingers on the desk. He was obviously making a great effort to say the right thing, and the intensity of the effort annoyed and then angered Barwick. Finally Salt swung back to him: "I must ask you whether you realize what you're doing. Cleves, you can't propose to marry a refugee you never heard of before. You have no idea what you may be letting yourself in for."

"George, I beg you, don't go on. Don't say something which will be irreparable between us. It's my business, and mine alone. Leave it at that," Barwick said, getting up.

"Now don't leave," Salt said, hastily lighting a cigarette. "Help me to understand what you're saying." He smiled weakly.

"Not difficult to understand. I met a beautiful woman and asked her to marry me. She's many times too good for me and my only worry is she won't have me in the end."

"I feel as though you were my own son whom I cannot permit to make this mistake. Doesn't your father feel the same way?"

"He doesn't know yet."

Salt leaped at the opening. "If you were really sure of what you're doing, you'd have been bursting with pride to tell him and your sister and me at lunch Sunday. I plead with you, Cleves, don't do some irrevocable thing that will wreck your career — "

"What are you talking about?" Barwick said in a cold fury.

"Whatever you've done, you have only to tell me and I'll stand back of you. If it's a question of settlement, just say so."

Barwick answered in a low voice. "You pleaded with me, just now. I had already begged you not to say the irreparable thing. Well, you've chosen to, and you'll take the consequences — "

"Then so will you," Salt said. In an instant he swept away the last 20 years. "No wonder you couldn't put the concession over; no wonder Carew's coming back here. I should have known by the way you talked from London that you had lost your head. Do Carew and his crowd know this?"

"No."

"If you weren't ashamed of it — "

Both men were on their feet like pugilists, eying each other. Then Barwick turned and strode out of the room.

George Salt sank down in his chair. He had a terrible desire to go down the hall and smash the model plant with a hammer. When he had begun, he had not been sure this Mrs. Linka was a common woman. Now, he had convinced himself of it. A wave of self-pity roared over him. His heart had first gone out to Cleves; he had only wanted to save him. Now there was more than him to think of. The man he had made the heir apparent had failed him. He would himself be made ridiculous before the Allied Board for his mistaken judgment of a man. They would lose the Carew process. He thought a moment. There could be no doubt that Barwick would resign. He knew him that well. Mrs. Donaldson would probably bring word in a few minutes. "You will never get over this," he said aloud to himself.

There was a knock on the door. "Mr. Barwick asked me to give you this personally, Mr. Salt," Mrs. Donaldson said.

He nodded and took the envelope addressed to him. The slip of paper inside read: "I assume it is agreed we will outwardly conduct the affairs of the Company so that the staff is not aware of the personal rupture between us. Cleves Barwick."

For one instant before he opened it, he had been sure Cleves had recovered his senses and was telling him he would give this woman up. And he had thought he would go into his office, thank him and tell him that he knew these things happened. But this cool and impudent note, not only yielding nothing, but making clear that Salt was not master of Allied, infuriated him. If this was to be a fight for power, then he'd have even Barwick's heart's blood.

CHAPTER 10

IN HIS office Barwick realized that the intensity of Salt's feelings had not surprised him. That bountiful but ungenerous man, cushioned with power, always right in his own eyes, vain, prejudiced and possessive, could not be expected to react otherwise than he had — unless the plaintiff broke down and begged. Then all would be quite different. Almost the ugliest thing was the weathercock quality which let him immediately link Rachel to the negotiations in London. Undoubtedly Salt's mind was now seized with the idea of getting him out of Allied. Salt would regard it as something strong in himself that he could sweep away 20 years of affectionate friendship to do "what was best for the Company"—drive him out—and he would have no doubt he could fire Barwick, if Barwick did not leave first. He would start by forgetting that the firing would have to be by the whole board and, when he realized it, he would tell himself that they would, of course, go along with what the Chairman wanted.

Barwick reviewed the directors mentally. Some were, of course, in Salt's pocket. Some would be as outraged as he by the marriage. But it was very probable that a majority would feel Salt was out of step with the times.

That being probable, it might well end with Barwick as chairman, particularly if Carew stayed in line. To be chairman at 40, though, was a different matter from being chairman at Salt's age. Barwick as chairman would still, for 20 years, be the chief executive officer and not, like Salt, largely shielded from the exasperations of the day. And during those 20 years, what would Rachel do? However much his sister or the wives of men he knew filled their lives with "good works" or "broad interests," none of them provided a pattern which Rachel would find satisfactory.

A warm and pleasant feeling came over him. Marriage was surely not supposed to be finding a becoming pattern for a busy man's wife, but a long adventure of discovery and excitement. If large affairs weighed on him, all the greater the challenge to make a work of art of marriage.

Struthers came in at that moment. "Can I get those Carew papers with the flow-of-work chart and the budget?" he asked. "Mr. Salt wants a complete recast."

"What for?"

"I don't know, Cleves. I thought it was something you had agreed on. I wish you'd come back in with me. I never pretended to understand the technical side."

Barwick was determined that none of the staff should learn or guess from him that Salt and he were at odds.

"Oh, you don't need me," he said with a smile. "Get the papers from Mrs. Donaldson. You know how he likes to go into things."

He dictated to Mrs. Donaldson until noon and then went up to his club and lunched by himself. He decided that he must give Salt every chance to blow off steam before Carew's arrival. The Carew process was vastly important and it rested on a delicate structure of tact and judgment. Above all he must not let himself be confused in pursuit of his own objectives.

He was becoming more and more concerned, too, that he hadn't heard from Rachel. After lunch he wrote a cable: "Please do two things at once. Go to Embassy and ask for urgent visitor's visa. Second, telephone me at my apartment any time after nine your time tonight. I love you with all my heart. I am not in the least morose about our future and if you don't come I'll do what neither Napoleon nor Hitler could do – invade the British Isles."

Outwardly cold and grim, he handed the cable to the girl clerk who read it with increasing interest. "This is 'with all my heart'?" she asked, printing above it. "And that's 'Hitler,' like that Nazi?"

"That's right," Barwick said. "Full rate, urgent, please."

SALT had gone when he got back. He looked in on Struthers. "I don't know what I'm doing this for," Struthers said, pointing to the mass of papers before him, "but he wants it all done over and I'm to take it to his home tonight. Cleves, you haven't had a row with him, have you?"

"No, not a row. We've had a difference on something wholly unconnected with it. It will blow over. Don't worry so."

"I just don't like it," Struthers said, and shook his head. "You can't tell me any more?"

"You know, least said soonest mended." He looked at his watch and went to the Board Room to the weekly meeting with Production Department Heads. The meeting lasted until four, when he decided there was no time like the present and took a taxi to Steinway's. He asked a salesman how long it took to deliver a piano to a 12th-floor apartment after it was purchased. Less time, he was told, than it usually took the purchaser to decide that the tone was what was wanted.

"Have you, by any chance, a cutout I could put on the floor to see where it would go?"

"Certainly, sir. Let me give you these three patterns."

At his apartment he had some difficulty with his housekeeper. He had moved a sofa, a table and a chair, laid one of the paper cutouts on the floor and was visualizing Rachel at the piano when Mrs. Cody appeared with a cup of tea and a sandwich. She gave an habitual sniff of disapproval and started to bundle up the paper.

"No, no, don't touch that, please, that's a piano. Just leave it," he said hastily.

"They call this a piano?"

He explained the idea and said he'd been intending to get a piano for some time. She said it was queer he never mentioned it. She, for one, didn't know that he could play the piano. She said a man she knew had been killed by a piano being dropped out of a window on him. He said when, as, and if, the piano came it would be by the freight elevator. That, she thought, would track a good deal of dirt through the apartment.

At that point the telephone rang. "Cleves, are you free for dinner, my boy?" his father asked. He said with regret that he wasn't, and with more regret did not suggest his father's coming there, as he would have liked to do. He did almost say: "If I get the telephone call I hope for, I'll have wonderful news for you," but he felt afraid to tempt the gods even that far.

Later he ate his dinner without relish, paced restlessly around the rooms unable to read or relax, haunted by the mournful night sounds from the river, comforted, if bitterly, by the knowledge that on one woman, at last, all his hopes were fastened.

The telephone did not ring again all night.

The question of the letter for Carruthers racked Barwick. To bring himself to submit a draft of it to Salt was intolerable. But whom could he ask to sign? Dennison, as chief counsel for the firm? His brother-in-law, Len Ogilvy, as a director? Fred Johnson, as an officer? Whichever way he turned, he was in a maze, entangled with the interests of the company and other people. And there was no letter, no cable, no telephone call from

Rachel. Some small assurance there would have given him time to plan rationally, but her silence made prudence or waiting impossible. Wednesday night he called Carruthers at his home and told him that a situation had arisen making it impossible to get Salt to sign.

"Any senior officer will do, but I have to have a letter," Carruthers replied. "In fact, if I don't get it you've put me on the spot. I've gone ahead. Why won't Salt sign?"

"We've had a row."

"I don't see how that affects the facts you gave me. But you've got a big company. There must be somebody else. You better do something to get me off the hook."

As soon as he reached his desk in the morning, Barwick dictated the letter to the startled Mrs. Donaldson and told her to type it at once. When she brought it to him, he took it to Salt. "It's not easy or agreeable," he began, "to ask a favor of you."

"I never said I wouldn't do a favor. I'm trying to do you one."

"I must send such a letter as this to the State Department. I'd appreciate your signing it."

Salt read it through carefully, put it flat on his desk and read it again, following the lines with a finger. Then he handed it back.

"I can't sign it," he said. "I'll have nothing to do with it."

"George, whatever you may feel, whatever you want to do about it afterward, it has to be signed. I supposed, of course, you'd do it and Carruthers has acted on the assumption you would."

"Then he's made a big mistake."

"You can't put me in the position of getting Fred Johnson or someone else to sign it."

"He'll not sign it because I'll order him not to. Do you suppose I'm going to have the company compromised because you've chosen to compromise yourself?"

"This is the most incredibly petty revenge I ever heard of."

"You may be a judge of revenge. I'm not. I hope I'm a judge of my duty."

Barwick picked up the letter and left. He had to admit he was at his wits' end as he had never been before. If he let Carruthers down, not only was he doing a contemptible thing but its repercussions might well bar Rachel permanently. And around it all was this new and distasteful business of asking favors.

Meanwhile Salt, more worried and uncertain than he had appeared, took counsel with himself. He had the feeling that he might have gone too far. Carew would arrive the next day. If Barwick took it into his head to bolt, he, himself, was not prepared for the bargaining. Suppose he signed this letter under protest. It would put Barwick under heavy obligation. Salt could not then be accused of petty revenge.

He rang for Barwick and told him to bring in the letter.

Barwick, on the defensive, brought it in.

"Please sit down," Salt said with a deep sigh. "I should like to read that letter again. You tell me you have committed yourself to sending such a letter." He read it again carefully. "This says nothing of a marriage being contemplated."

"No. If it did, a visitor's visa would not be granted."

"Then that's intended to deceive the Government? Perhaps you better not answer that," Salt said and reached for a pen. "I am signing this under protest, with every feeling that I am doing an unwise thing. I am laying myself open to criticism or worse." He signed his name, and handed the letter to Barwick. "I would rather you did not thank me," he concluded, raising his hand. "I have done it only to protect your word to Carruthers."

"Nonetheless I *do* thank you. I am sure in the end you will be glad you did it." He turned away with the letter and then stopped. "George, why don't we forget the last couple of days? They have made me unhappy. I should think they would have made you so."

Salt had wondered how to end with a grievance. "I am afraid," he said, "I have been too deeply hurt. You've had your way as you always do. Let it go at that. I'll meet you at Idlewild in the morning and we'll bring Carew and Pitt-Sempill back in my car. Is that all right?"

"Yes, quite," Barwick replied.

"We dine at the Union Club at eight and break it up early. We'll meet here at ten Saturday morning to begin our talk. There's nothing else, is there?"

"Not that I know of." Cleves left the Chairman's office.

THERE was a long wait for the plane at Idlewild the next morning and it was close to one o'clock when the travelers came through the customs door, Carew and Pitt-Sempill in the wonderful, well-worn clothes in which an English gentleman travels, Chutwell spruced up, and Everett looking as though he had slept in his clothes for a week. Salt was impeccably cordial and casual. "Perfectly delighted to see you back, Carew. Hello, Les. Mr. Chutwell, I've heard a good deal about you — and Mr. Pitt-Sempill. Well, let's get along to the cars. You're to be my guests at the Waldorf. Now is that all right with you?"

"Very much so," Carew said.

"Then, if it's satisfactory to you, I thought we'd all have dinner at my club tonight with Guy Eliot, a friend of ours, president of the Founders Trust. I wanted Dennison, our counsel, but he's out of town. Absolutely no business. And then in the quiet of Saturday morning we could have a talk at the office."

"We're in your hands. If they have running water at the Waldorf, that's all I want," Carew said.

They flocked out to the cars. At the door Everett detained Barwick. "Cleves, I don't think I can face Montclair."

"Of course you can. Everything's very quiet," Barwick said.

"I know, but could I possibly stay at your apartment tonight?"

"Certainly, if you think it's wise."

From the talk on the way to the city no one would have suspected that the four men differed on any subject. Salt handled himself well. When they left the visitors, Barwick drove with him to the office and they spoke normally.

Seeing the visitors so recently from London made him think all the more of Rachel and he suddenly rang and asked Mrs. Donaldson for a cable blank.

"Sit down, please," he said. "I'd like you to take this downstairs and send it." He carefully printed Rachel's name and address.

"If you cannot come here I can be in London to marry you within fourteen days. Thereby all visa questions obviated. Please cable you will come or agree. With deepest love, Cleves."

He handed it to Mrs. Donaldson. "You're sure," she asked, "you won't be sorry I've read it?"

"Quite sure," he said. "You may read it now."

She did so and put out her hand. "Oh, I'm so glad. I wish you every happiness. Have you a picture?"

"I haven't, as a matter of fact; only a mental one."

When Everett reached Barwick's apartment, about six, he looked like a man going slowly to pieces, or like a battered doll held together with adhesive. His bodily motions were almost painfully restrained, as though moving hurt him.

"Would you like a drink?" Barwick asked him.

"No, thanks," he replied, as though the words were in separate sentences. "I'll just have a bath and get dressed."

"Now take your time."

"I'm afraid about tomorrow. Brain's tired."

"Look, relax. Lie down for half an hour." Barwick picked up the suitcase and led him to the guest room.

It was twenty minutes of eight before Everett came out. "I'm afraid," he said, "I am terribly afraid I'll kill Ella."

Barwick had talked to people, Everett included, who contemplated suicide. But never to one who believed he would shortly be a murderer. Beyond a conventional "You're tired. . . . You'll see it differently in the morning. . . . Things work themselves out. . . ." he could think of nothing to say. He did not take it very seriously nor were his sympathies deeply touched.

They arrived at the Union to find Salt, looking Olympian, standing before a bright fire in a private dining room and talking to Carew and Pitt-Sempill. Everett went at once to join Struthers and Chutwell and, as Barwick stopped to say hello to them, he got the impression Chutwell had already had a good deal to drink. Barwick noticed Carew glancing over his shoulder at him, as Guy Eliot joined them and shook hands with the Englishmen.

"George," Eliot said, "your invitation said that if I mentioned business, I'd pay for the dinner. Well, it's worth that, to say one thing. I think this is a magnificent project you and Mr. Carew have in mind and I drink to your success."

"That is very gratifying, Mr. Eliot," Carew said, glancing again at Chutwell who had uttered a very hearty "hear, hear."

Dinner, if a little showy, was magnificent. The talk went well, Salt with his skilled manners bringing each of them into it. Even Everett, looking better, was prodded by Salt to tell an anecdote. Barwick noticed the growing glaze over Chutwell's eyes.

They had got up to go into the sitting room for coffee, brandy and cigars. Salt seated himself on a sofa and told Chutwell to join him. "You're the man they've been telling me about. I want to hear all about you," he said. Carew and Pitt-Sempill asked a waiter where the washroom was and followed him out to it.

Chutwell sank back on the cushions, crossed one leg over the other and slapped his thigh. "We've heard a great many stories tonight, Mr. Salt," he began in a ponderous throaty voice, "and I'm not here to deny they were good stories. But I'm a bit surprised no one has asked me for a story." He was obviously quite drunk. "I'm going to tell you a true story about my native city, London." At that his head rolled as though it were going to fall off.

"St. George," Struthers said, "how about a breath of air?"

"Oh, no. Mr. Salt, you would never condemn a man for having himself a time — wunnerful expression — having himself a time in a foreign city, now would you, Mis' Salt?"

"Certainly not," Salt replied with pained heartiness.

"St. George," Everett said quietly.

"Not talking about you, you — rogue," Chutwell said, wagging his finger at him. "Talking about our bitters, I mean betters."

"Your first time in America, Mr. Chutwell?" Eliot asked him.

"I rather not be interrupted," Chutwell said to him.

Salt laughed a little nervously. "Go right ahead, my dear fellow."

"Very pleased to, with Mr. Barwick's gracious permission. Well, gentlemen, Mr. Barwick's a sly rogue. He said to me, 'Oh, I can't possibly do that, Mr. Chutwell.' I'll never forget it. 'Can't possibly.' Too good for us, I suppose. A man's a man, though. I know, because I got the reports direct — "

"Come on, St. George," Everett said, tugging at his arm.

"Go with you right away, anywhere, Lester. Then Mr. Barwick can tell them all about his refugee. Poor girl, lost her job but gained a friend. Wha' a friend we have in Barwick. Isn't that right, Mr. Barwick? Mr. Great Heart who doesn't care if you're a Commie or what you are. Mustn't blame him. No man, Mr. Salt, should judge another man where a woman's concerned — " He wrinkled his face and regarded them all. Salt got up angrily.

"But this woman is a — you wanna hear this?"

With amazing vigor and quickness, Everett brushed Barwick aside, had Chutwell under the arms and on his feet, and led him to the door. "I'll get him to bed," he said.

"Tell you rest later," Chutwell called over his shoulder. "Lots more, but my eyes are very, very heavy."

As the door closed behind them, Carew and Pitt-Sempill strolled in. "Where's our colleague?" Carew asked.

"He was a little tired. He's gone to bed. Everett went with him," Barwick said.

Guy Eliot, pleading fatigue, said good night quickly and left. Carew noticed the frozen smiles on the faces of the others.

"I'm afraid I must apologize."

"Not at all. Very interesting fellow," Salt said. "Very."

CHAPTER 11

THE Saturday morning quiet of the Allied offices, manned only by the skeleton crew Salt had ordered to report, was as oppressive as a graveyard to Barwick. It now appeared that if Salt wanted him out he would have to go because, all else aside, Chutwell's drunken outburst would put an almost impossible strain on Carew when he learned of it. All would agree that personalities had entered in so strongly as to make business dealings with Barwick almost impossible. At the best, Carew would say, "Our embarrassment over this matter puts us at such a disadvantage that we have no choice but to try elsewhere."

If to win Rachel he had to leave Allied he would not hesitate. Yet Allied was a mighty matter to him, to his pride and love of power.

Everett had not returned to the apartment the night before and Barwick presumed he was still at the Waldorf, caring for Chutwell. Toward the latter Barwick felt deep, almost murderous, anger on Rachel's account, but little on his own. The irony of it was the way it bore out Salt's theory of never letting a man you wouldn't want in the Racquet Club get too far ahead.

No one was at the reception desk and, as he entered the inner office, the only person he saw for a second was John Lamey staring out the window. Then in a corner he saw three girls from the stenographic pool whispering. They glanced at him and turned quickly away. Struthers was not in. Mrs. Donaldson's purse was on her desk beside a pile of unopened letters. He glanced through them. There was none from London.

A man clerk, looking frightened and uncertain, came toward him. "I'd like to speak to you a minute, Mr. Barwick."

"Can't it wait? I'm busy," he said and then recovered himself. "All right, come in. You haven't seen Mr. Struthers or Everett?"

"No, sir. I have a message for you from Mr. Struthers. He won't be in but he will telephone you as soon as he can."

"Is that all?"

"No, sir. I don't know how to tell you. Mr. Everett committed suicide last night. He jumped out of a fourteenth-story window at a hotel. Mr. Struthers is there now, making arrangements."

Barwick heard it without changing expression. During the war he had steeled himself against such news, for the sake of self-preservation. He must somehow block the torrent of retributive guilt that would otherwise engulf him and those around. "I'll tell Mr. Salt," he said. "He's just come in."

Salt, coat and hat still on, was in the doorway, face and manner cold as the Arctic.

"You had better come in and close the door," Barwick said.

"I can hear no explanation now. I'll need all I've got to talk to Carew. I don't have to tell you, I hope, that anything about the Founders is over. Eliot telephoned me this morning."

"I have no intention of explaining, but I'm sorry to have to add to your worries. Lester Everett committed suicide last night."

"Oh my Lord, what next? Is it in the papers?"

"It wasn't in mine."

"Why should he choose to commit suicide at such a time?" Salt demanded. "The whole thing, every step of it, ties up to you and your incredible disregard for the people who have made you what you are. I thank God I'm not in your shoes. What's to be done, will you tell me that?"

"I should think the first thing was to keep your head."

"Don't talk to me that way. Are you without a shred of gratitude for all that's been done for you? Are you without a shred of remorse for poor Everett who tried to protect you last night?"

"Whatever I am, you'd better think about Carew and Pitt-Sempill. They'll be here shortly. We'd better let them come, tell them the situation and put everything off until next week."

"As far as I'm concerned it can be put off forever. I've brought this business where it is, and I can take it where it's going and it doesn't need Englishmen or anybody else. Who's doing anything? Is everyone just sitting here?"

"Struthers is out about it now."

Salt turned and strode away.

Carew and Pitt-Sempill arrived without Chutwell. They accepted the news as men of the world. Salt said that Everett was a great loss, company-wise and personally. He felt sure himself it had been an accident though they all knew that Everett's sensitiveness over his growing deafness and his over-application to his work had brought about a nervous condition.

Carew spoke of the sense of loss Everett's many friends in London would feel. He said he realized that Allied would need time to turn around, and that Pitt-Sempill and he would suit their convenience. At that they took their leave and Barwick went back to his office. In a few moments Mrs. Donaldson entered. "Mr. Pitt-Sempill is on the wire and would like to know if you could meet him somewhere alone right away."

"Yes, tell him the Racquet. And, if Mr. Struthers comes in, tell him I'll be back shortly."

At the Racquet, Pitt-Sempill and he found a quiet corner, and ordered coffee. "I didn't tell Roland I was meeting you, Cleves," Pitt-Sempill said, calling him that for the first time, "and I would like this to be between you and me. Both Roland and I have a strong suspicion that while we were out of the room last night, something was said by Chutwell which ought not to have been said and we're deeply worried about it. Will you please tell us?"

"You put a hard problem to me. It concerned me. As far as that goes, I've forgotten it."

"It could have in no way induced Everett's death?"

"Everett was in a very emotional state and I'm afraid he thought what Chutwell said cut off a last chance for happiness."

"Let me ask this. Is it entirely personal, something you're generously prepared to forget — or will it affect our negotiations?"

"Unfortunately, it will affect them, not because of how I feel, but because Mr. Salt and Mr. Eliot were there and it confirms what Mr. Salt already feels about me. I met a lady in London whom I intend to marry. This has, for the most preposterous reasons, enraged Salt against me. Chutwell, in a drunken stupor, spoke of the lady in an offensive way."

"The damn blackguard. My dear fellow, I am sorry from the bottom of my heart. I should like to say this, though: if the lady was the one you dined with at Claridge's, I also congratulate you from the bottom of my heart."

"Thank you very much," Barwick said with a smile. "It is not sure that she will have me."

"How much may I tell Carew?"

"As much as you feel you must, subject, and this is definite, to there being no permanent reprisals against Chutwell."

"He'll get more consideration than he deserves. I think it's best for us all to think this over until after the funeral."

Struthers was waiting back at the office. "I feel awful bad, Cleves," he said.

"I know; so do I. Poor guy."

"I got his will out of the safe. Everything to his wife. Cleves, did you know he had a girl in London?"

"Yes, I did. He had told me he wanted to marry her. By the way, is Mrs. Everett bearing up?"

"Oh yes, neighbors all in, you know. The poor guy. I suppose he just couldn't go back to Ella. How did the Chief take it?"

"As you'd expect. You were there when Chutwell had his say."

Struthers chewed his mouth. "What's it going to mean with Carew? Of course, they need never know what Chutwell said."

"They know. They suspected something. Pitt-Sempill asked me and I thought it best to tell him."

"It's not going to make any difference in the Company, is it?"

"It has. It'll make more but not before the funeral, I imagine."

"I don't know whether this will make any difference to you, Cleves," Struthers said, going to the door, "but, whatever happens, I go with you if you'll have me."

AT THE Waldorf Pitt-Sempill had told Carew the story. "The bloody fool," Carew said. "I don't know how many times Dunstanley has warned me that we must not let Chutwell loose. I don't see a hope, Rags, of our coming to terms now. And if Barwick should be out, I'm not sure I want to. How I loathe beginning all over with Rutkin or someone else."

"I've been thinking about that. There's this to it. If we began all over with someone who wanted Barwick, as will certainly be the case, it might be a solution for everyone," Pitt-Sempill replied. "Rutkin?" he asked in a moment.

Carew made a grimace. "I dread it but I suppose I'd better ring him up and propose myself for a drink."

St. George Chutwell was having a late lunch by himself as the day drew on. He couldn't see what there was of fair play in the way he was being treated. Lester Everett had been like a brother to him. Nobody seemed to consider how he felt about his bereavement. He would have thought Walter Struthers would have called, but no, not a word. Ingratitude, that's what hurt a man. It was all around him. A form of jealousy because even now — and more so with Les gone — who knew the Carew process as he did? He might have said too much the night before. He wasn't sure just what he had said, but whatever he said, it came out — *in vino veritas* — because his moral sense was outraged. One thing he couldn't stomach was a hypocrite. Barwick's "I couldn't possibly, Chutwell." Bah! Too good to go on a party — but not too good to sneak that woman, that holier-than-thou do-gooder, into the Savoy the night his friends were out.

Although Cleves Barwick's father was retired, he was still a busy, important and distinguished man of whom Cleves and his sister, Barbara, were enormously proud. Seated now in his father's study, in the kindly lamplight, Cleves filled his pipe and said to him: "I came to tell you I am in love with someone I met in London and I hope to marry her."

"My dear boy, I'm simply delighted."

"Before you say more, I want you to know she is Jewish, I have known her one week, she is a refugee, a musician, without money, doesn't like America or Big Business, and is so beautiful she makes the heart ache and is as unpurchasable as you are."

"Well, good for you, Cleves."

"I'm not sure she'll marry me," Cleves said, grinning.

"Nonsense. She'll marry you if we have to storm Jerusalem. Where is she and when is it? Have you a picture? Shall we call Barbara or does she know?"

"She doesn't know. I have no picture. Rachel's in London. I may have to go back for her. There are several darker aspects to it. I've told Salt and it has caused a break between us."

"What? I never heard of such effrontery in my life."

"Father, this makes me very happy but how does it happen you accept it all on faith with this enthusiasm?"

"My dear boy, if a son of your mother can't pick the perfect wife for himself at forty, I shall cease to believe in humanity. But there's more to it." He got up and pointed to a semicircular genealogy chart framed over the bookshelves behind him. "Here are ten generations of Barwicks who have lived in this country, nine of them born here. Look at the family names of the women they married. Not one from outside the British Isles. We have long needed an Eastern Mediterranean strain in our blood, a fair daughter of Zion, a rose of Sharon. Now about Rachel, what's best for me to do? Cable, write, telephone?"

"There's nothing to be done until I hear from her."

"I'm dining with Barbara and Len. I may tell them?"

"Yes, I'd like you to. But tell them nothing is to be said about this to anyone. I'd like to tell you this, however. At a dinner last night for our English friends, their engineer while drunk said something about Rachel—I could have killed him without hesitation. Salt and Guy Eliot heard it. It was all Salt needed. It enormously complicates our business relations with the other Englishmen. I just wanted you to know."

Dr. Barwick knocked out his pipe. "Good. Now I know and now I must go and change if I'm to see the grandchildren. Barbara's sending the car. God bless you. I'm very happy myself and very happy for you."

CLEVES was waiting for his dinner when the telephone rang.

"My dearest brother, Father has told us and we're all very happy and eager to see Rachel. Len wants to speak to you," Barbara said. "All my love and best wishes. Here's Len."

There was a long pause before Len spoke and Cleves got the impression he was waiting until Barbara was out of earshot. He congratulated him in a conventional tone, paused and said in a lower voice, "It was not wholly unexpected. I think you ought to know that George has spoken to me about it. You and I better have a talk alone."

Barwick had a good deal of respect and affection for his brother-in-law, in many ways the archetype of the wealthy man of good will and good works, but at times of an intolerable conformity.

"Len," he said angrily, "I have no doubt your saying that is well meant, but I will not 'have a talk alone' with anybody. I'm sorry to lose my temper, but—"

"All right. As you like, of course," Ogilvy replied.

"Don't be so damned judicious about it. As far as I'm concerned Allied and the Founders—"

"I'm afraid our dinner is served and I shall have to hang up. Good night and good luck," Ogilvy said.

As Barwick slammed the telephone back in its cradle he heard Mrs. Cody answer a ring at the door. She brought in a cablegram.

The message read:

> IF YOU STILL WANT TO THEN TELEPHONE ME AT THE LONDON CHIEF OFFICE IN KING EDWARD STREET BEFORE MIDNIGHT TONIGHT RACHEL.

CHAPTER 12

GOING to King Edward Street, Rachel was fearful of being robbed. She was carrying more money than she had ever had at one time. As she waited in the empty Chief Office, uncertain and unsure, she almost wished she would be robbed, because then flight would be impossible. And the call might not come. Barwick's patience might be exhausted. She had not written him—unable, in her inner confusion, to reply to his cables.

She was angry at herself for the way she had been managed all day like a refugee. The Guaranty Trust Company man arriving before she was up, to tell her to take her passport and come with him. The visitor's visa calmly issued without explanation at the Embassy. Surely it had not been she who had gone in a daze to the Guaranty office to sign receipts for money and traveler's checks while air passage for Sunday was arranged!

"My name is Rachel Linka," she announced at the desk. "I am expecting a call from New York sometime before midnight."

"If you'll be good enough to be seated there, we shall have no trouble finding you, and the booth there can be used."

She sat smoking. "You're sure there's been nothing?" she asked tremulously, at eleven.

"Nothing, Madame. I have twice inquired. Would you like a cup of cocoa? It comes around shortly."

When the wagon came, the cocoa, hot and sweet, did her a great deal of good. As she put the mug down, the man at the desk spoke into his telephone and said quietly to her, "I believe it is just coming through, now, Madame, if you will go into the booth."

Then he said into the telephone: "Yes, Mrs. Linka is here waiting. Quite ready, America."

"Yes, yes, I am Mrs. Linka. Oh, Cleves. Oh my darling, what can I say?"

"Say you love me."

"Oh, I do. You still love me?"

"My darling, more every minute."

"I can come in the morning by air if you still want me. I can't live any longer without seeing you — "

"Nor I."

"But, my dearest, you must not press me. I cannot promise I will marry you, even if you want to when you see me. It has all been so — oh, I can't tell you — may I come that way?"

"Of course. All will be well. Have you money and everything?"

"Yes, everything except knowing what to do. I'm trying to stop crying or laughing or whatever it is. Please help me be sane."

"Come," he said.

"Darling. You are still crazy. Now listen. I go to a place called Idlewild, such a funny name. Do you know where it is? And have you ever heard of Hampshire House? They have a room for me and that is where I'll stay until we can decide. Is it miles from you? Are you sure you want me to come?"

"Not miles. Very sure."

"It's BOAC Flight 37 and it's Monday morning."

"Monday morning here?"

"Yes. Good-bye, my darling. I hope you are not sorry."

Not until after breakfast Sunday morning did Barwick realize that he would have to be at Everett's funeral at the very time that Rachel was scheduled to arrive. It was more than dismaying. Surely any woman not knowing the full circumstances would say, "But what could be more important to you than meeting me?" And for Rachel, with her extreme sensitiveness, would it not be almost fatal to their reunion? Yet he was bound by every consideration of decency and decorum to go to the funeral services.

He telephoned his father. "Will you do something for me?"

"I think it's very likely," his father replied.

"Rachel arrives at Idlewild tomorrow around noon. The customs and immigration will take at least an hour. I must be at the Everett funeral and cannot meet her. Will you? And take her to Hampshire House?"

"The prayers of a just man are heard. Yes, of course. Barbara will come along."

"Now I don't want Barbara or you — "

"My dear boy, when you have shepherded as many sheep as I have, you won't need a stripling of forty to tell you what not to do. I shall simply tell the young woman that you are far too good for her, you were a lovely baby, your mother's pride and joy, and that losing you in my old age is a sad bereavement."

"But you hope to gain a daughter?"

"That's right. What is the flight number?"

"Thirty-seven. BOAC."

"And I take it you will be at Hampshire House in due course?"

"Yes. Oh, one thing more; don't say anything about Everett or that he was in London."

UNDER a blanket of fall flowers, Lester Everett rested in a funeral chapel in Newark. Left of the aisle sat Salt, Barwick, Johnson, Struthers, the other Allied officials, and Carew, Pitt-Sempill and Chutwell. Back of them were at least a hundred of the office staff, representatives of various engineering societies, Stanley Rutkin himself and his engineers.

Heavily veiled and weeping, Ella Everett came up the aisle on the arm of her niece. She paused at the entrance of the pew to look at the floral tributes from the fundamental industries of the country. As she had said to everyone the last two days, "He had so many friends." She threw back her veil and Barwick, glancing at her, saw something of what Everett must first have seen.

"I don't need to go and say anything to her, do I?" Salt whispered in loud tones to Barwick when the service was over.

"No, I shouldn't think so. Struthers and Chutwell are going to the cemetery with her." They walked out to the steps where people were waiting for the hearse to leave, the New Yorkers glancing anxiously at their watches.

"Do we have to wait till this is over?" Salt asked impatiently. "I don't know why Stan Rutkin and his crowd felt it necessary to come. Look, Carew's talking to him." Salt shouldered his way toward the gate, and Carew, seeing him, said good-bye to Rutkin and followed.

Rutkin glanced at Salt and came over to Barwick. "Room for you in my car, Cleves," he said.

"I've got mine. Thanks just the same."

It was ten minutes after four when Barwick got back to New York and, as he headed for Hampshire House, he could not deny his heart was in his mouth. This is probably the worst ten minutes I'll ever have, he thought.

"Keep this car here somehow for a few minutes," he told the doorman at Hampshire House and gave him five dollars. He straightened his tie and went into the lobby.

RACHEL, wearing the scarlet toque he had seen before, came out of the elevator. She made some little deprecatory gesture with her hand and hurried halfway to him. He kissed her, as dear old ladies and even the cynical bellboys watched them with approval.

"You're all right? You did understand my not coming?"

"Darling, of course. Oh, it's so blessed to see you, and I'm in love with your father."

"Any trouble with immigration?"

"Not trouble, but so many questions and I can only stay sixty days. And when I came out and didn't see you, I died a little and then your father and your sister rushed up and kissed me and I began to cry, and your father is just like you, he gave me a big white handkerchief and I blew my nose and we all laughed."

"How much do you love me?"

"You say first."

"With all my heart."

"And I with all mine, but now, nothing is settled. Remember that."

He glanced at her hand on his arm. It was ringless. "I want to talk quietly about settling things. Will you come to the apartment?"

"Of course. I can hardly wait to see where you live."

They got in his car, with her close to him. "We've never been in a car alone before. You must keep track of all our firsts, my darling," she said. The great apartment house by the river impressed her duly and as they got out of the elevator she said, "Darling, are you terribly, terribly rich? It worries me."

"Oh no. Just a living wage. The take-home pay is small." He unlocked the door. "I will carry you over the threshold at a later date." He led her into the living room, the curtains still open on the river and the city. Then she saw the piano pattern on the floor and turned back to kiss him.

"Oh darling, it will be so terrible if I must decide no. How did you think of the piano? I'll never get over it."

"No reason to. You can go and pick it out in the morning and put it wherever you like."

He took her on a tour of the place, explaining the changes there would be, pausing in each room for a wild embrace.

"I *am* all yours," she whispered to him. "I have been since the moment I saw you. I want to forget everything and be here with you forever. Be gentle and understanding until I am more at peace, please. You will never be sorry."

He let her go with a heavy sigh. "Why don't you go into the library and I will bring us a drink. What would you like?"

"May I have a whisky, please—with some of those beautiful pieces of ice?" He mixed the drinks, put them on a tray and went into the library. Rachel was standing at his desk, reading *The Times* folded to the story about Everett. Mrs. Cody, ever alert to his interests, had left it. "It was his funeral?" she asked.

He nodded.

"He was one of those in London who went with Chutwell?"

"Yes."

"You see, I knew it was all quite hopeless for us," she said. "All we were talking about was a dream."

He tried to realize she was exhausted from the flight, still in a way a stranger, filled with apprehensions, sensitive to beauty and hence to ugliness. He had realized from the instant he knew about Everett the effect it could have on her, but now he was angry that she should turn it against them. It had nothing to do with people like them or love like theirs.

"You must not say that nor think it," he said.

"Don't give me commands about what I shall think. It does bear on you and me. I heard from Berta about him. Was she a very different person from me? An American became infatuated with her. He told her he loved her. Yet when he had seen New York again for less than a day he killed himself. He must have realized his horrible mistake. No, do not come near me."

"You can't stop loving me this way in a minute. Please understand this has nothing to do with us. Everett had had a desperately unhappy home life for years."

"But the paper says he had dinner with all of you. Did something happen there, did one of the Englishmen speak of Berta?"

"No, not at all."

"You're being honest with me, now?"

"Yes."

"I have the queerest feeling you aren't." She took a sip of her drink and then said, "Darling, let us dispose of this now — because there are many other things in the way, too. You say nothing was said about Berta. Was anything said about me?"

"Nothing," he said, the first lie he had ever told her. He saw no alternative to it, but he swore to himself it would be the last. He crumpled up *The Times,* used it to light the logs in the fireplace and started to draw the curtains.

"Leave them," she said, kneeling on the couch at the south windows. "I've never been so high above a city. It's very thrilling. Kneel beside me and tell me about it."

Gradually, a great calm settled over the room. In the quiet firelight he told her that he thought they could go to Quebec in a few days to be married and re-enter the States without difficulties.

"If I try very hard to be the wife of a businessman, will you be patient? I don't see how I can do it, though. I can't imagine being interested in it. Will there be only stuffy people?"

"There won't be anyone you don't want."

"Suppose I wanted musicians here to play? Suppose I had them here and wanted them to stay to dinner?"

"Look," he said, "are these the mammoth difficulties you're worrying about? I never supposed musicians didn't get hungry. Have the whole Philharmonic in for breakfast." He kissed her. "Will you marry me as soon as possible?" he whispered.

"Yes, if it's all legal."

"Where is the ring?" he asked.

"Inside my dress. I'll get it and you may put it on."

CHAPTER 13

At breakfast on Tuesday morning Cleves broke the news to Mrs. Cody, telling her that Rachel begged her to stay if she would. To his relief the housekeeper beamed. "Quite a change for me," she said. "Ladies are more refined than gentlemen, if I may say so, Mr. Barwick, though I have always found you neat."

He then telephoned to waken Rachel at Hampshire House.

"My, you're brisk in the morning," she said sleepily after his informing her that he loved her. "I'm usually cross."

"I'm brisk because if I relax I'll come to see you and I have to work. I'm going to the office now. You're lunching with Barbara and I will be at the hotel by five or before. Wish me luck."

"Oh darling, with all my heart. Good-bye, Briskness. I love you."

He found the business of Allied Materials, large and small, going its efficient way when he arrived at the office. Struthers was superintending two porters packing Everett's personal things in transfer cases. Everett's secretary was telling Delehanty, who was to be Everett's successor, what her usual lunch hour was. Delehanty asked when the Englishmen would be in to see the model room. Barwick said about ten, and walked down the hall to see Salt. John Lamey looked up from his desk as he passed and said, "Good morning, sir," in his thin pathetic voice.

Salt received Barwick with a look of bitter grievance and a reference to himself, standing alone.

"This is all quite unnecessary," Barwick said, "and you might as well understand I have no intention of getting out of your way. I will admit in the first shock Saturday morning I thought I might have to. I no longer feel so."

"No," Salt said, banging the glass of the desk. "You don't because now you've got that woman set up in New York — " He stopped short, apparently a little frightened by what he had said.

Barwick held himself in check. "I have repeatedly told you I'm prepared to forget all you've said in the interest of harmony, but you make it impossible." He turned to go but Miss Tibbetts met him at the door and through it Carew and Pitt-Sempill called cheery good mornings.

Before they had left the Waldorf, they had had Chutwell on the carpet to tell him in cold, curt terms he was going home the next day without good-byes to anyone. They had not made the decision solely on the basis of Pitt-Sempill's talk with Barwick. That same afternoon, to Carew's amazement, Stanley Rutkin had given him the gist of what had been said at the Union.

"I don't want you to think I have a pipeline into Salt's organization but, one way and another, I manage to know what's going on and I was not surprised when you called me," Rutkin said.

Carew told Pitt-Sempill Sunday morning, "I do not like the

way I've got into the situation, but it may be providential. Rutkin repeated he was a taker on our terms. I am not sure I'd do it with Rutkin alone, but he seems to feel he'll have small difficulty now bringing Barwick over with him. He tells me the breach between Salt and Barwick is not going to be healed. Naturally, I only listened. You know, I read once that Americans are not allowed to have private lives. They have to have secret lives."

From the easy way both Salt and Barwick came forward to greet them, neither of the Englishmen could see there was any trouble between them. "Tell Mr. Delehanty we'll be right there, if he's ready," Barwick said to Miss Tibbetts. "Before we start talking, we want to show you some West African real estate. It's just down the hall, here." He led them to the storeroom.

The office force could see that all was well as the four men passed, talking animatedly.

"What do you think Mr. Chutwell will think of this?" Salt asked heartily, when the lights were switched on.

"He's had to go back, unfortunately," Carew said, bending over the table. "Well, it almost looks as though we were in business."

"Let's get down to it," Salt said. "Want to join us, Barwick?"

The sudden rudeness of his tone was astonishing. Actually he was feeling a good deal better. His reference to Rachel as "that woman" had shocked even himself. He had been very close to apologizing. But the impulse had gone almost instantly. The concept of the model plant, which so impressed these people, was his. He felt sure now he could handle Carew alone, if necessary. They all went back to his office and sat down.

"At the risk of seeming abrupt," Carew began, "I think it best to tell you that our attitude about the concession is unchanged, and that we have nothing to suggest. At the same time, and I put this to you as strongly as I can, we do not want to go elsewhere."

Salt hesitated. He had always relied on Barwick to come in at such a moment and involuntarily glanced at him, but Cleves was observing the New Jersey skyline. Salt cleared his throat. "We — have gone as far as we can and — are satisfied no one else of our standing will go further. Now, the advantage to you is — "

"You see," Carew said quickly and confidently, "that is just what we do not admit. We have every assurance of an acceptable taker. Now do we leave it at that or do you want more time?"

Pitt-Sempill glanced at his watch as though to emphasize time was running out. It was effective, and disturbing to Salt. It made him a little panicky. Why didn't Barwick say something?

"If we're in agreement on everything but the title, isn't it a mistake to let that one little thing stand in the way?" Salt said feebly, looking at each of the three impassive faces.

"To us it isn't one little thing," Carew replied.

"We couldn't but observe, sir, that the American flag was flying alone over the model plant," Pitt-Sempill said.

Salt had insisted on that. If there's going to be a question about the American flag, Salt thought angrily, let them go elsewhere.

"My own feeling is this," Barwick said quietly. "If there is a drop in world prices then it leaves you, our friends, in debt to us in a way friends should not be. I think that's the issue." He blamed himself for not having seen that as the issue from the start and based the demand for the title on it openly and originally. Rutkin might be willing to take a gambler's chance on it but he was sure Carew and Pitt-Sempill were too smart not to see how paralyzing it could be to them. He felt sure they would concede now, Rutkin notwithstanding, if he could offer something that would leave their prestige unaffected. It had to be the sort of thing that came in a luminous flash and which could be accepted without discussion. The sort of thing you could do by yourself alone with them if you were given unrestricted discretion.

Salt said, "I'm afraid our full Executive Committee will have to consider this. It may take a day or so to get them together."

"All right," Carew replied, "why not leave it at that? If you hear we've gone elsewhere, you may be sure we shall come back to you before we close."

They parted cordially enough, Cleves taking them to the elevator. When he came back, Salt was standing in his door and motioned to him to come in.

"I'll call the Committee together but I think it's out the window. It needn't have been this way, you know," he said accusingly.

Barwick thought for a moment and then went to his own office and telephoned Malcolm Tierney to have lunch with him.

MEANWHILE, like Salt, Chutwell's mind and heart were filled with bitterness and a sense of man's ingratitude. He had been made the scapegoat of another man's shortcomings. A mere slip of the tongue had been pounced on to ruin him. Because his origins were humble, because he had made something of himself under terrific odds and in face of the entrenched privileges of Cambridge and Oxford, he was the victim, the outsider, who could be discarded and forgotten, left alone in a hotel sitting room. And all because of a woman, a woman with a serpent's tongue. He had heard that even now she was in New York, staying—where was it?—at the Hampshire House. As he weighed the issues, he saw two possible courses of action. One might save him and the other would at least comfort him in bringing Barwick and Rachel down with him. The main difficulty was being in the dark as to the extent of the damage he had already done. Carew and Pitt-Sempill had been very closemouthed.

Now wasn't it good sense to see this woman and say to her, "Look here, you and I have had our differences in the past and you've won out. Anything I said or did was never meant to be offensive. I made a mistake, yes. We all do at times. But Mr. Barwick needs me. Why can't you ask him to forgive me?"

Suppose she refuses. Well, then, what do I do? I tell her, "Look here, you look pretty secure, but are you? Do you realize what you've done? Your affair with this man will ruin him. The only thing for you to do is to get out, just as I'm being made to get out . . . ." That's my general line with her.

CLEVES reached Hampshire House at a quarter of five in fine spirits. Malcolm Tierney had been responsive to the idea he had presented and, on his own, had said: "What amazes me is that George seems to have no conception of the magnitude of this thing and as far as I can see is prepared to lose it to get even with you. I'm beginning to get some idea of what you must have had to put up with all this time. It must be particularly trying to you with Rachel here and all this on your mind."

"It's a queer position," Cleves said, "to feel sure Carew won't double-cross us and be afraid George will. I'm not entirely sure, of course, that Carew won't close with Rutkin, but I *am* sure that he won't without a final refusal by us."

"You may get a flattering offer from Rutkin, you know."

"There happens to be a very good reason why he can make no offer I'd accept," Cleves replied. "Mrs. Cleves Barwick-to-be does not like him."

"Good," Tierney said. "Then we're safe."

From a house phone Cleves happily called Rachel in her room. She asked him to come up. He found the door open and went in.

"Leave the door open," she said.

"What's the matter?" he asked, going quickly to her.

She turned away. "Everything. Why did you lie to me? I think I could have stood anything but that." She pulled off her ring and looked at it. "All the beautiful things, the ring, the piano, the Ogilvy children, your father. Here," she said, holding out the ring. "Please see if there's air passage back tonight."

He went over to close the door. "Now tell me what's happened."

"Chutwell has just left me. You told me he had not spoken of us. I gave you every chance to tell me the truth. Now I know what he said in front of them all. It was horrible hearing it from him — "

"I was sure you would never hear it. I simply could not tell you. Could you have told me?"

She looked at him in dismay. "I don't know. What matters is that he made it clear that I have ruined your career, that your chairman is bitterly against you because you have disgraced him, that all you went to London for is lost because of me. Happiness will be impossible. Only by disappearing can I save you."

"You infuriate me," he said. "I thought something was really the matter. One question. Do you still love me?"

"I can't turn on and turn off love."

"This has been horrible for you, I know," he said. "Now, there are two alternatives. I can go to the Waldorf and beat Chutwell up or you can forget it."

"Don't you see that I can't ruin your life, have people think you're the victim of an infatuation for what he thinks I am?"

"I suppose not, if it were going to happen. But, my darling, your prospective husband has a great store of combativeness and energy, which he enjoys using. It seems quite easy now—it was impossible the other night—to admit that Salt *is* in a rage because I didn't ask his permission to fall in love with you. My brother-in-law, as nice a stuffed shirt as you will meet, is not in a rage, but may be in distress. There may be others. Such, as somebody said, is the impact of beauty on the lives of men. Now you told me less than five minutes after we met that artists were the people who had the brightest hopes for life. Do you mean to tell me that you, an artist and a rebel, are going to run away and let a lot of conformists say, 'Well, we stopped beauty in its tracks that time. Barwick is a very sensible fellow, after all.' "

"Oh, dear, I suppose not," she said, leaning against his shoulder, "but I wish it didn't have to be quite so hard." He kissed her. "I thought before you came our next kiss would be the last. Darling, you do have a gift for making things clear and easy."

"Now, where would you like to have dinner?"

"That is already decided. Your father telephoned to ask us when I was at Barbara's. To think, just before you came I was going to telephone him to say good-bye."

CHAPTER 14

CAREW and Pitt-Sempill spent Wednesday morning in the library of Stanley Rutkin's apartment on Fifth Avenue. If he valued his Bellinis at only one dollar, still the rest of his art collection and rare books would bring him a half million under the hammer, he told them, and they accepted the figure. Rutkin was a medium-sized, almost boyish-looking man of 50, whose face shone with health and benevolence. Until he got down to business, he was a little loud, a little too much of a breezy good fellow. But he soon slipped a grave and guarded life mask over his grinning face and began to talk about his companies.

Granted, they were young. But they were growing and they had plenty of money. He, of course, "made it a rule never to talk against a competitor and there is certainly nothing I could say against Allied. As a matter of fact, if Cleves Barwick were the head of Allied, I wouldn't have asked you gentlemen to come here. But, luckily for me, he isn't. Salt is, and behind Salt are others like him, only more so." Strongly as he felt, he would say right now that if the telephone rang and he were told that George Salt had dropped dead, he would chuck in his hand. That's what he thought of Cleves Barwick.

Now as to the present situation, he did not need to tell "you gentlemen" what was going on. One way and another he heard a good deal, and it was common talk there had been a wide-open break between Salt and Barwick. Some people thought Barwick would be forced out. Personally, he hoped he would, because he could tell Barwick where to come. He could park his car in his lot 24 hours a day. That wasn't the point. The point was that whether Salt won or Barwick won — and you couldn't be too sure of the latter — it would take months or even years to reunify the management of Allied. And in the meantime the drift and indecision would be catastrophic in any new venture.

It was his intention, unless "you gentlemen" said no, to ask Barwick to drop in at the apartment that afternoon, to put all his cards on the table — this bound them to nothing — and he was fully convinced that the four of them would be sitting right here, with their heads together, before many days.

"You have no doubt of your being able to carry the heavy commitments involved," Carew asked, "to a magnitude of ten million dollars?"

"Not the slightest. Double it if you want to."

"I think," Carew said to Pitt-Sempill in the taxi afterward, "that after that interview we poor foreigners ought to know pretty well whom we want to do business with. The only reason he seemed to have for our coming was that Barwick may be there."

"I feel sure Barwick could never stomach the fellow," Pitt-Sempill said. "All that oratory!"

"It does seem unlikely, but we don't know where the control lies in Allied. Suppose Rutkin does persuade him. Where are we then? Perhaps we should tell Barwick we're against Rutkin, come what may. But then what? We're completely vulnerable."

MEANWHILE Salt's only communication with Cleves was the typed notice of the Board Meeting on Friday. Both Malcolm Tierney and Ogilvy were more concerned over the outcome than Cleves appeared to be and even they, in spite of good will toward him, agreed that it was most unfortunate that he should be distracted, however happily, by Rachel. On the other hand, their wives were furious with them for letting "poor darling Cleves" be worried about business "at such a time."

"I wish you wouldn't be mad at me," Tierney said pathetically to his wife. "I simply made an observation. I'm going to do all I can. I'm going to move at the meeting that the whole business be referred to Cleves with power. You can't ask more than that."

"Well, I hope you'll get all the rest to vote with you."

"I will certainly try," he promised.

IN answer to a handwritten note from Rutkin, Barwick spent about an hour with him late that afternoon. To begin with, Rutkin said he understood congratulations were in order — and here they were. Mrs. Rutkin and he were particularly "intrigued" that his fiancée was a pianist. They were great concertgoers themselves. Then he began speaking very rapidly.

"I don't mean to beat around the bush, Cleves. You knew I was in London while you were, and I knew I lost that round. I know what's happened since. I want you to join us, and we'll have Carew. Write your own ticket. We haven't seen a great deal of each other but you must have known how I felt about you."

"Well, that's very nice of you, Stan," Cleves said, "but I don't see how I could consider it at a time when we're both after Carew."

"You mean you wouldn't feel it was ethical to quit your crowd right now."

"Yes, call it that."

"I admire that in you but I think you carry it too far. You've made Allied. Now don't deny it. The man who has profited most by it has turned on you in the most sacred matter of a man's life. Correct me if I'm wrong."

"I don't think I can discuss that," Cleves replied.

"Admire you for that, too, but, if anybody had dared to interfere with my marrying my wife, I'd make him regret it till his dying day. Look here, I know perfectly well that, except for that, George Salt would have yielded to you on this concession title and you'd have Carew. You know they've been talking to me and I can tell you they've said as much."

"What's your own position on the title?"

"Simple enough. I'd let 'em have it," Rutkin said with a smile. "Now, isn't it a fact that you'd waive title if it was in your hands and that George has got you hog-tied?"

"Not entirely."

"Admire your loyalty. Does you credit, but here's what you can't deny. You'll never be happy again at Allied. If by a miracle you should get the process, George will make it unbearable for you because you opposed him. If you don't get it — which I have very sound reasons for believing you won't — you'll never hear the last of its being your fault. You can't deny that, Cleves."

This was almost the only sensible thing Rutkin had said, and was not without its effect. What worried Barwick most was whether Carew and Pitt-Sempill believed in this fellow. All the admire-you-for-that's, the mock regret in the "we haven't seen much of each other, but — " Had Rutkin actually made a reputed personal fortune of five million dollars by such means? Did he really believe Barwick would not see through his advances to the truth that Rutkin had no cards at all?

"The whole thing needs thought," Cleves said.

"Well, just as you say, of course. It's you I'm worried about. I've watched this thing develop and I want to see you getting what you should have."

"That's very nice of you," Cleves said, and shook hands. It was quite clear to him now that his own self-interest corresponded to what was best for Allied and all concerned. But, on the way to the Racquet Club, where he was to join Tierney and Ogilvy in rehearsal for the morrow, it suddenly came to him that, in spite of everything he might do, and every consideration of corporation advantage, Salt might still control enough directors on Friday to force him out. No great disaster for him would follow, but it was unbearable to think Salt would be able to believe and convince others that he had been right about Rachel, that his intolerable insults needed no retraction.

Tierney greeted him. "Sit down and relax. I hope, when this is over, Rachel and you will take an extended honeymoon while we all recuperate."

Barwick grinned. "Where's Len, by the way?" he asked.

"He's meeting Dennison who's arriving from Washington."

"What's he in Washington for?"

"Carew and his concession, I suppose."

"I don't know about this. Whose idea was it?" Cleves asked. It was a considerable shock to hear something had been done without consulting him. Suppose Salt and Dennison had agreed to frame a question to the Government so that the answer would be, "Well, we think you'd better not go ahead at all at this time for these reasons. . . ."

"I don't know. I suspect George and he decided on it."

"I don't like it."

"Well, you can't expect to fight George and be in his confidence at the same time. Why don't you ask me about my carefree day?"

"What about it?"

"It has been spent largely in the entertaining company of Mr. William Adams Lejeune who, as you may have heard, is a director and very large stockholder in your company. All he said to me was that, if Henry Dennison agreed, he was prepared to vote power to you. If Dennison is against us — and he's never been crazy about you, frankly — then George has the majority because Channing will vote whatever way gets the meeting over the quickest. If my motion is defeated, you're done, as I see it. Are you ready for that?"

"Yes, I am."

"Now, Cleves, you really feel you'll get Carew if this goes?

Because we'll look awful, awful bad, if you get the power and we don't get Carew. It gives me the horrors, I may say."

"I am very sure."

"And the title to us?"

"Yes."

"But how? Why will they change? Don't say it's just a hunch."

"They will. We've waited them out. When do we see Len?"

"We're to wait for him at your apartment. Let's get going," Malcolm said, looking at his watch. "Actually I have a hunch it will go. I think George had it coming to him."

As they came downstairs they saw Salt at the desk under the membership board and waited till he went to the elevator. "Mr. Salt wasn't looking for me, was he?" Tierney asked the desk man at the membership board.

"No, sir. For Mr. Lejeune."

When Ogilvy arrived at Barwick's apartment, Dennison was with him. The latter's manner was one of chilled but polite annoyance. "I suppose, Cleves," he began, "you want to hear how I feel about all that Len has told me and I may tell you right away I'm not very happy. I'm not very happy that he came privately to me and that you, Malcolm, saw fit to go privately to Lejeune."

"Well," Tierney said, filling his pipe, "we just saw George going to see Lejeune privately, so I'd say we're all even. And it's due Cleves to say he did not ask us to see you."

"No," Dennison replied, "but I presume you were sure it would be satisfactory to him."

"I had certainly talked to them both and asked their support," Cleves said. "I would not have done so except for George's unwarrantable attitude toward a private matter of mine."

"I am afraid, Cleves, I shall have to ask you very frankly about that," Dennison said. "When a man of George Salt's position and experience — a man who has been a devoted friend for twenty years — feels he must violently oppose your marriage, your associates are bound to feel he has reasons that have to be heard."

Cleves interrupted him. "I know the reasons, and they are absurd. The fact is simple. I've met a lady who has honored me by agreeing to marry me."

"Isn't that all there is to it, Henry?" Ogilvy asked.

"I'm afraid not, as regards the Company. Cleves has chosen to act impetuously. But Leonard comes to me and says, 'Let's throw George Salt out and entrust everything to Cleves.' I'm afraid no very good reasons have been shown me for such an action. Am I to say, 'Why certainly, Cleves is a charming fellow and all the world loves a lover?' Or am I to think back to a certain telephone conversation which Salt had with him from London, when he displayed an amazing irritability, and to conclude that a very unfortunate sequence of events appears to have ensued and that I am not justified in entrusting Allied's great interests to someone so impetuous? In all frankness and good will, I do not see how I can be expected to agree."

"Then you will not agree?" Ogilvy asked.

"On the evidence before me I do not see how I can be expected to. But I should hope it would not come to that."

"What's that mean?" Cleves asked.

"I will admit I have felt for some time that George should become Honorary Chairman. I will go so far as to say that, unless we brought someone in from outside, I know of no one but you, Cleves, fitted for the post. I should be willing to think it over, provided you could categorically satisfy me on one point."

"What is it?" Cleves asked eagerly.

"Have you satisfied yourself, by your own investigation, that absolutely no question as to subversion can be raised regarding Mrs. Linka?"

"Certainly I'm satisfied."

"But," Dennison expostulated, "I didn't ask that. I asked 'by your own investigation.' Now I realize you feel like telling me to mind my own business, because of course you have investigated or caused to be investigated. In that case, you have only to give me your word that is so, and I shan't press for detail. Isn't that perfectly fair, Len?"

"Well, yes," Ogilvy replied.

"I simply want to know that, if anything comes up, Cleves has the answer," Dennison said blandly. "Put it this way: when you asked George to sign the letter for the visa, when you talked to Howard Carruthers about it, you unquestionably told them exactly why you knew it was proper to ask this of them. You wouldn't have asked such a thing of your friends unless you had proof positive they could trust what you said. I repeat, give me your word and that ends it. I shan't mention it to either of them. I give *you* my word for that."

Cleves saw instantly, as did the other two, that for some reason Dennison was offering an out on a silver platter. The other two knew that he could not truthfully answer yes. But Dennison was making it temptingly easy to say, "Why, yes, of course I did. I wasn't born yesterday." As such things went, the lie would not be wholly black and they were ready to let him tell it.

I could say it and settle it and who would be the wiser, Cleves thought. But someone he knew to be unpurchasable would soon be sitting across this room, piano notes rippling from her fingers, and he would not be able to listen if he could be purchased.

Dennison had risen and was studying the seascape over the fireplace. "As I said to you," he said without looking at Cleves, "one word and I'm satisfied."

"I made no investigation," Cleves told him, "and I said no more to Salt or Carruthers than I have said to you."

"Then I can be on my way!"

With strained politeness they all said good night and Barwick took Dennison to the elevator. When he came back, Ogilvy and Tierney were moving around the rooms like goldfish in an aquarium tank.

"He seemed quite anxious to make it easy, Cleves. Couldn't you have satisfied him?" Ogilvy said.

"How? By lying about it?"

"It didn't have to be much of a lie considering all that's at stake," Ogilvy said. "Form of words, as far as I see."

"Why should there be this pressure on me? Did anybody ask you to investigate Barbara? She was Red as hell at Vassar."

"The case is a little different," Tierney said. "She was in the Social Register and her father was in *Who's Who.*"

"I still don't see what Dennison went to Washington about. Did he say anything about it?" Cleves asked Ogilvy.

"No, he didn't, but I may have given him little chance by talking too much. We better face it. It looks as though we'll be defeated tomorrow, 4-3. Lejeune and Channing will follow Dennison. Where will you be if anything comes up, Cleves?"

"I'm going to meet Rachel. I almost wish Dennison had asked if she was staying here. Then I could have tossed him in the river. I'll be back here after dinner."

AFTER a long, leisurely dinner with Rachel, during which she told him in detail about all the sights she was seeing in the city, Barwick returned to his apartment and found a note from Mrs. Cody that Operator 114 had left word to call her. Operator 114 said Quebec had been trying to reach him and she would complete the call. It was McNishie, from Allied's Canadian affiliate.

"Hello, Mr. Barwick," he said. "We got your letter and all arrangements are made. It was quite simple. Two of us post bonds of a thousand dollars that there is no legal impediment, and you can get your license in a matter of hours and be married as soon as you like. Very pleased at being called on in such a happy occasion. Now, when will you come? We're holding two bedrooms and a sitting room at the Frontenac for you, as you request."

"That's marvelous," Barwick said. "I think we'll fly up Saturday."

"The bonds couldn't be placed until Monday."

"That's all right. I'll telegraph you by three o'clock tomorrow afternoon. Is that all right?"

"Splendid. Look forward to seeing you," McNishie said.

With his heart's desire so soon to be fulfilled, Barwick should have been in flaming spirits. He paced the room, however, in a very bad temper. It was intolerable to have to "think" at such a time, when all he felt was the desire to go and waken Rachel with the glad tidings. Why in the world was he the only man who in effect had to say to a variety of people, "I should like to get married in Quebec next Monday, subject, of course, to its not interfering with business?" Was this the price he had to pay?

Even if tomorrow's meeting went in his favor, which, after Dennison's talk, seemed unlikely, he still had Carew to deal with. Could he settle in an afternoon? If Carew wanted more time, what sort of marriage would it be from which you packed up and hurried back to the office? But suppose all went right for him at Allied and with Carew, could he then say, "Now, of course, you're in New York and there is much to iron out, but I'm going off on a wedding trip, so would you mind coming back, say in two weeks?"

If he yielded to any of this, what of Rachel, left dangling in New York? The more he thought, the clearer it became that what he really wanted was to have all the rest go against him and be left with life with Rachel before him and a free choice.

He was starting to undress, when the telephone rang.

"Mr. Barwick?"

"Yes."

"This is the 18th Precinct, Lieutenant Cosgrove speaking. We're holding a man here named John Lamey, that's L-a-m-e-y."

"You're holding John Lamey? Whatever for?"

"Well, I'm not quite sure yet. He's in a state of collapse. He says he knows you and he begged me to call you. I can get a squad car at your door in three minutes."

"But what's he done?"

"I don't think he's done anything. Look, come over, will you? He had a fire in his room. There was a girl with him. He got out. She's badly burned, but not fatally."

"Good Lord," Barwick said. "All right, send a car."

Samaritanism was a noble practice, but was there no limit to it? Why had Lamey turned to him? After all, Lamey worked for Salt and Dennison, not for him.

The idea of Lamey and a girl was so grotesque that Barwick almost convinced himself on the ride that there had been a mistake in identity. "There must be some mistake, Lieutenant," he said at the station. "The Lamey I know is a timid little clerk. He couldn't have had a girl in his room."

"Well, he did, Mr. Barwick."

"Was she a tenant in the building? He's a sort of receptionist there at night."

"No, sir."

"He must have taken her there to pray, then. He's really a very nice old fellow. Practically never speaks."

"He speaks all right. 'True Confessions' if I ever heard them. Nobody loved him, he says. Had no friends. For years he's watched young couples come laughing into his building, he says. And lately his loneliness has become worse. He mumbles something about the pretty girls in their coats with scarves over their heads hurrying into warmth and lamplight and somebody waiting for them — and he has no one. Apparently some dissension at your office has unnerved him further and sent him off the deep end. Evidently this office is his whole life. He says he just wanted to spend an hour with someone who would listen to his troubles. He got most of his money, it wasn't much, out of his savings account and walked along the street until he found this girl. Up in his room, she dropped a cigarette in a wastebasket. It blazed up. Caught a curtain. Lamey ran out but the girl couldn't get the door open."

Barwick shook his head. "What am I expected to do?"

"Well, like I said, I don't want to book him, but he wants to kill himself. Do you know a man named Salt? Lamey talks like Salt was going to massacre him. He's incoherent."

"Where's the girl?"

"Bellevue. She'll be all right."

UNDER the ugly lights and in front of the placid detectives, Lamey looked like the final derelict. The Lieutenant had understated his incoherence. He grabbed Barwick's hand, mumbling that Mr. Salt must never know. He wanted to die, to have them shoot him because he could never look Salt in the face again.

"Isn't there a place we can take him?" Barwick asked a detective.

"Bellevue," he replied with a shrug.

Barwick turned to the Lieutenant. "Do you know any private hospital I could put him in for a couple of days?"

"I can call a place on East Sixty-first Street. It'd be expensive."

"Call them. I'll talk to him," Barwick said. "Now Lamey, sit up and get yourself together. Be thankful your companion's not dead and that you're not under arrest. I'm going to take you somewhere where they'll look out for you for a day or so. Now, here's your coat. Stand up."

"I can't face Mr. Salt," Lamey sobbed.

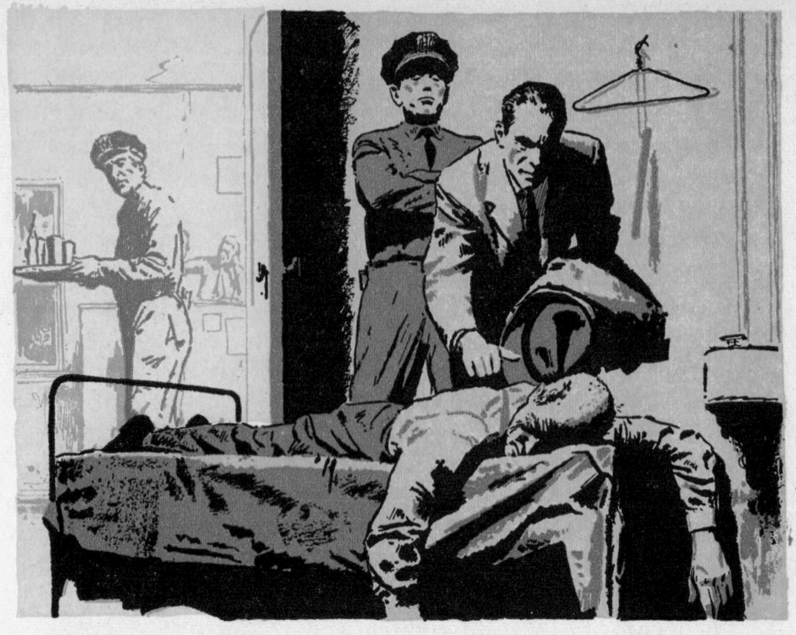

"Look, Lamey, either you walk out to the car or I'll call Mr. Salt to come down here. Now suit yourself."

"Don't do that, Mr. Barwick. He must never know. He's taken care of me all these years, had faith in me, done everything for me. Now I've lost my position and my room and my things, and all I've got in the world is $135 in the bank and Mr. Salt's good opinion. I can't lose that."

"Come on now, Lamey, be a man. Never mind Mr. Salt. You've got to have a rest and maybe get another job. You are a man with responsibilities. You've got to pay the medical bills for that burned girl. That's what a man does, that's what you'll do — "

"Mr. Salt mustn't hear this, Mr. Barwick. He's been heartsick about you. I couldn't help hearing it."

Barwick thought to himself, I'd like to call my father and put this problem in Christian ethics up to him. He felt absolutely no obligation for this man. If he stayed by him, a whole gamut of responsibilities would be his. Any sensible man would walk out and let the police, the Welfare, the Social Services, take over. But if he left him, what was the poor little guy going to do?

The cop and he led Lamey out to a taxi and at the sanatorium Barwick paid $30 in advance for his care. Then he went wearily home to bed. It was past two o'clock.

CHAPTER 15

When Barwick arrived at the office next morning, Mrs. Donaldson smiled and held up crossed fingers. "Slept with them this way," she said.

In spite of his late night, he felt very well. He had had a merry exchange over the telephone with Rachel in which he told her about the plans for Quebec. She had announced that unless she could convert her own pounds into dollars for the purchase of a dress to be married in, she probably would not marry him, as otherwise her independence would be affected. Did he know a Greek who would buy them? No, she would not use any of his charge accounts.

"I shall be out all day. I have to buy several things. Good-bye, Pompousness. I'll wait at the apartment."

It was hard to believe that the outcome of his life's work hinged largely on this bride-to-be to whom the increase in power and riches, or their loss, mattered so little. And, except that people could say his infatuation for an unknown refugee had lost them for him, they mattered less to him than they ever had. The careerist in him, however, had not wholly departed. The prizes and honors *did* matter, if Salt or Dennison proposed to take them away from him.

Salt, too, arrived very confident. Looking back, he did not see why he had worried so about the meeting. He would be in a position to swing it either way. It was obvious the only directors who would side with Barwick were his brother-in-law and Tierney.

Edward Channing arrived and said he hoped the meeting was not going to take all morning. William Adams Lejeune passed the door and Salt was a little surprised he did not come in. Tierney and Ogilvy arrived together and called good morning to him. Good sign, that. Made him feel a little sorry for them. He knew how they felt, having to go through the motions of supporting something their judgment told them was all wrong.

Tierney, waiting for Barwick in the doorway of the Board Room, said very quietly, "Dennison just asked me to make the motion as early as possible. He's very grim. I'm afraid it doesn't look too good."

They took their places, Dennison, Ogilvy and Tierney to Salt's right, Lejeune, Channing and Barwick facing them.

Dennison looked around the table with a feeling of profound sympathy for himself. The last 24 hours had been fuller of unpleasant things than any day he remembered. This meeting would be most unpleasant and it was now inevitable that he should lead it to a decision. The others knew Barwick had never been a favorite of his. Nor had he been more than lukewarm about the Carew process. And his essentially legalistic mind was troubled about the sequence in which he should present all the evidence he now had. He had been at breakfast when the tabloid reporter was announced. He had better tell the others about that at once, he decided.

"A newspaper reporter came to my house this morning with a story about our company," he began. "The fellow was a police reporter who was at the 18th Precinct last night when John Lamey was brought in."

"Who, not our John Lamey?" Salt asked. "Dead?"

"Don't tell me the old boy was drunk and disorderly," Channing said with a grin.

"John Lamey," Dennison said, tapping a finger on the table, "had a woman in his room. There was a fire. Lamey got out. The woman was trapped and badly burned."

"Good heavens," Lejeune said. "You told the reporter we didn't know him, didn't you?"

"Unfortunately, from papers in his wallet, they learned he was employed by us. The reporter said my name was on a company leaflet Lamey had. He wanted to know what we had to say about it."

"I can't believe it," Salt sputtered. "I've known him forty years. Always been perfectly satisfied — unless, of course someone made him dissatisfied. This on top of everything else."

"There's more to it," Dennison said, "and I will ask someone who was there to fill us all in."

"Yes, I will," Barwick replied. "The police telephoned me and I went there and did what I could for Lamey. He's in a private hospital."

"My Lord, they haven't got your name, too?" Salt demanded.

"I make no apology for going to the help of a man in distress," Cleves replied. "But no doubt I should have let you go."

"I should not have gone," Salt announced. "I should have had some regard for public opinion and the interests for which I am a trustee. But it all fits the picture." He looked down at the papers before him. "I'll talk to you after the meeting, Henry, as to what statement we are to make."

Cleves lit a cigarette. This pointed interjection of Lamey could hardly have been made for friendly reasons, yet for Dennison to use it against him seemed incredible. But looking at Dennison's flushed, angry face and Tierney's crestfallen one, he thought it did mean he would.

Salt, badly shaken, sat back in his chair and began to deal out the envelopes containing directors' fees. Under his sense of outrage he almost felt sorry for Cleves. What could have caused this sequence of wrongheaded behavior, going back to Everett and his abominable wife? Was he, Salt, to blame in not seeing the first symptoms of some sort of breakdown?

The boyish heartiness with which he usually spoke had gone out of his voice as he said, "You have before you Struthers' estimates of what the Carew process can mean to us. As you know, we had every grounds for believing it was in our hands. For a variety of reasons, having nothing to do with it, we now stand to lose it, unless we allow them to keep title to the concession. You are asked to decide whether we yield or tell them to take the business elsewhere. More important is the question, in either case, of who shall tell them and thereby have the last word. I must add this," he said, his voice gathering strength: "I have been reluctant to force myself into the negotiations. I now feel I must."

"Just let me understand this clearly," Lejeune said ponderously. "If they retain title, we advance them some ten million dollars and hope they'll pay it back. If we have title, we risk that amount but we are in control. Now is that the way it is?"

"That's close enough."

Channing interrupted. "I thought Cleves was handling these Carew birds. What's the matter, has he got too much else to do? Doesn't this Carew fellow like him, or doesn't Cleves like the process any more?"

Dennison looked over at Tierney, who said slowly, looking Salt full in the face, "Mr. Chairman, I move the whole matter be referred to the Vice-Chairman with power."

Salt clamped his teeth together.

"What's up?" Channing said in a very audible undertone.

"A motion has been made," Salt said as Ogilvy lifted a finger to indicate a second.

"I should like to ask at this time that the Chairman be good enough to withdraw from the room," Dennison said.

Salt looked at him uncertainly. Any such previous request had been for the purpose of voting him a six-figure bonus. Dennison must now intend something of the sort, perhaps with an exposé of the whole Barwick dereliction.

"Certainly," he said, getting up. As he did, Barwick also pushed back his chair, looking questioningly at Dennison.

"Yes, you'd better go, too," Dennison said, as though he were speaking to a child.

Salt went to his office, Barwick to the north anteroom. That Rachel might be under discussion behind that door infuriated him.

Behind the door Dennison was saying: "I must explain that I asked Malcolm to make his intended motion thus abruptly so that I could at once ask the others to withdraw. A personal situation has arisen between them which not only endangers our getting the process but which makes it impossible for them to remain effectively in their present positions. We must deal with it and choose between them. You all know the Vice-Chairman intends to marry someone of whom the Chairman violently disapproves and that this has caused the break."

"What's all this?" Channing exclaimed. "You say 'we all know' —I never heard of it."

"Well, will you please take it as fact and let me go on?"

"I don't know that I will. What's the objection? What right

has George to object? I'm not going to be a party to a sanctimonious wagging of heads."

"It's rather more than that. The lady in question is a refugee. When Salt gave a dinner at the Union for the Carew people, one of them spoke offensively about her."

"I should think Cleves would have knocked his head off—"

"I was not there," Dennison said, "but it is agreed he showed admirable self-control. Salt and he were already at odds about her. But that very night, after hearing it, Everett committed suicide. Salt saw it as a consequence."

"He said that to me and I didn't follow it," Lejeune said. "Just put it together for us to complete the picture."

"Salt said that Everett, as an engineer and an Allied officer, felt the Carew process was the greatest thing Allied had ever gone after. When he heard this about Barwick, Everett realized what he had set his heart on was lost. He was in a highly nervous state from overwork—and, well, there you are. He also worshiped Barwick."

"Certainly an unfortunate thing," Channing agreed.

"Unfortunate but untrue," Dennison continued. "I saw Cleves' father last night. Before Everett went to London he had threatened suicide as a result of a long and, I understand, frightful domestic situation. Except for what Cleves did at the time, he might have killed himself then."

"Of course George didn't know this?" Lejeune asked.

"He knew it. He knew everything about it and he tried to cover it up," Dennison replied. "But however we feel about that, there is another aspect on which George stood on solid ground. Put bluntly, there was an intimation that the future Mrs. Barwick was a Communist or a sympathizer. To this Cleves did not make any satisfactory reply, beyond saying she wasn't."

"I should think that was a complete answer," Channing said.

"It was simply an assertion of faith based on no investigation. Now as Allied directors it would be our duty to dismiss any official about whose wife any such question could arise without our having a probative answer. That has been my worry, and that is what faces us."

"Where was she, during the war?"

"In a concentration camp. To contemplate adverse action against Cleves in view of this Lamey matter is particularly unpleasant. Frankly, I do not know another man who in such circumstances would have responded so quickly, effectively and generously as he did. He feels bitterly toward Salt. All he had to do was to say, 'No, I won't come, but call Mr. George Salt,' and Salt would have been sent for and would have made a spectacle of himself. You heard from George himself what he would have done. However, I was not surprised at Cleves."

"You haven't forgotten they're both out there sweating, have you?" Channing asked.

"That's the price they pay," Dennison told him. "This is not a matter to be hurried. When I say I was not surprised about Cleves, I do so as the result of a talk with him last night."

Tierney and Ogilvy were instantly on the alert.

"The future Mrs. Barwick is in this country," Dennison continued, "on a visa secured by Cleves from Howard Carruthers, a friend in the State Department, backed by a letter which he wrote for George's signature. Now I found it hard to believe the State Department would have granted it merely on Cleves' say-so as to her nonsubversiveness. The more I thought about it the more it worried me. I hope you will all feel I did the right thing in going to Howard Carruthers and asking him exactly what had been said. What else could I do? As director and general counsel, I had to protect the company's name."

"I think you did exactly the right thing," Lejeune said.

Dennison would have preferred having someone else say it, but the others had pushed their chairs back and were regarding him coldly.

"Carruthers said to me that in talking to Cleves it had been quite hopeless to get anything helpful out of him. Of course, he could not authorize a visa in such circumstances but he did not want to come right out and say so. So after Cleves had gone he got on the teletype to Vienna and asked for Mrs. Linka's record. They had it from the day she came out of Regensburg.

"The record showed that she came out of Regensburg penniless and without any family at all. She first got a job playing the piano in a night club in Vienna. The club was frequented by American and British officers. All women employes were expected to entertain the clientele. She refused and lost her job. The usual story, but the Russians heard of it. They knew that at Regensburg she had been one of the camp leaders, a woman of very strong qualities. The café owner was told he must get her back. She was to be paid extravagantly; except for playing the piano, she need do nothing except talk to American or British officers in the club, and report what they talked about to the Russian Intelligence. They were smart enough to see that, if her virtue appeared unassailable, she would attract more attention. Well, I won't bother you with the lurid details — "

"Oh, do bother us with them," Channing said.

"No," Dennison said, shaking his head. "I will only say that this lady informed them she was not to be bought, and reported the matter to our people. They immediately urged her to accept and report to them. She repeated she was not to be bought. There was every chance of the Russians grabbing her. In the face of it, she remained in Vienna working in the child-relief section of UNRRA. Well, there it is."

"Henry, couldn't you have told us this last night?" Tierney asked. "No doubt you had your reasons, but — "

"Do you take it Cleves didn't know this?" Channing asked.

"He did not know it," Dennison replied. "As to your question, Malcolm, I hope you are going to feel I was justified. You all know that in the last eight years I have at various times had doubts about Cleves. I got the feeling that when he wanted something he was quite unscrupulous about how he got it. I am frank to say now I never had anything specific to base it on. But last night I felt I must know this — if it were made temptingly easy for Cleves to say he had investigated this lady and if he were told that would satisfy me without further question or mention of it, would he say yes to get what he wanted? I put the temptation to him as appealingly as I could. Without hesitation Cleves said he had not done so. I am ashamed of myself but I feel for the first time I know the type of man Cleves is."

"I could have told you that," Channing said.

"I am not just sure where this leaves us," Lejeune said.

"There was never any question as between the Chairman and Vice-Chairman as to who was the better businessman," Dennison replied. "In my mind there was a question of character. I have been deceived in both men. In the last few days I have found that a man I have known for forty years is vain, vindictive, even a liar to serve his purposes. More than that I see he's a moral coward and a Pharisee. Even this morning, had he shown a shred of Christian charity toward this poor Lamey wretch, as Cleves did, I should have been willing to compromise. But now I want him out of here. I want us to elect Cleves forthwith."

"That's pretty extreme. I said I'd follow you, but — " Lejeune said.

"I think what Henry's said is smart," Channing said. "In an impasse like this, there's nothing like having something new to go back with. The Englishmen will deal with a man they already know and like, and they'll see we have every confidence in him and think he needed more power, more discretion. It's exactly the thing to do."

"What about a vote?" Tierney asked.

"Well, I want to look at the bylaws, which of course aren't here," Dennison said, reaching under the table for the bell, "but I take it I have five votes for a new chairman and a resignation."

"I suppose if you all feel that way, yes," Lejeune said, nodding assent.

"Go and break it to George, Mal," Channing said. "After all — "

Dennison nodded. "And send Cleves in with the bylaws."

"Sit down, Cleves," Dennison said gravely. Tierney had only indicated by a gesture as he passed that Cleves was to go in. He sat straight up, shoulders back, to take it. "During your absence, the rest of us have taken two very grave decisions. We wish you to understand that both have been taken solely as representing what we feel is best for our company. We expect they will be so received by Salt and yourself."

Channing sighed noisily.

"Malcolm is now telling the Chairman that we request his full resignation. It is our intention immediately to name you as his successor."

Cleves sat up even straighter as Channing patted him on the back. An undeniable wave of triumph swept over him. "I shall do my best, and I am very grateful to you," he said, as they all shook hands with him. "Is my election official?"

"Well, it will be when I find the covering bylaw. Who drew these up, anyhow?" Dennison asked testily.

"Your office," Cleves replied with a grin. "It was before my time. Are there any instructions before I call Carew?"

"He's all yours," Dennison answered.

"Then I'll call him now. Will one of you tell George I'd like to talk to him?"

"WELL, Mal," Salt said cordially, when he saw Tierney at the door of his office, "are they ready for me?"

"Not quite, George," Tierney said. "They asked me to have a word with you first. Cleves has just gone in."

"I'm sorry for him, of course, but he has only himself to blame. First he lost his head about a woman. As a result he messed up the situation in London and when he saw the consequences I've learned he high-tailed it to Rutkin. When that failed, he turned on me and tried to get Len and you to bail him out. Then there's this reckless conduct with Lamey. I must say it was very considerate of Henry to spare my feelings about it, when everybody knows how I felt about Cleves. Even now I'm not going to see him go begging."

"You see, George, it hasn't worked out quite that way."

"What do you mean?"

"They've asked me to prepare you for their decision. We hope you'll take it as a purely business decision for the good of the company. We all feel it best that you resign."

Salt's face whitened. Well, he thought, they've at least done it the way I've always done things like it: no beating around the bush, no palaver, no emotion. He was oblivious for a moment to what it meant to him.

"Dennison voted with you? And Bill Lejeune?"

"Yes."

"Dennison takes my place?"

"No. Cleves."

Salt drew a deep breath. What an irony that others who had often been lukewarm about Barwick should now have given him what he had once looked forward to giving.

"When Cleves leaves the meeting, I wish you'd come back with me," Tierney said. He knew that on every ground the dismissal was right but there was something repulsive – like witnessing an electrocution – in seeing a man suddenly divested of the power he had held so long. Even his cocksure speech pattern would have to change. His idiosyncrasies would no longer be looked at with amused but respectful tolerance. Above all, there would be the shattering realization that people had not really thought about him what he had supposed they did.

In the Board Room all of them, even Channing, spoke softly, almost deferentially to him, while devoutly praying he would not make a scene. Dennison moved quickly from the head of the table to his own chair.

"Now don't sit below the salt, Henry," Salt said and they all laughed as if it were the funniest line they had ever heard. They were very gentle with him.

It was almost one o'clock before Salt came out to Barwick's office. "Henry would like you to look over these resolutions to see if you have any changes," he said.

Barwick looked at them. They covered his election, the with-power resolution for him as chairman, action on Salt's resignation, and the vote of thanks to him for his long services which took note that he "would continue to be available for advice."

"What about the Honorary Chairman?" Barwick asked.

"I said I would decline if it was offered. I don't want it."

"It reads as though you weren't going to remain as a director. I hope that isn't so."

"It is. I am through," Salt said. He had sat down, looking out the window, drumming on the desk with his fingers. "Well, you've got it all," he said. "You're pleased, I suppose."

"Yes, I am. I'd be more pleased to hear you say we're still friends."

"I find I haven't any friends. Cleves, tell me this. Where have I gone wrong?" His tone was almost confidential. "I can't see where. Everything I have done was done because I thought it was right. You know that. I suppose I've made mistakes, yes."

"We all have," Cleves replied.

"Even with you, I certainly never intended — well, never mind. I suppose that John Lamey's in the papers by now. I suppose that — "

"George, why don't you go to see Lamey? You're the only person who can get him on his feet. Tell him you'll give him the money for the girl's hospital, get him a job out of town. There must be a woman his age somewhere who's also lonely. Above all, show him how *you* take things. Now who but you can do that?"

"By George, I suppose that girl and he have got to be taken care of. Cleves, you're right. I'll do it. And another thing I want to say. If you like, I'll tell Guy Eliot I want you on the Founders."

"Look, don't do that. I don't want the Founders. I won't have time for it."

"I suppose you'll be seeing Carew this afternoon," Salt said.

"Yes, I am, at three."

"Well, you might give me a ring afterward. Where's this place you've got Lamey?"

Barwick wrote down the address. Salt put it in his pocket. He paused at the door. "Things have been lax around here, I suppose. I was mortified that Dennison had to send for the bylaws. Must have wondered what sort of a shop we were running. I intend to speak sharply to the office manager. If I've said once — "

The sound of his voice seemed to waken him to the realities of his position. He cut off his own words the way a radio program is interrupted, staring at Barwick, his lips silently forming the rest of the sentence.

"My God," he said in a whisper, "I'm done. I can't speak to him. I'm — why, I'm forsaken, aren't I?"

"Not at all," Barwick said. "You're free to do new things, instead of the old ones, over and over."

"Walk to the elevator with me, will you? The office mustn't suspect anything," Salt said.

WHEN Rachel telephoned Cleves about the wedding dress and hat he was already in conference with Carew. Mrs. Donaldson gave her the news and thought her a little vague about such magnificence. "Can I tell him where to meet you, Mrs. Linka? Or is there anything I can do?"

"Oh, thank you very much, no. Perhaps you'll tell him I'll go to the apartment about five."

"Yes, I will. Mrs. Linka, would you like to know we have your plane tickets for tomorrow?"

"How nice of you. I *am* so grateful. It is all quite wonderful, isn't it? Thank you again."

The day had been wholly divine. A beautiful fitted dressing case had arrived from Cleves before she left and she had found the perfect dress and hat, the sheerest lingerie and nightgown. Her heart was as high as the high blue sky. She reached the apartment at five and Barwick arrived soon after.

"Well, you've heard?" he said.

"Oh yes," she said, kissing him.

"No congratulations?"

"Yes. Many. Darling, I am very happy for you. I don't understand it all yet except that I am afraid it means you're more important and I'll never see you. Vivian and your family all telephoned to congratulate you."

"I've just left Carew and we may be delayed getting off. But only until Sunday at the latest. You do understand?"

"I have to," she sighed.

"Darling, please don't be that way about it—it will be over tomorrow or Sunday."

"But suppose it isn't? We can't go on much longer this way. And will you rush back from Quebec to the office? Isn't any time ours? It's like the stories you read about American men and their business."

"It's only that a great deal has happened at the same time," he said wearily.

"But can't someone else wait? What's the use of what's happened if it keeps us apart?"

"It won't," he said, putting his arms around her.

She was kissing him when the telephone rang. "Don't answer it," she said. "Tell Mrs. Cody you're out, whoever it is."

But at that moment Mrs. Cody came to the door and said it was Mr. Stanley Rutkin. Would Mr. Barwick call him at home?

He could feel the Arctic in the silent room. He dreaded what Rachel was going to say, dreaded it most because he would not be able to control his own temper if she said it. No love worth having could survive an endless I-told-you-so, or stay poised on a razor's edge. He could not go on protesting and explaining that Salt, that Everett, that Chutwell, that Rutkin were other people. He stood looking down at the river, his back to Rachel. He heard her make a sound. Then she came quickly to him, took his hand, pressed herself against him. He realized she was laughing.

"My poor angel. Stop worrying. I think it's very funny — "

"You're not really in a state?" he asked.

"Of course not. Call the wretch if you want to. I'll make love to you while you do. What a joke on him."

CHAPTER 16

"OF COURSE," Carew said to Pitt-Sempill, after Barwick had left them Friday afternoon, "this change puts a very different aspect on things. I'm frank to say I always found Salt a tiresome old fool. We must consider what was in their directors' minds. They obviously felt a change was called for, and they must have complete faith in Barwick as a man to make the change. After listening to him this afternoon I can see why. You know, when he talks on a drop in world prices, he's very impressive."

"Yes, I agree with you."

"I must say I liked the way he took the whole responsibility for not telling us about the title to start with. Obviously it was Salt's idea. But we must not make this easy for him."

"No. You realize Rutkin's been on the phone twice?"

"Yes. Well, we have nothing to tell him yet."

BARWICK's thoughts at dinner and afterward kept turning to the settlement with Carew. All else will be simple, once I am sure of Rachel, he so often had said to himself. Now nothing seemed surer than that they would be married on Monday, but it made the concession title no easier to solve.

He scarcely touched his dinner and gradually felt what he was saying to Rachel getting thinner and thinner, felt ashamed of himself for it and made some half-formal apology. As he did, she pushed back her chair and came around the table to him, took his hand and drew him to her. "You make me feel very maternal," she whispered. "You don't have to be bright and entertaining." She kissed his cheek, put her arm around his waist and led him to the living room. "Cleves, you must go to bed and be fresh for tomorrow. Go and undress and I'll come and say good night in a minute and then I'll go — "

"Of course I won't," he said.

"But my darling, of course you will, because I insist on it. Now run along quickly while I speak to Mrs. Cody. Cleves, obey me at once. You were up most of last night."

Five minutes later she knocked on his door and went in, carrying a glass of water. "Open your mouth and close your eyes and I'll give you something to make you wise — and make you sleep, too," she said.

"I can't sleep, I have to think," he said.

"Do you want a kiss or not? If you don't, of course, don't take this. Raise your head — "

"I never take medicine," he said ruggedly.

"All right, no kiss, and it was going to be a nice one."

He reached for the glass and the tablet.

"Be sure you swallow it. Now lie down," she said, sitting on the side of the bed. "Once there was a little boy who grew up and thought he was the only person who could do things right. And he met a poor girl who he thought had to be taken care of and protected, so he asked her to marry him. And she said yes. Do you know why?"

"Loved him?"

"Oh no, that was a mere detail. She felt sorry for him. She

knew he couldn't run a big business without a wife like her to help him. In the first place, he was a spendthrift who bought letters by Chopin and pianos by Steinway, while she was a great hoarder and saver of money. Everyone saw *her* head was on the right way. His directors began to say, 'Great thing for this great company that a refugee came along and married our Chairman.' Your eyes are drooping," she said, leaning over to kiss them.

"I thought it was to be 'a nice one.' "

"It is," she replied. "Nicer than you know. Good night."

BY 11 o'clock Saturday morning it seemed clear that settlement that day was out of the question. Yet it was also clear that both the Englishmen were very tired. "See here," Carew said. "If it will help it any, I'm frank to tell you we are not going to Rutkin. You must see from that admission how anxious we are to settle with you. But really, my dear Barwick, you do not make it easy. Every concession has come from us. You seem to be blind, if I may put it so, to the value we put on what we have discovered and developed in West Africa. True, we find ourselves unable financially to carry it through unaided, but must that mean we have to give up every symbol of our achievement?"

Barwick glanced at his watch, excused himself and went out to Mrs. Donaldson.

"Cancel my flight reservations, please," he said solemnly.

"Oh, I am so sorry."

"It can't be helped. Tell them to make it tomorrow and bring a note in if it's confirmed and call Mrs. Linka and tell her, please. Better let Mrs. Ogilvy and my father know. They were going to drive us out."

"Are they being impossible in there?"

"No, not impossible," he said with a sigh and went back.

They separated for lunch at one o'clock and resumed at three with the Englishmen evidently revived. When one considered, they said, the magnitude of what they were both proposing to do, one asked oneself if it was wise to force a decision. The process was secured by inviolable patents and neither Allied nor they were in such a situation that an immediate decision was necessary.

They asked themselves whether the sensible thing was not for them to return to London, leaving both sides to think it over.

Mrs. Donaldson came silently in and handed him a slip of paper. "Can I speak to you? *Very* important." He asked the two to excuse him again, and went out. "What's the matter?" he asked.

"Mr. Barwick, there are no Sunday flights to Quebec."

"No flights? You mean no seats? There must be flights."

"No, there aren't. No planes on Sunday. Religious reasons."

Business, immigration laws, the power of the Church, powers temporal, power spiritual—was there any end to the coalition against love? "Is all Canada closed down?" he asked.

"No, you could get to Montreal."

He did not want to go to Montreal. He had picked Quebec for its unique beauty. He wanted to go to rooms high on the river side of the Frontenac, after Rachel and he had had tea in the vast lounge, where they still made toast on the end of a great fork held over the fire.

Nevertheless, he said, "Telephone the Mount Royal, reserve the same thing you did at the Frontenac. Call the Frontenac and tell them I still want the suite Sunday, even if I'm not there."

Barwick went back and apologized for the interruption. "Now you were saying you could go back to London. I think it's a good idea. It's now ten minutes of four. If you agree, I can have Dennison here in fifteen minutes and this is the settlement I propose. The concession company will be called Carew-Allied Concession. Car-All-Con. All stock, except directors' qualifying shares, will be held by us and we will find all the money and take the risk. But the Chairman of the Board will be Mr. Roland Carew. Will that do it?"

As Barwick began, Pitt-Sempill had started to put his papers in his dispatch case and Carew to rub out his cigarette. Both stopped as he put the question. A smile lit up Carew's grave, handsome face and Pitt-Sempill brushed his papers aside.

"Done," Carew said. "This is very gratifying. I say, why didn't you tell us this to start with?"

"If you must know, the exact form of words just came to me

and I think we had to go through all we did in order to understand each other. You agree to my calling Dennison?"

"Most certainly."

"While I'm out, would you like to open that secret panel and make us all a drink?" Cleves asked.

"Rather," Pitt-Sempill said. When they were alone, he turned to Carew. "Well, Chairman? Say when." He poured from a decanter.

"Oh, splash it in," Carew replied. "This isn't a day for prudence."

WHEN Dennison arrived, Barwick went outside to tell him what he had done.

"I consider it absolutely brilliant, Cleves. I find a little personal satisfaction in the fact that I helped remove the only obstacle to it." They joined the others, Dennison all affability, even to the point of accepting a drink.

"Now, gentlemen," he said, "we are all most grateful to you for the patience you have shown with this delay. I have my two best young men on their way here to get at the drafting. They feel they can have things in shape for initialing sometime tomorrow. If we are ready by eleven o'clock, will you be?"

"Quite."

"I shouldn't think we would need more than an hour to read and initial, would you?"

"No," Carew said.

Dennison looked positively impish as he smiled at Barwick. "I press the point," he said, "because Mrs. Donaldson has just informed me that our friend here must leave the city not later than a quarter past two. Let us drink to the long life and happiness of him and his bride."

"Well done," Pitt-Sempill said as Carew reached out to shake Barwick's hand. "Why didn't you tell us, my dear fellow? This wrangle must have been perfectly intolerable to you."

"That," Dennison said, "is the sort of man he is."

All papers had been signed by noon on Sunday and they came out to find Dr. Barwick waiting to go to lunch at the Ogilvys' with Cleves. When the good-byes to the Englishmen had been said, Cleves took his father back into his office.

"Well, tell me about them," he said. It was to his father he had turned over the lost sheep of the last few days.

"I am a little dismayed," his father began, "when I realize that while both of the people you sent me to really needed spiritual inspiration and rehabilitation, all I have talked to them about is money. The girl at Bellevue is very pretty and they seem to feel she will not be disfigured. I must say I liked her and found her very responsive. I think we can find something for her."

"Lamey?" Cleves asked.

Dr. Barwick sighed and shook his head. "What is one to say? When does the soul enter the body? Did it ever enter his? A pitiful case. I saw him off to his sister's in Indiana. Incidentally, Henry Dennison had to send a check to Salt to sign. It had all slipped his mind. I may say we did not spare the moneybags."

"What will become of them?"

"Oh, I shan't leave matters where they are, though they must take some thought for themselves."

"I blame myself now that I didn't do more about poor Everett. I felt it particularly this morning when I thought of how happy it all would have made him."

"You did all you could. You mustn't have vain regrets today of all days. Rachel called me early this morning to say how much she loves us all."

OGILVY, Tierney, Barwick and his father waited for the ladies to get ready after luncheon for the ride to Idlewild. Suddenly the three Ogilvy children cascaded downstairs yelling for coats and caps. Barbara, Vivian and Rachel followed.

"Len," Barbara said, "Rachel, Cleves and the children in our car. The rest of us in Mal's. Do you mind terribly, Cleves?"

"He'd better not mind," Rachel said. "Have I ever had such an honor?" She looked radiant, in her small red cap, white orchids on her coat. Cleves had never seen her with children before. All the way to Idlewild she devoted herself to them and their endless questions, reaching across them from time to time to touch his hand and smile happily at him. He had it all, Salt had said, and soon he *would* have it all, all his heart's desire forever. He could even smile about the closed airport at Quebec.

At Idlewild he enjoyed the conventional seeing-off. It was conformity of the pleasantest sort—father, sister, friends and the delightful children. It seemed impossible that the routine call for their departure meant their whole new life's start. There was great kissing. Through the gate they went, to shrieks of "Good-bye, Aunt Rachel, good-bye, Uncle Cleves, good-bye, Aunt Rachel. . . ."

The plane was blessedly full of empty seats and as it mounted in the cold, clear air they could see the Atlantic far to the eastward. They sat for a long time, their fingers entwined, before either spoke.

"Dearest," Rachel whispered, "is everything but us forgotten?"

"Everything."

"We've been very good. I've conformed in every way, or tried to. It's been very nice, much easier than I expected. Do you know what I wish next?"

"Say."

"That you'd be that mad, absurd man you were in London, only more so. Be pompous first, then be competent, then be crazy."

"It is an error of judgment — " he began.

"That's it, go on."

" — for rebels and those who are artists at heart to be conformists too long."

"Um," she murmured inquiringly. "What should they do?"

"I can't tell you," he said, laughing at her. "You're too proper."

"What can you mean?" she asked in mock seriousness, turning around to face him. "Oh, darling," she said, kissing him. "How many more minutes?"

He glanced at his wrist. "About a hundred and forty to the airport."

"And then?"

"About thirty-five to the hotel."

"And then?"

"Six."

"Interminable. Is anybody watching us kiss?"

"A few people."

"Who cares?"

Howard Swiggett

A NATIVE of Ohio, Howard Swiggett grew up in Indianapolis and Brooklyn and was graduated from Yale in 1914. He returned unscathed from service in World War I only to be seriously injured in the famous Wall Street bomb explosion of 1920 in which 40 people were killed and 800 hurt. After a long convalescence he took up a business career; by World War II he was managing partner of one firm, president of another. In the week of Dunkirk he joined the British Purchasing Commission, later became Deputy Director General of the British Supply Mission. For these services he was made a Commander of the Order of the British Empire.

Besides *The Power and the Prize* Mr. Swiggett has published seven historical works and three novels of adventure. He has recently retired, after thirty successful years in business, to devote his full time to writing.

Illustrations by J.PAGÈS

The Duchess and the Smugs

A condensation from
"A Wreath for the Enemy" by
PAMELA FRANKAU

"A Wreath for the Enemy," copyright 1952, 1954, by Pamela Frankau, is published at $3.50 by Harper & Brothers, 49 E. 33 St., New York 16, N. Y.

THE THEME of an adolescent's yearning for conformity is familiar, but seldom is the adolescent so bewitching a child as 14-year-old Penelope Wells, heroine of this charming story.

Penelope, daughter of an English poet who runs a small hotel on the French Riviera, is enthralled by the orderly existence of the Bradley family in a neighboring villa. She longs to be like the Bradleys and is embarrassed by the unconventional atmosphere of her home, in particular by the presence of a favorite guest, the eccentric Duchess di Terracini.

Then, one fateful night, Penelope makes a discovery, and thereafter nothing seems quite the same. *The Duchess and the Smugs* is a wise and tender story that delights the reader at the same time that it expands his awareness of life.

CHAPTER 1

THERE had been two crises already that day before the cook's husband called to assassinate the cook. The stove caught fire in my presence; the postman had fallen off his bicycle at the gate and been bitten by Charlemagne, our sheep dog, whose policy it was to attack people only when they were down.

Whenever there were two crises my stepmother, Jeanne, expected a third; *"jamais deux sans trois,"* she said. This morning she and Francis (my father) had debated whether the two things happening to the postman could be counted as two separate crises and might therefore be said to have cleared matters up. I thought that they were wasting their time. In our household things went on and on and on happening. It was a hotel, which made the doom worse; it would have been remarkable to have two days without a crisis.

I was not very fond of the cook. But when I was sitting on the terrace in the shade working on my Anthology of Hates, and a man with a bristled chin told me in *patois* that he had come to kill her, I thought it just as well for her, though obviously disappointing for her husband, that she was off for the afternoon. He carried a knife that did not look particularly sharp; he smelled of licorice, which meant that he had been drinking Pernod. He stamped up and down, making speeches about his wife and Laurent, the waiter, whom he called a *salaud* and many other words new to me and quite difficult to understand.

I said at last, "Look, you can't do it now, because she has gone over to St. Raphael in the bus. But if you wait I will fetch my father." I took the Anthology with me in case he started cutting it up.

I went down the red-rock steps that sloped from the garden to the pool. The garden looked the way it always looked, almost as brightly colored as the post cards of it that you could buy at the desk. There was bougainvillaea splashing down the white walls of the hotel; there were hydrangeas of the exact shade of pink blotting paper; there were huge silver-gray cacti and green umbrella pines against a sky that was darker blue than the sky in England.

I could not love this garden. Always it seemed to me artificial, spiky with color, not quite true. My idea of a garden was a green lawn and a little apple orchard behind a gray stone house in the Cotswolds. It was my Aunt Anne's house in the village of Whiteford in England. I saw that garden only once a year, in September. I could conjure it by repeating inside my head,

And autumn leaves of blood and gold
That strew a Gloucester lane.

Then the homesickness for the place that was not my home would make a sharp pain under my ribs. I was ashamed to feel so; I could not talk about it; not even to Francis, with whom I could talk about most things.

I CAME to the top of the steps and saw them lying around the pool, Francis and Jeanne and the two novelists who had come from Antibes for lunch. They were all flat on the yellow mattresses, talking.

I said, "Excuse me for interrupting you, but the cook's husband has come to assassinate the cook."

Francis got up quickly. He looked like Mephistopheles. There were gray streaks in his black hair; all the lines of his face went upward and the pointed mustache followed the lines. His body was dark brown and hairy, except that the scars on his back and legs, where he was burned when the airplane was shot down, did not tan with the sun.

"It's a hot afternoon for an assassination," said the male novelist as they ran up the steps together.

"Perhaps," said Francis, "he can be persuaded to wait until the evening."

"He will have to," I said, "because the cook is in St. Raphael. I told him so."

"Penelope," said my stepmother, sitting up on the yellow mattress, "you had better stay with us."

"But I am working on my book."

"All right, *chérie;* work on it here."

The lady novelist, who had a sparkling, triangular face like a cat, said, "I wish you would read some of it to us. It will take our minds off the current bloodcurdling events."

I begged her to excuse me, adding that I did not anticipate any bloodcurdling events because of the battered look of the knife.

Jeanne said that the cook would have to go in any case, but that her love for Laurent was of a purely spiritual character.

I said, "Laurent is a smoothie, and I do not see how anybody could be in love with him."

"A certain smoothness is not out of place in a headwaiter," said the lady novelist.

Retiring from the conversation, I went to sit on the flat rock at the far end of the pool.

Francis and the male novelist returned very soon. Francis came over to me. I shut the loose-leaf book.

"The cook's husband," he said, "has decided against it."

"I thought he would. I imagine that if you are really going to murder somebody, you do not impart the intention to others."

"Don't you want to swim?" said Francis.

"No, thank you. I'm working."

"You couldn't be sociable for half an hour?"

"I would rather not."

"I'll write you down for RCI," he threatened.

RCI was Repulsive Children, Incorporated, an imaginary foundation which Francis had invented. According to him, RCI did a tremendous business and there were qualifying examinations wherein the children were tested for noise, bad manners, whining, and brutal conduct. I tried to pretend that I thought this funny.

"Will you please let me work for a quarter of an hour?" I asked him. "After all, I was disturbed by the assassin."

"All right. Fifteen minutes," he said. "After which you qualify."

In fact, I was not telling him the truth. I had a rendezvous at this hour every day. At four o'clock precisely I was sure of seeing the people from the next villa. I had watched them for ten days and I knew how Dante felt when he waited for Beatrice to pass him on the Ponte Vecchio. Could one, I asked myself, be in love with four people at once? The answer seemed to be yes. These people had become a secret passion.

The villa was called La Lézardière; a large, stately, white shape with a pink roof; there was a gravel terrace, planted with orange trees and descending in tiers to a pool of smooth gray concrete. At the tip of this pool there was a real diving board. A long gleaming speedboat lay at anchor in the deep water. The stage was set and I waited for the actors.

They had the quality of Vikings; the father and mother were tall, handsome, white-skinned, and fair-haired. The boy and girl followed the pattern. They looked as I should have preferred to look. (I was as dark as Francis and much too thin. And not pretty. If my eyes were not so large I knew that I should be quite ugly. In Francis' opinion, my face had character. "But this, as Miss Edith Cavell said of patriotism," I told him, "is not enough.")

Oh, to look like the Bradleys; to be the Bradleys, I thought, waiting for the Bradleys. They were far, august, and enchanted; they wore the halo of being essentially English. They were Dad and Mum and Don and Eva. I spied on them like a huntress, strained my ears for their words, cherished their timetable. It was regular as the clock. They swam before breakfast and again at ten, staying beside the pool all the morning. At a quarter to one the bell would ring from the villa for their lunch.

In the afternoon the Bradleys rested on their terrace in the shade. At four they came back to the pool. They went fishing or water skiing. They were always doing something. They would go for drives in a magnificent gray car with a white top that folded back. Sometimes they played a catching game beside the pool; or they did exercises in a row, with the father leading them. They had cameras and butterfly nets and field glasses.

I took Don and Eva to be twins; and perhaps a year younger than I. I was just 14. To be a twin would, I thought, be a most satisfying destiny. I would even have changed places with the youngest member of the Bradley family, a baby in a white perambulator with a white starched nurse in charge of it. If I could be the baby, I should at least be sure of growing up and becoming a Bradley, in a white shirt and gray shorts.

Their magic linked with the magic of my yearly fortnight in England, when, besides having the gray skies and the green garden, I had acquaintance with other English children not in the least like me: solid, pink-cheeked sorts with ponies; they came over to tea at my aunt's house and it was always more fun in anticipation than in fact, because I seemed to make them shy. And I could never tell them that I yearned for them.

Now it was four o'clock. My reverie of the golden Bradleys became the fact of the golden Bradleys, strolling down to the water. Dad and Don were carrying the water skis. I should have only a brief sight of them before they took the speedboat out into the bay. They would skim and turn far off, tantalizing small shapes on the shiny silky sea. Up on the third tier of the terrace, between the orange trees, the neat white nurse was pushing the perambulator. But she was only faintly touched with the romance that haloed the others. I mourned.

Then a most fortunate thing happened. There was a drift of strong current around the rocks and, as the speedboat moved out toward the bay, one of the water skis slipped off astern and was carried into the pool under the point where I sat. Don dived in after it; I ran down the slope of rock on their side, to shove it off from the edge of the pool.

"Thanks most awfully," he said. He held onto the fringed seaweed and hooked the water ski under his free arm. Now that he was so close to me I could see that he had freckles; it was a friendly smile and he spoke in the chuffy, English boy's voice that I liked.

"It's rather fun, water skiing."

"It looks fun. I have never done it."

"Would you like to come out with us?" He jerked his head toward the boat: "Dad's a frightfully good teacher."

I groaned within me, like the king in the Old Testament. Here were the gates of Paradise opening and I must let them shut again, or be written down for RCI.

"Painful as it is to refuse," I said, "my father has acquired visitors and I have sworn to be sociable. The penalty is ostracism." (Ostracism was a word that appealed to me.)

Don, swinging on the seaweed, gave a gurgle of laughter.

"What's funny?" I asked.

"I'm terribly sorry. Wasn't that meant to be funny?"

"Wasn't what meant to be funny?"

"The way you talked."

"No, it's just the way I talk," I said, drooping with sadness.

"I like it awfully," said Don. This was warming to my heart. By now the speedboat was alongside the rock point. I could see the Viking heads, the delectable faces in detail. Mr. Bradley called: "Coming aboard?"

"She can't," said Don. "Her father has visitors; she'll be ostracized." He was still giggling and his voice shook.

"Oh dear, that's too bad," said Mrs. Bradley. "Why don't you ask your father if you can come tomorrow?"

"I will, most certainly," I said, feeling as though I had been addressed by a goddess. Don gurgled again. He flashed through the water and they pulled him into the boat.

I had to wait for a few minutes alone, hugging my happiness, preparing a kind of visor to pull down over it when I went back to the group on the yellow mattresses.

"Making friends with the Smugs?" Francis greeted me.

"What an enchanting name," said the lady novelist.

"It isn't their name; it's what they are," said Francis.

I heard my own voice asking thinly: "Why do you call them that?" He shocked me so much that my heart began to beat heavily and I shivered. I tried to conceal this by sitting crouched and hugging my knees. I saw him watching me.

"Well, aren't they?" he said gently. I had given myself away. He had guessed that they meant something to me.

"I don't know. I don't think so. I want to know why you think so."

"Partly from observation," said Francis. "Their gift for organized leisure; their continual instructions to their children; the expressions on their faces. And the one brief conversation that I've conducted with Bradley — he congratulated me on being able to engage in a commercial enterprise on French soil. According to Bradley, you can never trust the French." He imitated the chuffy English voice.

"Isn't 'commercial enterprise' rather an optimistic description of your hotel?" asked the lady novelist, and the male novelist laughed. Francis was still looking at me.

"Why do you like them, Penelope?"

I replied with chilled dignity: "I did not say that I liked them. They invited me to go water skiing with them tomorrow."

Jeanne said quickly: "That will be fun. You know, Francis, you are becoming too intolerant of your own countrymen: it is enough in these days for you to meet an Englishman to make you dislike him." This was comforting; I could think this and feel better. Nothing, I thought, could make me feel worse than for Francis to attack the Bradleys. It was another proof that my loves, like my hates, must remain secret, and this was loneliness.

CHAPTER 2

I AWOKE next morning full of a wild surmise. I went down early to the pool and watched Francis taking off for Marseilles in his small, ramshackle seaplane. He flew in a circle over the garden as he always did and, when the seaplane's long boots pointed for the west, I saw Don and Eva Bradley standing still on the gravel terrace to watch it. They were coming down to the pool alone. They waved and beckoned and shouted.

"Is that your father flying the seaplane?"

"Yes."

"Does he take you up in it?"

"Sometimes."

"Come and swim with us," Don called.

I ran down the rock slope on their side. I was shy now that we stood together. I saw that Eva was a little taller than Don; that she also was freckled; and that they had oiled their skins against sunburn as the grownups did. Don wore white trunks and Eva a white swimming suit. They laughed when I shook hands with them and Don made me an elaborate bow after the handshake. Then they laughed again.

"Are you French or English?"

That saddened me. I said, "I am English, but I live here because my stepmother is a Frenchwoman and my father likes the Riviera."

"We know that," said Don quickly. "He was shot down and taken prisoner by the Germans and escaped and fought with the Resistance, didn't he?"

"Yes. That is how he met Jeanne."

"And he's Francis Wells, the poet?"

"Yes."

"And the hotel is quite mad, isn't it?" He turned to look at the painted blue sign that announced: "Chez François."

"Indubitably," I said. It was another of my favorite words. Eva doubled up with laughter. "Oh, that's wonderful. I'm *always* going to say indubitably."

"Is it true," Don said, "that guests only get served if your father likes the look of them, and that he charges nothing sometimes, and that all the rooms stay empty for weeks if he wants them to?"

"It is true. It does not seem to me the most intelligent way of running an hotel, but that is none of my business."

"Do you go to school in England?"

"No," I said, handing over my chief shame. "I am a day boarder at a convent near Grasse. It is called Notre Dame des Oliviers."

"Do you like it?"

"I find it unobjectionable," I said. It would have been disloyal to Francis and Jeanne to tell these how little I liked it.

"Do they teach the same things as English schools?"

"Roughly."

"I expect you're awfully clever," said Eva, "and top at everything."

How did she know that? Strenuously, I denied it. Heading the class in literature, composition and English poetry was just one more way of calling attention to myself. It was part of the doom of being noticeable, of not being like Other People.

God forbid that I should tell the Bradleys about winning a special prize for a sonnet; about being chosen to recite Racine to hordes of parents; about any of it. I defended myself by asking questions in my turn. Eva went to an English boarding school in Sussex; Don would go to his first term at public school this autumn. I had guessed their ages correctly. They were just 13. "Home" was Devonshire.

"I would greatly love to live in England," I said.

"I'd far rather live in an hotel on the French Riviera. Lucky Penelope."

"I am not lucky Penelope; I am subject to dooms."

"How heavenly. What sort of dooms?"

"For example, getting an electric shock in science class, and finding a whole nest of mice in my desk," I said. "And being the only person present when a lunatic arrived believing the school to be Paradise."

"Go on. Go on," they said. "It's wonderful. Those aren't dooms, they are adventures."

"Nothing that happens all the time is an adventure," I said. "The hotel is also doomed."

"It can't be doomed," Don said. "Don't famous people come here?"

"Oh yes. But famous people are more subject to dooms than ordinary people."

"How?"

"In every way you can imagine. Important telegrams containing money do not arrive. Their wives leave them; they are recalled on matters of state."

"Does Winston Churchill come?"

"Yes."

"And Lord Beaverbrook and Elsa Maxwell and the Duke of Windsor and Somerset Maugham?"

"Yes. Frequently. All their signed photographs are kept in the bar. Would you care to see them?"

Here I encountered the first piece of Bradley dogma. Don and Eva, who were splashing water on each other's hair ("Dad is most particular about our not getting sunstroke"), looked doubtful.

"We *would* love to."

"I'm sure it's all right, Eva; because she lives there."

"I don't know. I think we ought to ask first. It is a bar, after all."

"Oh, do let's chance it," said Don.

"I don't believe we ought to."

Mr. and Mrs. Bradley had gone over to Nice and would not return until the afternoon, so a deadlock threatened. The white starched nurse appeared at 11 o'clock with a Thermos flask of cold milk and a plate of buns. I gave birth to a brilliant idea; I told her that my stepmother had invited Don and Eva to lunch with us.

It was a little difficult to convince them, after the nurse had gone, that Jeanne would be pleased to have them to lunch without an invitation. When I led them up through our garden, they treated it as an adventure, like tiger shooting.

Jeanne welcomed them, as I had foretold, and the lunch was highly successful, although it contained several things which the

Bradleys were not allowed to eat. We had the terrace to ourselves. Several cars drove up and their owners were told politely that lunch could not be served to them. This delighted Don and Eva.

I took them on a tour of the hotel. The salon was furnished with some good Empire pieces. The bedrooms were not like hotel bedrooms, but more like rooms in clean French farmhouses, with pale walls and dark wood and chintz. All the rooms had balconies where the guests could eat breakfast. There were no guests.

"And Dad says people *clamor* to stay here in the season," Don said, straddled in the last doorway.

"Yes, they do. Probably some will be allowed in at the end of the week," I explained, "but the Duchess is arriving from Venice at any moment and Francis always waits for her to choose which room she wants, before he lets any. She is changeable."

Eva said, "I can't get over your calling your father Francis. Who is the Duchess?"

"The Duchessa di Terracini. She is half Italian and half American."

"Is she very beautiful?"

"Very far from it. She is seventy and she looks like a figure out of a waxworks. Once she was very gay, but now she loves only roulette." I did not wish to be uncharitable about the Duchess, whose visit was to be dreaded. The only thing in her favor was that she had been a friend of my mother, who was American and utterly beautiful and whom I did not remember.

"A great many people loved the Duchess desperately," I said. "She was engaged to an Austrian Emperor; he gave her emeralds, but somebody shot him."

"Oh well, then, she's practically history, isn't she?" Eva said, looking relieved.

CHAPTER 3

I MIGHT have known that the end of the day would bring doom. It came hard upon the exquisite pleasure of my time in the speedboat with the Bradleys. This was even better than I had planned it in anticipation, a rare gift. I thought that the occasion must be under the patronage of a benign saint or what the Duchess would call a favorable aura; the only worry was Mrs. Bradley's worry about my having no dry clothes after swimming; but with typical Bradley organization there were an extra white shirt and gray shorts in the boat. Dressed thus I felt like a third twin.

The sea changed color; the sea began to be white and the rocks a darker red.

"Would you like to come back and have supper with us, Penelope?"

I replied, "I can imagine nothing that I would like more."

"She *does* say wonderful things, doesn't she?" said Eva. I was drunk by now on Bradley admiration and almost reconciled to personal remarks.

"Penelope speaks very nice English," said Mrs. Bradley.

"Will you ask your stepmother then?" she added as we tied up the boat. I was about to say this was unnecessary when Don gave my ribs a portentous nudge. He said quickly, "Eva and I will walk you up there." It was obvious that the hotel exercised as much fascination for them as they for me.

When the three of us set off across the rocks Mr. Bradley called, "Seven o'clock sharp, now!"

Eva made a grimace. She said, "Wouldn't it be nice not to have to be punctual for anything?"

"I never have to be," I said, "except at school, and I think that I prefer it to having no timetable at all."

"Oh my goodness? Why?"

"I like days to have a shape," I said.

"Can you just stay out to supper when you want to? Always? Without telling them?"

"Oh, yes."

"What would happen if you stayed away a whole night?"

I said that I had never tried. And now we went into the bar because Don said that he wanted to see the photographs again. We were lingering beside Winston Churchill when the worst thing happened. I heard it coming. One could always hear the Duchess coming. She made peals of laughter that sounded like opera; the words came fast and high between the peals.

And here she was, escorted by Francis. She cried, "Ah my love, my love," and I was swept into a complicated, painful embrace, scratched by her jewelry, crushed against her stays, and choked with her scent before I got a chance to see her in perspective. When I did, I saw that there were changes since last year and that these were for the worse. Her hair, which had been dyed black, was now dyed bright red. Her powder was whiter and thicker than ever; her eyelids were dark blue; she had new false eyelashes of great length that made her look like a Jersey cow.

She wore a chiffon dress, sewn all over with sequin stars, and long gloves with her rings on the outside; she tilted back on her heels, small and bony, gesticulating with the gloves.

"Beautiful – beautiful – beautiful!" was one of her slogans. She said it now; she could not conceivably mean me; she just meant everything. The Bradleys had become awed and limp all over. When I introduced them they shook hands jerkily, snatching their hands away at once. Francis took the bottle of champagne that had been on ice awaiting the Duchess; he carried it to her favorite table, the corner table beside the window. She placed upon the table a sequin bag of size, a long chiffon scarf, and a small jeweled box that held honey drops, my least favorite sweets, reminding me of scented glue.

Francis uncorked the champagne.

"But glasses for all of us," the Duchess said. "A glass for each."

The Bradleys said, "No thank you very much," so quickly that they made it sound like one syllable and I imitated them.

"But how good for you," cried the Duchess. "The vitalizing, the magnificent, the harmless grape. All children should take a little to combat the lassitude and depressions of growth. My mother used to give me a glass every morning after my fencing lesson. *Et toi,* Penelope?"

"Oh, didn't you know? Penelope is on the water wagon," said Francis, and the Duchess again laughed like opera. She cried, *"Santé, santé!"* raising her glass to each of us. Francis helped himself to a Pernod and perched on the bar, swinging his legs. The Bradleys and I stood in a straight, uncomfortable row.

"Of youth," said the Duchess, "I recall three things. The sensa-

tion of time seeming endless, as though one were swimming against a current; the insipid insincerity of one's teachers; and bad dreams, chiefly about giants."

"What do you dream about now?" asked Don, who had not removed his eyes from her since she came.

"Packing; missing airplanes; losing my clothes," said the Duchess. "Worry — worry — worry; but one is never bored in a dream, which is more than can be said for real life. Give me your hand," she snapped at Eva. She pored over it a moment, and then said briskly, "You are going to marry very young and have three children; an honest life; always be careful in automobiles." Don's hand was already stretched out and waiting. She gave him two wives, a successful business career, and an accident "involving a horse between the ages of seventeen and eighteen."

"That is tolerably old for a horse," Francis interrupted.

"Sh-h," said the Duchess, "perhaps while steeplechasing; it is not serious." She blew me a little kiss. "Penelope I already know. She is as clear to me as a book written by an angel. Let me see if there is any change," she commanded, a medical note in her voice. "Beautiful — beautiful — beautiful! Genius and fame and passion are all here."

"Any dough?" asked Francis.

"I beg your pardon," said the Duchess, who knew perfectly well what dough meant, but who always refused to recognize American slang.

"I refer to cash," said Francis looking his most Mephistophelean. "My ambition for Penelope is that she acquire a rich husband, so that she may subsidize Papa in his tottering old age."

"Like so many creative artists, you have the soul of a fishmonger," said the Duchess. She was still holding my hand; she planted a kiss on the palm before she let it go. "I have ordered our dinner, Penelope. It is to be the *écrevisses au gratin* that you like, with small *goûters* of caviar to begin with and *fraises des bois* in kirsch afterward."

I had been anticipating this hurdle; she always insisted that I dine with her on her first evening, before she went to the Casino at nine o'clock.

"I am very sorry, Duchessa; you must excuse me. I am having supper with Don and Eva." I saw Francis raise one eyebrow at me. "I really didn't know you were coming tonight," I pleaded.

"No, that is true," said the Duchess, "but I am very disappointed. I have come to regard it as a regular tryst." She put her head on one side. "Why do you not all three stay and dine with me? It could be managed, Francis? Beautiful — beautiful — beautiful! There. That is settled."

"I'm most awfully sorry; we'd love to," Eva said. "But we couldn't possibly. Supper's at seven and Mum's expecting us."

"Thank you very much, though," said Don, who was still staring at her. "Could we do it another time?"

"But of course! Tomorrow; what could be better? Except tonight," said the Duchess. "I was looking to Penelope to bring me good luck. Do you remember last year, how I took you to dine at the Carlton and won a fortune afterward?"

"And lost it on the following afternoon," said Francis.

"I thought one never could win at roulette," said Don. "According to my father, the game is rigged in favor of the Casino."

"Ask your father why there are no taxes in Monaco," said the Duchess. "In a game of this mathematic there is no need for the Casino to cheat. The majority loses naturally, not artificially. And tell him further that all European casinos are of the highest order of probity, with the possible exception of Estoril and Bucharest. Do you know the game?"

When the Bradleys said that they did not, she took from her bag one of the cards that had upon it a replica of the wheel and the cloth. She embarked upon a roulette lesson. The Bradleys were fascinated and of course we were late for supper. Francis delayed me further, holding me back to speak to me on the terrace: "Do you have to have supper with the Bradleys?"

"Yes, I do."

"It would be reasonable, I should think, to send a message saying that an old friend of the family had arrived unexpectedly."

Of course it would have been reasonable; Mrs. Bradley had expected me to ask permission. But nothing would have made me stay.

"I'm extremely sorry, Francis; I can't do it."

"You should know how much it means to her. She has ordered your favorite dinner. All right," he said. "I see that it is useless to appeal to your better nature." He went back to the bar.

"Didn't you want to stay and dine with the Duchess?" asked Don, as we raced through the twilit garden.

"I did not. She embarrasses me greatly."

"I thought she was terrific. I do hope Mum and Dad will let us have dinner with her tomorrow."

I AWOKE with a sense of doom. I lay under my mosquito curtain, playing the scenes of last evening through in my mind. A slight chill upon the Viking parents, due to our being late; smiles pressed down over crossness, because of the visitor. Don and Eva pouring forth a miscellany of information about the Duchess and the signed photographs; myself making mental notes, a devoted sociologist studying a favorite tribe: grace before supper; no garlic in anything; copies of *Punch* and the English newspapers; silver napkin rings; apple pie. The secret that I found in the Cotswold house was here, I told myself; the house in Devonshire took shape; on the walls there were photographs of it; a stream ran through the garden; they rode their ponies on Dartmoor; they had two wire-haired terriers called Snip and Snap. I collected more evidence of Bradley organization: an expedition tomorrow to the Saracen village near Brignoles; a Current Affairs Quiz that was given to the family by their father once a month.

No, I said to myself, brooding under my mosquito net, nothing went wrong until after the apple pie. That was when Eva had said, "The Duchess told all our fortunes." The lines spoken were still in my head:

Don saying, "Penelope's was an absolute fizzer; the Duchess says she will have genius, fame and passion." Mr. Bradley's Viking profile becoming stony; Mrs. Bradley's smooth white forehead puckering a little as she asked me gently, "Who is this wonderful lady?"

Myself replying, "The Duchessa di Terracini," and Mrs. Bradley remarking that this was a beautiful name. But Mr. Bradley's stony face growing stonier and his officer-to-men voice saying, "Have we all finished?" Then rising so that we rose, too, and pushed in our chairs and bowed our heads while he said grace.

After that there was a spirited game of Monopoly. "But the atmosphere," I said to myself, "went on being peculiar." I had waited for Don and Eva to comment on it when they walked me home, but they were in a rollicking mood and appeared to have noticed nothing.

"Indubitably, there is a doom," I thought while I put on my swimming suit, "and, since I shall not see them until this evening because of the Saracen village, I shall not know what it is."

As I crossed the terrace, the Duchess popped her head out of the corner window above me; she leaned like a little gargoyle above the bougainvillaea; she wore a lace veil fastened under her chin with a large diamond.

"Good morning, Duchessa. Did you win?"

"I lost consistently, and your friends cannot come to dine to-night, as you may know; so disappointing, though the note itself is courteous." She dropped it into my hands. It was written by Mrs. Bradley; fat, curly handwriting on paper headed:

CROSSWAYS
CHAGFORD
DEVON

It thanked the Duchess and regretted that, owing to the expedition, Don and Eva would not be able to accept her kind invitation to supper.

I knew that the Bradleys would be back by six.

At half past four, to my surprise, I looked up from my rock writing desk and saw the Bradleys' car sweeping in from the road. Presently Eva came running down the tiers of terrace alone. When she saw me she waved, put her finger to her lips, and signaled to me to stay where I was. She came scrambling up.

"I'm so glad to see you. There's a row. I can't stay long. Don has been sent to bed."

"Oh, dear. I was conscious of an unfavorable aura," I said. "What happened?"

Eva looked miserable. "It isn't anything against you, of course. They like you terribly. Mum says you have beautiful manners. When Don and I said we wanted you to come and stop a few days with us at Crossways in September, it went down quite *well*. Would you like to?" she asked, gazing at me. "Or would it be awfully boring?"

I was momentarily deflected from the doom and the row. "I cannot imagine anything that would give me greater pleasure," I said. She wriggled her eyebrows, as usual, at my phrases.

"But of course it may not happen now," she said in melancholy, "although it wasn't *your* fault. After all, you didn't make us meet the Duchess on purpose."

"Was the row about the Duchess?"

"Mm-m."

"Because of her telling your fortunes and teaching you to play roulette? I did have my doubts, I admit."

"Apparently they were quite cross about that, but of course they couldn't say so in front of you. Daddy had *heard* of the Duchess, anyway. And they cracked down on the dinner party and sent a note. And Don kept on asking why until he made Daddy furious. Mummy said that the Duchess wasn't at all the sort of person she liked us to mix with, and that no lady would sit in a bar drinking champagne when there were children present, and that we shouldn't have gone into the bar again anyway. And Don lost his temper and was quite rude. So that we came home early instead of having tea out; and Dad said that Don had spoiled the day and asked him to apologize. And Don said a word that we aren't allowed to use and now he's gone to bed. Which is awful for him because he's too big to be sent to bed. And I'll have to go back. I'm terribly sorry."

"So am I," I said. "Please tell your mother that I deplore the Duchess deeply, and that I always have."

As soon as I had spoken, I became leaden inside myself with remorse. It was true that I deplored the Duchess because she was possessive, overpowering, and embarrassing, but I did not disapprove of her in the way that the Bradleys did. I was making a desperate effort to salvage the thing that mattered most to me.

In other words, I was assuming a virtue though I had it not and, while Shakespeare seemed to approve of this practice, I was certain that it was wrong. (And I went on with it. I added that Francis would not have dreamed of bringing the Duchess into the bar if he had known that we were there. Which was an outrageous lie.)

When Eva said that this might improve matters and might also make it easier for Don to apologize, because he had stuck up for the Duchess, I felt lower than the worms.

Which is why I quarreled with Francis. And knew that was

why. I had discovered that if one were feeling guilty one's instinct was to put the blame on somebody else as soon as possible.

Francis called to me from the bar door as I came up onto the terrace. He grinned at me.

"Be an angel and take these cigarettes to Violetta's room, will you, please?"

"I am sorry," I said. "I have no wish to run errands for the Duchess just now."

Francis, as usual, was reasonable. "How has she offended you?" he asked.

I told him about the Bradleys, about the possible invitation to Devonshire; I said that, thanks to the Duchess, my future was being seriously jeopardized. I saw Francis' eyebrows twitching.

He said, "Penelope, you are a thundering ass. These people are tedious *petits bourgeois,* and there is no reason to put on their act just because you happen to like their children. And I see no cause to protect anybody, whether aged seven or seventy, from the sight of Violetta drinking champagne."

"Mrs. Bradley said that no lady would behave in such a way."

"Tell Mrs. Bradley with my love and a kiss that if she were a tenth as much of a lady as Violetta she would have cause for pride. And I am not at all sure," he said, "that I like the idea of your staying with them in Devonshire."

"Do you mean that you wouldn't let me go?" I asked, feeling as though I had been struck by lightning.

"I did not say that. I said I wasn't sure that I liked the idea."

He could always make me feel a fool when he wanted to. And I could see that he was angry; less with me than with the Bradleys. He said, "I don't think much of the Smugs, darling, as you know. And I think less after this. Violetta is a very remarkable old girl, and, if they knew what she went through in Rome when the Germans were there, some of that heroism might penetrate even their thick heads. Run along with those cigarettes now, will you, please?"

I was trembling with rage; the worst kind of rage, hating me as well as everything else. I took the cigarettes with what I hoped was a dignified gesture, and went.

The Duchess was lying on the chaise longue under her window; she was swathed like a mummy in yards of cyclamen chiffon trimmed with marabou. She appeared to be reading three books at once: a novel by Ignazio Silone, Brewer's *Dictionary of Phrase and Fable* and a *Handbook of Carpentry for Beginners.*

The room, the best of the rooms, having two balconies, had become unrecognizable. Three wardrobe trunks crowded it; many dresses, scarves and pairs of small pointed shoes had escaped from the wardrobe trunks. The Duchess always brought with her large unexplained pieces of material; squares of velvet, crepe de Chine, and damask, which she spread over the furniture. The writing table had been made to look like a table in a museum; she had put upon it a small crucifix and two iron candlesticks, a group of ivory figures, and a velvet book with metal clasps.

"Beautiful – beautiful – beautiful!" said the Duchess, holding out her hand for the cigarettes. "There are the honey drops on the bedside table. Help yourself liberally, and sit down and talk to me."

"No, thank you very much. If you will excuse me, Duchessa, I have to do some work now."

"I will not excuse you, darling. Sit down here. Do you know why I will not excuse you?"

I shook my head.

"Because I can see that you are unhappy, frustrated and restless." She joined her finger tips and stared at me over the top of them. "Some of it I can guess," she said, "and some of it I should dearly like to know. Your mother would have known."

I was silent; she was hypnotic when she spoke of my mother, but I could not make myself ask her questions.

"Genius is not a comfortable possession. What do you want to do most in the world, Penelope?"

The truthful reply would have been, "To be like other people. To live in England, with an ordinary father and mother who do not keep an hotel. To stop having dooms; never to be told that I am a genius, and to have people of my own age to play with so that I need not spend my life listening to grownups."

I said, "I don't know."

The Duchess sighed and beat a tattoo with her little feet inside the marabou; they looked like clockwork feet.

"You are, beyond doubt, crying for the moon. Everybody at your age cries for the moon. But if you will not tell me which moon, I cannot be of assistance. What is the book that you are writing?"

"It is an Anthology of Hates," I said, and was much surprised that I had told her because I had not told anybody.

"Oho," said the Duchess. "Have you enough Hates to make an anthology?"

I nodded.

"Is freedom one of your Hates?"

I frowned; I did not want to discuss the book with her at all and I could not understand her question. She was smiling in a maddening way that implied more knowledge of me than I myself had.

"Freedom is the most important thing that there is. You have more freedom than the average child knows. One day you will learn to value this and be grateful for it. I will tell you why." Her voice had taken on the singsong, lecturing note that preceded a 15-minute monologue. "It is necessary to imprison children to a certain degree, for their discipline and their protection. In schools, they are largely hidden away from life, like bees in a hive. This means that they learn a measure of pleasant untruth; a scale of simple inadequate values that resemble the true values in life only as much as a plain colored poster of the Riviera resembles the actual coast line.

"When they emerge from the kindly-seeming prisons, they meet the world of true dimensions and true values. These are unexpectedly painful and irregular. Reality is always irregular and generally painful. In your case, Penelope, you will be spared many of those pains. Not only do you have now a wealth of freedom which you cannot value because you have not experienced the opposite, but you are also endowing yourself with a future freedom; freedom from the fear and shock and shyness which make the transition from youth to maturity more uncomfortable than any other period of existence. Francis is bringing you up through the looking glass, back-to-front. You are learning what the adult learns, and walking through these lessons toward the lightheartedness that is usually to be found in childhood but lost later. I wonder how long it will take you to find that out." She sat up on her elbows and stared at me again. "Do you know what I think will happen to your Anthology of Hates when you do find it out? You will read it through and find that these are not Hates any more."

CHAPTER 4

MY BEDROOM was on the ground floor, with a window that opened onto the far end of the terrace. It was late, but I was still awake and I heard Francis and Jeanne talking outside. I did not mean to listen, but their voices were clear and when I heard the name "Bradley" I could not help listening.

"I agree with you," Jeanne said, "that it is all an outrageous fuss. But these Bradleys mean a great deal to Penelope."

"Wish I knew why," said Francis. "They represent the worst and dullest aspect of English 'county'; a breed that may soon become extinct and no loss, either."

"They are the kind of friends that she has never had: English children of her own age."

Their footsteps ceased directly outside my window. I heard Francis sigh. "*Ought* we to send her to school in England, do you think?"

"Perhaps next year."

"That will be too late, beloved."

I had heard him call Jeanne "beloved" before, but tonight the word touched my heart, perhaps because I was already unhappy; it made me want to cry. "She will be fifteen," Francis said. "First she'll kill herself trying to fit into the pattern and, if she succeeds in the task, we shall never see her again. Heaven knows what we'll get but it won't be Penelope."

"She will change in any case, whether she stays or goes, darling; they always do."

"Perhaps I've done a poor job with her from the beginning,"

Francis said; he spoke my mother's name. And then I was so sure I must listen no more that I covered my ears with my hands. When I took them away Jeanne was saying, "You are always sad when your back is hurting you. Come to bed. Tomorrow I'll invite the Bradley children for lunch again; on Thursday when Violetta's in Monte Carlo."

I wept because they destroyed my defenses; my conscience still troubled me for the speeches of humbug that I had made to Eva, for quarreling with Francis, and for being uncivil to the Duchess. It was a weary load. If the Bradleys accepted the invitation to lunch, it would seem that God was not intending to punish me for it, but exactly the reverse, and that was a bewildering state of affairs.

By morning, however, God's plan became clear. Jeanne brought me my breakfast on the terrace. She sat with me while I ate it. I thought, as I had thought before, that she looked very young; more an elder sister than a stepmother, with her short, flying dark hair, the blue eyes in the brown face, the long slim brown legs.

I could hardly wait for her to tell me whether she had healed the breach with the Bradleys. But I dared not ask. Their talk on the terrace had been too intimate for me to admit that I had heard it. She said, "Penelope, the situation with your friends at La Lézardière has become a little complex."

My heart beat downward heavily and I did not want to eat any more.

"I thought that it would give you pleasure if I asked them to lunch and would perhaps clear up any misunderstanding. But I have been talking to Mrs. Bradley and apparently she would prefer them not to visit the hotel."

I did not know whether I was blushing for the hotel, for my own disappointment, or for the Bradleys; I was only aware of the blush, flaming all over my skin, most uncomfortably.

"Mrs. Bradley was friendly and polite, you must not think otherwise. She wants you to swim with them as much as you like; she said that she hoped you would go out in the speedboat again. But her exact phrase was, 'We feel that the hotel surroundings are just a little too grown-up for Don and Eva.' "

I was silent.

"So, I thought that I would tell you. And ask you not to be unhappy about it. People are entitled to their views, you know, even when one does not oneself agree with them."

"Thank you, Jeanne. I am not at all unhappy," I said, wishing that my voice would not shake. "And if the Bradleys will not come to me, I am damned if I am going to them." And I rose from the table. She came after me, but when she saw that I was near to tears she gave me a pat on the back and left me alone.

THIS was the point at which I discovered that hate did not cast out love, but that it was, on the contrary, possible to hate and love at the same time. I could not turn off my infatuation for the Bradleys, much as I longed to do so. They were still the desirable Vikings. It hurt me to shake my head and retire from the flat rock when Don and Eva beckoned me. They seemed to understand quickly enough, more quickly than their parents did. Mr. Bradley still called, "Coming aboard?" and Mrs. Bradley waved to me elaborately on every possible occasion. The children turned their heads away. For two days I saw them all like figures set behind a glass screen; only the echo of their voices reached me; I gave up haunting the beach and worked in a corner of the garden; the regularity of their timetable made it easy to avoid the sight of them. I told myself that they were loathsome, that they were the Smugs, and I even considered including them in the Anthology of Hates, but I found it too difficult. Now they had indeed become the moon that the Duchess told me I cried for. I cherished dreams of saving Don's life or Eva's at great risk to myself, and being humbly thanked and praised by their parents. Then I hoped that they would all die in a fire or, better still, that I would die and they would come to my funeral.

I found that I was seeing Francis, Jeanne and the Duchess through a grotesque lens; they were at once complete strangers and people whom I knew intimately. I could place them in a Bradley context, thinking, "That is Francis Wells, the poet, the poet who keeps the mad hotel. He always seems to wear the same red shirt. He looks like Mephistopheles when he laughs. And that is his wife, his *second* wife; younger than he is; very gay always, isn't she? What very *short* shorts. And there goes the Duchessa di Terracini, rather a terrible old lady who gambles at the Casino and drinks champagne; doesn't she look ridiculous in all that makeup and chiffon?" And then I would be talking to them in my own voice and with my own thoughts and feeling like a traitor.

I knew that they were sorry for me; that Francis above all approved my defiant refusal. I was aware of their hands held back from consoling gestures, to spare me too much overt sympathy. Even the Duchess did not speak to me of the Bradleys.

For once I welcomed the crises as diversion. And these two days naturally were not free from crises; a British ambassador and his wife found themselves in difficulty at our gates. All the entrails of their car fell out upon the road and we were obliged to give them rooms for the night.

This would not of itself have been other than a mechanical crisis, because the ambassador and Francis were old friends. Unfortunately the ambassador and the press baron from Cap d'Ail, who was dining with the Duchess, were old enemies. So a fierce political fight was waged in the bar, with both elderly gentlemen calling each other poltroon, and they would have fought a duel had not the electric current failed and the hotel been plunged in darkness till morning. (My only grief was that Don and Eva had missed it. All roads led to the Bradleys.)

On the third morning, which was Thursday, doom accelerated. I woke to find Francis standing beside my bed.

"Sorry, darling; trouble," he said. "A telephone call just came through from Aix; Jeanne's mother is very ill and I'm going to drive her over there now. Can you take care of you for today?"

He never asked me such questions: this was like a secret signal saying, "I know you are miserable and I am sorry."

"But of course. Please don't worry."

"There are no guests, fortunately. Violetta's going over to Monte Carlo; Laurent will be in charge tonight. You might see that he locks up, if I'm not back."

"I will do that. Can I help Jeanne or do anything for you?"

"No, my love. We are off now. I'll telephone you later." He ducked under the mosquito curtain to kiss me.

"You must pray rather than worry," the Duchess said to me, standing on the doorstep. "Death is a part of life," she added, pulling on her white gloves.

I could feel little emotion for my stepgrandmother who lived in seclusion near Aix-en-Provence, but I was sorry for Jeanne.

"The best thing that you could do, Penelope," said the Duchess, grasping her parasol like a spear, "would be to come over with me to Monte Carlo. We will lunch on the balcony of the Hotel de Paris; then you shall eat ices while I am at the tables; then a little stroll and we could dine on the quay at Villefranche and drive home under the moon. The moon is at the full tonight and I look forward to it. Come, child," she added, holding out her hand.

I thanked her very much and said that I would rather stay here.

THE first part of the day seemed endless. I sat in the garden on a stone bench under the largest of the umbrella pines. That way I had my back to La Lézardière. I could hear their voices and that was all. When the bell rang for their lunch, I went down to the pool and swam. I swam for longer than usual; then I climbed to the flat rock and lay in the sun. I was almost asleep when I heard Eva's voice. "Penelope!"

She was halfway up the rock; she said, "Look; we are so miserable we've written you this note. I have to go back and rest now." She was like a vision out of the long past; the freckles, the sunburn and the wet hair. I watched her scuttle down and she turned to wave to me from the lowest tier of the terrace. I gave her a half wave and opened the note.

It said:

DEAR PENELOPE,

Please don't be cross with us. Mum and Dad are going out to supper tonight. Don't you think that you could come? They have asked us to ask you.

Always your friends,

DON AND EVA

I wrote my reply at the *écritoire* in the salon. I wrote:

> Much as I appreciate the invitation, I am unable to accept it. Owing to severe illness in the family my father and stepmother have left for Aix. I feel it necessary to stay here and keep an eye on things.
>
> PENELOPE

To run no risk of meeting them, I went into the bar and asked Laurent if he would be so kind as to leave this note at La Lézardière.

After I had answered the note, I alternated between wishing that I had accepted and wishing that I had given them more truthful reasons for my refusal.

Later, I sought comfort by writing to my Aunt Anne in England; I sat there conjuring the fortnight as it would be and putting in the letter long descriptions of the things that I wanted to see and do again. It helped. I had covered 12 pages when the telephone rang.

Francis' voice spoke over a bad line: "Hello, Child of Confusion. Everything all right?"

"Yes, indeed. Nothing is happening at all. What is the news?"

"Better," he said, "but Jeanne will have to stay. I may be very late getting back. See that Laurent gives you the cold lobster. Jeanne sends her love."

Nothing would have induced me to ask Laurent for my dinner, but I was perfectly capable of getting it myself and the reference to cold lobster had made me hungry. No reason why I should not eat my dinner at six o'clock. I was on my way to the kitchen by way of the terrace when I heard a voice calling me:

"Penelope!"

I turned, feeling that horrible all-over blush begin. Mrs. Bradley stood at the doorway from the salon onto the terrace. She looked golden and statuesque in a white dress with a scarlet belt. The sight of her was painful. It seemed as though I had forgotten how lovely she was.

"May I talk to you a moment, my dear?"

"Please do," I said, growing hotter and hotter.

"Shall we sit here?" She took a chair beneath one of the red-and-yellow umbrellas. She motioned to me to take the other chair. I said, "Thank you, but I prefer to stand."

She smiled at me. I could feel in my heart the alarming collision of love and hate and now I could see her in two contexts; as a separate symbol, the enemy; as a beloved haunting of my own mind, the Mrs. Bradley of the first days, whom I had made my private possession.

"Can't we be friends, Penelope? I think we can, you know, if we try. Don and Eva are so sad and it all seems such a pity."

I said, "But, Mrs. Bradley, you made it happen."

"No, dear. That is what I want to put right. When I talked to your stepmother, I made it quite clear that we all hoped to see much more of you."

"But," I said, "that Don and Eva couldn't come here. As though it were an awful place."

She put her hand on mine; she gave a soft low laugh. "Penelope, how foolish of you. Of course it isn't an awful place. You have just imagined our thinking that, you silly child."

"Did I imagine what you said about the Duchess?"

Still she smiled and kept her hand on mine. "I expect that what I said about the Duchess was quite a little exaggerated to you by Eva and Don. That was an uncomfortable day for all of us. We don't often quarrel in our family; I don't suppose that you do, either. Quarrels are upsetting to everybody and nobody likes them."

"Certainly," I said, "I don't like them."

"Let's try to end this one, Penelope."

Did she guess how badly I wanted to end it? I could not tell.

"Supposing," she said, "that you let me put my point of view to you, as one grown-up person to another. You are very grown-up for your age, you know, and just because you are so grown-up and this place is your home, you have a very different life from the life that Don and Eva have. Now, my husband and I have to judge what is good for Don and Eva, don't we? You'll agree? Just as your father and stepmother have to judge what is good for you."

"Yes. I agree to that." It sounded reasonable; the persuasion of her manner was beginning to work.

"Well, we think that they aren't quite grown-up enough yet to understand and appreciate all the things that you understand and appreciate. That's all. It's as though you had a stronger digestion and could eat foods that might upset them. Do you see?"

When I was still silent, she added, "I think you should. Your stepmother saw perfectly."

"I suppose I see."

"Do try."

In fact I was trying hard; but the struggle was different from the struggle that she imagined. I felt as though I were being pulled over the line in a tug of war. Inside me there was a voice saying, "No, no. This is wrong. Nothing that she says can make it right. It is not a matter of seeing her point of view; you *can* see it; she has sold it to you. But you mustn't surrender." Oddly, the voice seemed to be the voice of the Duchess. I felt as though the Duchess were inside me, arguing.

I looked into the lovely, smiling face. "Do try," Mrs. Bradley repeated. "And do please come and have supper with the children tonight. Let's start all over again; shall we?"

When she held out both hands to me, she had won. I found myself in her arms and she was kissing my hair. I heard her say, "Poor little girl."

CHAPTER 5

ONLY the smallest shadow stayed in my heart and I forgot it for long minutes. We talked our heads off. It was like meeting them again after years. I found myself quoting in my head: "And among the grass shall find the golden dice wherewith we played of yore." They still loved me; they still laughed at everything I said. When I ended the description of the ambassador fighting the press baron and the failure of the electric lights, they were sobbing in separate corners of the sofa.

"Go on; go on. What did the Duchess do?"

"I think that she enjoyed it mightily. She had an electric torch in her bag and she flashed it over them both like a searchlight."

"You do have the loveliest time," said Eva.

"Where is the Duchess tonight?" asked Don.

"In fact, I think I heard her car come back about ten minutes ago," I began —

"Hark, though," Don interrupted. "There's a car now." He ran to the window; but I knew that it wasn't the Duchess' Isotta-Fraschini. It was the putt-putt noise of Laurent's little Peugeot.

"How exactly like Laurent," I said. "As soon as the Duchess gets home, he goes out. And Francis has left him in charge."

It occurred to me now that I should go back. I reminded myself that Charlemagne was an effective watchdog. But I was not comfortable about it.

"D'you mean you ought to go and put the Duchess to bed? Undo her stays; help her off with her wig?"

"It isn't a wig; it's her own hair, and she requires no help. But I do think I should go back."

"Isn't there anybody else in the hotel?"

"No."

"Oh, you *can't* go yet," said Eva.

I sat on a little longer. Then I knew that it was no good. "I shall have remorse if I don't," I said, "and that is the worst thing."

"All right, then. We'll go with you."

"Oh, Don — " said Eva.

"Mum and Dad won't be back yet awhile," said Don, "and we'll only stay ten minutes."

"They'll be furious."

"We won't tell them."

Eva looked at me. I said, "I cannot decide for you. I only know I must go."

"Of course if you want to stay behind . . ." Don said to Eva.

"Of course I don't. What shall we say to Nanny?"

"We can say we went down to the beach."

We crept out, silent in the spirit of adventure. The moon had risen, the full moon, promised by the Duchess, enormous and silver and sad; its light made a splendid path over the sea; the palms and the orange trees, the rock shapes on the water, were all sharp and black.

I could hear Don panting with excitement beside me. Almost, their mood could persuade me that the hotel was an enchanted place. We came onto the terrace and darted into the empty bar; Laurent had turned off the lights; I turned them up for the Bradleys to look at the photographs.

"What'll we drink?" said Don facetiously, hopping onto a stool.

"Champagne," said Eva.

"If the Duchess was still awake, she'd give us some champagne," said Don. "Where is she?"

"Probably in the salon," I said. "She never goes to bed early."

I put out the lights again and led them to the salon by way of the terrace. The salon lights were lit. We looked through the windows.

"There she is," said Don. "She's lying on the sofa."

They bounded in ahead of me. I heard Don say, "Good evening, Duchessa," and Eva echoed it. There was no reply from the Duchess. With the Bradleys, I stood still, staring at her. She was propped on the Empire sofa; her red head had fallen sideways on the stiff satin cushion. Her little pointed shoes and thin ankles stuck out from the hem of her shantung skirt which drooped down to the floor. A green scarf hung loose about her shoulders. A bottle of champagne stood in an ice pail; the glass had fallen to the floor; since one of her arms dangled limply, I thought that she must have dropped the glass as she went off to sleep.

"Please wake up, Duchessa; we want some champagne," said Don.

He took a step forward and peered into her face, which was turned away from us.

"She looks sort of horrid," he said. "I think she's ill."

For no reason that I could understand I felt that it was impertinent of him to be leaning there so close to her. When he turned back to us, I saw that his face was pale; the freckles were standing out distinctly on the bridge of his nose.

"She is ill, I'm sure," he said. "She's unconscious." He looked at the bottle of champagne. "She must be — " He stopped. I saw that he thought that the Duchess was intoxicated and that he could not bring himself to say so.

"Let's go," Eva said in a thin scared voice. She grabbed Don's hand. "Come on, Penelope. Quick."

"But of course I'm not coming."

They halted. "You can't stay here," Don said. Eva was shivering. There was no sound nor movement from the figure on the sofa. I said, "Certainly I can stay here. What else can I do? If she is ill, I must look after her."

I saw them straining against their own panic. Suddenly they seemed like puppies, very young indeed.

"But *we* can't stay here," Eva said. "Oh, please, Penelope, come with us."

"No indeed. But you go," I said. "It's what you want to do, isn't it?"

"It's what we ought to do," Eva stammered through chattering teeth. Don looked a little more doubtful. "Look here, Penelope, you needn't stay with her. When they — they get like that, they sleep it off."

Now I was angry with him. "Please go at once," I said. "This is my affair. And I know what you mean and it isn't true." I found that I had clapped my hands to shoo them off; they went; I heard the panic rush of their feet on the terrace. I was alone with the Duchess.

Now THAT they were gone, I had no hesitation in approaching her. I said softly, "Hullo, Duchessa. It's only me."

I lowered my head until my ear touched the green frilled chiffon at her breast. I listened for the beat of her heart. When I could not hear it, I lifted the little pointed hand and felt the wrist. There was no pulse here that I could find.

I despised myself because I began to shiver as Eva Bradley had shivered. My fingers would not stay still; it was difficult to unfasten the clasp of the green velvet bag. I thought that there would be a pocket mirror inside and that I must hold this to her lips.

The mirror, when I found it, was in a folding morocco case with visiting cards in the pocket on the other side. I said, "Excuse me, please, Duchessa," as I held it in front of her face. I held it there a long time; when I took it away the bright surface was unclouded. I knew that the Duchess was dead.

A profound curiosity took away my fear. I had never seen a person lying dead before. It was so strange to think of someone I knew well, as having stopped. But the more I stared at her, the less she looked as though she had stopped; rather, she had gone. This was not the Duchess lying here; it was a little old doll, a toy thing of which the Duchess had now no need. Where, I wondered, had she gone? What had happened to all the things that she remembered, the fencing lessons, and the child's dreams, and the Emperor? What happened, I wondered, to the memories that you carried around in your head? Did they go on with your soul or would a soul not want them? What did a soul want? Theology had never been my strongest subject and I found myself baffled by the rush of abstract questions flowing through my mind.

Then I became aware of her in relation to me. It was impossible to believe that I would not talk to her again. I was suddenly deeply sorry that I had not dined with her on the first evening. She had asked me to do this; she had asked me to come to Monte Carlo with her. Always she had been kind. I had not. I had never been nice to her because she embarrassed me and now I should never have another chance to be nice to her.

Automatically I began to perform small meaningless services. I covered her face with the green scarf, drawing it round her head so that it made a dignified veil. I fetched a rug and laid it across her feet; I did not want to see the little shoes. I carried the untouched champagne back to the bar. I lifted her tricorn hat, her bag and gloves off the table; I took them up to her room. It was more difficult to be in her room, with the bed turned down and the night clothes laid there, than it was to be in the salon with her body. I was running out when I saw the crucifix on the table. I thought that she might be pleased to have this near her ("Although," I said to myself, "she isn't there any more, one still goes on behaving as if she is"), and I carried it down; I set it on the table beside her. There seemed to be too many lights here now. I turned off all but one lamp; this room became a suitable place

for her to lie in state, the elegant little shell of a room with the Empire furnishings. I pulled a high-backed chair from the wall, set it at the foot of the sofa, and sat down to watch with her.

Outside the windows the moonlight lay in the garden. I heard her saying, "The moon is at the full tonight. I look forward to it." I heard her saying, "Naturally, you cry for the moon." I heard her saying, "Death is a part of life," as she pulled on her white gloves.

Sitting there so stiffly, I became terribly tired. "But it is a vigil," I said to myself, "and it is all that I can do for her." It was not much. It was no true atonement for having failed her in kindness; it could not remit my having betrayed her to the Bradleys. It seemed hours since I had thought of the Bradleys. Now I wondered whether the parents had returned and, with the question, there came incredulity that Don and Eva should not have come back. They had simply run off and left me, because they were afraid. The memory of their scared faces made them small and silly in my mind. Beside it, I uncovered the memory of my talk with Mrs. Bradley: the talk that had left a shadow. I admitted the shadow now: it was the note of patronage at the end of all the spellbinding. She had called me "poor little girl."

"You never called me 'poor little girl,' " I said in my thoughts to the Duchess. She had called me fortunate and a genius. She had spoken to me of the world, of freedom and maturity. That was truly grown-up conversation. In comparison the echo of Mrs. Bradley saying, "As one grown-up person to another," sounded fraudulent. Some of the magic had left the Bradleys tonight.

I was so tired. I did not mean to sleep, because this was vigil. But I found my head falling forward and the moonlight kept vanishing and the Duchess' voice was quite loud in my ears. "Of death," she said, "I remember three things; being tired, being quiet and being gone. That's how it is, Penelope." She seemed to think that I could not hear her. She went on calling, "Penelope! Penelope!"

I sat up with a start. Somebody was in fact calling "Penelope": a man's voice from the terrace. I climbed down stiffly from the chair. "Who's that?" I asked, my voice sounding cracked and dry. Mr. Bradley stood against the moonlight.

"Are you there, child? Yes, you are. Come along out of this at once." He looked large and golden and worried; he seized my hand; then he saw the Duchess on the sofa.

"Lord," he said. "She's still out, is she?" He started again. "Did you cover her up like that?"

"Yes. Please talk quietly," I said. "She is dead."

He dropped my hand, lifted the scarf a little way from her face, and put it back. I saw him looking at the crucifix.

"I put it there. I thought that she would like it. I am watching by her," I said.

He looked pale, ruffled, not the way, I thought, that grown-up people should look. "I'm terribly sorry," he said in a subdued voice. "Terribly sorry. Young Don came along to our room, said he couldn't sleep for knowing you were over here with her. Of course, he didn't think — "

"I know what he thought, Mr. Bradley," I said coldly. "Don and Eva are only babies really. Thank you for coming, just the same."

He said, in his officer-to-men voice, "Out of here now. There's a good girl."

"I beg your pardon?"

"You're coming to our house. I'll telephone the doctor from there." He took my hand again; I pulled it free.

"I'll stay with her, please. You telephone the doctor."

He looked down at me, amazed, almost smiling. He dropped his voice again. "No, no, no, Penelope. You mustn't stay."

I said, "I must."

"No, you mustn't. You can't do her any good."

"It is a vigil."

"That's just morbid and foolish. You're coming over to our house now."

"I am not."

"Yes, you are," he said, and he picked me up in his arms. To struggle in the presence of the Duchess would have been unseemly. I remained tractable, staying in his arms until he had carried me onto the terrace. He began to put me down and I twisted free.

"I'm not coming with you. I'm staying with her. She is my friend and she is not your friend. You were rude about her, and stupid," I said to him.

He grabbed me again and imprisoned me with my arms to my sides.

"Listen, Penelope, don't be hysterical. I'm doing what's best for you. That's all. You can't possibly sit up all night alone with the poor old lady; it's nearly three o'clock now."

"I shall stay with her till dawn; and she is not a poor old lady, just because she is dead."

I was aware of his face close to mine, the stony, regular features, the blue eyes and clipped mustache in the moonlight. The face seemed to struggle for speech. Then it said, "I don't want insolence any more than I want hysteria. You just pipe down and come along. This is no place for you."

"It is my home," I said.

He shook me gently. "Have some sense, will you? I wouldn't let my kids do what you're doing and I won't let you do it."

"Your children," I said, "wouldn't want to do it anyway; they are, in vulgar parlance, a couple of sissies."

At this he lifted me off my feet again and I struck at his face. I had the absurd idea that the Duchess had come to stand in the doorway and was cheering me on. And at this moment there came the miracle. The noise of the car sweeping in from the road meant that Francis had come home.

The headlights swung yellow upon the moonlit garden. Still aloft in Mr. Bradley's clutch I said, "That is my father, who will be able to handle the situation with dignity."

He set me down as Francis braked the car and jumped out.

"That you, Bradley?" said Francis. "What, precisely, are you doing?"

Mr. Bradley said, "I am trying to make your daughter behave in a sensible manner. I'm very glad to see you. There's been a tragedy here tonight, I'm afraid. Just doing what I could to help."

"I will tell him," I said. I was grateful for Francis' arm holding me; my legs had begun to feel as though they were made of spaghetti.

"You let me do the talking, young woman," said Mr. Bradley.

"If you don't mind, I'd prefer to hear it from Penelope," said Francis.

I told him. I told him slowly, leaving out none of it; there seemed less and less breath in my lungs as I continued. "And Mr. Bradley called it morbid and foolish and removed me by force," I ended.

"Very silly of you, Bradley," said Francis.

"Damn it, look at the state she's in!"

"Part of which might be due to your methods of persuasion, don't you think? All right, Penelope, easy now." I could not stop shivering.

"Leaving her alone like that in a place like this. You ought to be ashamed of yourself," Mr. Bradley boomed.

"Quiet, please," said Francis in his most icy voice.

"Damned if I'll be quiet. It's a disgrace and I don't want any part of it."

"Nobody," I said, "asked you to take any part in it, Mr. Bradley."

"Hush," said Francis. "Mr. Bradley meant to be kind and you must be grateful."

"I am not in the least."

"Fine manners you teach her," said Mr. Bradley.

"Quiet, please," said Francis again. "Penelope has perfect manners, mitigated at the moment by perfect integrity and a certain amount of overstrain." Looking up at him, I could see the neat Mephistophelean profile, the delicate shape of his head. I loved him more than I had ever loved him. Mr. Bradley, large and blowing like a bull, was outside this picture, nothing to do with either of us.

Suddenly he looked as though he realized this. He said: "I don't want my wife or my kids mixed up in it, either."

"Mixed up in what, precisely?" Francis asked.

I said, "It is possible that he is referring to the inquest. Or do you mean mixed up with me? Because if you do, no problem should arise. After tonight I have not the slightest wish to be mixed up with them or you."

It would have been more effective had I been able to stop shivering; I was also feeling rather sick, never a help when attempting to make dignified speeches.

Mr. Bradley faded away in the moonlight.

Francis said gently, "Did you mean it? It is easy to say those things in anger."

"I think I meant it. Was the vigil, in your opinion, the right thing to do?"

"It was. I am very pleased with you."

"They can't *help* being the Smugs, can they?" I said suddenly, and then for the first time I wanted to cry.

"They're all right," said Francis. "They are merely lacking in imagination."

I managed to say, "Sorry," and no more. I knew that he disliked me to cry. This time he said, watching me, "On some occasions it is better to weep."

I put my head down on the table and sobbed, "If only she could come back; I would be nice."

Francis said, "You gave her great pleasure always."

"Oh, not enough."

"Nobody can give anybody enough."

"Not ever?"

"No, not ever. But one must go on trying."

"And doesn't one ever value people until they are gone?"

"Rarely," said Francis.

I went on weeping; I saw how little I had valued him; how little I had valued anything that was mine. Presently he said, "Do you think that you can cry quite comfortably by yourself for a few minutes because I must telephone the doctor?"

Though I said, "Yes, indeed," I stopped crying immediately. As I sat waiting for him, I was saying good-bye, to my first dead, to a love that was ended, and to my dream of being like other people.

The next day I tore the Anthology of Hates into pieces and cast the pieces into the sea. I did not read through the pages first, so certain was I that I had done with hating.

Pamela Frankau

PAMELA FRANKAU published her first novel when she was 18, and has rolled up the formidable score of 23 books. Born and educated in England, for the past ten years she has been a resident of the United States, where she is equally at home in Martha's Vineyard and California. She is best known to the American reading public for her successful novels *The Willow Cabin* and *To the Moment of Triumph.*

"What makes her such a good writer," says Storm Jameson, another distinguished novelist, "is not only that she has wit, irony, rare gifts as a storyteller, but that she has a heart."

The only interruption in her record of literary production came with the outbreak of World War II when she enlisted in the A.T.S. (the Auxiliary Territorial Service of the British Army), where she attained the rank of major.

She confesses to a weakness for cooking, crossword puzzles, canasta, and air travel. One of her unfulfilled ambitions is to make a parachute jump. Friends of this intrepid and lively lady will not be surprised to learn of her doing it any day now.

Illustrations by Ed Vebell

TOMORROW!

A condensation of the book by

PHILIP WYLIE

"THIS is a CONELRAD Radio Alert. Enemy bombers are approaching. Take cover immediately. This is not a practice. *This is real.*"

Tomorrow! is Philip Wylie's white-hot evocation of what could happen in the event of a massive Russian air attack on the United States. River City and Green Prairie are twin cities in the Middle West; their citizens are as recognizable as your next-door neighbors. There are the Conners, pillars of Green Prairie's Civil Defense organization; the Baileys, social climbers whose frantic drive to "keep up" involves them in one crisis after another; the Williams family, who "know all about" Civil Defense and aren't having any; powerful Minerva Sloan, whose wealth and influence prove no protection against X Day.

When the nightmare atomic attack, unexpected, devastating, lands in the midst of these lives, it brings to the reader a shocking realization: *This could happen here!* But Philip Wylie is not prophesying doom; he is pleading for preparedness. *Tomorrow!* combines high drama with notable public service.

"A book with stunning impact for the American reader."—Val Peterson, Federal Civil Defense Administrator, in the New York *Times Book Review*

"Terrifyingly real and true and close and possible . . ." —Al Hine in *The Saturday Review*

X Day Minus Ninety

CHAPTER 1

THE Conner family lived in a frame house, circa 1910, set back in a big lawn on Walnut Street in the "residential section" of Green Prairie. A population approaching a million was shared by Green Prairie and its twin, River City, which lay across the Green Prairie River and in another state. Some of these residents were rich and powerful; some were poor; but most were ordinary people — prospering modestly, loving freedom, hating interference, intelligent by the lights of their society, fair citizens and superb neighbors.

The Conners were such a family. At first glance they were indistinguishable from millions in the nation — yet, like the millions, on any second look more individualist than most other people of the earth. At the end of the Second War, during the great expansion, the Conners had thrived. But like all their fellow citizens, and more keenly than many, they shared the doubts and anxieties of the new age.

Its very voice influenced their lives, even their domestic lives, as the years chased each other swiftly, rewardingly, after the century's mid-point. Green Prairie and River City were halves of a happy, urban world, separated by a river and a political boundary but united by bridges both actual and spiritual. Typically American, content, constructive, the Conners, too, were happy. And yet . . .

THE SOUND came through the open windows of the dining room. Each of the five members of the Conner family was differently affected. Henry, the father, stopped all movement to listen. His wife, Beth, looked out through the screened windows, frowning, as if she wished she had never heard a siren in her life. Nora, who was 11, exclaimed, *"Brother!* You can hear it *this* time, all right, all right!"

Ted Conner pushed back his chair, stood, started to go, then snatched a fresh roll before his feet took the stairs with the noisy incoherence of a male high school student in a hurry.

Charles, the older son, smiled faintly. This was the first evening of his leave and the first time he'd worn home the proud silver bar of a first lieutenant. The dinner — especially the roast beef which had filled the kitchen with a hunger-begetting aroma all afternoon — was a celebration for him. Now the sound surging over the city would interfere with that homely ceremony. Charles's smile expressed his regret. "Can I help?" he asked his father, who had risen.

"Guess not. This is a civilian party!" Henry Conner took the stairs in the wake of his younger son, but more deliberately.

"It's a shame it had to be this evening," Mrs. Conner said. "Still, Nora and you and I can at least eat."

"Aren't you in it?" Charles asked.

"I'm in the first-aid group, yes. But we don't have to answer this call. This is just for air-raid-warden practice."

The siren gathered strength and volume. Its initial growl and its first crescendo had seemed far away; soon its slow rise and fall became pervasive and penetrating; the human head was invaded not just by noise, but by what seemed a tangible substance. "This new one," Nora yelled above it, "sure is a lulu!"

"They must have hung it on a tree in our back yard," Charles replied loudly.

His mother shook her head. "It's on the new TV tower, out on Sunset Parkway by the reservoir."

Henry Conner came down the stairs two at a time. He opened the front door and called from the porch, "Here comes Ed!" He raced down the driveway, waving. The effort caused his crimson arm band, on which the word "Warden" was stenciled in white, to slide off his arm. When he bent down to retrieve it, his World War I helmet clattered on the sidewalk. At the same time, Mrs. Conner called, "You forgot your whistle!" and ran indoors to get it. The lieutenant hastened to help his father reassemble his gear.

At the dinner table, alone in the presence of a feast, Nora made a hasty survey and passed herself the jam. She piled an incredible amount on half a slice of bread, tossed her two braids clear for action and contrived to crowd the mass into her mouth.

"Everything's cold," Mrs. Conner said ruefully as she and Charles returned to the table.

"Far from it," her son answered. "Best meal I've looked at in six months." He sliced a square of thick and juicy beef. "Best I've *ever* tasted!"

Her rewarded look was warm, but it vanished as she noticed the diminished aspect of the jelly dish. *"Nora . . !"*

In the car, as he sped down Walnut Street beside Ed, Henry Conner was thinking about the wild-strawberry jam and the roast beef, too. His companion had identical sentiments: "Caught me," he said, as he slowed to cross Lakeview Road, "just as we were sitting down to dinner."

"Me, too. Guess they figured everybody would be doing the same. Ought to be a good turnout, on account of it."

Ed slammed on the brakes in time to avoid the chemical engine of Hook and Ladder Company Number 17. It pounded across the intersection, its lights on in spite of the fact that the sun still shone, its clanging bell drowned by a whoop of the siren. "Something *else* to think about," Henry yelled, letting his nerves down easy. "When those sirens are going, you can't hear car horns or even fire-truck bells!"

Ed wiped a little diamond dust of sweat from his forehead. "Could have been closer, Hank."

"Oh, sure."

The sedan turned into South Hobson Street and slowed. The school was only four blocks distant, and converging Civil Defense cars were piling up, even though volunteer "police" were blowing whistles urgently and waving their arms. They could see, now, hundreds of cars parked and being parked in the playgrounds of the South High School. They could see the "wrecked" corner of the gymnasium where, later in the evening, the fire fighters and rescue squads would rehearse under conditions of simulated disaster, including real flames and chemical smoke. The very numbers of the congregating people stimulated them. That stimulus, added to a certain civic pride, helped Hank Conner and Ed McWade to forget they were middle-aged businessmen, middle-class householders, who for weary years had periodically and stubbornly pretended that their city in the middle of America was the target of an enemy air raid.

Before Ed parked the car, Henry leaped out and went to his post to assemble his block wardens. One of them, Jim Ellis, proprietor of the Maple Street Pharmacy, was incensed. "You know what, Hank? This is my druggist's night off. I had to shut down the prescription department since I can't be there to roll pills myself! Probably cost me twenty, twenty-five bucks. Maybe customers, even. Next time we have one of these fool rehearsals — "

"You shouldn't be here, anyway, Jim. How come?"

"I phoned headquarters when the letter about this new drill came. They told me whenever the sirens went to report here — "

"Well, I'll be responsible for that. You get your car and go back to the pharmacy. In a *real* raid you'd be indispensable there."

"That makes sense!"

Hank's easy voice rose to a pitch of command: "Sykes! Evans! Maretti! Get Jim's car cleared of the parking yard and see him around to Baker Avenue!"

A woman wearing a warden's arm band rushed up from a knot of people gathered around a placard that said "Station 42." She cried anxiously, "Mr. Conner! I left rolls in the oven!"

Henry drew a breath, expelled it. "How often do we have to go through the routine, Mrs. Dace? You're supposed to check all those things before you jump in a car and start for your post. You'll have to get a phone priority slip and tell your neighbors to turn off the gas."

Hank began searching the school grounds for somebody connected with telephone priorities. He wondered with a kind of good-humored annoyance how in hell the citizens of Green Prairie would learn to save lives when they couldn't remember to salvage biscuits.

In that segment of the attic which had long ago been converted into "the boys' room," Ted Conner worked feverishly amid a junklike jumble of wires, dimly glowing tubes, switches, dials, condensers, transformers and other paraphernalia with which gifted young men — specialists at the age of 16 or so — are able to communicate with one another, often over distances of hundreds of miles. Ted Conner was a member in good standing of the

American Radio Amateurs' Society. He was also a volunteer member of Civil Defense, Communications Division.

To Ted, more than to any other person in the family, the rise and fall of the siren spelled excitement. It was his instant duty to rush to his radio set and tune in headquarters. It was his additional assignment, every five minutes on the second, to listen for 30 seconds to his opposite number in Green Prairie's Sister City, directly across the river.

Ted sat now with one leg hooked over the arm of a reconstructed swivel chair, his blue eyes shining, his usually clumsy hands turning the radio dials with delicacy. He was oblivious to everything in his environment: the pennants and banners on the wall; the stolen signs that said "Danger" and "Do Not Disturb" and "Men"; the battered dresser and its slightly spotted mirror framed in snapshots — snapshots of girls in bathing suits, and girls with ukuleles, and a burning B-29.

He did not see any of it. To Ted Conner, who was 16, a hideous danger now menaced Green Prairie and River City. To Ted, the theoretical enemy bombers were near. To him, brave men like his brother Chuck (though Chuck, actually, was a Ground Force officer) were even now climbing from nearby Hink Field into the stratosphere to engage atom-bomb-bearing planes that winged toward Green Prairie.

This stage setting was necessary to accompany the rest of the dream he had, every time there was a drill:

One enemy bomber was getting through. Man after man was trying for it and missing. Its bomb-bay doors were opening. The horrendous missile was falling. There was an earth-shaking explosion. Half of Green Prairie and even more of River City were blotted out. Now, Ted Conner was alone — alone at his post in the attic. His family had been evacuated. The place was a shambles and on fire. But there he sat, ice-calm, sending and giving messages which were saving uncounted lives — to the last. They would put up a monument for him later — when they found his high school ring, miraculously unmelted in the ashes of the Conner home.

His earphones spoke. "Headquarters. Condition Red! Condition Red! Stand by, all stations."

Ted felt goose flesh cascade down his back. He stood by. Headquarters had been saying that off and on for 20 minutes. And not much else.

Downstairs, Nora asked if she could have another piece of pumpkin pie and whipped cream. Mrs. Conner said, "Absolutely not."

"Then I'll go out and play till it's dark."

"You'll do your homework, that's what you'll do!"

"Mother! It's *ridiculous* to ask anybody to study during an *air raid.*"

"It is ridiculous," her mother replied, "to think you can use a drill for an alibi. Now go do your arithmetic, Nora."

"I hate it!"

"Exactly. So — the sooner you do it . . ."

Chuck grinned reminiscently and excused himself. He went through the kitchen to the back door. Queenie, the Conner tomcat, was meowing to be admitted. The lieutenant let him in, marveling briefly over the mistake in gender which had led to the original name, and his young sister's defense, which had permitted the misnomer to stick.

"A cat," Nora had said long ago, "can look at a queen. So, he'll *stay* Queenie, even if he has got a man sex."

Dusk was gathering in the yard. Chuck could smell rather than see that his brother had recently mowed the lawn. He could see, however, that Ted hadn't trimmed the grass along the privet hedge which separated the Conners' yard from the Baileys'. Chuck reflected that in his boyhood he had been a precise trimmer and clipper. But then, he'd always wanted to be what he would be now, were it not for his uniform: an architect. And Ted was different: he wanted to be an inventor — at least right now. Inventors were probably not much interested in tidy lawns.

Chuck stood in the drive and looked uncertainly at the Bailey house. Time was when his family's house and the residence next door had been quite similar — ordinary American homes — but the Baileys had "modernized" their place just after World War II. The front porch had been carted away and the front façade remade with imitation adobe bricks and a picture window. The vegetable garden in the back had vanished and in its place were a summerhouse and a barbecue pit where, wearing a chef's hat and an apron with jokes printed on it, Beau Bailey, Lenore's father, sometimes ruined good beefsteak while his guests drank Martinis in the gloaming.

All in all, Howard Bailey (who was called "Beau" even by the president of the bank where he worked as cashier) had spent a lot of money for his remodeling job and failed to fool anybody. Putting on "side" was Chuck's opinion — and it characterized not only Beau, but his wife.

Lenore was different.

At least, Chuck hoped she was different still.

For Chuck could hardly recall a day in his life when he had not been in love with the Baileys' only child. Propinquity might have explained that: there was no day when Chuck had not lived next door to Lenore. But propinquity was not needed to explain the attachment.

Lenore long ago had won a "Prettiest Grade School Girl" contest that had included River City as well as Green Prairie. At 18 she had been May Princess at the South High School, which meant she was the most attractive girl in her senior class. And she had been voted the "Most Beautiful Coed" when she had graduated from State University. But Lenore's desirability involved more than her loveliness. She happened to be bright and, in addition, she was sweet and gracious, democratic and sincere.

Chuck and Lenore had always been "friends." As "friends" they had enjoyed an intimacy of a particular sort. Chuck was sure, for example, that he was the first boy who had ever kissed Lenore; but it was not very impressive assurance. He had kissed her when they were both six years old. Though Chuck recalled the episode with warmth and savor, his close amity with Lenore at six did little to bolster his confidence at twenty-four.

He examined the Bailey house. There was a Buick parked at the curb — "a Buick," his father often said, "trying to look like a Cadillac" — and a Ford in the back yard. That meant all three Baileys were probably at home: Beau, Netta and Lenore. But it didn't mean Lenore had no date that evening or that Chuck could simply enter without even knocking as he'd done when he and Lenore had studied algebra together.

He had about decided to go back in the house and phone formally when a door opened and somebody came out wearing a yellow plastic jumper with a hood that covered the head. The person was carrying a box with wires attached to it and a silvery gadget dangling from the wires. This figure turned toward the open door and called in a husky, pleasant voice, "Don't wait up for me. I've got a date — after."

It was Lenore's voice. Chuck shouted, "Hey!"

The box with its attached gadgetry was set on the lawn. The voice now floated toward him. *"Chuck!* When did you get back?" Lenore ran toward him. "What a wonderful surprise! Why didn't you let me know?"

Lenore was dressed as if she were going to crawl under the Buick and fix it — a chore of which she was capable; but it was not for that, Chuck knew. He knew it if for no other reason than that neither her mother, whose social ambitions were limitless, nor her father, who had matching financial desires, would let their daughter play mechanic in the street. It was only when they touched hands there in the gathering twilight — when they felt warmth and strength each in the other — that Chuck associated the girl's astounding regalia and recent events.

"Ye gods!" he cried, letting go of her, "a *Geigerman!"*

She nodded, a little impishly. "Isn't it becoming?" She pirouetted like a model. "Yellow," she went on, "is the fall color. The material is simply amazing. Not only weatherproof and mothproof, but fire-resistant, too. Absolutely dustproof. No common chemicals can damage it. The hood" — she pulled it farther over her face and drew down a green, transparent visor which sealed her from view — "provides adequate protection from the elements, *all* the elements, including their radioactive isotopes!" She broke off, pulled down the hood, disclosed blue eyes, tumbling dark hair, crimson lips. "Oh, *Chuck!* I'm *so* glad to see you! Kiss me."

He tried to kiss her cheek and she made that impossible. She held the kiss, besides, for a long moment and when she settled on her heels she whispered, "Welcome home."

He dissembled his feelings, pointed. "How come?"

"This?" She looked at the radiation-safety garment. "Spite."

"Spite?"

"I'll explain. I've got to take off in a sec—South High. Want to drive me there?"

" 'Whither thou goest...' and so forth," he answered.

Chuck carried the Geiger counter to the car, climbed in and backed down the driveway. He switched on the headlights and started slowly along Walnut Street. "How are things?" he asked.

"Just the same." She shrugged one shoulder somewhere under the coverall. "But absolutely, painfully the same. Possibly a shade worse. Dad seems to be drinking a little too much. And Mother keeps crowding me a little harder all the time."

"Why don't you go away?"

"Away like where?" she asked. "Didn't we kick that around till it got lost, the last time you were home on leave?"

"I kept thinking about it—at the base."

"I didn't need to. The family didn't let me study what I wanted. Couldn't afford graduate courses. You know that. They hate the very thought that their darling daughter has a knack for science instead of a knack for rich men. So why should I go away, to New York even, and work at something I'd detest? Being a secretary. Or a model. Phooie!"

"Anyhow," he said, not happily, "you'll make a damned good Geigerman."

She ignored the hurt tone. "Won't I? And doesn't it burn Mother to the core!"

He swung into South Hobson Street. It was solid with cars. From time to time they moved up a few inches. In the distance, the playgrounds of South High, floodlighted now, were swarming with people, most of whom wore brassards and helmets. Whistles blew. Teams of various sorts formed and marched together toward a place where flames licked around a huge heap of broken boxes, barrels, old lumber. Hoses played. The thrumming of a fire-engine pump could be heard. A searchlight snapped on somewhere and threw so much light on the simulated burning wreckage that the flames became invisible and only the smoke showed.

Chuck fixed an eye, half-humorous, half-melancholy, on the scene. It was just a little like basic training, when you crawled along under live bullets from real machine guns and when you ran through actual poison gas, wearing a mask. But, he thought, it was nothing whatever like a real city after the detonation of a real bomb — even a high-explosive bomb. "Terrific," he said.

Lenore raised her eyebrows. "Ridiculous, too?"

"Just what do you do?"

"We form," she answered, "exactly one hour after the siren. I'm late, but everybody in my section will be because they can't get their counters working right, or can't find where they put them, or took them over to the lab for repair. Then we approach the 'simulated radioactive site.' Tonight, they told us, they will actually have a small chunk of radiating metal somewhere. We're supposed to probe around till we find it."

He shook his head, inched the car up, braked again and watched as she opened the door. "Carry on!" he said, saluting her with mock solemnity.

She laughed a little. "I've got myself in this, and a date later, when what I want to do is see more of you."

"I'll be home," he answered, "any evening for the next thirty."

"And as soon as Mother knows it," she answered, grimly, picking up her instrument, "she'll raise heaven and earth to make it as nearly impossible as she can for me to see you at all."

"Still — you being twenty-four — "

"But jobless and dependent." She slammed the door. "I can't fight them to the point where I'm really kicked out."

He wanted to ask why she couldn't. He wanted to say, as he had said before, that there were young women, lovely ones, who managed to live on a lieutenant's pay. But he knew what would follow any such suggestion. It began with the reminder that, when he ceased being a lieutenant in one more year, he wouldn't have an income at all. When he was settled in civilian life, it would at first be on the minute income of a draftsman in some small architectural office in River City or Green Prairie. "Barely enough," Lenore had said once in a bitter moment, "to pay my dry-cleaning bills."

"Do I call back?" he asked.

"I'll get a ride. This monkeyshine won't break up till around eleven. Then we go to somebody's house for what the older veterans of Civil Defense call refreshments and jollification."

"Ducky."

She stalked down South Hobson Street, making better time than the traffic.

He parked her car beside her house and saw, through the picture window, Beau Bailey asleep with the evening paper in his lap, a highball by his chair. Hurriedly he crossed the lawn to his own yard.

CHAPTER 2

Beau Bailey woke up with a start because Netta had spoken to him—yelled, rather, *"Telephone!"*

He got out of his chair and gulped down his highball. He picked up the instrument and cleared his throat. His tone was suddenly buoyant and friendly: "Howard Bailey speaking."

"This is Jake."

If Netta had been in the hall, she would have seen that Beau's face lost all its color. The whisky, too, went out of his brain. Nothing was left but a pallid and wobbling man's body, frantic eyes—but the voice intact, for Beau knew his wife would be listening though she could not look. She always listened.

He said, after a pause, "Oh, yes. How are you?"

A businessman, Netta decided upstairs. Somebody of whom Beau was slightly afraid, which didn't mean much, since he was somewhat afraid of everybody.

The voice that reached Beau was level, a little too level and, though not foreign, it used English in a fashion alien to Green Prairie—in a way which anyone familiar with American dialects would have identified as related to Chicago, to the South Side, to the period of 1920-1930. "Shallcot Rove ran fifth today, Mr. Bailey."

"Yes, I know. Of course."

"It puts the total up to five thousand, even."

Beau gave a little laugh. "As much as that, eh? I wouldn't worry. I expect the market will take a turn for the better — "

"No more 'market,' Mr. Bailey, until you pay up."

"I'll come down and have a conference in a day or two. . . ." Beau could feel the sweat forming and he could hear Netta on the stairs.

"Yes," the voice of Jake said flatly. "You come down to The Block tomorrow, to the horse room, Mr. Bailey. And I think you better bring the five thousand. If not all, then at least half. And half later — but soon. And no more bets. Frankly, I told the Bun not to take bets from you last week till you paid. I was sore at him for doing it against orders. He is home sick now because I was so sore. I made him sick."

Jake hung up.

So did Beau. He hung up fast and found, by listening to his wife's tread, there was time to get back through the archway into

the living room (sunken two steps since the remodeling) with the appearance of casualness. The wall then hid him long enough so that he could whip out his handkerchief and wipe his face. He could see in the mirror wall around the fireplace that he was pale.

When Netta Bailey came downstairs, she was occupied by nothing more than a marriage-long habit of anxious inquisitiveness and a very slight feeling, not that the phone call was of a serious nature, but that her husband had been a little more obsequious than usual. She saw now that Beau was frantically afraid. His effort to dissemble went to no purpose. She said, "What's wrong?"

"Nothing. Nothing whatever."

"*Beau.* You can't fool me."

"I'm not trying to!"

Netta walked around the bleached-mahogany table in the room's center. Her eyes needled. She was somehow made more ominous, where it would have rendered most women ineffective, by the fact that she had been "experimenting" after supper with creams and lotions: her rusty-musty hair overtopped a towel and dangled from it and her face gleamed greasily. "Okay," she said steadily. "*Who* was it?"

"Netta, please! It was a business call."

"Your business, though. Not the bank's."

Beau made a tactical error. "How can you tell?"

"So it was personal. Beau! What have you been up to?"

"Nothing, I tell you. Nothing."

Netta sat down on the arm of the huge, flower-print-covered divan the decorator had chosen for them. "You can tell me now or you can argue awhile. Either way, Beau, I'll find out from you."

His voice suddenly filled the room, taut, shrill, surprising him even more than Netta. "None of your damned business!"

"It's really bad trouble, isn't it?"

"Who said it was trouble?" His face had puckered like the face of a baby trying to decide whether to produce a tantrum or a spell of pitiable tears.

"How much is it going to cost us?"

"Netta — stop jumping to such crazy conclusions!"

She could tell, to a decibel, a hairbreadth, when he was lying and when he was not. She went on implacably, "If you've just hocked something — or borrowed on the cars . . . "

"What have we got to hock that isn't already hocked, including the cars?" He stared at her with momentary self-righteousness.

She said, "Then it *is* money?"

"Quit hounding me." He reached for the bottle.

"No more drink until you explain."

He put the bottle down. Another man might have continued the defense for hours, even for days. Beau himself might have gone on fencing for a time, save for the fact that he was now far more afraid of another person than of Netta. He took a chair. He lighted a cigarette. He looked at his intent wife and said, "Okay. You brought it on yourself. This time we really are in a jam."

"I brought it on myself! *We* are in a jam! Speak for yourself, bright boy!"

"I'll tell you," he said, "just how bad a jam it is. If I hadn't borrowed up to the full value on my insurance . . !" He pointed his forefinger at his temple, cocked his thumb in a pantomime of shooting himself.

"How *much* money?" she asked again, unimpressed by his drama.

"Five thousand dollars."

Netta moaned softly, sagged, slid from the arm of the divan onto the cushions. "Five — thousand — dollars." She murmured the words, wept them. "Even one thousand the way we're fixed . . !" Then she screamed, "How in the world do you owe that?"

Tears filled Beau's eyes. "All my life," he recited, "I've done just one thing and one thing only: scrimped and sweat and slaved and hit the old ball, so you and Lenore could have a fine life. I have no pleasures of my own, no vices, no indulgences — "

She was looking at him, white-faced, oblivious to his stale stock of good providing. "Those . . . 'bonuses'! The 'little windfalls,' you *said!* The fur coat you got Lenore! The new Deepfreeze you made a little killing just in time to pay for! All *that?"*

"A man," he responded in a ghastly tone, "can get so devoted to his family he'll stop at nothing for their sake — "

Netta said, "You've been gambling!"

"How do you know?"

"Horses!"

"And I did all right." Her guess seemed to release him. "And if I had some *real* dough to lay on the line, I could get back what I'm down — !"

"Where? What bookie? Was it *Jake Tanetti?* That was *Tanetti* on the phone!"

Now, for the first time, Netta was more frightened than angry. "Beau, do you really owe Jake Tanetti five thousand dollars?"

"I didn't think it was that much. I thought — around three. But *he* says five."

"Then it's five." Netta sat silent for a moment, her chest heaving. Once or twice she looked speculatively at Beau. Finally she smiled at him wanly. "Come over here. Sit beside me."

"Net, I don't want to. I'm too ashamed."

She beckoned. Heavily he rose and cautiously approached. He seated himself as gingerly as if the divan had been an electric chair. But Netta just took his hand and held it in her own and stared at it and finally said, softly, "Beau, my boy, you've done some dumb things in your day, but this is really Grade-A trouble. I'm not sore. I'm sorry."

She meant it. Meant the compassion she displayed, the calm. Intellectually, Netta knew that the only way to manage Beau now would be with gentleness. Anything harsh might easily snap the thin threads of his remaining pride and cause him to do something still more rash. Not suicide. But he might confess to Minerva Sloan and throw himself (and her and Lenore, as incidentals) on the mercy of the old woman.

The widow of Emmet Sloan, the richest man in the Sister Cities, board chairman of the Sloan Mercantile Trust, was Beau's boss. Minerva had become head of the Sloan holdings when Mr. Sloan died in 1935 — "of Roosevelt," they said. There was no such thing as mercy in Minerva, Netta knew.

"You're the cashier of a big bank," she said carefully, "so you *can't* gamble. That means this business *must not come out."*

"If I don't pay Jake — "

"Sure. If you don't — it will. So he has to get paid."

"How?"

"That's what we've got to figure. He'll probably take something down. . . ."

Beau brightened a little. "He said he would. Half now. Half later."

"Okay. All you need right off is $2500."

He shrugged. "Might as well be two million."

"I've heard you say, Beau, you could lay your hands on fortunes, and nobody would be the wiser for years."

He pulled away from her. "The *bank?"*

"You said . . ?" she gestured casually.

"Good lord, Net! I *said* so, sure. Portfolios full of negotiable stuff that I check, sometimes. You could slip out millions and borrow on it — cash it in — and nobody would know till somebody looked. Maybe six months, maybe a year, or longer. But that's out!"

"You got any better ideas?"

"That one isn't even an idea. Look, Net. I appreciate the way you're taking this. I — I — guess I thought you'd just kick me out on the street if you got the facts. But I'm not borrowing from the bank without notice. No embezzlement. No. I could go to *jail!"*

"Have you thought what could happen if you didn't pay Tanetti? They say he's put men in the Green Prairie River in a barrel of cement for less."

"Maybe Hank Conner . . ?"

"Look, Beau. You borrowed five hundred from Hank last year. Remember? And eight hundred, two . . . three years before that."

"Sure. But — "

"But what? Hank's generous. He's a damned good neighbor in a lot of ways. He's come to your rescue five or six times. And you never paid him back a cent."

"Sure, but he knows I'm good for it. Someday I'll — "

"Someday you'll — nothing! You don't even know how much you've borrowed, over the years. Okay, go to Hank. If you get the twenty-five hundred, I'll really think he's crazy. If you don't . . ." She broke off. She had already said enough about his access to inactive portfolios. To Netta, being in trouble with Jake Tanetti was far more dangerous than lifting a few bonds from a bank — especially when one way or another you would make sure to get the bonds back before their absence was checked.

Had Netta been reared in a strict, upright family, her ethics would probably have been different. Unfortunately, her father, a railroad brakeman who had seven other children, had been an alcoholic. Her mother, though sporadically pious, was a woman with a chronic weakness for receiving and returning affection — due, perhaps, to the small amount she ever received from or gave to her husband.

As a child Netta had learned all there is to know about the flea-bitten ways of life. Her world had been a mean street, seen through secondhand lace curtains darned not to show. She had worked her way through normal school, but she had never intended to make a career of teaching. Normal school had been the only feasible way of acquiring something resembling education.

She was pretty as a young woman; she was also durable and indomitable. She grew up with one determination: to have nice things someday. The method was always apparent: marriage. At 17 she had barely escaped marrying a drummer of 40 who had what she thought of at the time as "money." But she marked down Howard Bailey as a good thing within ten minutes of their first meeting, at a picnic in 1928. Beau Bailey had been the handsomest senior in his high school (where the nickname had attached) and his father, who owned an automobile agency in River City, was wealthy.

Netta and Beau were married — and there Netta's luck failed. In 1929 Beau's father, following historic Black Friday, shot himself. Beau was left with nothing but his job in the Sloan Mercantile Trust Company. Curiously enough, Netta discovered that, though the self-evident thing to do was to get divorced and find a new spouse whose bonds and stocks had not been touched by the market collapse, she was by then attached to Beau in a way she could not fathom. His very weakness, his dependency, made her postpone repeatedly even talk of divorce.

Beau and Netta Bailey were not intentionally evil people. Like many, they were engaged in striving toward that place in life where their hypocrisies, small dishonesties, speculations and shady deals would become "unnecessary." To them not only "keeping up" but "getting ahead" had priority over conscience. Theirs were the vices of ambition, which has come to be identified with progress, thus obscuring its other name — greed.

Beau drew a long breath, exhaled, picked up the bottle, saw that Netta was not going to forbid him and mixed a highball. Casting the whole burden away from himself, he said relievedly, "Brother! Are *we* in a mess!"

In the hall, the front door closed with a click. Lenore came in, tiredly, her coverall over her arm. She set down the Geiger counter. "Is there anything unusual about the Baileys being in a mess?"

"This time," her mother said, "it's a real one. Beau . . !"

His eyes implored. *"Don't* — Mother! Not to *Len!"*

Netta brought to an end her state of uncompromising sympathy. Beau deserved to be punished. She said, "Your father, Lenore, has at last succeeded in making the priceless kind of fool of himself I always expected."

The girl dropped on the divan near her parents. "Now what?"

Netta told her in a few flat sentences.

Lenore said nothing. Her eyes filled and overflowed. She didn't look at her mother or her father. She just sat still, crying silently. Her anguish was an intolerable spectacle for her father.

"Don't, baby," he kept saying. "Don't cry. Net and I will find a way out of it. We always have."

But she kept on crying. After a while she rose and went to her room and left her parents sitting together, not talking.

Beau had a drink.

CHAPTER 3

THE Green Prairie Civil Defense "practice alert" had repercussions.

These repercussions had long heralded their approach, in complaints and criticisms and threatened suits. To be sure, Green Prairie took pride in its Civil Defense outfit for the reason that its state was one of the top-ranking five in the "National Ready Contest" — and the Green Prairie organization was the best in the state. The perpetual competition between the Sister Cities furnished a further motive for local pride and support: the six hundred thousand inhabitants of River City, being citizens of another state, shared the views of its thrice-elected governor, Joseph Barston, that Civil Defense was "a waste of money, a squandering of public energy, a meddlesome civil intrusion into military spheres and, all in all, just one more Washington-spawned interference with the rights of common man."

Loath to enter into the costly, intricate affairs of Civil Defense, the gentlemen in the state legislature had been only too glad to follow the governor's lead and table as many bills referring to CD as possible.

As for the politicians of River City, though it was obviously the only worthy "enemy target" in the state, and though a hit across the river would damage them, their feeling was that for once they were off the hook. Here was a chance to compete with Green Prairie by doing nothing. Instead of laboring mightily to construct a CD outfit equal or superior to that in Green Prairie, they had only to relax — and make jokes about the earnestly rehearsing citizens across the river.

The truth was that after a number of years (and even though Green Prairie had rescue teams, hordes of auxiliary fire fighters and police, tons of medical supplies and the like) almost nobody believed there was any danger. The passage of many years of "cold war," "border war," satellite seizure, international tension, international relaxation, deals made and broken, had convinced most people that Russia and China were without the technical means to wage a large-scale war, would never undertake one, relied wholly on prickly politicking and small grabs to exhibit power.

People for the most part have little imagination and less will to use it. The prairie cities were far away from the border of the sea; the air ocean over their heads they regarded as a kind of property; they thought, indeed, it differed wherever they were, so that a special blueness canopied the Sister Cities and their sovereign states. Everyone in the region talked about "Missouri skies" and "Kansas skies" as if the atmosphere had taken cognizance of political boundaries.

Every day, many times over, planes left the local airports to fly nonstop hops longer than the distance from the Sister Cities to the closest potential "enemy" air bases. But such facts, determined by the simple shape of the planet, were dismissed with a single popular word: *globaloney*.

WHAT actually precipitated the "Civil Defense Scandal" was a trifle. When the snow's right, however, a cap pistol can bring down an avalanche.

Minerva Sloan, on the afternoon of the practice alert, attended a directors' meeting in the Mercantile Trust Company which lasted until six o'clock. When she left the bank, she could not immediately find her limousine. A large, a very large woman — tall and fleshy, an English bulldog of a woman — she paced the wide sidewalk angrily.

Finally, she saw her car and ran out peremptorily, holding up her pocketbook to bring the heavy afternoon-rush-hour traffic to a stop. She took her time about getting into her car. She sat back, unrelaxed. "Willis," she said, "where were you?"

"The police," he answered, "made me move from Adams Avenue."

"Didn't you tell them *whose* car — ?" Minerva's further words were interrupted, suddenly, by the beginning growl of sirens. The limousine had gone less than a block meanwhile. One of the largest sirens was on top of the Sloan Building, which Minerva owned. It was a double-horn, revolving type, with a ten-horsepower motor. This was its first test.

As the growl of the siren intensified, traffic stopped dead. Minerva had time to say, "What on earth is that?"

Willis had time to shout back, "Air-raid practice."

Minerva's infuriated rejoinder was lost in a crescendo of pitch and volume that yodeled through the streets, the vertical valleys, the stone labyrinths. Car doors, truck doors, popped open. People ran toward the vaulted entries of the tall buildings, following instructions printed in the papers bidding them, if caught in their cars by the surprise alert, to pull to the curb, park and take cover. It was, of course, impossible to pull to the curb in the rush hour on Central Avenue, so people just stopped where they were and piled out.

The first sound apex of the siren was not its best effort. Even so, Minerva was obliged to wait till the head-splitting scream diminished before she could make herself audible. "Willis," she bawled, "get us out of this!"

"I'll find an officer," he said and jumped out with alacrity.

Minerva leaned back on the cushions of the car. The siren went up again and this time the noise, surging through the canyons of the city, was literally painful. Her ears ached. One of her fillings seemed to vibrate, hurting her tooth.

The scream held until she thought she could not bear it and then descended the scale. Around her, now, was a sea of cars and trucks and buses, all untenanted. For a moment, she couldn't see a soul. Then she caught sight of two men approaching, men with brassards and helmets.

"Wardens," she said with the utmost disdain. "Oh, the idiots! The meddlesome fools!"

The wardens were looking into the cars. They spotted Minerva and swung through the stalled cars toward her. They opened the door politely enough. "Madam," one of them said, "you'll have to take cover."

Minerva sat like a she-Buddha. "I will not."

They were obliged to wait — wardens and the obdurate woman — for another crescendo of the siren. "Rules," the spokesman of the paired youths then said. "If you'll step into the Farm Industries Building here, it'll all be over in twenty minutes."

"Twenty minutes! I haven't got twenty minutes. I have ten people coming for dinner at eight o'clock. I'm Minerva Sloan."

They looked blank. She supposed there were people in Green Prairie, newcomers and illiterates, who didn't know her name. She waved at the 35-story stone edifice on the corner behind the limousine. *"Sloan Building,"* she bellowed. And then, because the tearing sound was rising again, she pointed at herself.

It didn't mean anything to them. They in turn pointed to the entry of the Farm Industries Building, which was newer — and loftier — than her own structure. She shook her head and covered her ears with gloved hands. It helped. The pressure of sound finally waned.

"We'll have to call the police, if you refuse," the warden said.

"I wish to God you would!" she answered.

They went away. The siren didn't stop.

Stopping it became a goal for Minerva. She was shaken by it physically and emotionally. If a thing like that went on very long, she thought, it would drive a person mad.

The paired wardens, who Minerva was later to claim had "forcibly restrained" her, found two policemen sitting in a squad car, smoking, gazing with rapt amazement at a city jam-packed with cars in which there was nobody at all. "Big fat woman in a limousine up the line won't take shelter."

The cops eyed the wardens. "Carry her into a building," one cop suggested.

"Says she's Minerva Sloan."

The cops both lost their grins. "Let her sit," one said.

The warden protested in an eager-beaver tone, "We're supposed to get everybody — but *everybody!* — off the streets. And the police are supposed to help — if people refuse. . . ."

The older cop batted his cap back on his head and blew smoke. "Look, bud. In this territory, if Mrs. Sloan says she won't coöperate, there will be no coöperation, believe me."

Minerva was obliged to wait the full 20 minutes. The sirens stopped, but nobody came. Then the hideous horns tootled at broken intervals and people swarmed back, including Willis, who had been thrust into a shelter by two wardens paying not the slightest attention to his protests.

But it was 40 minutes before the stream of traffic downtown moved at all; thereafter, it crawled. Someone would pay for this infamous trick, Minerva vowed. She sat back firmly, snugly, in the limousine, studying out possible victims and suitable means. Two blocks short of James Street, traffic was fouled again.

"Go investigate!" Minerva bellowed.

It was now nearing eight o'clock and darkness had fallen. She would definitely be too late to dress for dinner but with luck she would be at home in time to greet her arriving guests. When Willis returned, that hope expired.

"The bridge," he said deferentially, opening the rear door, "is destroyed."

"Whatever . . ? Oh! For heaven's *sake!* You mean this — this moronic game is still going on?"

Willis peered through the car and across the eastern edge of Simmons Park to the curving facade of the "Gold Coast" hotels which glittered above the silhouettes of park trees. "The whole area is supposed to be totally destroyed, ma'am. Vaporized."

Minerva did not rant or upbraid any longer. She thought. The next bridge over to River City was at Willowgrove Road which became Route 401 to Kansas City. At the rate traffic was moving, it would take an hour to get there, to cross and to come back through the slums of her city to her residence on Pearson Square. For all she knew, Route 401 might also be in the area of imagined total destruction.

"Willis," she said presently, using the speaking tube, as the car budged along in 50-foot starts and stops, "we won't go home. Instead, I'll phone. My guests will have to make the best of it with Kit for host. Drive to the Ritz-Hadley."

The hotel doorman greeted Mrs. Sloan with a soothing word. She swept up the marble steps, across the red-carpeted foyer and into a phone booth. She dialed her home, grimly relieved to find the phone system had not been "vaporized." She told Jeffrey Fahlstead, her butler, to do the best he could with her guests, the dinner, the musicale. She spoke briefly with her son.

She then dialed the offices of the Green Prairie *Transcript,* in which she was a majority stockholder. She asked for Coley Borden, the managing editor, and soon heard his crisp, "Yes, Minerva? How's things?"

"Things," he quickly learned, were not good. "This business has got to stop, at once," she began.

"What business?"

"This Civil Defense nonsense!" She began to talk.

She was angry. She was very angry. It was not unusual.

He argued, but to less than no avail. He pointed out that it was *Transcript* policy to back up CD in Green Prairie, that she had her River City paper in which to condemn it.

Minerva was not moved, not moved at all.

He had never heard her more furious, or more irrational:

"Two of the biggest cities in America," she thundered, "blocked up for hours!" Green Prairie and River City, together, added up to one of the 20 or 30 largest American municipal areas. Minerva always spoke of them, however, as if they were aligned just behind New York, Chicago, Los Angeles and Philadelphia. "You know what it is, Coley? It amounts to sabotage! Sabotage left over from the imbecilities of Harry Truman's administration! It wastes millions. It squanders billions of man-hours. For what? Absolutely nothing whatsoever! Do you know what I suspect about Civil Defense, actually?"

"No, Minerva." His tone was wary.

"That it's Communist-inspired. All it does is frighten people." She warmed to the idea. "Terrorizes them by making them react to weapons the Reds probably don't even own. Meanwhile, they are completely diverted in their attempt to wipe out dangerous radicals at home. The last thing a sane government would do would be to get its citizens playing war games in the streets . . . !"

Coley said, "Hey! Wait up!" because he was extremely well acquainted with the old lady. "Doesn't it go the other way round? Doesn't the failure of the American people to get ready for atomic warfare reflect *lack* of realism and guts? Isn't Green Prairie rather exceptional—because it *is* sort of ready, after all these years? If you were the Soviets, wouldn't you rather America neglected atomic defense? You bet you would!"

There was quite a long pause. Minerva's voice came again, as quiet but as taut as a muted fiddlestring. "Coley, am I going to have to replace you?"

Sitting in his office in the new Transcript Tower, which he'd helped build by building up the newspaper, Coley felt the familiar whip. "No," he said. "No, Minerva."

"All right, then! Stop arguing—and get to work on the kind of job you know how to do!"

She swept from the phone booth into the main dining room of the Ritz-Hadley and ordered a meal of banquet proportions.

Most of Coley Borden's leg men were out on assignments having to do with the air-raid drill. Some were at dinner. Around the horseshoe of the rewrite desk a half dozen men worked. They were in shirt sleeves; some wore green visors. The managing editor walked toward them, beckoning to others, who looked up from their typewriters. He sat on the end of the horseshoe. "How's the drill going?"

The night city editor grinned. "Dandy! About an eighty-percent turnout. That means over thirty-five thousand volunteers actually participated."

"We're going to blast it."

For a moment, no one spoke. Then the city editor said, "Why?"

"Minerva's mad."

"You can't do it!" Grieg, a reporter, a man of 40 with graying red hair, made the assertion flatly. "The whole town's proud—except for the usual naysayers. It's the best CD blowout ever staged in the Middle West. About the least popular thing you could do would be to blast it."

"Civil Defense," Coley answered, with nothing but intonation to indicate his scorn, "is Communist-inspired."

"What!"

"So Mrs. Sloan claims."

"I always predicted," Grieg moodily murmured, "they'd come for that moneybag with nets someday. Men in white."

Payton, the city editor, said, "Just what do you want, Coley?"

The managing editor sighed. "I merely want to undo the work of about forty thousand damned good citizens—not to mention a like number of school kids—over the past years." He considered. "Every day in Green Prairie, people get hurt in car crashes. All people hurt this afternoon will be victims of our crazed Civil Defense policies. Any dogs run over will be run over because of air-raid rehearsal. Likewise any fires started. If anybody died in the hospitals, it will be because the traffic jam held up some doctor."

Grieg whistled. "The works, eh? She *must* be mad!"

"She didn't get home for dinner," Coley answered quietly, "and she had guests."

"Has she got a fiddle?" the reporter inquired.

"Fiddle?" some one echoed.

" — in case Rome burns?"

Coley looked out over the big room. "I was thinking that. Now look, you guys. Payton, spread this. No clowning. You could overdo CD criticism in such a way as to make everybody realize it was orders, and that the staff disagreed. I don't want it! When we obey orders of this kind, we really obey 'em. Run only stuff that actually seems to indict CD."

"A lot of pretty devoted people are going to hate it. Have you considered mutiny?" Payton asked.

Coley said, "Yes."

He went back to his office. Later, he silently approved the morning lead:

SIXTEEN HURT IN CD ALERT
Sister Cities Paralyzed
"Outrageous and Unnecessary"
— Says Mayor

September 21: Air-raid sirens, sending the population of this metropolis cowering into "shelters," keynoted at six p.m. yesterday the onset of a great fiasco in which 16 persons were injured and large but unestimated damage was sustained by property. . . .

CHAPTER 4

THIS HAD not been one of Nora Conner's lucky days. She had been ill-prepared for geography recitation. She had, very honorably, opened her book the previous evening. But she had pored over other matters than home industries and resources: matters contained in a paper-back volume entitled *Sin in Seven Streets.* This item, borrowed from a classmate in return for the use of Nora's mother's necklace at a party, purported to be "a frank, factual account of the shocking traffic in womanhood by a team of world-renowned journalists."

This morning Mrs. Brock had breathed with enthusiasm, "Our *own* industries. Just think, class! We've studied the imports and exports of dozens of foreign lands and of the nation and *now* we're going to memorize all we do right here in Green Prairie!"

"All we do in Green Prairie," Nora had murmured, thinking of an overheard parental discussion of gambling, "won't be in any musty old geography book."

Mrs. Brock had diminished her smile and said with slight sharpness, "Nora. Did you speak?"

"Possibly," Nora answered.

"What did you say, Nora?"

"I wasn't aware," Nora responded thoughtfully, "of saying it aloud. Pardon me."

Mrs. Brock meditated, and pursued the matter no further. The last time she had persisted in probing Nora's murmurings, Nora had reluctantly vouchsafed their subject: certain frank facts of natural history gleaned from idle reading in a book on pig breeding. Mrs. Brock resumed the mien of good will related to home industries.

She would like, Nora thought judiciously, to teach us *something;* it's just that the poor woman doesn't know anything worth teaching.

It was not a good day. Later, Nora was unable to define "commission government" in civics and she got three dates wrong in the history test. After school, when she stopped beside the fence to argue with Judy Martin on the meaning of "morphodite," Billy Westcott crept up behind her, tied her two long pigtails together and hung them over an iron picket. When she began to walk away, her head jerked back nastily, and only a fast scuffling saved her from falling and hanging ignominiously by her braids. Furthermore, on her way home, a bus hit a puddle at the Spruce Street intersection and spattered her dress.

Her inner condition was mediocre when she reached home. She was about to open the front door when her father drove into the yard with a sound of brakes that meant he was mad. Very mad.

"Nora," he said, "I want you to stay outdoors this afternoon! I'm having a meeting."

"It's impossible," Nora responded.

Thus challenged, he took closer cognizance. "You sick? It's a perfectly swell, hot day!"

"My dress is filthy—through the fault of the Green Prairie Street Transportation Company."

"Well, go round the back way then. I expect a lot of people here shortly."

"Where's Mom?"

He went in. "How do I know? I just got here, too! Making sandwiches, I hope."

"What's the meeting for?"

"Civil Defense indignation meeting. My section. We may all decide to cancel our subscriptions to the *Transcript*."

"Civil Defense—*that* old stuff!" Nora murmured. She brightened. "Anyhow—if it ever *did* happen—it would probably be a hydrogen bomb and there wouldn't be a stone standing in the uttermost corners of the County."

He stared at her. "Sometimes," he said gently, "I feel that would be best."

He slammed the door. His daughter shrugged and tittered. Inasmuch as her mother was making sandwiches, Nora went dutifully around back. She was given a cheese-and-jelly and a cold-meat.

These she took into the yard. Queenie was stalking a bird—a small one with red on it. Nora followed him through the hedge, skirted the summerhouse and came to rest, kneeling, behind the chimney of the Bailey barbecue pit. She ate thoughtfully, taking care to make no sudden movement. It was a fairly fascinating thing to see, and she hoped old Queenie would get the bird because she had never seen a cat eat up a bird and never even really got a good look at a bird's insides.

Thus Nora was where she was with reason. She was merely watching her own cat hunt, while she ate her own sandwiches. She was not engaged in eavesdropping, hiding in bushes, or any other such furtive occupation when Lenore Bailey and Kittridge Sloan descended upon the summerhouse.

Lenore, wearing a sweater and a skirt, was laughing. The man—Nora at that time did not know who he was— had a mustache, black, small, twisty. She failed to observe that he was more than six feet tall, about thirty years old, built like a first baseman and dressed in sports clothes. She did notice that he wore three gold rings and looked like a "Mexican movie actor."

"I haven't got long," Lenore said. "I have to go to a meeting. . . ."

He looked across the lawn at the Conner house and said, "You really mean you intend to go?"

"Certainly. I'm in Henry Conner's sector."

He laughed. "And I've invited you to the club!"

"I know. But this is important. The *Transcript* was perfectly *beastly* this morning and . . ." She broke off. There was a pause and she said, "I'm sorry."

That made him laugh even more, and Nora could see the dark young woman was relieved. The man said, "That's Mother's doing. She was trapped downtown last night. Brother! Did she ever boil!"

"She has a right to her opinion, but I don't agree — "

The man took Lenore by the shoulder and shook her gently, so that her dark hair swung and her worried expression faded. "I certainly am glad I went shopping today. Ye gods! Imagine you being around town — and me not knowing it! How long . . ?"

"I graduated over a year ago, Kit," she said.

From behind the barbecue pit and sundry rose bushes Nora reflected that his name, anyhow, was Kit, like first-aid kit.

"And I didn't know!" He peered at her with what the fascinated onlooker regarded as an oozy look. "You realize, don't you, that you've turned into the most beautiful creature in two states?"

Lenore moved away from him and sat down. She said, "Nonsense!" She paused and went on, "Besides, you *have* seen me, or could have, when you were in town last winter — at the Semaphore Hill Club Christmas party. Several places. Only — you were busy."

"I gave you up three years back because — "

"Because I wouldn't — give."

"Still the same old Lenore."

She nodded. "You bet. Untarnished. But with a gradually souring disposition perhaps."

He shook his head in mock sorrow. "The end product of spinsterhood," he said.

"Are you going to be in River City long?"

"Living with Muzz," he nodded. "For how long? Search me! You know, Lenore, *you* could have something to do with that! Let me ask you something. Is your health good?"

"Why? Of course it is."

"Grandparents long-lived? Have many children?"

"Just what . . ?"

He grinned. "Tell me."

"One had five and Dad's family has four, *all* living. Why?"

He leaned back. "Mother is getting very insistent these days. You know — the family line must be continued. I must find somebody steady, intelligent, healthy, good family, sound stock — you'd really fit the whole catalogue."

"Did she say anything about the girl being willing?"

"Nope. Mother rarely does. Just that she be found by me. The presumption is that the rest can be managed."

Lenore nodded across toward the Conner house where cars were parked. "I really have to go."

"All right," he said reluctantly. "I'll phone you tomorrow."

She thought about it and nodded. They got up.

Kit grabbed her and gave her a long and large kiss. Nora edged up a little higher on her knees to evaluate it. You could tell, she felt, that Lenore wasn't particularly keen about the kiss. But it went on for so long that Lenore seemed to weaken a little. And when he let her go she looked at him with a very odd expression. He said, "See you!" and ran away.... Then his car started. Lenore just sat down.

By and large, Nora thought, the beautiful girl next door was one of the best types of grown-up people. She paid some attention to others. She could tell when a person was discouraged or being put upon and, if she wasn't busy, she would do something about it. Buy you a sundae, maybe, or even take you to the movies. Right now, for instance, Lenore was on Nora's side against Nora's mother on the matter of braids. Lenore argued, sensibly, that braids were a bother to kids.

On the other hand, this business in the summerhouse, Nora felt, was definitely on the two-timing side. Lenore was Charles Conner's girl and always had been and they would be married someday and, in Nora's opinion, Lenore was about as good as her brother could be expected to do.

She sat in the grass until Queenie made his pounce at the bird and missed. Queenie sat down and groomed his tail, glancing once at Nora with the look of a cat who was fooling anyhow and merely enjoyed scaring hell out of birds.

Nora went home. She stopped at the dining-room doors, but they were drawn together. She listened to voices.

"Henry, you're the leader here! I say we need help from Washington and you ought to phone."

"I say, let's start a campaign to boycott all advertisers in the *Transcript.* We've given years to this organization. It's intended to save Green Prairie in case of an emergency. We cannot allow a newspaper to ridicule us, censure, blame. . . !"

Nora went upstairs slowly. Music drifted from Ted's radio in the attic. The day, all of it, had blanked from Nora's mind, save for one thing: her braids. She felt she was a neglected child and would have to take care of herself. She went to her mother's sewing basket, found the big shears and cut off both braids, hastily, lest she change her mind.

They did not cut easily. She had to hack them off, one strand at a time. When she finished, an expression of purest delight set Nora's light-blue eyes dancing. *She had done it.* She had done it by herself, because it was her hair and it was unbearable, and nobody else but herself cared what happened to her. She ran skipping to see the effect in the long mirror in her mother's room.

And when she saw, she was horrified. In her mind's eye, she had overlooked the present phase — the ragged, wrong-length, hacked locks that were not a recognizable bob of any kind but merely the plain evidence of devastation. A long, low cry escaped Nora and rose to a penetrating wail of dismay. Beth Conner heard it first and hoped it would subside.

Henry heard it and went on for a moment: ". . . it's my feeling that we shouldn't appeal to Washington. We ought to handle our problems at home. People always kicking about too much central government hadn't ought to yell for federal help the minute anybody tramps on their toes. . . ."

He stopped and smiled at his wife. "It's Nora," he said. "I guess you better go up." He went on, "So I think we ought first to get hold of Coley Borden and ask him what he thinks he's doing. After all, there isn't one of us here but knows and loves Coley."

Beth hurried up the stairs, following the steam-engine wail. She found Nora lying on the double bed, on her back, a braid in each hand.

For a moment, Beth nearly burst into laughter. She had liked the child's long hair, but she had been on the verge of conceding to Nora's demands that it be cut. Now, hearing the agony in Nora's voice, Beth lost her smile. She did not conceal it; a genuine, deep sympathy banished amusement. She picked up the girl bodily and hugged her. "Nora. You mustn't cry. You're just upset because it looks so funny at first. I'll take you right straight over to Nellie's and we'll have your hair fixed to look *lovely!*"

Hope and wonderment stirred Nora. She checked her grief. "It'll *never* look lovely!"

"Come along. My! Your dress is a mess. Never mind. . . ."

Beth beckoned her husband to the front-hall door. "I've got to take Nora on an errand," she said.

"Is she sick?"

"No. But — "

"Ye gods, Beth! This is an important meeting. And somebody has to serve the refreshments afterward."

Beth shook her head. "Nora's important, too! Lenore can serve. She knows where everything is, Henry. Tell her the refrigerator — and the plates are all stacked in the pantry. Oh, *she'll know. . . !*"

CHAPTER 5

CHARLES CONNER's mother had repeatedly reminded him that he would have to pay a call on his aunt. He had at first agreed gladly, for he had always liked his mother's sister and her family. Perhaps it was the kids he had particularly liked, for the father, Jim Williams, wasn't actually much: an archetypical nobody, a little gray chap who would get lost in a crowd of two. And Beth's sister, Ruth, though she had been blonde and pretty at twenty, was careworn now. No wonder, with so small a salary and six kids.

Still, he boarded the Central Avenue bus reluctantly. He'd been home for a week now, and he'd had only one real date with Lenore. The rest of the time she'd been busy — or had merely dropped in for an hour, or had permitted him the same privilege. There was a tension in the Bailey house he didn't understand, though the Baileys had always been tense. And there was a kind of — distance — about Lenore: an attitude he'd never before seen in her.

The bus plugged across the river and on for half a mile, through a run-down section, competing with trolley cars, trucks and hordes of pedestrians. Out of the slums at last, it made better time and soon covered the distance to Ferndale, River City's oldest suburb. Charles walked the short way to his aunt's house.

He was sighted in the distance by twelve-year-old Marie. In a moment, four of the young Williamses came down the sidewalk under the catalpas, yelling, he thought affectionately, like Indians. As the youngsters caught his hands and poured forth questions about his family, about the armed forces, Charles lost some of his feeling of forlornness.

He loved kids. He had liked being one, through all the wonderful epochs of childhood from the day of his first sled to the day his father had given him a fly-casting rod and thence to the magical evening when his dad had said, "Well, Chuck, looks like the ducks might be coming in around dawn tomorrow and, if you look in the broom closet, you may discover something resembling a brand-new, sixteen-gauge, over-and-under. . . ."

What in the world, Chuck thought, turning into the Williams's walk, was life all for — if not this: kids to pass on kinship to?

When dinner was over and the youngest children were asleep, Chuck, with a tumbler of elderberry wine, sat with Ruth and Jim.

"We haven't seen much of Beth and Henry." Ruth sounded apologetic. "Time was when Ferndale seemed practically next door to Walnut Street. But now" — she sighed — "by the time I get the kids organized, or a few hours of an afternoon, it seems a million miles off."

"I know," Chuck nodded. "Took me an hour and a quarter to get over here."

"Mercy!"

"Both cities," Jim said, "were horse-and-buggy designed. I read the other day that cities are strangling themselves. Green Prairie and River City sure are!" Yielding his moment of pontification, Jim asked, "What do you think, Chuck?"

"You'd believe so, if you could hear Dad and his wardens talk! They jammed up Green Prairie, but good, last week."

Ruth said, "I wish Hank Conner would get out of that thing!"

Charles lit a cigarette. "Why? He loves it. Dad's a kind of natural leader of folks."

"Think of the effect on Nora, though — and Ted — "

"What effect?"

Jim put in anxiously, "You see, we're not allowed to mention atom bombs or anything having to do with them in this house."

"It's emotionally destructive," Ruth Williams said emphatically. "I can show you the scientific facts, in the PTA *Bulletin!* Every time they run off a series of atomic tests anywhere, the kids of the United States show a marked rise of nervousness, of nightmares, of delinquency. The Rorschach Tests prove it!" She shuffled in a stack of papers, schoolbooks, bills, checkbooks, women's magazines on the top of a radiator.

"I suppose kids do," Charles agreed. "They react to things. Nevertheless, we have to run the weapons tests, don't we? If only to try to keep ahead of the Reds."

"I thought we were making peace with the Reds!"

"We've been 'about to' ever since I was in high school."

"Peace, peace, peace!" she said heatedly. "Why don't we accept this last offer? The one they made in August?"

"We're trying to, Mother." Jim was obviously endeavoring to divert his wife. "The United Nations is trying."

"Maybe the Reds are right," she said. "Maybe the military men and the big steel manufacturers don't really want peace."

"It isn't that, Aunt Ruth." Charles tried to be lucid. "Every single time we've thought we were on the verge of an understanding with the Kremlin — whammo! They broke loose somewhere else. Stop them there — get a deal set — and bingo! They hit in China again. Burma, the Balkans — "

"So what? Are those people worth dying for? Worth making permanent nervous wrecks of all the children in America and a lot of grownups besides, like your father?"

Charles considered the idea of his father as a "nervous wreck"; he chuckled. "I know how you feel, Aunt Ruth. After all, it's why I have to spend time in service. But look. There's one thing the Soviets have never offered — offered and meant it. That's to let the world come in and inspect them and make sure they aren't stockpiling mass-destruction weapons. Right?"

"They've offered, time and again, to inspect themselves! I don't see why, for the sake of ending all this crazy strain, we can't try having just that much confidence in them. What would you feel if you were a whole government, and another government flatly refused to take your treaty oath and your word?"

"The Soviet Government," Charles replied, "goes on the principle that its own word is no damned good whatsoever. That's why we can't trust their mere promise to disarm. That's why we have to test A-bombs and keep up a draft army and remain powerful, until and unless Russia permits the world to see for itself that it is doing what it has promised to do. There's no other way! Our government would have found it long ago if there had been."

"You're wrong!" Ruth was shaking with anger.

Marie had come in the front door and was standing in the hall, holding the hand of six-year-old Don when Chuck noticed them.

Don began to whine. "Stop talking about atomic bombs."

"Why?" Charles asked calmly.

The little boy's face twisted. "It scares me. I don't want to hear about it. I hate talking about cities blowing up."

"You see?" Ruth said.

She said it as if every point she had brought up had been proven beyond further debate. Annoyed by this narrowness, this ingrained sense that River City would always be there because it always had been there, Charles took up the challenge again. "I *don't* see, Aunt Ruth. So long as even the potential threat of A-bombs on America exists, nothing we can do in the way of arming ourselves, of testing weapons, of Civil Defense, is too much. I think little Don here is jittery because you've made him jittery. I think — "

Jim said, firmly, "Cut it, son! Mother's mad."

She *was* mad. She controlled her temper long enough, however, to order the wide-eyed Marie to take her brother upstairs and put him in bed. Then she whirled on her nephew. "I know you're a soldier. That's no excuse for your coming to a quiet, peaceable, domestic scene and scaring little children!"

"Somebody ought to be scared," he answered.

"*You* should be! People like your crazy father, stringing along with that everlasting play acting about sudden death! A fine way to bring up a whole generation, watching grown men and women make like they are dead and dying. I tell you, Charles Conner . . ."

". . . and I tell *you,* Aunt Ruth, you ought to go get those old newspapers out, where they announced Russia had exploded an H-bomb, and reflect on what that means to your kids — "

" 'Bout time," Jim Williams said, mildly still, "for you to be running along, isn't it, Chuck?"

He went.

He had walked a mile down Willowgrove Avenue before his vexation abated. Then he laughed a little. Most people took it the way Ruth did. They were frantic inside themselves and trying, somehow, to fight off the feeling, simply because they couldn't, or wouldn't, nerve themselves to look squarely at the cause.

Twelve blocks of walking took Charles well into River City. He decided he might as well walk the rest of the distance. It was only 9:15. He turned into Mechanic Street, known as The Block. Here, in small, brick-fronted buildings that once had been homes, the nefarious part of River City's life was conducted. Charles knew Pol Taylor's place was somewhere here — and so was Jake's. It was here he saw Beau Bailey. Beau stumbled down three steps to the sidewalk, nearly fell — a man in conspicuous trouble.

Charles hurried. Beau, looking wildly up and down the street, rushed away, not recognizing Charles. The younger man stopped. Several things had become plain to him in that instant. Beau's eye was cut and bleeding and his nose was bloody. But he had not been looking for help. His face, in the arc light, had been tormented by fear; he had been furtive.

Charles walked across the bridge slowly, toward home. On Walnut Street he saw a Jaguar parked in front of the Bailey house. He slowed to admire the red-leather upholstery, the complex controls panel. He wondered whose it was and saw the monogram: KLS.

Kit Sloan.

When Charles entered his house and his mother called, "You're back pretty early!" he concealed an emptiness. "Yeah. Got in a bicker with Ruth about the world situation. Jim politely threw me out. Remind me to phone and make up in the morning."

He started upstairs. "Guess I'll turn in."

But not to dream, he thought; not even to sleep. Kit Sloan.

Across the lawns, on the second floor of the Bailey house, Beau was daubing cotton soaked in ice water on his cuts and talking to his wife. "That's what happened," Beau repeated shakily. "I asked Jake for thirty days more and he told Toledo to 'impress' me with the situation." He didn't seem even aggrieved, merely resigned. "He slugged me. I tried to hold myself together, Netta, I really did. I told him nobody could assault an officer of the Sloan Bank and get away with it — "

"What'd he say?" Netta had to know every detail.

"He said he only wanted his five thousand. He said I wouldn't *be* a bank officer — any day he wanted to lift a finger!"

"I thought you were going to speak to Henry Conner — "

"I did. Yesterday. He offered me five hundred. Said, with taxes the way they are, it was all he could spare."

"Skinflint!"

"Maybe it was the truth."

"Henry Conner," Netta said, "probably still has the first dollar he ever made! Look at the cheap way they live. I bet he has a tidy sum stashed away."

"Well — *we* haven't." He shuddered. "Look at me! What'll I say at the bank?"

Netta was bitter. "Oh, *heavens*. Say you fell down the cellar stairs. Say a mouse pushed you. We've got to plan, Beau!"

"How in hell can planning materialize five thousand?"

"Don't talk so loud, Beau. Kit might hear you." She changed moods briefly. Her eyes became exultant. "They're together on the big divan, pretending to look at TV. I peeked." Her mood shifted back. "Go lie down in your bed. Take a towel, so you won't stain anything. I'll get you a drink. Thank heaven, you had the sense to sneak home the back way! If Kit Sloan had caught sight of the mess you've made of yourself . . ."

When she re-entered the beige-and-scarlet bedroom, she carried a strong highball and a weak one. Beau was handed the latter.

"Now *look!*" Netta began, and he knew it was the prelude to something that would go on half the night. "Everything depends on playing our cards right. I couldn't believe our luck when I learned Kit was interested in Lenore again."

"He's just interested in pretty girls."

She waved that away. "Lenore won't be able to accomplish anything fast enough to help you in this Jake business — "

"She doesn't even much like the guy."

"That's neither here nor there!" Mrs. Bailey talked on, persuasively. "A woman *learns* to like a man. Now, Beau, you've absolutely got to do something yourself about this gambling debt. We can't afford to have Lenore's chances with Kit Sloan ruined because some petty racketeer disgraces you! All you need to do is something temporary. Something that would hold the fort, until Lenore could get — "

"Get what exactly? Disgraced herself?"

"Now, Beau. This is the twentieth century, not the Victorian Age. You've got to be realistic."

"Listen, Net. I'm not going to let my daughter haul me out of this by making herself into a tramp."

"What I'm asking is, are you going to stand in her way of making what might be a brilliant — and happy — marriage? A marriage that would move you into a real house in, maybe, the Cold Spring section. Don't you realize *everything* would be utterly different, if the Sloans and the Baileys had a hyphen between the two names, owing to Lenore?"

He was smiling a little. "Maybe it would at that!"

"I'll get you another highball."

"Yeah," he said, absently. "Please do. My face hurts like mad." He called after her, "And make it stronger than iced tea."

It was going to go on all night.

But Beau began to think, began for the first time to let himself think, that life might not forever be a round of hard work, of figures and facts and statements, of the aching anxiety of home finance and stretched funds, of eternal self-sacrifice for a wife and daughter 365 days a year, with only an hour snatched here and there for personal pleasures.

Things could be better. He deserved them better.

And a man, a self-respecting man, couldn't take a slugging lying down.

X Day Minus Sixty

CHAPTER 6

It was a peculiar farewell. Chuck thought it was probably like thousands of farewells said by soldiers.

He had been raking leaves when she came into the yard. She was wearing an orange-red knitted suit. He could feel his nerves jump.

"You're going tomorrow, aren't you, Chuck?"

"So Uncle Sam says."

She looked at the fire as if it were a work of art. "Nice and warm," she said. "I've been over in Coverton, watching State play Wesleyan."

"Who won?"

"We didn't stay to see the end. State was ahead — thirty points — at the half. And Kit wanted a drink."

"He didn't bring you home," Chuck said.

"We had a fight." She kicked a spruce cone into the fire. "About you."

"Me?" He leaned on the rake, slender, dark, smiling.

"I said — you and I had a date for tonight."

"Do we?"

"Heck, Charles! You're going back tomorrow. I sort of assumed we'd spend the evening together."

"Swell."

"And, anyhow, he doesn't *own* me."

The fight, then, had been a mere declaration of independence, not of special loyalty. "I'll borrow Dad's car."

"Don't bother! I've got my Ford. And your old man needs his these days. Running around . . ."

Chuck nodded. "He's working hard. And to darn little purpose. People are deserting his organization like . . ."

"I know. Well, what time shall I call for you?" She laughed. "Say, eight?"

THEY drove down to Lee's Chinese Inn and danced a while. But the place, in spite of the Oriental lighting, the orchestra and the waitresses in Chinese costumes, didn't have the necromancy that had invested it when they had been high school kids. They were both restless.

"Let's go," she suggested, in the middle of a fox trot, "on out the river, the way we used to, and park in that spot where the mill used to be."

It was crisp and cool out there and bright with moonlight. The heater had warmed the car. They pointed its nose so they could see the water shimmering in the ruined flume.

"Remember when we came here after the basketball game?"

He said, "Remember the night you and I — and Wally and Sylvia — went swimming?"

"If Dad had seen us down there, he'd have skinned me alive!"

The recollections bubbled up, glimmered, broke.

"How long will you be gone this time?" she asked.

His shoulders shrugged a little. "No telling. Six more months — but I'll be out, all things equal, in eight more."

"It seems a long time!" She picked up his hand. "A long, long time, Chuck. It *is* a long time, don't you think?"

"Yeah."

"I wish you weren't going away."

"See any beggars riding, these days?"

"If wishes were horses?" Lenore shook her head. "You know what I'm thinking about."

"Guess I usually do, Lenore."

"I guess you do. It's Kit — of course. Partly."

"And partly you?"

Her head shook, and the small motion seemed to diffuse in the night an additional quantity of the perfume she wore. It came from her hair, he thought, her midnight, wavy hair. "Not me, exactly," she said in a speculative tone, and added defensively, "Kit's a lot of fun."

"Why not? He's never had experience in much else."

"He has so! He does plenty of difficult things, too. Climbs mountains. Flies. He was a war pilot. He has a pound of medals."

"Shall I try to get wounded?"

"No," she smiled, uninjured by his sarcasm. "Not even — emotionally, Chuck. Do you think you could put yourself in my place for a few minutes?"

Charles laughed. "I could come mighty close!"

"You sit still. I mean — look. I'm twenty-four. Right?"

"Practically senile. Right."

"You're the same. You've got nearly another Army year. Then, some architectural office, and maybe — maybe in ten years — you'd have enough to — "

"To what? I've got Dad and Mom. In a year, Lenore, I could have a house in Edgeplains, maybe. And if I didn't, the folks would see to things till I got started."

"Would I like it?"

He said soberly, "Don't think I haven't wondered. Some parts, you'd surely like."

She murmured, "Let's skip those parts, Chuck. I know about them. Like the poem. There is some corner of Lenore Bailey that is forever Chuck. The part of me that grew up with you. Skip that."

"I don't know about the rest of it, from your angle," he said. "Being married, making your way in the world, having kids is one hell of a hard assignment."

"I can tell you." Lenore listened to the ghostly, tinkling waterfall a moment. "For six months, maybe a year, I'd love it. We'd get the Edgeplains cottage. I'd fancy it all up. I'd make do with the clothes I have — plenty, God knows, for a long while. Then I'd see our cottage was just a dreary little bungalow, in a row, with dozens like it — and dozens of young women imprisoned there like me. Then I'd start to hate it. Mother and Dad, of course, would be completely off me, taking my marriage to you as their final, personal disaster."

"Is that any reason why you . . ?"

"No. It isn't. But look at it another way. They spoiled me. They saw to it, all my life, I had everything a girl could want, to look luxurious, feel luxurious, be luxurious — "

"You were going to throw it overboard in college to be a scientific research worker. . . ."

"I talked about it. But I didn't *do* it, did I, Chuck?"

"No. Marriage is important, too, though. And so is love."

"Look at it the other way. Suppose, just suppose Kit ever proposed and I said yes. A whole lot of very important problems would come to an end forever. I'd have everything in the world, and so would my folks, and I wouldn't be a physical wreck. I wouldn't love him — no. I wouldn't have as many things in common with him as with . . . other men I know. One other, anyhow. But at least I'd never be in a spot where I'd wilt at the sight of my own house and hate myself for working so hard and despise never getting ahead fast enough to keep up with the bills. Don't you see, Chuck, either way it wouldn't be a perfect deal?"

"This is all a lot of nonsense," he said.

"Women," she answered, "shouldn't ever try to tell men what they really think! What they have to consider — when men won't!"

"Some men consider other matters more important than living-room drapes."

"Don't you think I do, too!" Her voice was urgent. "Why do you think I've gotten to be twenty-four years old without marrying? I'll tell you. *You*. I've had plenty of offers and chances to enlarge a friendship into a gold hoop. Rich men, bright men, men in college, men from Kansas City, New York, even. Only first you had to take another year for architecture. Architecture, of all the hard-to-learn, hard-to-rise-in things! Then, two years for the Army. And now, who knows? What if they start a new little war someplace? Maybe I'll be *fifty* when you can afford a wife." She stopped very suddenly, caught her breath and stared in the dimness. "Charley," she whispered, "you're crying."

He blew his nose. "Maybe I was," he said unevenly. "It's a little hard to take it—like that. Brick by lousy brick. Maybe, Lenore, you better give up the marathon. Maybe you *are* right. It's so damned hard for a guy to separate how he feels and what he wants—from the facts."

She came close to him, familiarly, because she'd been close to him often before, in cars, on hay rides, at picnics, in movie theaters. "It's a rotten time for young people."

"For *people,*" he agreed, putting back his handkerchief.

"Charles?"

"Right here." He kissed her forehead.

"Tomorrow, you'll be gone."

"Don't remind me."

"Charles. Why do we have to do like this all our lives?"

"For freedom," he said. "For God, for Country and for Yale."

"Can I ask you something?"

"You always do, Lenore."

"Have you made love to other girls?"

"Some," he admitted.

"I mean—really. Actually."

"No."

She hesitated. "Me—either."

"I know," he nodded, his head moving against her dark hair. "That, I always knew." He kissed her on the lips. "I love you, baby. I always will." He managed to grin. "And now, I'm taking you back home."

CHAPTER 7

MORE and more, Coley Borden had taken to standing by the window, especially at night when the big buildings were lighted. Sometimes he'd sit on the sill—27 stories above the street, above the people-ants, the car-beetles—watching the last thunderstorm of summer, for instance. He'd be there when fog rolled in or when the wind picked up dry earth from between the myriad acre-miles of corn stubble and plunged the cities into the darkness of a duster. He'd watch rain there.

Sometimes the men at the city desk would say, "Coley's getting a bit odd."

He was standing there one night, looking at the moon-lacquered panorama, when he heard his door open.

"Mr. Henry Conner's here to see you," Mrs. Berwyn, his secretary, said. "And it's almost ten o'clock."

Borden smiled. "Hank Conner? Tell him to come right in."

"You haven't had supper yet, Mr. Borden. Would you like .. ?"

"Later." He snapped on lights and sat down at his desk.

Hank came in and Coley noticed a new, unwelcome diffidence about him. He sat down uncomfortably in the walnut-armed, leather-upholstered chair beside the desk. "Good evening, Coley." He didn't add, "You old type-chewer," or anything.

"Like a cigar?"

Hank's head shook. "Brought my pipe. Came to talk about Civil Defense, Coley."

"I know."

"Kind of hate to. Always liked the *Transcript*. Respected it." Hank lit his pipe. "Of course, I know Minerva Sloan was responsible for your policy change."

"Yeah."

"But it's doing us bad harm. Real bad." Hank mused a while. "Called a meeting of the whole gang at the South High yesterday, Coley." Hank looked at his pipe. "Forty-three people showed up."

"Good Lord!"

Henry sighed. "We usually turned out around five, six hundred."

"What do you want me to do, Henry?"

The bulky man stirred in his chair, frowned and said, "Talk, first of all. Get out from behind Minerva Sloan's skirts and talk! I've always had a good deal of respect for you. You've been right about things in this man's town – sometimes when I was wrong. You've got a good mind, Coley. You've read a lot of history. You know a lot about this science stuff. Your paper's been wide-awake. Now, all of a sudden, because we jam up traffic – and it's not the first time we've done it – you change tack on us."

Coley Borden's face wrinkled with intensity. "I can imagine how you feel, Henry."

"The point is — why I came here, is — what do *you* really think? I've talked to lots of people, last few weeks. People in CD and even people from River City who think the whole show is some kind of boondoggle. I talked to Reverend Bayson, he's a fire fighter in my outfit. I talked to a couple of professors. I kept asking, 'Should we go on? Is it worth it? Are we doing anything valuable? Or are we what they call us — a bunch of Boy Scouts?' I decided to put you on my list of people to talk to."

"Thinking of quitting, yourself?"

Henry Conner looked squarely at the editor. "That's it." He recrossed his legs as if his body dissatisfied him. "Not right off. I don't mind looking ridiculous to other people, so long as I don't feel that way myself. Well. What about it?"

"If I were you," Coley said, "I wouldn't quit if hell itself froze over."

HENRY CONNER had gone, saying it was past his bedtime, chuckling. Coley Borden sat a while and then buzzed for Mrs. Berwyn.

"Get your book, Bea," he said over his shoulder. He was standing again, looking along shelves for a volume which, presently, he took down. When he turned, she was sitting; she had brought her pencils and stenographic notebook with the first buzz.

"We're going to do some work. An editorial."

"For morning? The page is in."

"Yeah. If it comes out right, it'll be for morning. I'm kind of rusty, Bea. But I'll take a crack at it and maybe I'll run it. Ready?"

She nodded.

He began to walk in front of his desk and to dictate:

"Ten years ago and more, this nation hurled upon its Jap foe a new weapon, a weapon cunningly contrived from the secrets of the sun. Since that day the world has lived in terror."

Coley paused and Bea looked up. When he did not immediately continue, she said, "I think if you asked the first hundred people on the street if they were terrified, they'd laugh."

"That's a fact. Good suggestion." He went on:

"The more civilized a man may be, the less readily he will admit panic. That is what 'civilized' means: understanding, self-control, knowledge, discipline, individual responsibility. What happens, then, if a civilized society finds itself confronted with a reasonable fear, yet one of such magnitude that it cannot be tolerated by the combined efforts of reason and the common will? Such luckless multitudes, faced with that dilemma, will have but one solution. Feeling a gigantic fear they cannot (or they will not) face, they must pretend they have no fear. They must say aloud repeatedly, 'There is no reason to be afraid.' They must ridicule those who show fear's symptons. To act otherwise would be to admit the inadmissible, the fact of their repressed panic.

"Thus a condition is set up in which a vast majority of the citizens, unable to acknowledge with their minds the dread that eats at their blind hearts, loses all contact with reality. The sensible steps are not taken. The useful slogans are outlawed. The proper attitudes are deemed improper. Appropriate responses to the universal peril dwindle, diminish and at last disappear."

Coley sat down on the edge of his desk and dictated more quietly, sometimes kicking his heels against the bleached mahogany:

"We, the people of the United States of America, have refused for more than a decade to face our real fear. We know our world could end. Every month, every year, several nations are discovering the instruments which make that ultimate doom more likely. The antagonism between a free way of life and a totalitarian way is absolute. And it appears to be unresolvable owing to the expressed, permanent irreconcilability of Communism.

"What have we done about all this? The answer is shocking. We have failed to meet the challenge. We have shirked the duty of free men. We have evaded every central fact. We have relied on ancient instruments of security without examining the new risks—reinforcing military strength while we left relatively undefended the targets of another war: our cities, our homes."

His eyes focused on space. "On our prairies," he dictated, "farmers, fearing the onslaught of the wind, dig cyclone cellars. They rod their barns and ground their aerials, lest the lightning strike." He looked far away, to his right. "Downstream on the Green Prairie River, and below on the Missouri, men have erected great dams, set up levees, against flood. In our cities, lest fire break out, we maintain engines and men to save us from burning. We have appraised many dangers and prepared against them in these and a hundred other fashions. *What of the peril of world's end?*

"Today in Washington, men argue interminably concerning how doomsday may be resisted or put off. We maintain a navy—against what may never move by sea. We levy vast armies and hold them the final arbiter of every battle even though, just the other year, an empire called Japan fell to us with never a foot soldier of ours on its main islands. We believe our airplanes can deliver stroke for stroke, and better, but we will not count the effect of strokes upon ourselves. We admit our radar screen is leaky. We have dreamed up—and left largely on drawing boards—such weapons as might adequately defend a sky-beleagured metropolis. In sum, we face the rage of radioactivity, the blast of neutrons, the killing solar fires, with peashooters and squirt guns."

He paused a full minute.

"Anything else?" Mrs. Berwyn asked.

"Just a paragraph or two." His desk chair received him, squeaked a little as he tipped it back and spoke:

"The sands of a decade and more have run out. In 1945, or 1946, or even 1947, America had—and missed—its only golden chance. America then was the earth's most powerful nation, Russia was devastated. We could have dissolved the Iron Curtain by a mere ultimatum. Now we cannot challenge without venturing the world's end. Quite possibly our death notice is written. But the only question before you, citizens of Green Prairie, of River City, of the wide prairie region, of this momentarily fair nation and the lovely world, is this, apparently:

"What new idiocy can you dream up, with your coffee, your porridge, your first cigarette, *to keep yourselves a while longer from facing these truths?*"

Coley fell silent.

"What do we do with it?" Mrs. Berwyn asked, a little stunned by the blunt finale.

He was looking at her perplexedly. "I told you. It's tomorrow's editorial."

"You're kidding." She stood up and came to the side of his desk.

"You quitting the *Transcript,* Coley, after you spent your life to build it?"

"Maybe."

She was close to unprecedented tears. "Do me a favor. Do us all a favor, Coley. Wait till tomorrow. Let everybody mull it over—"

"Remember, Bea, back in 1943? When I went abroad?"

"What's that got to do—"

"To England," he said musingly. "The whole Middle West refused to believe in the blitz. The folks were deluded then, the same way. I went over, just so they could read the stories of a typical Middle Western editor—written from London, while the fire bombs fell. Remember?"

"Sure," she said.

"I went because I'm an *editor*. Because I thought an editor, an American editor, was obligated to help the American people face facts. I *still* think so!"

"Even, Coley, if it means you commit newspaper suicide?"

He rocked forward in his chair and began, delicately, to align the objects on his desk: clock, calendar, inkstand, memo pad, the engraved paperweight given him by the YMCA Newsboys Club.

He said, "Sure. Even if it marches me off the stage."

Coley watched dawn invest the cities.

Life returned to the great building. The presses, underground, shook it a little. Doors slammed. Elevators hummed at intervals.

When the sun cut deep into the man-made canyons, shining on windshields, bus tops, palisades of glass windows, Coley knew Minerva would be awake. She would be ringing for her maid. Getting coffee and a folded copy of the morning paper which she owned.

His phone rang. " 'Lo?"

"This is Minerva Sloan."

"Morning, Minerva. How—"

"You're fired, Coley."

He put on his hat and coat and went out.

CHAPTER 8

IT WAS not until the last week in October that Beau Bailey, made desperate by a series of ever-more-menacing (and constantly harder-to-explain) phone calls, decided to act. Jake and Toledo had taken to phoning him at the bank and their voices were not the sort Beau wanted to have the operator hear. Like many who commit crime, however, Beau was brought to the actual deed by idle opportunity as much as by resolve.

It was a period of pre-Christmas inventory. From the vaults, with armed guards watching, a number of portfolios were fetched for checking. These were metal boxes containing lists, account books, receipts, letters, orders and sheaves of certificates.

And it was while this routine checking was in progress late one afternoon that Miss Tully's mother got a sudden appendicitis. The hospital promptly informed Miss Tully an emergency operation was imminent; that distracted woman, who had served the bank for 27 years (with a total absence of but 11 days), appealed to Beau. He was not very nice about it, but he let her go.

It was 3:15, a rainy, raw afternoon, and the main floor, with cages all around and stand-up desks in rows in the center, was already empty of customers. When Miss Tully departed, Beau was left in his office with three large deposit boxes and Miss Ames, his secretary. He set himself to do the checking which had engaged Miss Tully, leafing in a desultory way through the amassed holdings of one John M. Jessup, of Larkimer County, a livestock dealer. If Beau remembered rightly, Jessup was about seven feet tall, had a sparrow's voice, wore glasses, had cleaned up on beef in the First World War, and hadn't been in the bank since Truman left office. In Beau's hands were ten $1000 bonds, issued by Hobart Metal Products when they had expanded the works on the west side of town.

Just half of these, Beau thought, would get me out of all my worries. He glanced at Miss Ames. "How would you like," he said, "to go through the passageway to Sherman's and get me—*us*—some coffee?"

When she had departed, Beau studied the opaque glass walls of his cubicle and decided they were, indeed, opaque. After that he tried to remember the present market value of Hobart Metal bonds. He thought it was par but wasn't sure. If he were going to borrow five, he might as well be certain and take six. He tucked them carefully into an inside breast pocket. Only then did he remember his exposure in the window. He whirled with horror and stared up at the panes across the street. Lights shone in every one and rain poured between. There were faces and people moving, but no one seemed to be interested in him, in anything in his direction.

He took the inventory list and correctly reduced the number of listed bonds from ten to four. He then made out, in a disguised writing, a receipt for six bonds and signed it with an indecipherable scrawl, using a bank pen and bank ink. He pulled out the nib afterward, put in a new one and pocketed the old. Nobody, he thought, could prove who had written the receipt or show with what it had been signed. Not even experts. And, anyway, the absence of the bonds would go unsuspected.

It took two more days to complete the transaction and set his mind at rest. Or momentarily at rest.

The following morning was still rainy. Taking Netta somewhat into his confidence, he explained it would be "useful" if she alibied him with a slight cold. She did not inquire more deeply. She called the bank and talked about "a couple of degrees' temperature" and "doctor's orders."

It happened, owing to Country Club contacts, that Beau knew an officer in the Ferndale Branch of the Owen National Bank of Commerce, who was a "good man to go to in a tight spot." His name was Wesley Martinson. Beau had cultivated the man, played a few rounds of golf with him, come to call him Wes.

Wes greeted him without surprise, ushered him into a private room, performed smoking amenities and said, "Well, Beau, what can we do for you?"

Beau had pretty much taken the measure of his man, through the medium of a hundred off-color stories retailed by Wes with relish. Beau therefore chuckled and said, "Frankly, I want you to help me perform a small robbery."

Wes chortled. "Son, that's what banks are for. And you've come to the right banker."

Beau took the bonds from a very old and battered big envelope which bore his name and in which for years he had kept unpaid bills. It looked exactly like something that had lain in a vault a long while, holding bonds. He threw the parchment-stiff, aging paper on Wesley Martinson's desk. "Want to borrow on these."

Wes picked them up, studied them and said, "They don't *look* counterfeit."

Beau chuckled. "Nope. Something I stashed before the tax rate knifed us. Trouble is, I don't want the little woman to realize I'm borrowing on them."

The other man frowned. "I see."

"Oh, no you don't! However, I'll let you in on the sight, one of these days. She has — " Beau made curves with his hands.

As Beau knew, the invention suited his own need for cover as well as the other man's mind. Wes chuckled. "I guess Owen National can help you. Security's okay. You know the rates."

"I should!" Beau said and took the proffered pen.

Not that evening, but the next, Beau made his way to The Block. He was determined to expose himself to no further risks. So he approached by bus, then taxi, and then a second taxi and at last on foot.

Jake was there, in his littered office. He took the five $1000 bills without comment. He dug in a greasy file for some time, produced Beau's IOUs, handed them over, and then looked across his cigar stub. "Where'd you get the dough?"

"Borrowed it," Beau answered cheerfully.

"Off who?"

"Friend."

"What friend?"

"I can't say. It was—a woman." Beau was suddenly very nervous. He had thought that all Jake wanted was the money.

"What woman?" Jake said.

"I told you . . . Look! I paid. We're square. So what?"

Jake didn't have a mean face, a vicious face. He looked like every man who stands in a dirty white apron beside a green-grocery stall in an open market. He hardly lifted his voice. "Toledo," he called, and Toledo, who did have a vicious face, came in from the dark hall.

"I just want to know," Jake said, "if this is hot money. Ask him, Toledo."

Before Beau could cry, "No!" the first blow knocked him off his feet and halfway across the dirty, worn carpet. He got up. He got out a handkerchief. Shaking like a rabbit in a snake's mouth, he said gaspingly, "Okay. I had to borrow a couple of bonds from a dead account at the bank."

"Whose account?"

"I forget," Beau said.

"Ask him whose account, Toledo."

Beau managed to stave it off this time by darting to the farthest corner as he said, "John Jessup."

Jake nodded thoughtfully. "So okay. What are you hanging around here for?"

Beau ran out of the room, ran down the stairs, tripped, almost fell, and found the gloomy sanctuary of night. He hadn't gone many blocks before he realized clearly that now—and forever—Jake really had him over a barrel. Sweat broke out over him; for several blocks he couldn't remember which street led back to Market.

Two weeks after his dealings with Jake, Beau walked across the marble floor of the bank, on the way to lunch. He had decided, as usual—after a struggle, as usual—that he'd have two Manhattans; weather was really cold now.

His eye detected a singular customer among the queued scores, the dozens writing at the desks.

It was a very, very tall man, wearing glasses, waiting in line at one of the "Trust Funds" windows.

It was John Jessup.

X Day Minus Thirty

CHAPTER 9

At eight o'clock on a cold evening shortly before Thanksgiving, Kittridge Sloan sat opposite his mother in the shadowy dining room of the Sloan mansion, gustily spooning soup.

"Have a good day, son?"

"Passable."

"Any plans for the evening?"

"Thought I'd pick up Lenore Bailey. . . ."

That suited Mrs. Sloan for an opening. Her eyes fastened briefly on her son and moved thoughtfully into the distances of the formal room where the gold rims of plates gleamed from china racks, and cabinets of cut glass sparkled dully.

"You've seen a lot of the Bailey girl, lately."

"Yeah."

"Does that mean anything, Kit?"

He smiled at his mother. "Ask Lenore."

She passed that up with a gesture that was partly disdainful and partly indulgent. She thought, with pride, that the Sloan men had always possessed a way with women. She was able to feel pride, not rancor, now that her husband was occupying a plot in Shadyknoll, with a 30-foot obelisk to mark the grave of a great industrialist, banker and rakehell. Her son's "conquests," as she thought them, did not in her opinion belong in the same category as her late husband's "vices." There was the mitigating fact that Kittridge was an "irresistible young man"; her spouse had been an "old fool."

"You in love with Lenore?"

"Muzz, I love 'em all — if they're pretty. If they're as pretty as she, I love double."

"She's an interesting girl."

"How do you know so much about Lenore?" he inquired.

"The girls that interest you, Kit, naturally interest me." She sighed slightly. "I'm getting older every year. . . . And as to Lenore, it's very easy. After all, her father's in the bank."

"So he is! Old — what's it? — old Buzz — no! Beau Bailey. He's cashier, or something. . . ."

"That's correct." Mrs. Sloan tinkled a coronation hand bell and the soup was removed. "The girl's not merely pretty as a movie star. She's bright. Did some really good work in college. Science, I believe. I like a scientific-minded woman. Sticks to facts. Realist."

Kit grinned agreement.

"She's high up in the brains department. You want to know why water expands when it freezes, or all about hydrogen bombs —Lenore can tell you."

"And quite good at athletics," Minerva said.

"What is this? You're talking about the woman I love—at the moment—as if she were something entered in a state fair."

"She wouldn't make a bad entry. And that's what I mean, in a way. Because there must be children, when you marry. They will be needed in the future. Our holdings—the businesses—"

"I know! But—"

"A day," his mother said firmly, "is surely coming when you cannot temporize. You're well over thirty, Kit, and I'm aging. . . ."

"Have you ever thought Lenore might not be interested? If you want to know, Muzz, I'm fairly crazy about that girl, and she is totally uncrazy about me. I made an inquiry—and found out."

Mrs. Sloan considered that for a full minute. "An odd thing has happened at the bank," she said, her tone altered.

Kit instantly understood the slight change; it showed in her physical bearing. There was tension, now almost visible—a bringing together of her features, a tightening of muscles in her big shoulders, a slight narrowing of eye.

"As I said, an odd thing has happened at the bank."

"Really? What, Muzz?"

"You know John Jessup?"

He shook his head.

"You should remember him from childhood. An old horse thief—and one of the smartest men in Larkimer County! Made millions, in cattle mostly. He was one of your father's cronies, years back. It's not important. The thing that's important is this: the bank takes care of his holdings. He doesn't even look things over for long periods. Trusts us, of course, and leaves us free to make certain kinds of changes, so his holdings are open always."

"Somebody cleaned him out!" Kit guessed.

Minerva's eyes acknowledged the guess. "Not cleaned him out. Just took $6000, in bonds."

"Who?" And, of course, he knew. "Beau Bailey! But he's been with you forever, Muzz!"

"There is no proof, as yet, and Beau denies it, of course. But I have found out more about him than he knows. For instance, I learned—after all, a bank has to have connections with all sorts of people—that Beau's been betting the horses for some time. And losing."

"So? What's it got to do with Lenore? She never struck me as lacking in guts. If her dad's disgraced, I can imagine she'd bear it. Get a job. She's had some dandy offers for everything from modeling in New York to working in labs at Hobart Metal."

Minerva chuckled. "Be ironic, wouldn't it? Beau took Hobart bonds."

"I don't see — "

"I've decided it's past time for you to marry, Kit. I merely felt I should make sure, by a heart-to-heart talk with you, that you really liked Lenore Bailey."

"Would the daughter of a bank thief be suitable?"

"Her father isn't what people generally mean by a thief. He's merely ambitious; he's got more ambition than moral strength. He probably found himself in a situation he thought desperate and sold his soul for a miserable $6000 in bonds. I've seen brighter men do it for less."

"And so there might be a nice little shotgun wedding—with both barrels pointed not at the groom but the bride's papa."

"I said, Kit, that I wanted to know how you felt about Lenore. And then I wanted you to *act*—not fiddle years away."

It was all there, he thought, laid on the table, right in front of the centerpiece. Well, it was quite an idea.

"I'll have to think about it, Muzz," he said. "Lenore is pretty headstrong and independent. If we ever married, I'd *need* a way to handle her!"

"I think," his mother answered, "we've discovered a way."

The vast airfield shook with motor noise in the gray, windy afternoon. A dozen huge bombers had left the hardstands and roared out on the runways to take off on a regular training flight. Each one had six propellers. Each prop sent back a wash of air and dust and din, adding it to the boring Texas Wind.

Lieutenant Conner entered the colonel's conference room at headquarters and saluted. There were four men in the room: Colonel Eames, the Commanding Officer, Major Wroncke, Major Taylor and Captain Pierce. They looked more serious than usual. Usually, nobody took the weekly Intelligence meeting with any seriousness at all.

The colonel, sitting at the head of a worn conference table, returned Charles's salute. Charles sat down and unlocked his brief case. He was acting for Major Blayert, Staff Intelligence Officer at the base, who had been detached, temporarily, for duty in Flagstaff.

"We have," the colonel said, "some new, secret orders. From Washington." Eames looked at the officers. "They are pretty elaborate and they mean plenty of work here at the base."

Nobody appeared to be overjoyed at that news.

"As you know, condensation trails have been spotted for years, over Alaska, over Canada. In other words, we've known for a long time the Russkis have reconnoitered our northern defense perimeter. Lately" — he tapped his own brief case — "they have moved in over the United States."

"Is that positive?" Major Wroncke asked sharply. "Rumors—"

"I know." The colonel hesitated. "Civilian spotting has fallen down badly. And with the last appropriations cut by Congress, the radar defense has had to be reduced."

"What have they got on it?" Major Taylor asked. He was a fussy man who constantly tried to "move things ahead" — equipment, people, plans, conversations.

"Plenty," Colonel Eames answered. "And not Flying Saucer material, either! Contrails over Nebraska, Iowa, Ohio and all the states down here in the Southwest. Definitely not our own."

"Any contacts?" Major Taylor asked.

"None. Radar blips, though."

"Plane types?"

The colonel frowned faintly at his impatient staff officer. "I'll boil it down to this. GHQ is satisfied that there have been, for some months, numbers of Red planes over this country, flying very fast at very high altitude — probably turboprop types — probably photograph recon. None of our interceptors has so far gotten up to one fast enough to take a good look. We do have a few rather definite photographs, taken at long ranges with telephoto lenses from our own planes."

"That's pretty definite," Captain Pierce murmured. "What's the interpretation?"

Colonel Eames turned away and frowned. "The Pentagon feels that this business of Russian reconnaissance is one more stupid action, one more mere crude breach of ordinary international etiquette. They spar for peace, but they can't resist the improved chance it gives them to sneak a few photographs. However, we're being ordered to put on a big show. For the next six weeks there are going to be 'air exercises.' That's what the world at large will be told. We'll get everything in the air we can, as high as we can, with cameras and arms, also. We are expected to keep open eyes, to photograph anything unidentified we see, to fire on it when and if we can overtake it. Bombers are to do the job, not interceptors. The bombers can go up, stay and cruise."

Major Wroncke whistled.

Colonel Eames smiled without pleasure. "In a nutshell," he said, acknowledging the whistle. "At this base, it means a lot of partly trained crews are going to have to fly some of the latest equipment. It means a logistic problem, just to keep what we've got up and on patrol. Six weeks is a long time. We aren't supplied for it, so we have to get supplied, fast. It means we've got to expand the Intelligence side; an Intelligence officer is supposed to fly in every plane."

Captain Pierce laughed. "That's going to chop up the Lieutenant, here, mighty fine."

Charles also laughed a little.

"Orders," the colonel said dryly. "Any more questions, gentlemen?"

There were none.

THE Mildred Tatum Infirmary for Colored was a large, brick building which Emmet Sloan, motivated by a genuine, if somewhat patronizing, liking for Negroes, had rebuilt out of a foreclosed rayon-knitting mill in 1937.

On a Wednesday, as usual, Willis drove Minerva Sloan across town to the Infirmary punctually at three. Alice Groves, the head of the Infirmary, stood at the head of the stairs within the dingy building. She was dressed in powder blue which, Minerva noted, became her mulatto good looks. Behind Alice were the usual starched bevies of nurses, drawn up like a company for inspection.

Minerva made panting, reluctant rounds—baby wards and the new operating room. She drew the line at visiting the adult wards, and there were no private rooms.

"Right after Christmas," Alice Groves said pleasantly, as they finished the tour and started toward the bright, chintz-draped room where the "Wednesday ladies" sewed, "we're going to start a drive among our own people for $50,000."

"Good heavens! Can you raise anything like that?"

"Perhaps not. It's the amount we need to buy a little building in the country for chronics. There are so many!"

Minerva was thinking other thoughts. "That's really very enterprising and wonderful—"

"I'm delighted you approve. I was sure you would. In fact, I've told the press—"

"*What* have you told the press?"

"That you approved. In fact, I said it was your idea."

"No harm in that," Minerva murmured.

"You're always so kind, Mrs. Sloan!"

Minerva thought grimly that beyond doubt this "chronic home" drive would cost her the uncontributed balance of its quota. She had to admit Alice Groves was a good operator. Then she saw the hat — the sprouted fright — that Netta Bailey was wearing, and she went through the chatting, peanut-eating, one-day seamstresses with a booming, "Afternoon, everybody! Afternoon, Netta! So glad you're here. I wanted to have a private chat with you—church matters—before you left."

It was recognition that both delighted and alarmed Netta. Minerva seldom did more than nod to her, at a distance.

In the little talk that took place in the visitors' powder room half an hour later, Minerva explained her position, rapidly. "You see," she wound up, "my boy loves Lenore. Crazy about her.

Charming girl. I'm crazy about her myself. So unfortunate that dear old Beau would make a slip at such a time! I have no sympathy with crookedness, Mrs. Bailey. . . . "

"Of course not!"

Minerva squinted, but she could not prove irony in the response. She made a thin, tight mouth, a formidable mouth, and then let it relax into a smile. "However, it was only a slip, a little slip. But it must, of course, be his last. I can hardly send my son's future father-in-law packing off to prison—"

"God forbid!" There was, at least, no irony in that.

"On the other hand," Minerva went on, changing her tone to one of intimacy, intimacy tinged with potential regret, "we mothers understand things our children don't. Kit tells me Lenore doesn't seem to reciprocate his feelings. . . . "

"Oh! I'm sure she does!" Netta was alarmed, but not as much as she appeared to be.

"I can understand it. Kit's rather a—shall we say, frightening—young man, from the standpoint of an innocent young thing."

"Innocent as driven snow," Mrs. Bailey murmured.

"Kit's peremptory, bullheaded, reckless and foolish. I wouldn't have it any other way," Mrs. Sloan said sharply. "But you know and I know how love grows in marriage— "

"Indeed, I do!"

"—so I feel, a word from you, Mrs. Bailey—I must call you Netta, and you must call me Minerva—the *right* word . . . "

"I understand perfectly," Netta gulped. "Minerva."

"I'm sure you do!"

As soon as she decently could, Netta left the Infirmary and drove home at rocket speed. The first thing she had to do was to sober up Beau, who'd been drinking like a fish since coming home from the bank. Lenore could be tackled after that. Beau would sober up fast enough when she got through the fog with the news of reprieve.

Lenore would be a more difficult subject.

But Minerva stayed on quite a while, even sewed a little. When Willis drove her away, she waved from the window of the Rolls to a contented, gracious Alice Groves on the Infirmary steps.

Lenore said, "I won't!"

"I think you will," Netta said, "simply because I know you haven't lost your mind."

"Nevertheless, I will not marry Kit."

"It's so plain it hurts," Netta said. "You refuse Kit. Okay. Your father's in jail — five to ten years. Kill him sure."

"Maybe it would — what's left of Dad!"

"The house goes. Both cars. The furniture. Probably even our clothes, forced sales and repossession. Then we have nothing."

"But self-respect."

Netta said quietly, "You've never been poor. Flat. Broke. Without a friend or a dime — unless you hustle a friend and he gives you a dime."

Lenore thought that over. "I doubt it would happen. People would tide you and me over — "

"Who?"

Lenore looked through a window. "The Conners."

"The Conners — the Conners! I've heard it all my life. I'm sick to death of it. Who are the Conners? An accountant for a hardware firm, that's who! And a crazy young kid who thinks he'll be an architect in maybe ten years when you've got bags under your eyes."

Lenore felt frightened, cold, sick. She was trapped and she knew it as well as her mother. If it were just disgrace, as such, and poverty, that would be thinkable. But she couldn't face the image of her father in prison, marching in a line to eat, going out on the roads in stripes. She knew he was weak. But she knew, also, that he was kind. Kind and rather gentle and, in his own way, loving. Which her mother was not, unless, in some twisted way, she, too, cared for Beau.

Lenore was intelligent. She was realistic. She had been brought up to like and enjoy "nice" things and to want and to know how to use far more of them than her father could ever supply.

At this moment, however, she realized how very little "nice things" meant in relation to the whole of human life. Her very realism had showed her, long ago, that life was closing in on her. The sweetheart of her childhood had not turned into the dream prince of maturity. He was far away now, doing some sort of menial chore for the Air Force. Desk work. He'd grow up at a desk, drawing buildings that probably would never be constructed, because Chuck didn't seem to have even as much drive as his father. All Chuck's drive was in his head, his imagination. It never came out, never produced.

Long ago she'd begun saying to herself, Wise up, Lenore. He isn't for you. Find yourself another boy.

Well, her mother had found one. If it wasn't to be Chuck, did it matter so greatly who it was?

Lenore could anticipate the turnings of her mother's mind. She anticipated now, as her mother began, "After all, Lenore, in time . . ."

"I know. Divorce. With alimony. Abundant alimony."

Netta got ahead of her then. "Why not? People like the Sloans expect it."

"I suppose that sort of thing's been done, by plenty of women."

"Then you'll . . ?"

"I haven't said," Lenore answered. "I painted myself into this corner with my own little hand. If Dad isn't to go to prison right off, I suppose I've got to be engaged or, at least, have an understanding with Kit. You've got me in a spot where either I do that or Dad's jailed."

"I always knew my daughter . . ." Netta began rapturously, and rapturously she rose from her chair to bestow an embrace.

Lenore sat perfectly still. "Sit down, Netta," she said.

"Minerva will want to know!" Mrs. Bailey breathed, discomfited only momentarily.

"You call her and the deal's off. I'll tell Kit in my own time and my own way, and the terms won't be practicing matrimony from the moment he slips on the diamond, either! Sit still, Mother! I swear, if you put the needle in anywhere, one more time, I'll take a job in New York and be damned to you and Dad both!"

X Day

CHAPTER 10

CHUCK had come home for Christmas. Beth Conner's pleasure in having her son home again so soon was only slightly alloyed by his preoccupation. Twice, in the first four days after his homecoming, he'd put on his uniform and driven over to Hink Field "on business." Confidential business, business that upset him, Beth thought.

On Friday, the Friday before the Monday that would be Christmas, Beth was in the kitchen, working. Henry came in, blowing on his cold hands.

"Where's everybody?"

"They'll be in soon. Nora's over with the Crandon youngsters. I don't know where Ted is. And Charles is shopping."

Henry eyed a roll and restrained himself. "If Chuck's downtown, he'll be late. Never saw such crowds."

"I'm worried about him," Beth said. She sighed a little and tried the boiling potatoes with a fork.

"Ready?" he asked eagerly.

"Heavens no! Half hour till supper, and you know it. They have to be mashed and quick-baked, still. It isn't just Lenore. He's upset about something that has to do with the Air Force, too."

Henry followed the transition without difficulty. "Chuck's in Intelligence now, Mother. Guess he knows quite a few worrisome things. He has responsibility — with all these exercises going on."

"Shake the plaster off the attic someday, those jet planes will. Charles takes things slowly the way you do, Henry." She paused, thought, amended. "The way you do—*sometimes*. He's going to be a real long while getting used to the fact that Lenore Bailey is marrying Kit Sloan, not Charles Conner."

"Is she? You sure?"

"I'm afraid so."

"Won't be the merriest Christmas we ever had," he said quietly. "Take *me* a while to get used to the idea of not having Lenore for a daughter-in-law." He peered out the window at the prettily lighted snowscape, sniffed the steaming home smell of the kitchen, shook his grizzled head.

Nora came in.

That is, the front door burst open and stayed open long enough to send a few bushels of arctic air down the hall into the kitchen. Then the door slammed. Galoshes thudded as they were kicked into the hall closet. Then that door slammed. There was a long indrawn sniffle followed by a sneeze. Followed, in turn, by a *sotto voce* "Dammit!"

"Nora?"

"Yes, Mom. Not burglars and not the Fuller Brush man." The words sounded nasal. She came into the kitchen, saw her father. "Hi, Pop."

"You sound as if you were catching cold," Beth said.

"I'm not." Nora coughed defensively. "I feel fine."

"Say ah-h-h-h-h."

Nora stood under the center light, lifted her winter-rouged face, said the word.

"Look at this, Henry. She's getting a very red throat."

"It's not a bit sore," Nora asserted urgently.

Mrs. Conner suddenly sat down. "That's about the last straw! Henry, I just can't take her over to Ruth's if she's catching a cold. The new baby—the other children—"

"I knew it!" Nora said in a low, dismal tone. "I knew it all along. Like a prophecy! This Christmas is going to be utterly, totally wrecked for me."

"It isn't Christmas tomorrow; it's the Saturday before," Beth answered. "And it isn't being wrecked at all. You'll have to stay in tomorrow and not go to Aunt Ruth's dinner, so as to be perfectly all right again by Christmas! I'll have to find somebody to look after you tomorrow."

Nora threatened tears. "I'll miss the dinner we always have. I'll miss Santa Claus."

In Simmons Park, annually, the stores erected a giant mechanical Santa Claus whose arms moved to hand gifts to children, who talked over a loudspeaker in his midriff and who even sang carols. He was the Yuletide deity and big wonder of Green Prairie; a child who missed him was unfortunate indeed.

"You can stay with Netta, I'm sure," her mother said. "She's having a cleaning woman in."

"She's totally despicable! I abhor staying there!"

"She's minded your brothers, often. She's usually a pretty good neighbor when these problems come up." As an afterthought she added: "You can show her what a fine cleaning woman you are, too."

Nora said, "Phooie! Vixen. Shrew. Termignant."

"Termagant," Beth corrected absently. She moved toward the kitchen phone and began to make arrangements for the custody.

IT WAS a beautiful day—and that was the trouble with it.

So Nora thought sourly next morning as her family, muffled to the eyes, climbed into the Oldsmobile and drove off to Ferndale. To make matters worse, old lady Bailey was on her high horse, too. No sooner had Nora taken off her hat and coat in the Bailey house than Netta, her face covered with a greenish substance called Chloropack and her hair in curlers, said, "Upstairs in the linen closet are stacks and stacks of papers. The first thing I want you to do is to carry them down cellar. Pile them beside the ash cans."

Nora went up. The sloppy Baileys had simply tossed what looked like about 20 years' supply of papers and magazines in the closet. Nora figured it would take a person a thousand years to cart it all to the cellar. She put her mind on the problem. Downstairs, the vacuum was going. The colored cleaning woman was now in the kitchen, scrubbing.

She went into the front bedroom and looked out sorrowfully at her own yard. The Bailey cellar door was on that side, which gave Nora her idea. She opened a window. Icy air gushed in from the deceptively sunny outdoors.

Nora carried an armful of magazines down the hall. She pushed them over the window sill. They fell with a satisfying flurry. She brought another. In due time, she had amazingly depleted the stocks of printed matter in the closet. From downstairs came a voice. "What's that cold draft?" The vacuum stopped and feet pounded. Mrs. Bailey raced into the bedroom. "Good heavens, you idiot! You've chilled the entire upstairs. Don't you know how much it costs to heat a house, you lazy thing!"

"I wasn't going to keep it open any longer. Much. And I can drop the magazines again, into the cellar."

Netta Bailey was not in a good mood. Cleaning house was far from her favorite task. The new hired woman was proving incompetent. And having Nora about was a liability. The imp had cooled off the hall and bedroom, spread magazines over half the yard, and left a trail of papers from the closet to the window.

Nora, on her part, was not in a much better mood. "What I'm doing is efficient," she said calmly. "If you want me to slave around here for you all morning—"

"Shut up," Mrs. Bailey said. "Pick up everything in the hall. Then put your things on and go out there in the yard. You'll have to stack the stuff on the back porch now. Beau hasn't been able to get those outside cellar doors open for two years."

Fuming silently, Nora obeyed.

She was appalled at the amount of snow-covered lawn upon which the falling periodicals had been distributed. She began to pick them up in a desultory way.

A theory she had often entertained in the past now absorbed her: people picked on her. There was something about her—maybe she was a genius, and people cannot tolerate superiority—that caused everybody to want to hurt her feelings, make things difficult for her. By the time her family got back, old blood-eye Bailey would probably have locked her in a closet. Things seemed to work out that way for Nora.

The Lindner kids passed by, headed for Crystal Lake, pulling a Flexible Flyer.

"Whatcha doin', Nora?"

Nora stared across the Bailey yard, the snow-capped evergreens, the brown wrecks of last summer's annuals. "Blowing soap bubbles."

Annabelle laughed. "Where'd all those magazines come from?"

"Fell out of a Flying Saucer," Nora answered. "They're all printed in Martian."

Tim Lindner said, "Aw—you're crazy."

The sled banged and squeaked down Walnut Street.

Old needle-face, curler-durler Bailey stuck her pickle puss out the door and whoo-whooed *"Nora!* Hurry with those magazines! I want you to pull rugs while Harmony and I lift things."

And you couldn't pull them exactly *where* she wanted them, Nora calculated, if you measured with a solid-gold ruler. They'd be lifting and straining and getting red faces—old snoodle-snozzle Bailey would, anyway.

Nora didn't so much run away as drift away.

She didn't so much desert her assignment as take time out.

CHAPTER 11

At the Jim Williams home in Ferndale, Beth and Ruth, in the kitchen, were busy preparing the feast. A table, groaning already under stacks of plates, side dishes, preserves, silver, napery and favors, waited the onslaught of two hungry families. The new baby, Irma, was watching the process, round-eyed, lying in a baby pen. Ted Conner was upstairs helping Bert fix his radio.

The three men, Jim, Henry and Chuck, sat in the living room, killing time, talking about the Sister Cities' biggest Christmas boom in history.

When the phone rang, Jim went into the front hall and soon returned. He looked unhappy. "For you, Hank. Man who sounds upset."

Henry Conner lumbered into the hall and said cheerfully, half playfully, "Merry Christmas. This is Henry."

A very shaky voice came to his ears. "Henry Conner?"

"That's right. Who is it? What's the—"

"Been trying to reach you for half an hour! This is headquarters. Brock speaking. Condition Yellow."

Henry felt as if he'd been hit with a .45 slug. His knees wobbled and he sat down hard on the hall chair. Then he realized it must be either a gag or some crazy test. If it was a test, it was a terrible time for one. Next, he realized that this sort of situation had been envisaged, and a code designed to cover it, so only those who knew the code could check back on the announcement. For a moment, the proper words were swept out of his mind. He cudgeled his brain and said, in a voice that was nothing like his own, "How many sacks of potatoes?"

"Maine potatoes," the voice replied. "And Idahos. I've got to break off."

That was the question. That was the answer. It wasn't a grim practical joke. It wasn't a test.

It was Condition Yellow. *Real.*

So many things happened in his mind that he was astonished by the mere capacity to think of them all.

He would have to leave and so would Ted. Chuck could stay—no—Chuck was "military personnel" and entitled to the information.

It was going to ruin the pre-Christmas party.

What in God's name am I thinking about a party for? flashed in his head.

"Condition Yellow" meant that enemy airplanes had been recognized over continental U.S.A. It was an alert, currently confidential, which was intended to reach and mobilize all Civil Defense people, police, firemen and other city employes, as well as "key" technicians in industry. It meant that CD headquarters—and that meant the military—believed the risk was great enough to warrant the shock and disturbance of a complete, but quiet, official turnout on the Saturday before Christmas.

Henry thought of the Air Force "exercises" which had been going on for a month. With the skies above the continent crossed and crisscrossed by American flights, how could the military be sure this was an enemy attack? The probabilities were a hundred to one that some flight of our own bombers, off course somewhere, over California or New York or Alaska — anywhere — had been mistaken for enemy planes. Why wouldn't spotters be liable to error? After all, there hadn't been any sign of hostility whatever on the enemy's part. It was a thought that flashed through the minds of some millions of city dwellers who picked up telephones all over the United States and heard the two words: *Condition Yellow*.

Even men at the top of military and civilian intelligence agencies —men "cleared" to know all the known facts—hesitated. There had been nothing from behind the Iron Curtain to indicate the assembly of long-range planes, the gassing up, the bombing up, the vast number of activities required to launch a "surprise" attack. If this was "it," the experts thought, almost as one man, the Soviets had outdone the Japs in their surprise onslaught on Pearl Harbor.

The experts, however, reacted dutifully. Others did not.

In cities on the West Coast, the East Coast, and in the South and the Middle West, hundreds of thousands of ordinary persons, men and women, ready for Christmas, thinking the world on the verge of assured and eternal peace, decided for themselves. They were not as well indoctrinated in the meaning of duty as the professionals. It *had* to be an error, these myriads thought—and went back to lunch, to the TV set, to mowing the lawn in Miami and shoveling snow in Detroit.

Not Henry.

When his brother-in-law came into the hall and said, "Something wrong? You're ghost-white!" Henry smiled and nodded.

"Maybe, Jim. Look. Don't say anything to the women. Ask Chuck to step in, willya?"

Charles came. "Lord, Dad! What's wrong?"

Henry motioned. Charles shut the hall door. His father said, "Just reached me from CD. Condition Yellow, Chuck."

The soldier lost color, also. "That's—what—I've been scared of."

"You think it could be the McCoy? Or some error . . ?"

Chuck strode to the phone, snatched it up, thought a moment

and dialed. He waited, then set the phone down. "I called Hink Field—on a special number. Busy. So I can't say. But we can't take chances now."

"On the other hand, I'd hate like the devil to scare Beth and Ruth and the kids half to death—and find it was a bloomer."

"That's true. Suppose you take our car, and Ted—he's due to report, isn't he?—and go. I'll try the phone awhile. We can tell the folks it's a practice—for the moment."

"That'll do," Henry decided. He bellowed up the stairs, "Hey, Ted! Hurry down! The fools have called a practice alert and you and I have to make tracks!"

The door from the hall into the kitchen flew open. Two indignant women stood there.

"Henry," Beth said, firmly, "this is *really* too much!"

"Of all the idiotic ideas, on a Saturday, at dinnertime!" Ruth added.

Jim Williams came through the living-room door. "You two stay right here, Hank. This damn fool defense thing has gone too far."

"Long as I'm in it, I have no choice." Henry was shrugging into his coat. He threw a meaningful glance at his older son. "I'll rely on you, Chuck, for everything. Come on, Ted; get cracking."

CIVIL DEFENSE headquarters for Green Prairie had been originally located in the midtown area, near City Hall. Its transference to an old high school building, on the east side of town, had followed the gradual realization that, if Civil Defense were taken earnestly, the midtown area was no place for headquarters: it would constitute the target area of any enemy attack. The present headquarters, unused by pupils, was a superannuated, large, yellow-brick structure.

Henry drove into the parking yard on chattering tires. Other cars were ahead, behind, or waiting in line for space.

"Why don't I drive on home and get my set going?" Ted asked.

"You're too young to . . ." Henry grunted and turned from the line. "Take it home, son," he said gently. "And go easy. I'll hitch a ride from here to the South School to assemble my section. If you can, lemme know when the folks get home."

Henry said that over his shoulder. Men were running, like himself, into the lobby of the school building, where sector wardens were to report in an emergency.

Douglas McVeigh, the CD chief, was standing at the top of the steps on something—a table, maybe. He was stone-grim.

"How"—Hank struggled to phrase the burning question in every mind—"how *authentic* is it, Doug?"

McVeigh glanced around, waited for a half dozen new arrivals. "This is *it,* folks. A very large flight of long-range bombers is somewhere over Canada, right now."

A woman began to cry audibly.

"No time for that!" McVeigh said. "Get going, everybody!"

"Thank God we're only a Class-Two Target Area," a man beside Henry said.

Henry raised his voice. "Who's for South School? Henry Conner here. Need fast transportation!"

"Come on, Hank." Luke Walters ran through the growing crowd in the lobby.

They made it, at breakneck speed, to Hank's sector HQ. Cars were assembling there, too, and people, moving quickly, were streaming into the building like ants, taking the places they had learned through the years.

Hank went to the principal's office, shucked off his coat as he began giving orders, skimmed his hat at the rack and sat down. He rang a special number and reported himself at his post, his checkers at work, his people arriving in good numbers.

TED drew up at his house, his heart hammering and his ears crimson from the cold. It had been some drive, the way everyone was traveling. Looked as if quite a few were already making for the country. So it was evident that "security" about Condition Yellow was being partly violated.

He parked the car, face out, in the drive, as it should be in time of emergency. He was panting a little as he bounded up the porch steps. Then he remembered that nobody had thought to give him a key. He shattered the glass in a front window; he reached in . . . the lock turned.

He ran up both flights of stairs, threw himself into the broken swivel chair at his work table, clapped phones on his head and started to pull switches, turn dials.

Presently, a hysterical and varied chatter began to pour into his astonished ears.

"It's real," he whispered to himself. "It's—*it.*"

Anyone looking at the teen-ager in that transfixed moment would have thought that "it" was the most wonderful thing that the young man could have hoped for. It wasn't; but nobody could top it for pure, raging excitement.

In Ferndale, Chuck got through at last to Hink Field. Dinner was spoiled. His mother and his aunt were indignant; Ruth was, in fact, weeping with disappointment and rage. He could hear her say, over and over, "The fools! Oh, the fools! They're little boys, really. It's all a big game and they love it."

The baby started to cry as if she, too, realized the party was over, spoiled, done for.

That was when Chuck dialed for the twentieth time and got through.

"Captain Parker here," a voice said.

"Jeff? This is Chuck Conner—"

"Chuck? Report out here as soon as possible."

"Know anything?"

There was a minute pause—as if the captain had looked over his shoulder. Then his voice came, tense, low and fast. "Yeah! Only a Yellow alert, so far. First wave sneaked in low, somewhere above Great Slave Lake. Spread out and cruised slowly. They're split in pieces now and under attack. Thing is — thing that gets *everybody* — a wave is coming from the *south!*" The voice became flat again. "Okay, Conner. Report, Hink, instanter."

At that moment, Charles Conner had perhaps the most accurate information of any person within the main confines of the Sister Cities. He walked back into the distraught living room and said, casually almost, "Mother, I've got to report to Hink, myself. Guess I should take you home now."

"Take my car," Jim said.

Chuck looked at him. "Wouldn't you rather keep it, under the circumstances?"

Jim was sitting in his easy chair now, his face puckered with indignation and a glass of beer in his hand. "This phony-baloney? Take the car, boy."

"It may not be — phony. . . ." Chuck didn't want to frighten his uncle, merely to warn him. And he didn't want to violate his own trust.

Jim Williams stood up, his expression sardonic. "Did the Hink Field soldiers take it straight?"

Chuck nodded.

"Bunch of idiots!"

"Just the same," Chuck said, bringing his own and his mother's coats, "if you hear the air-raid siren, get down in your cellar with all the kids—and *stay* there."

Jim was grinning. "That's a hot one! Son, there aren't six sirens in all River City and the nearest one to Ferndale is audible in a strong wind only about to the reservoir."

Chuck had forgotten the great difference between the defense preparations of the two cities. He said, "Then promise this. Keep the radio on. If you hear a Condition Red, get in the cellar fast and stay there!"

He opened the door. "Promise?"

"Sure," Jim said negligently. "Gosh! I never realized I had such spooky, fool relatives."

In the Williams's car, Beth said, "It's real, isn't it, Charles?"

"Damned real."

"You were told—more than you can tell us?"

He avoided a speeding truck. "This is for you, Mother — and only you. There are two . . . three waves of bombers on the way and one's coming from the south — God knows why or how."

She didn't answer. She bowed her head and shut her eyes, and he realized, at first with a sense of shock and then with a sense of its fitness, that she was crying.

CHAPTER 12

NORA had kept on going. There was excitement in the air, and this was an adventure and besides, old lady Bailey would be really mad by this time.

All around, now, were the big buildings, the skyscrapers and the shops. The sidewalks, though broad, couldn't hold the people. They bulged out in the street, off the curb, and cars honked at them. Cars piled up at every cross street; people going over in big bunches sometimes made the cars wait through an entire green light, honking in fury, but helpless.

Simmons Park, where the giant Santa was, began to seem quite far away, though it was actually less than a mile. A mile was usually as nothing to a determined Nora. But a mile in a mob, with no lunch, was something else. She began to wonder whom she could find to help her.

She walked down Central, the biggest street, and presently found herself looking in the window of the White Elephant Restaurant, just beyond the Sloan Bank. At the sight of people eating, she swallowed several times. She pushed her nose against the cold glass and wondered if 18 cents was enough to give her entry.

Four very pretty women, not very old women, were eating their lunch right under Nora's nose. Her magnetized gaze traveled from sirup-dripping waffles to chicken salad. All of a sudden one of the women jumped up and came out the revolving door to the street and said to Nora, "You hungry, honey?"

"Yes, ma'am."

"Haven't you got any money or any folks around here?"

"I was Christmas shopping," Nora explained readily. "And I ran out of funds."

"What's your name, dear?"

"Nora Conner, and I live out on Walnut Street. That's near Crystal Lake."

"My name's Alice Groves and I'm having lunch with three nurses. Would you like to eat with us? I'll buy the lunch."

Nora hardly bothered to consider the fact that Alice Groves was colored and so were the other three women. Nora privately thought the majority of colored adults were a good deal more interesting than nearly any grown white people. She accepted.

They introduced themselves. It seemed they were all trained nurses at the Mildred Tatum Infirmary, which Nora knew about, and Miss Groves was head of the whole thing. They were off duty, Christmas shopping.

"Order anything you like, dear," Miss Groves urged.

Studying the menu, Nora asked, "Would it be all right if I had two sardine sandwiches and then waffles?" That came to 95 cents.

Alice Groves said, "It would be perfectly all right."

When Nora finished eating, the nurses asked her if she would like ice cream, but she said not, politely. Then they told her they were going to Toyland in Marker's store and she could accompany them and they would put her on a bus for home later.

Nora had forgotten all about the Santa Claus in Simmons Park. The nurses were wonderful people to be with, she thought, and there wasn't any great hurry about getting home because the snow had stopped and, if her family came home and worried about her any, it would serve them right for leaving her behind.

TED CONNER was alone in the attic on Walnut Street. At first, he had wished someone was there. The news was tearing in — the unbelievable news which he'd been trained to handle. You couldn't exactly tell what was happening from the reports, direct and relayed, that Ted tuned in on. But you could guess.

Denver had said somebody farther west had said they couldn't raise anybody in San Francisco. Or Los Angeles, either.

A guy he had often talked with in Omaha, an old gaffer named Butts, who had a sender with plenty of oomph, came in laconically. "Hello, Green Prairie. . . . Hi, Ted, son! . . . Seen anything?"

"Not here, not yet. Over."

"You will — and maybe we will, looks like. Dallas got it."

"Big Eddie? Over."

The Omaha voice, venerable, quavering with age rather than alarm, came dryly across the winter-swept plains: "Big Eddie among other things."

"Big Eddie" was the term CD ham operators in the region had come to use for "atom bomb."

Mr. Butts went on. "Station W5CED reported. He's outside the city some twenty miles. The blast wave bent his aerial, he claimed. One big flame is all he can actually see. Where Dallas is. Or was. As the case may be."

At that point, Ted wished the family was at home. It was an awful thing, he thought, to be sitting up there alone in the kind of dim attic room, with tubes glowing and word of practically the end of the world pouring in. But nobody to tell it to.

He considered running over to the Baileys' and getting Nora.

She was darn good company at a time like this. However, Nora would be an unauthorized person. That observation reminded him of duty. In Condition Yellow, he was supposed to get on the CD network with other locals and stand by for orders and relays.

He sighed heavily and tuned according to regulations.

The whole air around Green Prairie and River City was on fire with communication, all right. Somebody at headquarters — Al Tully, it turned out — soon was saying, "Station W Double Zero CDJ. Come in, Ted Conner. Over."

Ted's hands moved swiftly. His voice said in a businesslike way, "Conner, here. W Double Zero TKC. Come in, please."

"Where the hell you been? Nothing from your district at all. *Why?*" he asked.

"Dunno." At that moment, at Ted's side, an illegal phone, which he had installed himself and plugged in as he sat down, began to ring. "Here it is! Stand by. . . . "

He grabbed the instrument. To his surprise, he heard his father's voice. "That you, son?"

"Yes, Dad. Say! *Dallas* was hit! Frisco and LA don't answer."

"Good God!" Henry Conner was shocked to brief silence. His son, listening in on a ham radio set, *knew*. All Henry knew, in the principal's office in South High, was what came from State CD. Not much, nothing as appalling as the information Ted had tersely stated. "Mother home yet?" he finally asked, and Ted heard him swallow, it was so loud.

"Nope. Not yet. Nobody here."

Henry's voice was tighter, more brusque. "Okay. It's just as we figured. Phone lines swamped downtown. Can't raise HQ. We ought to have paid for a direct line, like I said, and the phone company's supposed to put us through. Try and do it. The whole thing's a mess."

"I got HQ here," Ted answered. "They want your report."

"Good kid! Tell 'em — in general — we're doing all right. We're about forty-five-percent mustered, at a guess. I'd say the doctors and surgeons are worst. Most of them haven't reported that they've followed the plan and gone outside town. But we're quietly getting all movable people out of Jenkins Hospital, into the homes around, with the homeowners mad as spit, even though they volunteered for it."

"Why," Ted passionately asked a question that had been burning in his mind, "don't they let go with the *sirens?"*

"You forget!" his father said. "Condition Red is only for the direct attack. Planes actually *headed toward us."*

"I don't forget," Ted answered. "I just suspect planes are headed for *everybody!"* He heard the slam of the front door and stood up, looking out a window. "I guess Mom just came in," he said. "I see Chuck in Uncle Jim's car."

Henry said, "Thank God! Shoot in the report, son — and I'll send you a runner soon if I can't get a wire."

CHARLES CONNER, on the way to Hink Field, after dropping his mother at home, had passed, and even been passed by, 30 or 40 vehicles, mostly private cars, bearing families, outward-bound and going like hell's chased bats. These obviously were people who reacted to the confidential news about Condition Yellow by packing up and getting out of town.

Beyond the tan fence and gates of Hink Field, a crescendo of noise told Chuck that the base was reacting. As he approached, accelerator on the floor, six jet planes came in low, cut around and climbed at full power. His pass put him through the gates and he parked in the section reserved for junior officers. He went into Flight Operations.

At the door of Control Ops, he was stopped by two soldiers with rifles in their hands and bayonets on the rifles. He wouldn't have got farther if Lieutenant Colonel Wilson, the commanding general's aide, hadn't come out to the water cooler while Chuck was arguing with the guard.

"Oh," the lieutenant colonel said, "Conner. It's you. Might as well come in and watch the shambles."

In the Operations room, on the left-hand wall, was a huge map of the United States, Canada and Mexico. On the right wall was a large-scale map of the Hink Field region, showing all of two states and parts of four more. Around the big map, in a cluster, were perhaps forty officers. Two of them were moving colored pins

and colored flags on the big map. Another was advising them, according to messages he received from headphones.

The group was absolutely silent. The flags moved toward Chicago, Chuck saw, and Indianapolis, Detroit and Toledo. There were scarlet flags on four cities — all of them, Chuck observed, coastal cities and big ones: San Francisco, Los Angeles, New York and Philadelphia. Finally, Major General Boyce spoke.

"It appears that the assault from the south is a small wave. Note it seems to have broken into three parts. Nothing coming this way. Both northern waves have split east and west. It would seem, gentlemen, that we aren't on the target list."

Those words were followed by a quiet murmur. That gave Charles a chance to say to the lieutenant colonel, who stood beside him, "What are the scarlet flags?"

"H-bombs."

Chuck felt sick. He didn't answer.

Now, to his astonishment, a civilian pushed out from the crowd.

Chuck recognized him, though he was ash-pale, almost blue-lipped. It was River City's Mayor Clyde. "I repeat, General," he said almost in a shout, "if we are not yet threatened, we must maintain Condition Yellow! You start those sirens and you sign the death warrants of maybe a thousand people. The whole population is jammed downtown, and they'd panic!"

The general followed the mayor and the men parted to make a clear path. "I know. I *know*. Any decision here depends only on emergency. Nothing has come through from Second Army. Zinsner!" he called.

The man with the headphones heard and removed them. "Yes, sir?"

"Anything from Colorado Springs?"

Zinsner spoke, inaudibly, into a mouthpiece he held in his hand, waited – while the room waited – and shook his head. "No word, sir."

General Boyce paced in front of a desk, on the thick carpeting.

Mayor Clyde followed him for a little while, gave up, leaned against the desk and wiped his face with a big linen handkerchief. He got out a cigar and lit it. The general faced the room abruptly. "What's your opinion, Berdich?"

A man wearing eagles, a man with a thin face and very white skin, said, "Can we properly call this an emergency? Our radar has a range of better than two hundred miles. So far, we have accounted for every blip — "

General Boyce lost his patience. "Good *Lord,* Berdich, I don't want a *résumé.* Just yes or no."

"No," Colonel Berdich said.

The mayor looked at him in a gratified but still-frantic fashion.

"Tetley?" asked the general.

A tall, dark man, who looked more like a college professor than a soldier, stepped forward through the group. He was a major. He said, "I say yes."

"Why?"

"From what we can gather, the little coming in, I suspect some of the attacks are by guided missiles, homing on the cities, launched from the air. Range could easily outreach our radar, and the speed would be supersonic. Even two hundred miles might not give us a Red Condition time of ten minutes."

"Ten minutes is still ten minutes," the mayor muttered.

Boyce whirled. "Ever try to empty a thirty-story building in ten minutes?" He began to pace again. "Trouble is, there's no official operational plan for precisely this situation!"

Another officer said, in a remarkably calm tone, "We've got the area ringed with search. No report. That gives us about *five hundred* miles."

"We'll wait," the general finally said.

As if that were a command, the men clustered around the map again, watching to see what changes were made according to reports relayed in a near whisper by Zinsner to the men who moved the pins and flags.

The difficulty at Hink Field was the difficulty experienced in those same hours at many other military installations. Stations that should have given reports had vanished. Cities close to command areas, like Denver, had been hit, and the news had not yet reached the right information centers; what had happened in Colorado's capital was unknown for 76 minutes at the military heart in Colorado Springs. The knowledge then arrived — as a rumor. Some command centers had, themselves, been stricken, and posts dependent upon them waited vainly for orders. Beyond that, some Air Force bases so concentrated upon defense activity that it was impossible to find wires for a steady alert service to nearby cities.

Faced by invasion with atomic arms, most military men reverted (as their long discipline had made sure they should) to conventional means and ends. This was war; this, therefore, was not the affair of civilians. Their often logical position was this: that it mattered more to bring down a grievously armed enemy plane than to keep any given city, only potentially menaced, in step-by-step contact with events, which occurred so fast in any case that the best-informed staffs were soon far behind.

Much defense matériel was expended in error. The rockets that ringed Detroit went up, after mistaken recognition signals, and destroyed seven American bombers two hours before the single Soviet plane launched its missile onto Detroit from a position far to the north, in Canada.

Of all the blunders, the most serious was that which derived from domestic politics. Civil Defense had always been considered a matter for states to organize and administer. The federal government had advised, urged, supplied research and data — and left most practical decisions to the states.

Some states had responded relatively well; others, where politics was the measure, hardly at all. Much had been done in Green Prairie for that reason; little, in its Sister City across the river. Thus the CD situation, from the military point of view, was all but hopeless. There was no way to standardize procedure. What Maryland was ready to do, Ohio had not yet even thought of. When, in the space of a dozen hours, the actual onslaught took place, the disorganized, decentralized, variable whole soon lost every tenuous relationship. For the enemy not only struck on a great shopping day and during generally poor weather, but in a period of imminent holiday when the military itself, bone-cut by tightened budgets, was cut again by holiday leaves. In many areas, the blow fell before a commanding general got back on duty, before enough technical sergeants were at their proper posts. Pearl Harbor on Sunday was far readier than the U.S.A. in that moment of hope concerning peace, that Christmas holiday.

Such thoughts passed through the mind of Charles Conner in the ensuing hour. He was, of course, like every sentient American that day, aghast and unable to weigh emotion. But, unlike most, he could set emotion aside, in a single area of his mind, and use the rest for reason.

He thought, toward the middle of the afternoon, that the Sister Cities would probably escape. Many other city areas of equal size stood unscathed, unmenaced. The enemy planes had flown far; they'd been in the air a long while; they had faced every form of interception America could muster. It was considerable. And pilots of jets, after the first few quarter hours, did not bother to press the triggers of their guns and rocket-releases. Wherever they saw the Red Star on alien wings, they plunged headlong. As they died, they knew they had struck a target which no man, with but his one life, could afford to miss.

In the general's Operations office, there was no true awareness of passing time. Outdoors, planes came in, refueled, took off. The cups on the wind gauge kept turning, the air sock streamed and the radar antenna swung in its interminable circle. The snow stopped; the clouds lifted but did not dissipate.

And then, in the gilded brightness of that winter day, certain pins on the great map turned from their coursing far below, to the south. They turned in a direction that made the room so still Chuck heard breathing, and nothing else.

CHAPTER 13

LENORE sat under the drier at Aubrey's Beauty Salon, on the eleventh floor of the Manhattan Department Store. She could see a line of other Christmas-primping women, chic women, for Aubrey's was the smart hairdresser of the Sister Cities, and she could see the magazine in her lap, *Harper's Bazaar* for January. She could reflect, if she wanted to, on why she had been handed the latest issue of one of the most modish magazines. In years past, they'd given her an old copy of the *Bazaar* or *Vogue* to read under the drier. But the mixture of gossip and dynasty is potent, and Aubrey's was a center of both. The fact that Lenore was probably soon to be the bride of Kit Sloan gave her a high priority.

"Francine," she called, "my nails are dry enough for the last coat. And I'm in a hurry."

She fidgeted in the chair. She had a headache. It would grow worse, she knew, on the floors below while she jousted with people around the counters, in the aisles. Then, worse still, over at the Ritz-Hadley, under the lush dim lights. They'd dance in too-crowded places, there and elsewhere. One Martini, two Martinis, three Martinis away from now, the headache would not be a pain but merely a sense of stiff places in the brain, waiting for tomorrow morning.

The feelings of confusion, the sense of trapped helplessness, that came over her every day were girlish feelings, maidenly sensations, no doubt. She almost regretted that she did not have her mother's attitude toward males. To Netta, they were commodities; humanity-in-pants. But to Lenore, one male remained stubbornly other.

Chuck, she thought, oh, *Chuck!*

The words were warm within her, stirred within her. The buzzing drier sang them for a little while. Chuck, oh, Chuck!

The drier went off suddenly. Unexpectedly, the effeminate voice of Aubrey came from behind her chair: "A call for you, Miss Bailey. I'm very sorry. I said you'd call back. But they insisted you be told it was your sector calling about some yellow goods, an emergency matter."

Lenore said, *"Wha-a-a-at?* It doesn't even make sense! *Wait!"* For it did make sense. She ducked out from beneath the drier and ran toward the phones.

"Yes? Lenore Bailey speaking."

The voice was flat, secretarial. "Have we been playing tag to reach *you!* This is Beatrice Jaffrey, Lenore. There's a" — her voice fell to a whisper—"Condition Yellow out. Has been, quite a while."

Lenore's answer was faltering. "Today? Good heavens, they can't expect us—unless it's—serious?"

"It's so serious," Beatrice replied, "I can't wait for your double-take. Make tracks, honey!" There was a click.

Lenore hung up. For half a minute, she merely stood beside the high shelf of the half-enclosed booth, her hand resting lightly on the mauve telephone. She was going to miss Thelma Emerson's party. The fact gave her such a sense of elation that all other facts and all other assumptions were crowded out of her mind. She was possessed by a kind of happiness, a surge of joy, something she had not felt for a long time.

I hate him that much, she thought with astonishment.

LENORE swung open the front door. "Mom!"

"I'm in here!" Netta was reclining on the divan. She had a magazine, a highball, a box of candy, a fire going in the grate, a radio on, and she talked in a barrage as Lenore stripped off her coat, gloves, galoshes. "What a hellish day! The new maid's *impossible!* That Conner brat ran away on me. I'm not through with cleaning. You'll have to do your own room, yourself, tomorrow. Why didn't you go straight to the Ritz?"

It no longer mattered to Lenore what her mother thought. She knew what her mother would say and try to do. That didn't matter, either. She answered, "Mother, I got yanked away from Aubrey's by Civil Defense."

"What?" Mrs. Bailey didn't understand; she was so completely baffled she could not even react.

"Now, Mother, take this calmly. I got an alert. It means nothing probably. Perhaps just a special drill—to see how we respond when we don't in the least expect it. But it meant going through the routine. Coming home. Getting into my clothes. Going over to the school—all such. I'm in a hurry."

By then, Netta understood. She understood and was calm. "I've been patient about this Civil Defense business for long enough, Lenore. I know you did it just to annoy me, anyhow. But you are *not* going to cut an important party and break a date with Kit, just because some fool rehearsal has been ordered. Get that straight."

"Get *this* straight," Lenore answered. "It's an alert. Official. I was summoned. As soon as I can change, I'm going. If you try to stop me, I'll — I'd even call the police!" She went.

MINERVA SLOAN found that afternoon, to her vast annoyance, four names on the lost leaf of her Christmas list which could not be ignored. That meant, in spite of the Saturday crowd, she would have to go out and make four purchases. She decided that she would shop in Green Prairie rather than River City. It was farther, but she could stop in at the bank and save herself another trip on the following Tuesday.

The moment she entered the Sloan Bank she knew things were wrong, very wrong. Too many clerks were rushing about; and they were rushing too hurriedly; besides, they were carrying too many things. She caught sight of Beau Bailey, looking white. She bawled, "Beau!"

He turned and hurried up. She stared at him as he drew near. The man, she thought, is mortally frightened.

"What the devil is the to-do about?"

"Minerva! Get home immediately! Condition Yellow — been in effect for hours! Don't you *know?*"

"Know what? What on earth are you talking about?"

He clapped a fat hand to his forehead. "Air-raid alert! The radio and TV aren't saying, but people keep calling. The most terrific rumors. Enemy planes everywhere! Many cities hit! Still Condition Yellow here, though . . . ! Thank God."

"Beau, listen. I don't know what you mean."

"Russian bombers," his voice answered, with a thin, squealing overtone, "are said to be attacking our cities. The CD people have given the bank its special alert! Evidently they've heard more than they're permitted to tell! But Condition Yellow is official."

"What in the world *is* this yellow condition?"

"The first air-raid alert. That's why everybody's rushing around here! Condition Yellow means we have to get all important papers down in the deep vault."

"See here, Beau," Minerva said solidly, "I don't know what's panicked you. But I do know nothing of the sort is happening."

"You do?" He seemed on the verge of inexpressible relief.

"I know it morally. I would have been notified! It may be that those incalculable damned fools have started some sort of a crazy air-alert practice again. They did it before, you'll remember. It could even be a real foul-up — an alert the military started, because they made some error. But — "

Beau's hope was perishing before her eyes. "If you'd step into Mr. Pavley's office, where there's a TV set . . ."

"I will," Minerva said. "Because, believe me, this hysteria has got to stop!"

Her first, creepy inkling came when she saw the live show in progress at the local station. The actors were saying their rather stupid lines, but merely saying them. Their gestures were somewhat alien to their words. And their eyes kept straying from the business in hand, as if they were watching something or somebody in the studio, rather than playing to each other.

Minerva picked up a phone. She dialed a number. It was busy, so she tried another. She gave that up because she got the busy signal with the first digit: the automatic switching station was busy as a whole. *"Something's* happening," she admitted.

She went out on the floor of the bank. Her eyes roved over the place slowly, from the vaulted windows to the huge light fixtures that hung on chains from the remote ceiling; she looked at the balcony that ran around three sides and at the figures moving there hurriedly. She gazed at the gleaming marble, big as a skating rink, usually peopled by hurrying depositors, people making withdrawals, people doing business — with her. From nowhere, unwonted, a line came into her mind: *This, too, shall pass away.*

It annoyed her greatly. But it alarmed her slightly, too.

Another thought entered her busy brain. Suppose, right now, the sirens let go? Whether in earnest or in some crazed drill, they would catch her here. Right here. In the middle of town, in the bank. At best, she'd be delayed for hours, getting home. At worst! But the worst was preposterous.

She turned to Beau, who had accompanied her, agitated, wringing his hands frequently, "I don't know what this is all about, but I think I'll go and find out. I'll phone you."

She left the bank, quite quickly.

After she had departed, Beau went back to his office. He put on his muffler, his rubbers, his coat and his hat. He went out on the mezzanine and down the stairs. Nobody saw him, nobody who had importance enough to question his going. He pushed through the crowds to the Kyle Parking Garage and waited an endless 40 minutes for his car to come down the ramp. He drove east, to the Wickley Heights section and so, circuitously, toward his home. His car radio played dance and Christmas music. The regular programs were no longer on the air. Just records, as if somebody in authority had ordered the change.

THINGS had been happening to Nora, inexplicable things. In the middle of the fun at Toyland, some colored girl in a yellow uniform and a thin coat had come up to Alice Groves. They had talked a minute. Alice had then yanked Nora out of the line of kids waiting to try the slide and said, "That was one of my probationers. They heard me say I'd be here in Toyland. I've got to go back."

"Why?"

"There's been an emergency."

So they were outside again, on the street in the mobs and hurrying. The nurses with them followed, as reluctantly as Nora. "You'll have to tag along with us," Alice had said, "and we'll telephone your people from the Infirmary. I haven't time to wait to get you on a bus. If I could find a taxi . . ."

They were still looking for an empty taxi when they passed the Sloan Bank. Minerva Sloan was just coming out and Alice stopped her. Nora didn't hear what Alice said because there was one of those tie-ups on Central Avenue, which set all the car horns blowing. But Mrs. Sloan nodded, though she looked mad. Nora, the three nurses and Alice Groves all got into the limousine.

Two nurses sat outdoors with the chauffeur. The car went to Central Avenue Bridge and over it and turned east and finally reached the Mildred Tatum Infirmary.

"I'll take the child to my home," Minerva said.

Nora thanked the colored girls deeply and sank back on the cushions. "This is very kind of you, Mrs. Sloan," she said in a pious tone. She was surprised to see that Mrs. Sloan didn't even hear her, hardly knew she was there at all. Mrs. Sloan's mind, Nora thought, was probably failing.

Coley Borden was walking in the Christmas crowd, too. He looked ten years older than he'd looked on the night when he had written the editorial that had ended his newspaper career.

He passed the Court Avenue entrance of the Transcript Tower and he stepped inside it, briefly, full of such recollections that he knew he should hurry on before one of the boys came by and caught him red-eyed. He felt an arm on his shoulder just then and he heard a familiar voice: "Hello, boss. Somebody tell you?"

Coley smiled and raised his head and there was Payton, the city editor, looking rather odd. "Tell me what?"

"Thought that was why you'd come down here." Payton glanced apprehensively at the streaming people and lowered his voice: "The whole country's under air blitz, Coley. They're holding it back here, to prevent panic, in the belief this area is not on the target list."

"What is this?" Coley asked softly. "April Fool?"

"It's *it,*" Payton answered. *"You* should know!"

Coley stepped back till he felt the firm stones of the skyscraper against his shoulders. "God help us!" he whispered. "God help us all." Then he snapped, "What's the *Transcript* doing about it?"

"Standing by — for the story."

"That maybe they'll never print! Well, get on, son. Don't waste your time with a broken-down old prophet!"

Payton patted his former boss on the arm and hurried off.

Coley stood awhile, without moving. Perhaps he was thinking. Perhaps he was merely summoning the strength to get going again.

He entered the building, finally. He took an elevator to the top. When he stepped out, the smell was familiar, the sounds were remembered and fond; the look of the place was home itself.

CHAPTER 14

CHUCK CONNER was still in Control Ops. The news came abruptly, repeated by Zinsner:

"Three planes — four-engined turboprop bombers — now diverted from main wing — Green Prairie-River City destination probable. Approach in Sector two-oh-nine. Repeat: two-zero-nine. Intercept at distance one hundred fifty miles minimum or combat probably ineffective. Bomb carrier probably equipped to launch medium-range missile. That is all."

General Boyce began giving orders which were swiftly relayed to all fighters aloft. Then he looked at the mayor of River City, but not with bitterness. "Condition Red," the general said quietly, "and God pity them!"

HENRY CONNER, at his desk, stiffened as the great wail of fright went over the city. It rose to a scream. Air-raid wardens in Henry's sector tightened their belts, pulled at their helmets, looked up at the still-bright sky and walked on. "Take cover!" they yelled at all other pedestrians.

Men in the rescue squads in the high school playgrounds began rechecking equipment. The engines of bulldozers and cranes roared into trial life and were stilled. In the gymnasium, below Henry, the Radiation Safety volunteers anxiously examined their monitoring gauges. Superintendents and head nurses began unlocking closets stacked to the ceiling with drugs, medicines, bandages.

At the Broad Street Police Station, all but three men had already reported and half had already been assigned to street duties. In the nearby firehouse, the men listened incredulously. They knew they were as ready as they could be under existing circumstances — and not ready at all.

Henry knew that. He went on with his work.

IN THE Conners' attic, on Walnut Street, the iron shriek hurt Ted's eardrums. "There she goes!" he murmured. "Oh, *boy!*"

His mother came upstairs, gray-faced. "I haven't found a trace of Nora," she said, waiting for a lull in the sustained bellow. "Nothing. Netta said she just *went.*"

"She'll be okay," Ted answered, feeling frightened. "Trust old Nora!" Mrs. Conner sat down on the bed. She held her hands together and didn't move at all during the next crescendo of the siren. "It's happening, isn't it?" she said, then. "It really is!"

Ted got up, shucked off his phones, gripped his mother's shoulders and said something, when the siren allowed it, which changed Beth. It was, under the circumstances, the right thing — and a remarkable thing for a 16-year-old boy to say. "Just about every other mother in America has a Nora, someplace, right now," he told her.

The woman stood up then, looked intently at her son, nodded slowly. Her answer was blotted out by the siren, but Ted knew approximately what it was: "I'm supposed to go over to the church." She smiled at him in a loving way and left the room.

He went back to his seat. His hands were getting slippery with the old sweat.

The limousine was moving through Pearson Square when the crescendo-diminuendo sound reached the chauffeur. He speeded up, ignoring Minerva's tap on the glass partition. He swung the big car into the driveway and leaped out nimbly for his age. "We better get in the cellar," he said.

"Nonsense!"

"I've kind of fixed it up, ma'am. With the help of Jeff and some other servants and the gardener. It's right comfortable."

Willis was waiting, holding the door, and yet looking away and upward toward the winter lace of treetops and the glimmer of high buildings in the distance.

"If any preparations were made in my cellar," Minerva said, "I should have been told!"

"We thought you might object, ma'am."

"I *would* have! Insane . . !"

"It was owing to the gardener's brother, mostly. He went through the blitz in the last war. Near London."

Minerva, scornful but shaken, said, "Very well. Come on, Norma."

"I'm *Nora.* Do you think there'll be an A-bomb?"

"I think," her august guardian replied, "there will be the biggest scandal in the history of this government! But Willis thinks otherwise, so we'll go to my cellar."

Beau Bailey had just reached his door, too, when the sirens went. He rushed inside. "Turn off the gas!" he yelled. "Where the hell is Lenore?"

"At the high school, naturally."

"At the . . ? Oh. You mean she went — with all that junk?"

"She really did. A long time ago. Come up here, Beau, and help me pack!"

"Pack? Ye Gods, woman, there's no time to pack. That's the Red alert! We're going down by the furnace!"

"And leave all my new clothes up here? I should say not!"

Beau stood at the foot of the staircase.

The siren rose and fell. Slowly.

On the radio the music stopped, and Jim Williams frowned. He did not know about *Conelrad,* the radio way of trying to baffle enemy bombers by putting all stations on two specified wavelengths. But he turned dials until he heard:

"Repeat. This is a CONELRAD Radio Alert. Enemy bombers have attacked the United States. A condition of confidential alert has existed for some hours. *This is not a practice. Not a drill. This is real.* Enemy planes, possibly bearing atomic weapons, are said to be approaching Green Prairie and River City. *Take cover immediately. Everybody. Take cover instantly! Condition Red is in effect!* Sirens are now blowing. Persons in cars draw to curb and wind up windows and get on the floor below the window glass. All persons near windows get below the level of the glass. Take refuge in cellars and basements, if possible. *Instantly.* Repeat — "

Jim switched it off. "Hey, Ruth," he called, "you hear that?"

She came from the kitchen. "Yes, I did. I don't believe it."

"Neither do I," Jim said. "Must be a walloping hoax." He went to the window in contravention of the radioed orders. He looked out. "Some cars are stopping though. Most aren't. Maybe they haven't got their radios on. Or radios in 'em at all." He snickered. "Just like that Martian gag!"

Ruth's hands were wet with dishwater. "What a day!" she said. "What a *crazy* day!"

He lighted a cigarette. "You think maybe we ought to go out and rally the kids and take 'em down cellar?"

"Let's see what the radio says now." She turned it on.

THE SIREN burst into his brain as Coley stood in the outer offices on the editorial floor. The effect was amazing. Everybody — secretaries and rewrite men, copy boys and stenographers, editors and sub-editors — streamed past the place where Coley stood. There were some 80 people on the top tower floor. It took about three minutes for them all to go. He just stood there, bewildered by the confusion, unrecognized by persons who were united in one idea: getting to the ground, or under it.

By and by, he went through the city room to his old office. There were papers on his successor's desk. There were copy and proof. There was a phone left off its cradle. Coley put it back.

The very walls, when the siren rose to its top pitch, seemed to vibrate. He walked to the familiar windows. He opened one and leaned out and looked up. The clouds were high and thin. It was going to be a clear night — clear and very cold. Here and there toward the west, blue sky showed through in slits and streaks, blue tinged with pearly colors. He could only see one airplane — a jet, from the speed — and it was going away, north and west, across River City.

A scarf of light fell down every skyscraper. The day was still bright, but waning. Coley wondered, as he stared at the infinitely familiar vista, what was happening elsewhere. He regretted, momentarily, that he would probably never know. Then, with the siren penetrating his very skull, he looked down.

"Great God," he whispered softly.

The cars in Court Avenue and on Madison were packed solid and standing still. The sidewalks were black with people. People who hadn't obeyed the shelter signs. People who wouldn't stay in the jam-packed stores. It was like looking down at ants in an anthill calamity.

Then, suddenly, the siren was still. It dropped its brazen voice, rattled death in its own throat and fell silent. But silence did not follow. From the streets below came the most bloodcurdling sound Coley had ever heard or dreamed of. The combined tumult of an agony of fear came up the building sides, up the concrete cavern walls, to Coley's ears, as one sound. He could not reckon with it in his mind. It was so awful he wanted to stop up his ears. He jerked his eyes away.

And thus he was one of the few, one of the very few, to see it coming. He would not even have seen it, so tremendous was its speed, had it not approached almost straight toward him, though at a higher level. *There it is,* he thought strangely.

It was quite long, dark,

but with a flare of fire at the tail end that shone palely against the winter sky. It had a place to go to, he supposed, and it must be near its place. The nose end was thin and very sharp. Then, where it had been, almost overhead by that time, a Light appeared.

It was a Light of such intensity that Coley could see nothing except its lightness and its expanding dimensions. It swelled over the sky above and burst down toward him. He felt, at the same time, a strange physical sensation — just a brief start of a sensation — as if gravity had vanished and he, too, were a rushing thing, and a prickling through his body, and a heat.

And he was no more.

IN THAT same part of a second the proud skyline of River City and Green Prairie smoked briefly, steamed a little, and no shadows were thrown anywhere in the glare. The façades — stone, concrete, brick — glazed, crinkled, and began to slip as they melted. But the heat penetrated, too. The steel frames commenced to sag and buckle; metal, turned molten, ceased to sustain the floors upon many floors. Peaks of skyscrapers, domes, steeples, square roofs, tilted sideways and would have toppled or crashed down, but gravity was not fast enough, not strong enough. For that part of a second the great region, built so slowly, at such cost, by men, liquefied and stood suspended above the ground: it could fall only 16 feet in that time. Then, in the ensuing portion of a second, the liquid state was terminated. The white in the sky bellied down, growing big and globular, a thousand feet across and more. The liquids gasified: stone and cement, steel and plaster, brick and bronze and aluminum. In the street — if anyone could have seen at all, as no man could in the blind solar whiteness — there were no howling people at all. None.

On the sidewalks, for a part of a second, on sidewalks boiling like forgotten tea, were dark stains that had been people, tens of thousands of people. The Light went over the whole great area, like a thing switched on. The air, of a sudden, became hotter than boiling water, hotter than melted lead.

Clothing caught fire, the beggar's rags, the dowager's sables, the baby's diapers, the minister's robe. Paper in the gutter burst into flame. Trees. Clapboards. The wires above 10,000 roofs — the TV antennae wires — glowed cherry-red, then white, then fell apart while slate beneath melted. Every wooden house for two miles began smoking. And tombstones in Restland Cemetery glowed dully, as if to announce the awakening of those they memorialized. In that second part of a second.

The plutonium fist followed:

It hammered across Front Street, Madison, Adams, Jefferson and Washington, along Central Avenue and rushed forward. Under the intense globe of light, meantime, for a mile in every direction, the city disappeared. In the mile beyond, every building was bashed and buffeted. Homes fell by thousands on their inhabitants. Great institutions collapsed.

The fist swung on, weaker now, taking the lighter structures and all the glass, the windows everywhere, hurling them indoors.

Invisible, from the dangling body of light, the radioactive rays fell. Men felt the fist, the heat, but not the unseeable death that rode in swift consort with the explosion.

River City, from the Cathedral on St. Mark's Street to the water, from Swan Island to the James Street Bridge, a mile-sized arc, with all the great skyscrapers it contained, was nothing. A flat place, incandescent.

Green Prairie, from Washington Avenue to the river, from Slossen's Run to the fashionable Ritz-Hadley, was gone. A vapor in the heavens. Beyond that, for a mile, each acre of land underwent such convulsions, such surges of heat and twisting avalanches of blast, as to leave little man might use.

The belly of the fireball flattened. An uprising dust column, assembled by the vacuum left behind the outracing blast, hoisted the diminishing white horror toward the heavens. It went out, leaving a glow of lavender and orange, ascending, spreading. Two great metropolises lay stricken below, as the mushroom soared.

The heart of the cities was gone. A third of their people were dead or dying or grievously hurt. A million little fires were flickering, anucleating, to form a great holocaust. And this had required the time in which a pensive man might draw a breath, hold it reflectively and exhale.

It

CHAPTER 15

HENRY CONNER's fingers drummed the table; his friendly eyes, narrowed with thought, looked unnoticing from his borrowed office on the top floor of the school. He was receiving a telephone report about the road patrol. The men were out on duty, the cars marked, all the necessary things done, and nearly three quarters of their assigned numbers on hand.

"Good," he said.

Even the siren's tearing willawa — the announcement, hooted across the city, that Condition Yellow had become Condition Red — did not entirely convince his inner self of reality. The long years of work were here to meet their meaning. Yet he thought of them as a dream. The committees and conversations, the drills and exercises, seemed like neighborly games, pleasant habits. They had gone on and on, in crackling autumns and the sweat of remote Julys. He could not think of their significance.

It was the Light that changed him.

The Light gushed over the trees. Outdoors, the view turned white; only degrees of whiteness existed. Henry's eyes beheld a scene like an exposed negative lifted up to the naked sun, a scene of trees and roofs and the front of the tall hospital, Crystal Lake and more trees, more snow-clad grounds beyond, white, brilliant, one step from transparency.

He shoved back his chair, fell on his face, crawled beneath the desk. The fist struck the building. It lurched. Steel-hard air ripped part of the roof away, went around walls, closed beyond and, driving and sucking, took the windows on one side across the schoolrooms to shatter and cascade along the walls, flung the rest out in the day.

Henry got up, looked at a crack through which the sky showed, watched plaster dribble, heard bricks cataract into the yard, stamped on a firebrand that dropped in the room.

He was all right. His staff people, scared, moving weakly, were coming back from a corridor where they had taken refuge when the siren sounded.

"There's a fire downstairs," someone said.

"Two men," someone else said, "are lying in the hall. Under bricks." They were looking at him.

"Okay," he heard his voice begin. "Trent and Dawson, see about the fire. The house crew'll probably be on it soon, but check. The house medical's in the gym. Send for them — start picking the bricks off the hurt men. Leete, inspect the other side and report back. Have the runners' information collated downstairs from now on; just bring me the main points."

Someone else said, "Maybe this building is no longer safe!"

Henry felt his lips turn into a grin, and the feeling buttressed him just when he needed support. "So what?" he replied. "It's still here! That's at least something."

People began to move, to do things — slowly, Henry thought.

TED CONNER went under his table. The Light came. The house bucked and screamed as if some cosmic claw hammer were trying to open it. A thud seemed to compress his body on all sides at once. His radio equipment, the precious store of instruments earned by hundreds of mowed lawns, was flung on the floor and smashed.

He picked himself up. His leg was bruised and bleeding. He drew out a jagged piece of Bakelite.

He went downstairs. The house was battered, but it was a house and their house still. His mother's china cupboard lay on its face; broken cut glass glistened on the carpet. The kitchen was a shambles of crocks and pots and pans.

He went out in the back yard, stupefied. The clapboards on that side of the house were scorched, but nothing was burning. The blast, he thought, had put out the fire. The building looked tilted a little and askew on its foundations.

Queenie came up to him, mewing.

He went back indoors, checked the gas and the lighting circuits (there was no power) and got his coat and hat in preparation for making his scary way over to the school to report.

It was what they had always planned he should do if his radio set was knocked out, or the power failed.

Netta Bailey had insisted on trying to get her clothes down to the cellar. She argued; Beau, increasingly panicked by the siren, had taken a reluctant armful down — and stayed in the warm company of the furnace.

For him, the Light was a stabbing bar that shot through the dirty coal windows and turned the place to day.

For Netta, still upstairs, it was incomprehensible, an irritant. Her reaction was to run to the window and gaze obliquely north toward the perplexing source. The blast brought the window in on her, slicing her face, her breast, her abdomen. She was doll-flung to the opposite wall, mercifully knocked unconscious.

Beau, calling, coming up afterward, found her. He assumed she was dead and looked at the bloody figure for no more than a moment. Then he tiptoed down the suddenly treacherous stairs and entered his living room. "Need a drink," he said quietly to himself.

He found a bottle finally that wasn't broken. He drank from it and, with it in his hand, without a coat, he went outdoors. He had a vague idea that somebody should do something about Netta.

As he left his house, not aware he was running, he kept calling, "Where's a doctor? Where's a doctor?"

Mrs. Conner was on her way to the Presbyterian Church, a fairly long walk. She was wearing her old winter coat — glad she hadn't given it away — and carrying a heavy suitcase. The suitcase was her own idea and she hadn't told Henry about it. In it were "odds and ends," assembled by Beth as she had listened over the years to Civil Defense talk about what might happen. She had slipped onto her arm the brassard of her volunteer corps: "Emergency Nurse" it said, in red, white and blue felt letters.

The sirens were screaming like wounded demons and the only other people on foot were air-raid wardens, here and there, who hurried toward her to tell her to take cover, then saw the arm band and grinned and called, usually, "Hello, Mrs. Conner!" or, "Watch it!" She answered mildly. She was thinking about Nora.

The Light caught her on Ash Street, near Arkansas Avenue. Henry had told her to get down in the gutter with the curb between herself and the hot whiteness, but she was afraid of the cars. There were, however, small terraces in the Wisters' front lawn. Beth dropped on her hands and knees, then flattened herself. The blast and the Wister windows and some of the tiles from the roof went over her and she was not hurt.

She got up and trudged on, carrying the suitcase still. When she reached Lake View Road, she saw that the windows of the Jenkins Memorial Hospital had been blown away; and the steeple of the Crystal Lake Presbyterian Church, her destination, a hospital itself in the event of emergency, had been broken off at the middle.

In Ferndale, Jim Williams's family assembled while the sirens wailed unheard, and only the ultra-calm radio voice gave a warning. Ruth, whoo-whooing, brought the older ones in. Jim hastily put some Coke in a pail — and some beers — and pulled out the screw driver which served as a bolt for the cellar door. The house was heated by oil stoves, so he'd had no occasion to go down to the cellar for some days.

When the door creaked open, he knew by the smell, however.

He switched on the light. Sure enough. Water had seeped in during the thaw, a week back. "Wait up, you!" he called, and went down the cobwebby steps. He found the handle of an old shovel and probed gingerly.

"Water down here," he reported disgustedly. "About a foot deep! We better stay upstairs after all."

Relieved, the entire family went back to the parlor. They sat around uncertainly, the kids, for once, quiet. Ruth, alone, stood. When the Light came, she snatched the baby from her pen.

Jim said, or began to say, with a still-unconvinced tone, "Maybe we should do like they told us — duck — "

The blast wave struck. The Williams house, more than a thousand yards nearer the place of the fireball than the sturdier Conner home, had its top floor mashed as by a mallet. The windows screamed into the room. And that year they were double; Jim had put on storm windows. All the children fell, bleeding. Jim lost much of his face.

Ruth was not hurt — not hurt at all, physically — the baby, now dead, had shielded her.

KIT SLOAN, on his way home from the River City Athletic Club, was in a temper even before the sirens started. The seasonal parties, dances, balls and festivities had given him an alcoholic nervousness. He'd decided that day to play squash early, get his rubdown, and come home to dress in time to make it over to the Ritz-Hadley for the Emerson cocktail thing.

But his customary opponents hadn't been on hand. There was a rumor going, about an air-raid drill; and the three best players in the club, Green Prairie men, were in Civil Defense. He'd been obliged to bat balls around by himself for an hour.

He drove vexedly in the Christmas crowds. It wasn't far from the club to Pearson Square, but the waits for lights, the bumper-to-bumper pace between lights, made it seem a long way.

When at last he reached the southeast corner of the square, he saw that traffic along the south side was so badly jammed he decided it would be quicker to run the Jaguar through an alley, and drive across the interior park itself, on a paved path meant for bikes and baby carriages. He doubted if the cops would bother him; he'd done it before, as a gag, at night. He figured he could blast a hole in the stalled traffic with his horn, thus getting into the Sloan driveway long before the log jam could be broken.

The decision saved him from swift death.

The siren caught him in the alley. He had to wait even there for three huge trucks, unloading behind the supermarket, to disentangle themselves and move down to the square. He followed. By then, a group of teen-age boys, attracted by the red car, were begging him to give them a ride. He ground up his windows in fury.

When the Light came, he didn't think at all. He shot to the floor of the car and covered his head with his arms: whatever it was, it was deadly. His reflexes so interpreted it. The blast followed. The supermarket behind him disintegrated, and bricks roared down upon his car, burying it. He lay in sudden darkness and the choking dust of mortar.

Trapped, hardly sensing as a special phenomenon the blast itself, Kit picked at the split glass of a window in his car. Bricks fell in on him but the illumination increased. Frantically, he pulled in more bricks. By and by he had a hole through which he could worm his way, hands first, tossing bricks aside.

ALL Nora knew, for sure, when the ground jumped, was that the atomic bomb must have hit.

They'd been in the subcellar, with candles, sitting in old, discarded chairs — Minerva and Willis and three maids and Jeff, the butler, and the gardener. All around them were racks of dusty wine bottles, barrels of wine and cases. They couldn't have been sitting there, Nora thought, for more than a minute. Then the whole place jumped and the candles went out and it was like being on the Whipsaw ride at Swan Island, and the maids screamed, but not like amusement-park screaming.

Then — the air full of moldy-smelling dust. And the maids were hollering their fool heads off. Nora's chair slid on the bare earth floor. Barrels fell and bounced and rolled.

Then Willis, his old voice fierce, yelled, "Quiet!" Peculiarly, Nora thought, the maids became silent. "Are you all right, ma'am?" Willis asked. Mrs. Sloan didn't answer.

A match struck. Nora noticed how it shook, how the hands that held a candle wobbled with it. The first thing Nora saw was the maids, hugging each other, pale as death. The next thing she saw was a big wine barrel that wine was gurgling out of. Then she

saw Mrs. Sloan, her legs pinned underneath it. Her eyes were shut.

"We'll have to get out of here," Willis said. "And get *her* out." He was kneeling, listening to Mrs. Sloan's heart.

From the door, which he'd opened, the gardener called, "Stairway's kind of blocked and it does smell smoky-like."

Willis said, "Well, clear a way through somehow!"

Pretty soon, they had moved the barrel. Jeff was looking at Mrs. Sloan's legs, holding another lighted candle and pulling up her skirts in a most casual manner. "Busted — smashed," he said. "Have to make a stretcher. Some weight!"

From the door, the gardener yelled, "We can get around this junk. But hurry! I hear it crackling up there!"

So they dragged Mrs. Sloan. The maids went first, though — they ran. And Nora was next to the gardener, who went last. As she followed the dragged woman, she saw Mrs. Sloan's pocketbook on the floor underneath the place where she'd been lying. Nora took it along and nobody paid any attention.

"Hurry up, kid," the butler said. That was all.

The cellar was half caved-in and you could see lines of fire, through cracks overhead. The smoke was awful. Nora ran past the men with their slow-moving burden to the square of outdoor light, and she raced up stone steps, gratefully, for she was at last outdoors. She hoped she was in time to see the mushroom cloud, and she eyed the sky eagerly.

She was in time. In plenty of time.

And she saw more. The whole city, to the south, seemed on fire. It was, she told herself, extremely spectacular. It was unforgettable. She took a good look so she would never forget.

Then she looked at the house. The great Victorian pile was also burning. Flames surged in the broken guts of the building and curled among the slates of the roofs and the many gables. It was all afire. The car that had brought them was on fire.

Willis said, "And the garage is blocked. We'll have to put her in a barrow, I guess, Jeff, and get her to the street. Maybe we can catch a lift — or borrow a parked car. . . ."

The men had a very hard time pushing the wheelbarrow. The ground was soft and there no longer was any snow — to Nora's surprise. On the drive, though, it went easier. The gardener helped, too, taking the longest turn with the wheelbarrow.

It would be dark presently, Nora thought. The light, at the moment, was pinkish, as if a sunset had begun. But it was not a sunset at all and came from the south. It was the start of a fire storm, she knew.

When they reached the street, they stopped.

It was the first time Nora had got a good look at any dead people and now there were so many she could hardly decide which ones to look at first. Some, she saw, weren't exactly dead, or completely dead. A few in cars were opening and closing their mouths or moving their arms feebly, and one girl about Nora's age kept bumping her head back and forth between the front and rear seats in a sedan. Some people in the park were crawling around and you could hear screams and groans, mostly from where some big store was crushed about flat.

Willis was walking along, looking at the cars that stood on their wheels and weren't full of glass or smoking or anything. At long last he got into a car and started it. Then he and Jeff got Mrs. Sloan in the back somehow and she moaned once but her eyes didn't open. Willis said, "Where to?" in a funny way and Nora thought probably he had a certain percentage of "shock." Maybe about forty percent, she thought, and she thought Jeff had about fifty and she had ten or maybe twenty percent at most.

The car started along the street very slowly, going this way and that, but the lights were smashed and you couldn't tell exactly what you were running over. Nora saw then that sweat was pouring down Willis's face and he was crying and the butler beside him was looking straight ahead at absolutely nothing. When they reached St. Paul Street, they couldn't make a right turn because of the rubble, so they went on north.

Finally Jeff said, "The City Hospital's the other way, Willis." He spoke quietly, as if he didn't want to hurt the chauffeur's feelings. But Willis wasn't making a mistake. He answered, "Jeff, there won't *be* any city hospital down there."

Jeff said, "Check," and sounded crestfallen. "Where you headed?"

"I thought we might break through farther up here and get to the Infirmary."

"Mrs. Sloan would be highly incensed — "

"I don't know if she'll ever be highly anything."

When they crossed Market Street they began to see a lot of people who weren't hurt at all, just running around. Many were going in and out of houses, carrying things, and some families already had beds and bedding and trunks and suitcases and piles of clothing out on the street. Quite a few had put things in handcarts and even on children's wagons, and they were hurrying along, pushing and pulling and carrying babies. Some blocks down, where the big Cathedral was plain to see because it was on fire and half-mashed anyhow, fire hoses were shooting up and fire trucks were all around.

"That's what comes," Willis said, "of having all Harps in the Fire Department. Save the Catholic church and let the city go."

Jeff said, haughtily, Nora noticed, "I guess it isn't important. Half the fire companies must have been wiped out and the rest couldn't do much. The flood that floated Noah couldn't put this out!" He laughed a little; cackled, Nora called it to herself.

They covered about three miles to go about one straight mile, and often they had to back out of streets because they could see they couldn't go through. Pretty soon they stopped.

They stopped because the street ahead was solid with people trying to get to the Infirmary. They were all hurt. A lot of people were already on the ground, unable to move, or dead, and nobody paid any attention to them.

"I'll have to get through somehow," Willis said.

"It isn't possible."

"We can't let her wait for her turn here. She'll die, most likely."

Jeff stepped out of the car. His hair started to blow and his coat flickered and Nora realized it was very windy. That would be the air moving in to feed the fire storm and it could reach hurricane force, her parents had often said. The butler took a look at the hurt people, who were all around him now, and a long look at the big torch in the sky, and he just ran, like the panicky maids.

"Smelled 'em, I guess," Willis said.

Nora stepped out. She felt the coldness of the pouring air on one side and the heat of the veritable Mount Everest of fire on the other.

Then a terrible thing happened.

Willis got out of the sedan, too, and suddenly grabbed his shoulder. His face became distorted and he tried to say something, tried to gesture, but he fell down. Nora squatted down and shook him and said, over and over, "Mr. Willis! Mr. Willis!" But he didn't say a word so she knew his heart had failed.

It wasn't surprising, she thought. He was a very elderly man. More people were coming into the street all the time, pushing toward the Infirmary. If she didn't want to spend the rest of the night right there, she'd have to move. She thought she might be able to go up the street again and around to the back or the side of the Infirmary. It was the only hope of getting a doctor for Mrs. Sloan, though she hesitated to try it, because now she would be all alone.

Beau was lost. How he got so far downtown he never knew.

He remembered the railroad tracks, because he almost got killed there. A train — covered with people like flies on flypaper — came around a bend, headlight shining, folks scattering ahead. Some got hit. The train gave a whistle blast and thundered by, out of the city, Beau guessed. Even so, he must have taken the wrong direction on the tracks afterward. It was hard to remember which way you'd faced, after you'd rolled down an embankment.

He was somewhere around the Simmons Park area, though, in Wickley Heights, he thought.

He stopped to take bearings. "Quite a night," he said aloud. Netta's dead, he thought.

There was a big apartment building, a swanky place, on this street, he noticed. It had broken windows, big ones, because the ground floor was for shops. He thought there might be a liquor store. He walked along in front of the fire-illumined building, waded, rather, in deep glass that was slippery. The trees on the street had been knocked over in neat rows pointing the same way.

He stopped. It wasn't a liquor store. It was a jewelry store.

The big window was just a glass jaw, like a shark's, that a man could step through. The glass counters were conveniently shattered. Inside, things glittered in the firelight, brighter than glass, and different colors. There was nobody around. Nobody at all.

Beau said dazedly, rather happily, "Well!"

He went in and picked up a bracelet and then a necklace. "Well, well!" he murmured. He commenced to stuff his pockets, humming. He hummed, "Happy days are here again. . . ."

Hook and Ladder Company Number 17 pulled back to Broad Street, according to plan. The sea of fire began at Washington, to the north. Nothing could be done to stop a fire storm. It had to burn itself out, leaving just ash, the Hiroshima effect. The temperature inside it would rise to 6000 degrees or better. Any people alive under that circle of flame would crisp and cremate, or, escaping that, in some deep cellar suffocate. For all the oxygen of the atmosphere nearby would be used by the fire. The "air" would be carbon monoxide and carbon dioxide.

They thought maybe they could save the Police Station and everything from there south. When they got to the station, they piled out. There were lights in the windowless building and even the green lights outside were burning again, thanks to an auxiliary power plant. Over toward Bigelow and Cold Spring, it looked comfortingly dark, though the firemen knew brands and sparks would be raining down there and probably clear to the city limits. The CD people would have to take care of that. The business of Number 17 was the big stuff, like the row of stores blazing on Broad. Fortunately, the wind blew toward the center of town from every compass point, feeding the fire storm; it made peripheral fire fighting practicable. If it hadn't been for that in-sucked wind, all Green Prairie would have gone.

The trucks fanned out. The growling sirens fell silent. Caps fell from fireplugs, hoses were screwed on, streams of water traversed Broad and crashed into the seething row of stores.

Lieutenant Lacey, looking military neat, came out of the Police

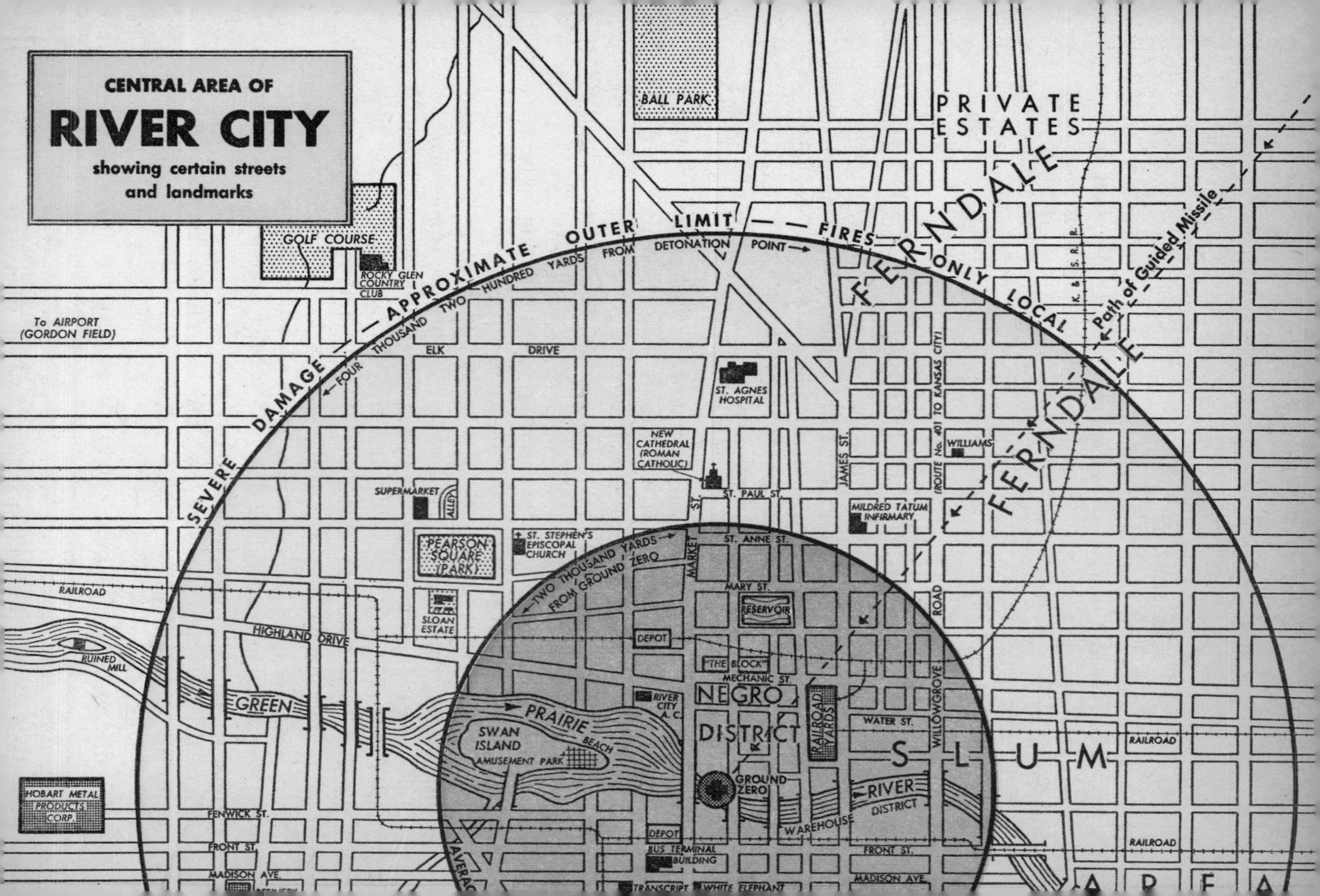
CENTRAL AREA OF
RIVER CITY
showing certain streets
and landmarks
BALL PARK
PRIVATE ESTATES
GOLF COURSE
ROCKY GLEN COUNTRY CLUB
To AIRPORT (GORDON FIELD)
SEVERE DAMAGE — APPROXIMATE OUTER LIMIT — FIRES ONLY LOCAL
FOUR THOUSAND TWO HUNDRED YARDS FROM DETONATION POINT
FERNDALE
FERNDALE
Path of Guided Missile
K. & S. R. R.
ELK DRIVE
ST. AGNES HOSPITAL
NEW CATHEDRAL (ROMAN CATHOLIC)
ST. PAUL ST.
JAMES ST.
(ROUTE No. 401 TO KANSAS CITY)
WILLIAMS
MILDRED TATUM INFIRMARY
SUPERMARKET
ALLEY
PEARSON SQUARE (PARK)
ST. STEPHEN'S EPISCOPAL CHURCH
TWO THOUSAND YARDS FROM GROUND ZERO
MARKET ST.
ST. ANNE ST.
MARY ST.
RESERVOIR
RAILROAD
SLOAN ESTATE
HIGHLAND DRIVE
DEPOT
"THE BLOCK"
MECHANIC ST.
WILLOWGROVE ROAD
RUINED MILL
GREEN
RIVER CITY A. C.
NEGRO DISTRICT
RAILROAD YARDS
WATER ST.
PRAIRIE BEACH
SWAN ISLAND AMUSEMENT PARK
SLUM
RAILROAD
GROUND ZERO
RIVER DISTRICT
WAREHOUSE
HOBART METAL PRODUCTS CORP.
FENWICK ST.
FRONT ST.
MADISON AVE.
DEPOT
BUS TERMINAL BUILDING
TRANSCRIPT
WHITE ELEPHANT
FRONT ST.
MADISON AVE.
RAILROAD
AVERAG
AREA

CENTRAL AREA OF
GREEN PRAIRIE
showing certain streets and landmarks
To FOOTBALL STADIUM
To GORDON FIELD (SISTER CITIES AIRPORT)
To HINK FIELD (MILITARY AIRPORT)
WASHINGTON AVE.
SUNSET PARKWAY
RESERVOIR
BYPASS)
SEWER AND STORM DRAIN
RUN
RESTLAND CEMETERY
FIRE HOUSE
PARKING GARAGE
SIMMONS PARK
SANTA CLAUS
TOTAL DESTRUCTION — FIRE STORM
JAMES ST.
HEIGHTS
APARTMENTS
WICKLEY
RITZ-HADLEY HOTEL
AND HEIGHTS HOTELS
BOULEVARD
JEWELRY STORE
WEST BROAD ST.
EAST BROAD ST.
BROAD STREET POLICE STATION
PUBLIC SCHOOL No. 44
(NEW SEWER)
SLOSSEN'S
HICKORY ST.
HOBART PARK
POND
GOLF COURSE
GREEN PRAIRIE COUNTRY CLUB
PLUM ST.
OAK ST.
SPRUCE ST.
PINE ST.
MAPLE ST.
WALNUT ST.
ASH ST.
SOUTH HIGH SCHOOL
CHASE DRIVE
OVERFLOW
SOUTH HOBSON ST.
BIGELOW AVE.
COLD SPRING ST.
COURT AVE.
CENTRAL AVE.
WILLOWGROVE AVE.
HOUSE
APARTMENT
DRUG STORE
BANK
ASYLUM
APARTMENT
CONNER
BAILEY
MISSOURI SIOUX R. R.
KANSAS AND SOUTHERN R. R.
EDGEPLAINS
CRYSTAL LAKE
ROAD JENKINS MEMORIAL HOSPITAL
CRYSTAL LAKE PRESBYTERIAN CHURCH
MANSE
VIEW
LAKE
DUMOND AVE.
ARKANSAS AVE.
RIVER AVE.
SEDMON AVE.
WINDMERE PARKWAY
COLD SPRING NURSERY
DECATUR RD.

Station and pointed at a huge lump of debris in the street—a tangle of metal, half-melted, unrecognizable, and as big as a small house. "It fell," he yelled in the fire chief's ear, "right after the blast. Think your men are safe around it?"

The chief stared. "Around it is where they gotta be, if they're going to keep this fire from spreading."

"I phoned the school," Lacey said, "for one of those radiation people. They haven't got many. And we need 'em in a million places!"

The chief nodded. A roof fell across the street and he ran from the station steps to deal with the changed circumstances. This conflagration would have been a three-alarmer, in ordinary times; it was a mere match sputter now.

The Ford came fast, considering the condition of the streets.

Somebody had stuck CD flags on both sides, so Lacey ran down and yanked open the door. "Big gob of metal dropped in the street," he said. "I've kept my men clear of it, but the firemen have to work beside it."

"I'll check."

Lacey stepped back and stared. It was a woman.

She piled out, wearing some sort of plastic thing that made her look like an Arab, and carrying a box with dials and wires. He followed her.

She didn't even glance at the fire engines or the men swarming in the street or the blazing buildings. She went through the puddles, in boots, to the mass he'd pointed out. She held a shiny metal rod out at it and began walking slowly around it. Lacey went right along with her. He could see, in the heaving firelight, that the dials on her gadget were jumping. But that didn't make her back away from the big slag heap, so *he* didn't back away.

"It's radioactive," she said. "Plenty. Looks like something blasted from a building. Steelwork and wiring. Balled up in the air and hurled out here."

"Is it killing the men?" he asked.

Lenore chuckled and shook her hooded head. "No. They'd be safe even sitting on it, for a matter of a few hours. But I wouldn't want it in my dining room for good."

"Cigarette?" Lacey asked.

Lenore unzipped her transparent face protector. "I'd love one! Heaven knows when I had my last one, and I've got a list of calls to make as long as my arm." She threw back her hood, inhaled and said, "Thanks."

"You're the Bailey girl, aren't you?"

"I am. Why?"

Lacey answered, "Thought you might like to know something. My men have searched from Broad, here, to Ash. Nobody at your house that we found. Your mother's up at the Crystal Lake Church."

"Dad?" she asked. He shook his head.

"Thanks, Lieutenant," Lenore said. She got into her Ford and went on to the next call.

Toward eight o'clock they brought food to Henry.

He had not left the room, had scarcely moved from his desk.

The high school's windows had been boarded up with plywood. A large kerosene stove was shedding heat and smoking slightly in the corner. Canvas had been nailed temporarily across the big crack in the roof. An engineer had made his inspection and assured everybody the high school wouldn't collapse. There were plenty of kerosene lamps. A bevy of determined housewives, wearing arm bands and having nothing better to do, had come in with brooms and dustpans, raised a fearful dust, and cleaned out the plaster and loose debris.

At a desk pushed up to face Henry's, Eve Sanders, acting as secretary, kept typing out notes — summaries of word that came over the walkie-talkies, and from the few ham radio stations still operable; and from runners from all parts of the area: boys on bikes mostly. The Motorcycle Club, having cleaned up the police auxiliary work in Henry's sector, was checking in now for message work.

On blackboard stands, beyond Mrs. Sanders, three men kept writing and erasing. Henry, just by looking up, could tell where his main crews were working. The Fire Department companies, after a two-hour fumble and an effort to run things their own way, were in direct liaison with him now, and some of the phone company linesmen were already making emergency connections on standing, usable lines that crisscrossed the sector.

Henry felt lucky, fantastically lucky.

Only a small arc of the area of very severe damage intruded into his sector. And the fires were being handled. He had plenty of casualties — glass, mainly — burns, next — shock — and miscellaneous. He also had approximately nine thousand very badly hurt people from the area closer in. There had been some panics, at first. CD crews had blockaded Dumond, Arkansas, River, Sedmon, Ames, VanNess, Bigelow and Cold Spring Avenues. That had stopped the cars mostly, though an undetermined number of people — "thousands" they said out along Decatur, exaggerating, no doubt — had got beyond the city limits, during the long span of Condition Yellow.

Where traffic piled up, the loudspeaker trucks had sailed in. Many fugitives, of course, had trudged ahead on foot. But the speakers had brought most of the panicky groups back toward town — toward the high flame, the radioactivity, the horror — by argument, cajolery and threat. There was no guarantee of a way to live in the countryside; but in the city, the loudspeakers bellowed ceaselessly, there were food, shelter, clothing, medical aid, all that people required.

The doctors and nurses in Henry's sector who had packed the prescribed medical and surgical equipment in cars, and driven to outlying areas during Condition Yellow, were now back in town at work. The doctors and nurses and other "key personnel" who had refused to respond properly to Condition Yellow were now dead, or among the casualties themselves, or trapped behind the irregular rim of fire that circled the fire storm proper.

Thousands of people had been rescued from homes, stores, apartments, factories, lofts, buses, trolleys, other spots suddenly rendered perilous. Thousands remained, even in Henry's area, in distress and danger. But the trained hundreds in his groups, with growing numbers of volunteer helpers from the unhurt, were tearing into every problem as they came to it, dousing fires, removing the injured, taking them to Crystal Lake. They were carting bulldozers and cranes on flat truck beds around the perimeter of ruin, smashing fire lanes, sweeping debris from trunk thoroughfares. They were sweating with the Water Supply people over emergency means to divert Crystal Lake to a hastily dammed gully where the fire hoses could feed. They were commandeering the contents of damaged stores, especially food stores and clothing stores, and bringing truckloads to Hobart Park where a vast "dump" of supplies was accumulating. They were — the women — tending the hurt, the shocked, the frightened, helping the surgeons and nurses, corralling the hundreds of lost children.

All that and more was happening when the food came for Henry. He took a big bite of hot corned-beef sandwich, swigged coffee and picked up a plate of beans.

"Why don't you come over to the other side," one of his assistants asked, "and take a look?"

Henry surveyed his assistants. They were working efficiently. Things, at the moment, were comparatively quiet. He said, "All right," and carried his plate and his sandwich into the corridor.

From an opposite, unshielded window, he could see.

Between this top-floor vantage point and the fire storm, nothing remained that stood higher.

The single flame of the burning city-heart could not be followed to its summit. It disappeared in smoke, in smoke so thick and dark, so folded and contoured it looked like a range of hills, illuminated by fire. The flame itself was yellow-white and solid, a curving wall that slanted in toward the center and could be followed for a thousand feet or more to the place where smoke screened it. Silhouetted against it, for a mile and a half, were the intervening buildings and homes, many burning with separate fires.

The city roared like a volcano and the night shook.

Henry stood still. He stopped eating. The heart and significance of the city were gone. It was his city, his life, his boyhood and manhood, and it had died and this was its funeral pyre — this tremendous thing. But its people, the majority of its human contents, could be saved.

"Okay," Henry said. "I've seen it."

He went back.

CHAPTER 16

TED CONNER was carrying a walkie-talkie with the mixed gang of firemen, cops and CD people who were trying to crash and beat their way down James Street to Simmons Park. It was outside his father's sector, in K. But the Sector K headquarters had been wrecked, and they were borrowing people from adjacent areas.

On James Street, the façade of the Shelley Garden Apartments had slid into the highway. Bulldozers began raging at the mountain of bricks. That meant a wait before the next advance. Ted sat down on the curb. A bank, with white marble walls, shielded him from the burning sky.

He unshipped his walkie-talkie because the straps were cutting into his thin shoulders. He got out a Hershey bar someone had handed him when they had mobilized for this job. It was limp from the heat but he ate it, wishing he had a drink of water to go with it.

Because of his job, he knew a great many miscellaneous facts — most of them relayed from Hink Field — that he had passed on to nobody, for lack of time and owing to the concentration everywhere on the struggle at hand.

New York was gone. H-bombed. The whole thing.

So were San Francisco and Los Angeles and Philadelphia.

About 25 other cities had been hit by fission bombs like the one which had struck the Sister Cities, "probably a secondary target or target of expediency," Hink Field had said.

Every state had declared martial law.

Two vast waves of Soviet bombers had come in across Canada.

Two enemy aircraft carriers, the existence of which had not been known, had made their way into the waters south of the Gulf of Lower California and launched planes equipped with robot missiles which were armed with "unexpectedly powerful" plutonium bombs.

The robot bomb that had detonated over Green Prairie River was now estimated at approximately 100 kilotons. The aiming point was thought to have been the Central Avenue-Market Street Bridge, and the actual Ground Zero, a few hundred yards west. The bomb had been launched at a distance of more than 100 miles and apparently guided by TV-radar devices. The launching plane had been brought down, in a suicide dive, by Captain Leo Cohen of Hink Field, only seconds after the discharge of its missile.

Ted knew (if he cared to think about it) that:

An all-out counterattack had been launched.

Moscow and Leningrad were gone.

Several other Soviet cities had been destroyed, the names of which he could not even pronounce, let alone remember.

The Eastern seaboard of the U.S.A. was in rout. The state of Florida had been declared a hospital area and casualties from the rest of the nation would be accepted there. Who in hell could reach Florida when we can't even get to River City, Ted thought.

The radio air was hot with speculation. Possibly the enemy had now exhausted his supply of hydrogen weapons. But he had obviously used only a small part—so far—of his plutonium bombs. The foe was believed to have launched his attack prematurely, in order to keep the United States from taking the additional time needed to build an immense arsenal of H-bombs. This was a Soviet "preventive war," many thought, a genocidal, 11th-hour gamble, undertaken with whatever the Russians had.

There was no longer a place that could be called Washington. The District of Columbia was a white-hot saucer, deep-hammered in the land. The Potomac and the tides, rolling back over the depression, were turning into mountain ranges of live steam. Where Philadelphia had been was a similar cauldron. Manhattan Island was gone—demolished, vaporized, pressed beneath the Hudson—and the sea was already cooling over much of Brooklyn, Queens, the Bronx, Staten Island and the Jersey marshes.

Ted heard all that, and more—more than the mind could grasp.

The President was dead.

Martial law wasn't working in many states because the National Guardsmen couldn't reach mobilization points or were too occupied dealing with situations right where they were to go anywhere else. People, by millions, were streaming in their cars and on foot and by boat and train and rail and ferry and bridge from all the cities of the U.S.A. Unhit cities feared momentarily that they would be next.

Ted sat on the curb for a while, thinking of these reports. Finally, he got up, feeling more tired than when he'd sat down. Just around the corner, he saw a drugstore, dark inside. He hurried toward it, licking his lips thirstily. The water spigot at the fountain didn't produce, but the soda spigot did. He filled a wax-paper cup and drank and drank until he was not thirsty any more.

Back on the corner, they were yelling, "Signals! Signals!"

He hitched into the walkie-talkie harness and trotted toward the men. "Here I am!"

"Dammit, stay in the main drag, willya? We needya."

OUT at Hink Field they were doing what they could. It wasn't much. General Boyce had ordered his Crash Plan into effect.

He had stripped the Base to send food and medical supplies, hospital corpsmen and medical officers into the cities. He had sent all the Base fire-fighting equipment. He had called up every enlisted man and every noncommissioned officer — paymasters, bandmasters, cooks, bakers, dental hygienists — every man in uniform except the regular guard. He broke out every weapon and all the ammo. He started officers organizing rescue and aid squads, emergency military police, technical-assistance squads. He sent all the communications and signal people he could spare to the Green Prairie CD authorities. River City's organization had collapsed; he couldn't raise anybody there who would accept that kind of help.

Chuck Conner had not been sent out on any of these patrols because orders for him to stand by had arrived from his home base. Although he protested that he knew River City and Green Prairie better than most of the men sent in to assist, they stuck to protocol, assigning him to the Operations room, pending the availability of transportation which would make it possible to carry out his orders. So Chuck saw the fire storm from a distance of many miles. But his knowledge of the two burning cities helped in shaping plans for reconnaissance and for airdrops of food and water.

He was aware, as the night progressed, that General Boyce held himself to blame — and himself alone — for the local delay in using the sirens. Chuck remembered the discussion in the afternoon, as if he were remembering something that had happened a year or two ago; he knew that the mayor of River City was responsible for the delay, if anyone could be held blameworthy.

"The old man," a captain said to Chuck as they studied the wall map, "is in poor shape. I never saw him so quiet. He thinks he lost the people in the shopping crowds."

"That's foolish!" Chuck answered, staring at the map, wondering if the K. & C. L. railroad embankment would make a firebreak of any lasting value. "Because, if the sirens had let go, they'd have just traffic-blocked themselves and been penned under Ground Zero all the same."

"You sound mighty calm about it all, Lieutenant!"

Chuck gave a ghastly smile. "That's the only way I dare be. All my folks are — yonder — in it."

"Oh." The other man tapped with a pencil. "Sorry."

A short time later, Chuck happened to be coming back from the latrine when he saw the general step out through the door onto the field. It was odd for him to be alone and Chuck stepped out to speak to him. But the general had already walked some distance onto a hardstand and was staring at the distant fire. He was wearing side arms. Chuck thought nothing of that.

General Boyce whipped out his .45 and shot himself through the head so suddenly that Chuck couldn't even shout. And before he reached his side, three grease monkeys had arrived and were kneeling.

Toward midnight, Chuck was assigned a patrol and ordered into River City to do what he could about panic, looting, whatever might be handled.

By what back streets and alleyways Nora had come, past what unspeakable sights, Alice Groves would never know, didn't want to know.

Nora's hair was burned ragged, her eyebrows were gone, her face, on one side, was red and peeling. Her mittens were two big holes through which her fingers showed, raw — from the broken masonry everywhere. Her shoes were slit and her feet bled. Nobody could have recognized her under the dirt. But her voice was about the same.

"Hello, Miss Groves. I left Mrs. Sloan in a big car up the street a few blocks. But it took *so* long to get here!"

Somehow Miss Groves ran her mind backward to the cities that were gone, the streets, the skyscrapers, the White Elephant Restaurant. "Oh," she said slowly. "What's wrong with her?"

"Her legs got mashed and she's unconscious."

"Is her body mashed?"

"Oh, no. She's all right. Her heart's going good."

One of the nurses said, "Let her die, the old rip!"

Alice Groves shook her head. "She — her husband — built us this place. And she maintained it."

She smiled at Nora. "Could you tell the nurses where her car is and what it looks like?"

"Oh, yes. It's a green Buick sedan and it's just this side of St. Angelica Street, a little on the right."

"Miss Ellman, see if Dr. Symes will come off a ward and take a bag and try to reach her. He used to play football and, if anybody could get through . . ."

A doctor leaned from the operating-room doorway. "Miss Groves, could you please! We've got a bad head wound here. . . ."

Alice nodded. "In a sec!" She addressed the nurse again. "Have we got a bed anywhere — crib — cradle — mattress . . . ?"

"Yours is still empty. . . ."

As the superintendent went back to work, she said, "Take the child up. Give her a shot — she's out on her feet."

KIT looked back. He could see the light of the fire still but not the flame itself. He didn't know where he was, just some place well to the west of the city. He didn't know the make of the car he drove — and recalled only dimly that he'd hit a fellow on the head to get it. He was about at the end of his rope, he felt; bushed. When he hit a stretch where he couldn't see a car ahead, or car lights in his rearview mirror, he watched along the side road and spotted a big, white farmhouse. He turned in the drive, switching his lights off. There were cattle in the barns, he could hear them. And light leaked around the front window blinds, so someone was in the place. He knocked.

The door opened a couple of inches. "I need help," Kit said. "I've got to rest a minute. Eat something, get a drink of water . . ."

A gruff, not inimical, voice replied. "Come from the city?"

"Yes."

"I'm sorry, mister. We don't dare let no one in. The radio tells us folks out here not to open doors or even show a light. There's gangs of hoodlums runnin' loose."

"I'm Kit Sloan; maybe you've heard the name."

"You mean — old lady — Mrs. Minerva Sloan's son?"

"Yes." Kit shivered.

Chain rattled. The door opened.

Kit's red eyes fell first upon a tall, bearded farmer with a shotgun across his arm. In the parlor behind him were four pretty girls and a plump, middle-aged woman who looked something like all four. Only one lamp was lighted and the radio was talking like firecrackers, but turned down low. The girls were young — perhaps 12 to 17 or 18. Kit said, "Thank you, sir," to the farmer.

"Guess it's all right," the man answered. "You ain't armed, even. Couple of fellows stopped by a minute ago — they were. I was kind of nervous, but they tried the door and then beat it. Your mother's bank holds our mortgage, Mr. Sloan."

The smiles of the frightened girls, the sturdy look of their mother, the composed tone of their towering father brought Kit part way back to his senses. He looked down at his clothes. They all looked.

"Marylou," said the bearded man, "run up and get something from Chet's closet. Mr. Sloan, here, is kind of dirtied up." He set the shotgun in the corner and turned to his unwanted guest. "My name's Simpson. Albert Simpson." He jerked his head. "The missus — my daughters, Mr. Sloan. The bank."

Kit said, "This is very kind of you."

"I'll get you something." Mrs. Simpson put a workbasket aside. Kit realized, with a kind of feverish resentment, that she had been listening to everything the radio must have been saying — and darning. "We have fresh milk . . . ?"

"If you have anything stronger . . ?" he ventured.

"There's brandy — in the medicine chest," Mr. Simpson said.

"Brandy would be fine."

"Sarah, go get it."

They stared while Kit poured all their brandy into a tumbler, which it half filled, and then drank it like water.

"We're prohibitionists here." Mr. Simpson smiled. "More or less. I don't suppose you'd care to say anything about — where you came from?" He saw Kit's immense shudder. "Likely not. What's *that,* now!"

He rose, grabbed the shotgun and went to the door. The sound of a big truck grinding up the driveway grew louder. Then it stopped on shrill brakes and many men's voices filled the night.

A knock at the door.

The farmer unlocked it, on the chain. "Who's there?"

They shot him through the head. They kicked in the front windows.

In a trance of horror, Kit watched the men enter. Two — then four or five — then a dozen. They were grinning a little. They were drunk. They were the kind of men who wear caps and work in alleys. They eyed the girls with joy.

On the staircase, Marylou stopped — a clean shirt and washed jeans folded over one arm. She started to back up the stairs.

Her mother and sisters said nothing, nothing at all.

"Come on downstairs, baby!" one of the men called, smirking.

Marylou backed another step. The man aimed a pistol and fired. The railing chipped. Marylou came on down then, still holding her brother Chet's clean clothes.

The women looked hopefully at Kit. He said, in a thin squeal, "You men move on."

"Oh, yeah?"

"This is a private home. You've just done *murder!*"

Kit threw himself on the floor. It was his idea to get out — nothing else. His powerful muscles sent him slithering toward the dark hall. He didn't even try to pick up the farmer's shotgun. He heard their shots and vaguely felt the referred impact, from the floorboards. He reached the hall. He half stood, unchained the door, ran out.

Somebody bellowed through the smashed windows, "Hey, Red! *Get* that jerk!"

Kit saw the trees against the luminous sky line, the square silhouette of the truck, the palely white porch banister. Flame squirted from the truck and his body was seared. He fell down the steps and lay, without moving, on his back.

He wished, seeing the stars as they began to swim and cavort, that he'd at least grabbed the shotgun and plugged a couple of them.

In the parlor, the men turned toward the rigid women. "Going to be a nice little party," one said, licking his lips. "Private-like."

Others laughed. One yelled, "Hey — Red! Come on in! We found *five* of 'em!"

They moved toward the four girls and their mother.

She said, softly, "Pray, children."

But nobody was listening to prayers that night.

CHAPTER 17

TOWARD morning, Henry left his second-in-command at his desk and went out in the night with the police lieutenant, Lacey. Some streets, some avenues, were slots leading arrow-straight to the fire storm, box-ended with flame. Other thoroughfares merely caught the downbeat of illumination. On them, great shadows danced as the grotesque, the monstrous pyre flickered in the sky. Here and there, a building or a home burning individually made a big candle for this block or that.

Because of the red headlights and the siren, they got across town to the Country Club, where a brief meeting was to be held. The clubhouse had no windows but it did have electric lights, which astonished Henry until he recalled that he had voted — years before, when he'd still had his membership — to put in a power plant simply to show a little spunk to the electric company.

They went into the main room, which seemed a bright glare after a night of emergency illumination. A few dozen of the scattered easy chairs had been pulled together and faced in one direction. Sighing, not removing his overcoat, Henry dropped into a chair. Lacey took a seat beside him. Perhaps 50 men were there already. They, like Henry, were just sitting, saying nothing.

The CD chief, McVeigh, came down an aisle left between the chairs. He was followed by two women who wore CD brassards. They pulled up a big library table, helped by the men in the front row. Then McVeigh faced the sector leaders and their delegates.

"We've had to pull out of headquarters," he said. "Fire storm making it too difficult to save the place." His face grimaced. "What was *left* of it, I mean to say. Here's why I asked you to come over. We've got it bad, but River City's far worse. The bulk of their fire-fighting apparatus lost. Most doctors dead or casualties. Short — almost out entirely — of every class of personnel. The whole city panicked. Point is, what can the Green Prairie outfit do to help — if anything?"

Not a man in the room spoke.

McVeigh nodded. "I know how you feel. I do myself. But what are we dealing with? Certainly not local pride. Simply human numbers. If you can save ten here, you let one go there. Right? All night I've been getting appeals from Jeffrey Allison — he's *their* chief. I can't decide alone. You'll have to help me. We never figured we'd have to salvage River City. It was their job, that they didn't prepare for. If you sector heads could spare even one person in ten, of every classification, beginning at dawn . . ?"

A man whom Henry did not know stood up. "I can't spare a man. I can't spare *myself here*. I can use ten more for every man and woman I've got!"

There was a sound of agreement.

McVeigh studied the faces for a moment. "About 50,000 people," he said slowly, "crowded into the ball park. God knows why. Somebody started it — the rest followed. Maybe a third were kids. They filled the field solid; then the bleachers caught fire and the whole mob stampeded. They're up there, what remains of 'em. Not one doctor. *Nothing*. That's how things are all over River City."

Henry stood up. "We'll tithe," he said.

Lieutenant Lacey grabbed his arm. "You can't do it, Hank! We're short on the medical end — "

"No medical end at all at the ball park."

"You'll be letting Green Prairie people die!"

Henry nodded. His eyes were empty. The room was listening to his private argument. "Sure. Green Prairie people will die. One for ten, didn't he say?"

Henry stalked from the room. Behind him, he could hear other sector chiefs making offers. It didn't hearten him. He felt no pride in having started the ball rolling. He'd never done a tougher thing in his life: he'd condemned some of the provident to save many of the improvident. He wasn't even sure it was just.

"Mr. Conner!" someone called from across the club porch.

"Yeah?"

The man ran up. "Thought you ought to know. Your son Ted was running a walkie-talkie down the line. Got buried in a brick slide. They're trying to dig him out now."

Henry took hold of a porch post. He felt Lacey's hand on his arm.

"I know about where that crew was," the police lieutenant said. "Let's go!"

Henry sobbed just once. He took one immense breath. His head shook. "What the hell extra could two of us do? Let's get on."

While Lacey drove, Henry used the car radio. He ordered his subordinates to take one tenth of the personnel — medical, rescue, first-aid, decontamination, and so on — off what they were doing. Quietly, firmly, he put down frantic protests. He arranged for the assembly of the selected people and said he'd be back as soon as he finished his inspection.

All night, from Bigelow Avenue, at the perimeter of the fire storm's edge, Henry had been besieged with calls for medical-aid people, for rescue and decontamination personnel as well as fire fighters. He and Lieutenant Lacey drove there now. It was the site of a number of apartment houses, vast structures, six stories high, brick on the outside, wood within. The bomb had not only collapsed these buildings on their tenants but hurled on top of them, by some freak of blast, the contents of a half dozen small factories and machine shops, closer in town.

There was no water pressure in the mains. They had been shattered. The fire companies had long since abandoned the scene. All that stood was a great moraine of debris.

Into it, during the night, spelling one another, men had tunneled their way. Wherever they had holed through to rooms, halls or their crushed remains, they had found the living and living-dead — these last because masses of metals in the machining area were close to the fireball; they had been violently irradiated and were giving back that deadliness now.

Henry had come to this place with a view to ordering his crews back farther. The proximity of the fire storm constantly threatened the rubble mass with burning, in which case it would become a mere addition to the central torrent of heat and flame. The general outdoor radiation level, high at many points near the fire storm, was endangering everyone who worked in this area for too many hours.

Shielding their faces, the two men approached a group of rescuers at work on the mountain of debris. One of them stepped forward, a man so black with soot and white with plaster as to be unrecognizable. He bellowed above the drum roll of the fire, "Hi, Henry! Ed Pratt."

Henry nodded. "What's the situation now, Ed?"

"About like our last talk. We got out over a hundred people, but we've only dug in about halfway." He gestured toward some men hauling, tug-of-war fashion, on ropes. "We're trying to deepen a passage now." The rope-pullers shouted in unison, heaved together, and from the hole in the mass they drew forth a huge fragment of floor and ceiling lumber. Henry could see that the opening ran for at least a hundred feet into the wreckage.

He went closer, followed by Lacey. "How hot is it?" He was not aware that he was shouting. The fire storm here was like near, continual thunder. But it was necessary to converse in shouts almost everywhere that night.

Ed waved at the blaze. "Gettin' warmer in there all the time. Awful-looking thing, ain't it?"

Henry hardly glanced at the intimidating fire wall. "I mean, *radiation hot.*"

"Oh! This new tunnel—I dunno. Got a monitor in there measuring. Here they come now!"

A figure—then another—showed in the ragged entrance of the tunnel. Behind trudged a third and a fourth. They carried flashlights. The broken, snaglike intrusions in the tunnel made their approach slow. The first one, Henry saw, was wearing the yellow plastic garments of a monitor and carrying a counter. This was the one who addressed Ed Pratt and, until he bent close, he didn't realize it was a woman. Even then he did not recognize Lenore.

"It's too high a level," she reported. "We got to a lot of metal and kind of a big cave beyond, but it's too hot to stick around. You can't send your people any deeper, Mr. Pratt. In minutes they'd get enough radiation to be sick — maybe die."

One of the three men who had made the perilous trek into the tunnel with Lenore said, "Pity. Beyond that opening she talked about, you could hear kids calling."

Henry looked with fear and horror at the demolished building, at the frightening flame. He looked at the rescue people, and they were eyeing him. "This whole crew," he yelled out, "will get in touch with my headquarters for another assignment!" He jerked his head. "Abandon this! You've done what you can."

That was that. Men nodded. One or two women cried. But people began throwing picks, shovels, crowbars, a block and tackle, other gear, into a truck. That was that — until Henry heard a shout near the tunnel mouth and saw two men rush in.

"They shouldn't!" the woman with the radiation counter exclaimed.

Henry recognized her then. "Lenore!" he whispered. He reached out and gripped her arm. Her teeth showed white in a kind of smile. Her face was black as a miner's.

"How about your family?" Lenore asked. She was hoarse from much shouted talk.

Henry felt the pain again. "I don't know, dear! I don't know!" He held his head close to reduce the need for bellowing every word. "Ted's under a brick slide. . . ."

"I'm sorry."

"Mother's up at the First Aid. Nora — search me! Chuck reported yesterday at Hink Field."

She nodded. She looked, briefly, but in a special way, at the fire storm. Henry knew what she was thinking: Chuck was not in there; he hadn't been caught downtown as she'd feared. But she didn't mention her feelings. "Gotta get cracking," she said and left.

"Shall we get along?" Lacey asked.

"Wait." Henry approached the tunnel, followed by the lieutenant.

"You recognize your neighbor? The Bailey girl?"

"Yes."

"Guts."

Henry didn't reply. He just nodded and bent to peer into the dark dreadfulness of the hole the rescuers had made and abandoned, the hole into which two men, against orders, had plunged. For what seemed a long time nothing happened. Then he saw a wink of lights and shadows moving. One man made his way to the tunnel mouth and put down the thing in his arms. It was a baby and it cried.

The man turned back.

"Got a torch?" Henry asked the lieutenant.

"*You* can't go in!" Lacey yelled back. "Too risky for you!"

"Got a torch?"

Lacey went to the squad car and returned. He followed Henry into the tunnel.

Far down, they encountered the other man, helping along two

children, who wept and shivered. Lacey, on Henry's orders, led them back.

It was quiet in there. One of the men said to Henry, "You stay here, sir. Beyond this point, the radiation's bad. There's only one more kid and Sam's getting her free. No use exposing yourself. We've already had the full dose and he won't need help."

The man left. He was gone awhile. Henry stood still, more frightened than he'd known he could be.

He could see, in the light of a lantern left by the tunnel-makers, what had happened. A weight of machinery and sheet metal had cut through the collapsing building and piled up, just ahead; that was the point of peak radioactivity, he was sure. Beyond, apparently with another lantern in it, he saw a kind of opening.

From the opening the second man came, with a form on his shoulder. A little girl, unconscious. As he passed the metal mass, he turned his back and put the inert girl in front of him, shielding her body with his own. Henry appreciated that what these two men had done might succeed, for the children. They might survive. But the men had quite likely received ultimately fatal doses of radiation when they tore a path around the intrusion of scrap metal.

Henry said nothing then. The man indicated the lantern with his toe. Henry picked it up, following. Soon they were outdoors in the light of the fire storm — in the strange night, where a cold wind blew on their faces and their backs were seared by heat. Lacey had loaded the other children.

The man carried the unconscious girl to the car and put her in, too. His brave companion was just standing by the fender, a smile of satisfaction on his face.

"I'll send a car back for you two," Henry said. "We'll do everything we can — over at the Country Club. Got good doctors there. They may be able to . . ."

One man said, "Thank you."

Henry gazed at them. "That was the finest thing I ever saw. Who *are* you two guys?"

The nearer one, a rather slight man, who was dabbing at the blood from a cut on his arm, laughed and answered, "I'm Jerome Taggert, minister of the Bigelow Avenue Baptist Church, and

Sam is Father Flaugherty of St. Bonaventure's Roman Catholic...."

Henry said, "Oh," and kept looking back at them as Lacey drove away.

Beth Conner trudged home, still carrying her suitcase, breathing whitely in the frigid air. It was Christmas morning, she thought dazedly.

When she saw the house, she stood for a long time, with tears in her eyes. It didn't sit quite right any more. A chunk of the roof was gone, up over the boys' room in the attic. The front yard was a pile of debris — some from the house, but most of it tree limbs shoved aside by bulldozers going down Walnut Street. The windows weren't there any more.

She went up on her front porch. The steps were loose under her feet and there was a big, white, printed sign nailed on the door. "Inspected," the sign said. "Safe for occupancy. Use extreme caution. Beware of fire." Underneath that, was written in red pencil, "Radiation level okay. Am okay, too. Love, Lenore."

"Bless her," Beth whispered. She went in and put down the bag tiredly. She'd had three or four hours of sleep, all told. In the kitchen she tried the gas stove; it didn't work. She went back to the hall and opened the suitcase. There was a Sterno stove in it, six cans of pink fuel, powdered coffee, sugar, tinned milk — among many other items. She took the things for coffee, and a flashlight, and went back to the kitchen and tried the water but that didn't run, either.

Downstairs, in the air-raid shelter Henry had fixed up years before, were the five-gallon bottles of distilled water he made her change every six months. She found a pan, went down in the cellar and poured some water. She went into the jelly closet, discovering that most of the canned things were still on the shelves where she'd placed them, labeled and tidy, all summer long. They could eat, then, without drawing from the Green Prairie food stocks.

She went up with the water, lit the little stove and put on the water. Someone knocked at the front door, frightening her. She ran to it.

"Hi, Mrs. Conner! Henry home yet?" It was Jed Emmings, from Spruce Street.

"Not yet."

"You all right?"

"Yes, thanks. Are you?"

"You bet — and thank God. So are my folks. I just came by to let you know your Ted's okay, too."

"Ted?" She stared at him perplexedly. He was filthy dirty, like almost everybody. "I didn't know," she said finally, "Ted was hurt."

"Hurt bad, Mrs. Conner. But he's over in the Green Prairie Country Club, getting real good care. I was on duty there. I talked to him."

"What happened?"

"Got buried in a brick slide. Broke both legs."

"But . . ?"

Jed Emmings smiled because he understood. "Absolutely okay, Mrs. Conner — or I'd have said so. No head injuries worth worrying about and nothing internal. Chipper and full of beans already. In traction, of course."

She said, "Thank you, Jed."

He nodded. "Glad to tell you. Glad to bring some good news to *one* door, anyhow!"

He went down the walk.

She noticed that the sun was shining. She hadn't really noticed that before. She felt almost surprised that the sun was still there in the sky in its place.

She was sipping her coffee, a little later, when she heard car brakes. I got home just in time, she thought. More visitors.

The car went on before she reached the hall and what she heard, she did not believe. It was Nora's voice calling, "Mummie! Mummie! Aren't you *home?"*

There she was, running up the walk, the way she always did, and Mrs. Conner felt things start to go black because she did not, could not, believe. But there was a car, going away, a colored girl at the wheel, and it wasn't quite the same Nora, coming up the steps on her spidery legs. She wore a different coat, too small for her, and a dress Beth didn't recognize. Her hat was missing and one side of her long bob had been chopped off short. There was a big pad of bandage on her right cheek. Mrs. Conner still wasn't absolutely sure, until she felt Nora in her arms.

"We thought — " she started to say.

Nora leaned back and looked up. "I had one *hell* of a time, I *really* did!" Nora said.

OUTSIDE of the place where Washington, D. C., had been, in a big house that had belonged to a famous 18th-century American, some 50 men held a meeting in the lamplit drawing room. The men came there by automobile, mostly; but three or four walked, and one arrived as the original householder often had, riding on a horse. Some of the men wore bandages, two were brought on stretchers, and all of them had to go through a considerable process of identification at check points around the estate.

When they had assembled, a man who wore the white garments of a doctor, and around whose neck a stethoscope hung, said to a man in slacks and a tweed jacket, "Mr. President . . ."

The man shook his head. "I haven't taken the oath yet."

The doctor shrugged. "Mr. Gates, then. I think you ought to start the meeting if possible. The Secretary of State is slipping fast."

Mr. Gates walked to the middle of the handsome drawing room and stood at the head of a carved mahogany table. He rapped with a gavel. Talk stopped. Every person present turned toward him.

"The meeting," he said, "will come to order."

Chairs moved. Attendants brought stretchers close.

Harry Jackson Gates was sworn in as President of the United States. It was done quickly, in low tones. The only Justice they could find administered the oath. When it was over, all but the new President sat down. He returned to the head of the long, gleaming table. On it there were only the gavel and a Bible.

"Our group," he began in a somber voice, "constitutes, as you all know, all the high-echelon members of the Government who could be assembled, this frightful Christmas Day." He looked at a notebook which he took from a jacket pocket. "Three members of the late President's Cabinet are here." He named them. "Supreme Court Justice Willard. Seventeen members of the United States Senate. Thirty-eight members of the House of Representatives. In an adjacent room, General Faversham and some other high military officers are waiting and I shall ask them in — with your consent. All in favor?"

There were grave "ayes."

The new President nodded to the guards at a far door and it swung back. The military men came in quietly, took chairs.

The President spoke their names, gave their rank, and continued:

"I shall be brief. As you know, panic reigns from coast to coast. Four great cities were totally obliterated by hydrogen bombs in the afternoon and early evening of the twenty-third. Washington met the same fate later. Twenty-five cities have been struck by plutonium bombs of exceptionally high power. Some twenty millions of us were killed or injured in the attack. It is the judgment of the military" — he paused, looked at the officers — "that weeks, if not months, will be required to restore order, and an indeterminate interval, many more months, to bring the nation back to a state of production and communication which will support the survivors at a survival level. I am sure you are, in general, familiar with those ghastly facts."

There were murmurs of assent.

"Three possibilities face the United States of America. The first is — surrender."

A heart-rending "no!" was wreathed in low-toned murmurs of rejection.

"The enemy," the President went on grimly, "has offered terms."

That, too, stirred the audience.

"They are quite simple. We are to surrender all atomic weapons, to dismantle all atomic plants and works, to allow enough of the enemy free access within this nation to ensure that the status is permanent. There will be no occupation, no tribute."

His eyes went over the room. Some of the haggard faces were stony. But some glowed with hope.

"A great predecessor of mine, in an hour of trial, once called an example of wanton assault 'a date that will live in infamy.' No phrase, in any language, can be made to speak the evil now done to this nation. I shall not try to give you any condemnatory words. But, let me point out, the offered terms *seem* reasonable. It is *only* a seeming. If we grant those terms, nothing — ever afterward — can prevent the enemy from working upon us whatever his further will may be. We know his philosophy. We bleed now under his treachery. Disarmed, we shall surely soon be enslaved. But surrender *is* one possibility.

"Another — is to continue the assault we are making. I assure you, the foe is suffering grievously. But his cities are so few, his dispersion of populace is so great, that our gallant Air Force cannot readily drive his people into the general panic that has uprooted this nation and destroyed its social organization. In time our effort might be equally effective. We must inquire if we have the time. The bombs, the planes, the determined men to fly them, we do have. But let us suppose the effort took thirty days. In the end, there might remain in both nations that utter wreckage of civilization which the few predicted for so long, and the many refused to believe. But that is a *second* possibility."

"The third?" a woman's voice called. "What's the third?"

For a moment, the new President reverted to his old habit as Speaker of the House. "The lady from Massachusetts asks the third. I'll explain as best I am able. I am not a scientist. The military will amplify."

He frowned, cleared his throat. "First, I must state that my late, great predecessor, though he worked hopefully for peace, somewhat feared a situation like this. He feared, as did his Chiefs of Staff, the very danger we have encountered. He, with them, prepared a threat of their own — of our own — a dreadful threat, intended only for use as a menace. You are familiar with the *Nautilus* —"

The silence in the old room was absolute.

" — the first of the atomic-powered submarines. As the recent 'peace' negotiations reached a high degree of intensity, it was felt in the — the" — he stumbled — "White House, that the enemy was probably sincere. But the possibility remained that such negotiations might be the immediate precursor to the disaster that now is fact. Consequently, the *Nautilus* was drydocked and secretly reconverted. She is still a submarine, still atomically driven, but she is also a bomb. She contains, now, the largest hydrogen bomb ever assembled, and around it and in her sides, replacing armor, and in her keel, for ballast, is the element cobalt with other readily radioactivated elements. She stands, this day, in the North Sea, awaiting orders. She could be sent swiftly into the Baltic. She could approach the ways to the enemy, dive to bottom and explode herself."

"The crew . . ?" someone interrupted.

Gates said nothing. His long, thin face turned toward the questioner and his hazel eyes burned into the man. Then, at last, he spoke again.

"This is one of the greater-than-super weapons mentioned at least as far back as the Truman Administration. Its exact effect is not known and cannot be calculated. A few scientists fear its detonation at sea bottom might actually set up planetary chain reaction. Most say not. I believe the latter. It would, however, unquestionably devastate a large part of the enemy's nation, and leave vast areas of enemy land radioactive, deadly even to vegetation.

"It might, according to the uncertain vicissitudes of weather, transport a large amount of this lethal material across the Pacific and conceivably leave here a lesser but real train of death and sickness, sterility, misery and additional fear. This is an indeterminate risk involved in the weapon's use. It is our third possibility — the only alternative I can offer to surrender or to a continuation of the existing holocaust with present weapons. I shall have a few of the military men and scientists speak to you. . . ."

An hour and a quarter later, it was voted to order the *Nautilus* to proceed — and to demolish herself, and the foe.

THEY could have seen it from the planets.

On Mars, if there are naked eyes, they could have seen it without other aid.

On that Christmas night, the Baltic Sea erupted. There was no warning. The faint signals the *Nautilus* received were not intercepted by the beleaguered but seemingly victorious Reds.

She penetrated the Gulf of Finland, dove to bottom and her skipper, summoning the men, prayed, flashed a last word and touched a small button, installed some hours before on the table directly below the periscope. The rays, the temperatures, vaporized that part of Finland's Gulf in a split part of an instant. The Light reached out into the Universe.

Kronstadt melted, Leningrad. The blast kicked up the ashes that once had been Moscow, collected the burning environs and pulverized them and hurled their dust at the Urals.

In the ensuing dark, a Thing swelled above the western edge of Russia, alight, alive, of a size to bulge beyond the last particles of earth's air. On the wind currents it came forward, forward across the north-sloping plains, a thick dust that widened to a hundred miles, and then five hundred, moving, spreading, descending, blanketing the land that night, and the day after and the next. It thinned, over Siberia, thinned and spread until it was no longer blinding, till men could no longer see it or smell it or taste it.

But still, where it rolled, day or night, they died.

The farther it surged from the reshaped Finnish Gulf, where the sea had come sparkling back, the longer men took to perish. But they perished. The radiation-emitting particles filled their lungs, contaminated their food, polluted their water and could not be filtered out. Men swallowed, ate, breathed, sickened and perished in a day, a week, two weeks — men and women and children, all of them, dogs and cats and cattle and sheep, all of them. Wherever they took refuge, they perished.

Surrender of those who survived, the southern dwellers of the nation, was delayed because they could not decide who should make the offer; they did not care how abject the terms might be. But days passed. A week. Two weeks. And the message winged from Tiflis. It was over.

The last war was finished.

CHAPTER 18

ON A sunny afternoon, just before June became July, during a Midwestern heat wave, a young man pushed a hand mower back and forth over a Walnut Street lawn in the city of Green Prairie. He looked to be 22 or 23 years old though, actually, Ted Conner was not yet 19. He had grown big, and there was something about his face (besides the scar on the forehead) which suggested more years than the teens. He limped, too.

He paused, took out a bandanna handkerchief and wiped his brow. He glanced at the house for a moment.

Two and a half years had passed, since The Bomb.

Only the attic windows were boarded up. Glass was still rationed — along with a hundred other things — but householders had enough, now, to take care of two floors per family. The Conners hadn't bothered yet to try to get the house back exactly on its foundations. Men had come, that first winter, with powerful jacks and pushed the frame building as near to its proper position as they could. "Temporary" foundations supported overhanging sills. A power pole leaned across the drive from a concrete base on the ground to the eaves, a brace against winter wind. Have to paint that pole, Ted thought; wouldn't want it to rot. He moved again, drowning out the cicadas in the trees.

His father had boarded up all the windows that first winter, when there was no window glass and when Ted had been in the hospital. At the Country Club, that was — with many other people. He was among the lucky. Plenty of them hadn't left that place alive. They'd died of about everything you could think of, injuries and burns, shock and even of radiation, like that Catholic priest and the Baptist minister. So *many* people . . !

For a moment, the fear of those days returned to him. No one had been sure of anything. Everything was short — food, blankets, bandages, medicine. Nobody knew whether the war was over or not; they knew only that the Soviet planes didn't come back.

That time passed.

Peace came. Then, for more weeks, the burying. It was still

going on when he could sit up in bed and look out the window. They made a new cemetery of the Green Prairie Country Club golf course, the last nine holes. Later that spring, in common with other bombed cities, they designed their Cenotaph and it stood now above the graves — a monument to the ninety-some thousand known dead of Green Prairie. There was one in River City —for a hundred and twenty thousand. At what had been the ball park.

When Ted finished the edge of the walk, he picked up a bushel basket. It seemed odd in his hands. It wasn't made the regular way and it didn't appear to be the right size. He saw faded stencil marks and read: *Produit de France*. The good old Frogs! he thought. In the "Aftertime" they'd kicked through — the French and, of course, the English, the Italians and Belgians and Dutch and the Latin Americans and about everybody else except the Russians — who almost didn't exist — and the satellite countries.

In the first dreadful winter, unreckoned millions of Ted's fellow citizens were saved by European bounty. He even recalled foreign labels on some of the medicine bottles at his bedside, when he'd been smashed up.

He raked up a green mound of fresh-cut grass and carried it, in the French hamper, to the chicken yard. The Conners now had more than sixty chickens and five pigs. Henry was even angling for a cow.

His mother came down the street, walking slowly because of the heat. When she saw the mowed grass, saw her tall, broad-shouldered son mopping his sweaty light-brown hair, she moved faster and smiled.

Ted said, "Hello! Been expecting you. Haven't we got company coming for supper?"

"A lot of people! Twenty-odd."

"Ye gods! I thought it was just us and the Laceys."

"I asked both families that have moved in the Bailey place." She glanced across. "They're new, and they don't know a soul in this part of town. I thought we'd get them acquainted. Their names are Brown and Frazetti. Have you seen the Brown girl?" His mother smiled.

"Didn't know there was one."

"She's sixteen. Blue eyes and the prettiest red hair I ever saw. If you aren't in love with her by nine o'clock tonight, I'll lose a bet."

"Phooie," he said.

"Wait till you see her! Name's Rachel."

Ted looked at the neighboring house. For a year and a half after X Day, it had been occupied by people billeted by town authorities. Then it had been roughly remodeled inside as a double house.

"I wonder what happened to Beau," he said.

She stopped in the screen door. "I doubt if we ever find out now!"

Lenore's mother had been sent to Florida and she was still there, undergoing plastic surgery. But Lenore's father had vanished. He was one of the anonymous dead. Or one of the unfound bodies. Or someone who had a new name and a new life somewhere else — because, after the shock, he had been unable to remember what his name had been — or because he wanted to forget.

Nora came home on her bike. She was fourteen now and trying to behave like eighteen. Occasionally, for minutes at a time, the effort was fairly convincing. She'd changed in two years and a half. She was hardly a kid now. There was something very precise and well-cut about her profile. Her nose didn't turn up so much. Her hair, light like Ted's, was wavy like their mother's. And her clear blue eyes were getting slanty — exactly as Nora would prefer it: slanty-eyed women got the dangerous men, she claimed.

At this instant, however, her behavior was on the kid side. "Mom!" she yelled through the kitchen screen, "Mr. Nesbit didn't have enough hamburger to make fifty patties. I got sixty hot dogs instead."

"That'll be fine, dear. And don't bellow."

She yodeled briefly, put away her bike, came around the house and greeted her brother, who was clipping edges. She assumed her pseudo maturity. "Good afternoon, *beast.*"

"Greetings. How's things?"

"Ted. Will you give me an answer to a serious inquiry?"

"Sure. Any old answer. What's your problem?"

"I'm not kidding. Do you think it's *inevitably,* in *any* case, a mistake for a fourteen-year-old girl to be engaged?"

He concealed his grin. "Is she deeply in love?"

"Very," said Nora in a deeply-in-love tone.

"Well" — he rose on his knees, thought somberly — "is the boy able to support her?"

"He will be someday. He intends to become an anthropologist."

"Be all right," he said, nodding in self-agreement. "That is, if the girl's going to have a child."

"Oh! You meanie! You evil thing!"

"If they're going to have a child," he asserted in an offended tone, "I really think they owe it to the little stranger to marry."

"There are times," Nora said, "when you ought to be afraid the earth would open and swallow you up! I'm talking about the sacred kind of love, not the profane kind!"

"What on earth," Mrs. Conner asked, "are you two fighting about?"

"Nora's life interest of the moment," Ted said, beating her to the reply. "Something people for years have been calling sex."

Beth chuckled. "You better get dressed. Your father will be along soon. And you still have to bathe, Ted."

HENRY CONNER signed his mail, said good night to his secretary and went down two flights of stairs to the ground floor of the West Side store of J. Morse and Company. The main building and the warehouses had, of course, vanished with The Bomb. They were using the West Side branch for business offices now and would go on doing so until the new Morse Building was finished. At present, it was a set of blueprints, the work of Charles Conner.

The Oldsmobile was parked behind the store, near the loading area. It gave him an almost sentimental feeling: it would be good for quite a few more years. He drove away in the hot sunshine, aware that its hotness was diminishing, that there was a breeze. He was scheduled to pick up Charles first, then Pad Towson and Berry Black, then Lenore. Next week the car pool would be Towson's lot.

Charles wasn't waiting at their meeting place.

Henry was glad. He parked the Olds and got out. He looked for a while at the building where his elder son worked. The Green

Prairie Professional Building had been the first one erected according to the new city plan and the first one to invade the "total destruction" area. It wasn't high, not a skyscraper, only four stories. But it was as tremendous as the Pentagon-that-was, in the Washington that-used-to-be. It was something like a ranch house, but blocks long, with many "L's" and "courtyards" between them, with gardens, patios, glassed-in restaurants, even a skating rink in one courtyard.

Someday Green Prairie and River City would have a hundred such buildings all around the circle of ruins. "Horizontal expansion" they called it. It replaced the vertical growth of the skyscraper which had let fumed air, heat and slums accumulate in its canyons. It had not been so difficult as many had expected to "sell" the once-crowded city dwellers on the new pattern for living. For nobody who had lived in a bombed city wanted to spend another hour, if he or she could help it, in such a deathtrap. To be sure, there was no menace, any longer, of bombs. But the memory pervaded the whole population.

Henry turned away from the structure where his son worked, walked to a fence, and drank in the scene opposite. He drew a big breath and expelled it with force. He never could get it through his head that something his living room could easily contain had removed the familiar cityscape, left it nude. And all in a night, consuming in hours what had taken men generations to put there.

Now, in summer, weeds were growing out there. The red-brown nothing was relieved by sprawls of green, bisected by the river's blue water. Everywhere, making a din, sending up dust, machines worked. Like men on Mars, they lumbered in this desert, disinterring and reburying, with mammoth indifference to all meaning. If one watched a particular dozer or earth-mover, one would see the substance of archaeology, the potsherds of recent 20th-century Americans. A refrigerator would be turned up, or a bathtub, or a kitchen stove. These would be pushed into shallows, crushed flat, covered again. Someday, where Henry looked at dusty nothing, a new city would rise.

He felt Chuck's hand on his shoulder. "A penny," Chuck said. He didn't wait for the thought he'd bargained for. "Great day,

Dad! Old Minerva Sloan finally accepted our drawings — mine, that is — for the new bank building! May mean a partnership! But, *brother!* Is that crippled old dame a sourball!"

Henry said, "Peachy!" He held his hand out, gravely.

They picked up Pad Towson and Berry Black and, finally, Lenore. The men were just two businessmen coming home from work, tired, looking forward to whatever home meant: a hot soak in a tub, slippers, a highball, a meal.

But Lenore was different. Excited. Privately excited, for she slipped into the front seat between Charles and her father-in-law and silently took her husband's hand.

They delivered their passengers before she began to tell, talking to Charles but permitting Henry to hear. "I've got news."

"I can see that!" Charles smiled.

"Good news."

Henry sensed the tenseness in his son's voice. "Are you going to *tell* it?"

"I'm pregnant."

Henry heard his own faint breath-catch. He slowed down, jostled, as Chuck wrapped his arms around her. "I thought . . ." Chuck broke off.

After they had kissed, she said, "So did I! So did Dr. Mandy, at first! I got so *much* radiation! Now we know different! I can have babies."

Charles whispered, "That's just too wonderful to believe."

Henry let go of the wheel with his right hand. He reached out, touched her dark hair. He didn't say anything more than the touch said. But she looked toward him fondly as she snuggled against Charles. It would be, she felt, the finest thing on earth to have a father like Charles. But, certainly, it would be almost as fine to have such a grandfather as Henry Conner would make a boy — or a girl.

AT THE house, they could see smoke from the fire in the barbecue pit. Henry went around and opened the car trunk. There was a keg of beer, wet with its own coldness.

"Give me a hand," he called.

But Chuck was already streaking through the hedge. "What do you think?" he called. "Lenore's going to have a baby! I'm going to be the father of a child!"

Mrs. Conner's eyes blurred with happiness.

Nora Conner's did not. "That's nothing," she said. "Queenie's just *been* a father — of five."

Henry came up. "Somebody help me with the beer. . . ."

Beth reached out, caught his sleeve and whispered, "A couple of professors here, Henry. They're making a survey of the region to find out why things went so badly in River City and so well, comparatively, over here. I asked them to stay for supper."

Henry looked across the lawn and spotted the men. "Time we quit talking about it!" he said. "Only difference was, some of us tried to swap freedom for security; the rest of us went on *fighting* for freedom, as usual."

"Tell them that," Beth said. "They'll never find a better answer, no matter how smart they are, or how long they ask."

Henry's eyes moved. "Who's that redhead Ted's mawking at?"

"Lives next door," Beth replied. "She's mighty sweet."

Henry stared at the girl a moment longer. Then his twinkling, affectionate gaze traveled on to the Bailey house. "Kind of where we came in, isn't it, Mother?"

"People don't change very much or very fast," she smiled.

Henry nodded and walked over to meet the professors and his new neighbors.

The sun went down and left the lawn in gilded light.

Philip Wylie

Philip Wylie was born in Beverly, Mass., the son of a Presbyterian minister and a mother who wrote fiction. After attending Princeton he held a wide variety of jobs — on farms, in Manhattan stores, in factories, on ships — before settling down to a successful writing career.

Generation of Vipers is perhaps his best-known book, but *Night Unto Night, When Worlds Collide* (written with Edwin Balmer) and *Opus 21* have also been best sellers. He has written hundreds of stories and articles for national magazines; his "Crunch and Des" fishing stories in *The Saturday Evening Post* are especially popular.

Mr. Wylie is thoroughly grounded in the subject matter of *Tomorrow!* As early as 1939 he wrote a short story about Germans making plutonium bombs in a Colorado cave. When magazine finally bought it, in 1945, it was sent to Washing- for clearance. To his amazement, the author was placed der temporary house arrest until FBI men satisfied themselves that the story was straight fiction — not the result of a security leak in the Government's top-secret atomic-energy project.

Mr. Wylie has been an expert in Civil Defense for ten years and serves the federal government as a consultant. This experience has convinced him that "so far, people have been ducking the idea of an atomic attack." He hopes that *Tomorrow!* will be "the *Uncle Tom's Cabin* of the atomic age."